Masculinity, Motherhood, and Mockery

Masculinity, Motherhood,
and
Mockery

*Psychoanalyzing Culture and the
Iatmul Naven Rite in New Guinea*

Eric Kline Silverman

Ann Arbor
THE UNIVERSITY OF MICHIGAN PRESS

2004   2003   2002   2001   4   3   2   1

A CIP catalog record for this book is available from the British Library.

Library of Congress Cataloging-in-Publication Data

Silverman, Eric Kline.
    Masculinity, motherhood, and mockery : psychoanalyzing culture and the Iatmul Naven rite in New Guinea / Eric Kline Silverman.
        p.   cm.
    Includes bibliographical references and index.
    ISBN 0-472-09757-1 (cloth : alk. paper) — ISBN 0-472-06757-5 (pbk. : alk. paper)
        1. Naven (Iatmul rite)—Papua New Guinea—Tambanum.   2. Iatmul (Papua New Guinea people)—Rites and ceremonies.   3. Iatmul (Papua New Guinea people)—Kinship.   4. Iatmul (Papua New Guinea people)—Psychology.   5. Women, Iatmul—Social conditions.   6. Masculinity—Papua New Guinea—Tambanum.   7. Motherhood—Papua New Guinea—Tambanum.   8. Patrilineal kinship—Papua New Guinea—Tambanum.   9. Ceremonial exchange—Papua New Guinea—Tambanum.   10. Tambanum (Papua New Guinea)—Social life and customs.   I. Title.
    DU740.42 .S57   2001
    306'.089'9912—dc21   2001000383

For Andrea. And for Sam and Zoe.

Contents

List of Illustrations   ix

Acknowledgments   xi

A Note to Readers   xv

1   Introduction: The Grotesque and the Moral   1

PART 1: COSMIC MASCULINITY

2   Food and Floods   15

3   Cosmic Bodies and Mythic Genders   27

4   Human Bodies   47

5   The Architectural Grotesque   64

PART 2: SOCIAL MASCULINITY

6   A Symbolic Forest of Kin   83

7   Oedipus in the Sepik   100

8   The Shame of Masculinity   116

PART 3: RITUAL MASCULINITY

9   Men and the Maternal Dialogics of Naven   133

10   Conclusion: Naven and the Pathos of Masculinity   159

Epilogue: Masculinity beyond the Sepik   174

Notes   179

References   203

Index   233

Illustrations

MAP

1 Sepik region of Papua New Guinea   16

FIGURES

1 Processing sago   19
2 Flute playing in the forest   34
3 The men's house   44
4 A house "mother"   65
5 A healthy gift of jewelry   93
6 Iai marriage and the repetition of names   107
7 The oedipal triangulation of iai marriage   108
8 Giving gifts after a naven ceremony   134
9 Mothers frolicking in a canoe   143
10 Honorific mud smearing   147
11 Women dance a naven with a spirit   153
12 The performance of nggariik   160

Acknowledgments

My greatest debt, for which I am both grateful and humbled, is to the very people whose conversations and lives I have tried to interpret: the men and women of Tambunum Village in the middle Sepik River, Papua New Guinea. Without their kindness, hospitality, unfaltering willingness to share their pains and passions, and, above all, extraordinary patience with my graceless presence and relentless questioning, none of this would have been possible. I can only hope that, after reading this book, they will greet my faults, as they did my successes, with good cheer. I wish I could think of an apt, or pithy, phrase that would adequately convey my deepest appreciation for the people of Tambunum—be it in English, tokpisin, the vernacular, or any other language for that matter. Alas, I am unable to do so.

I want to thank in particular various members of my adoptive household, including Yambukenandi, my father, and Agwi, my mother, who bestowed onto me the name of Kamikundiawan, or "one who talks like a fish"; Kara, Lecharimbo, Salapwaymbange, Salapwaymbo; Kamboi, Njoula, Miwai; Bonjoi, Mundjiindua, whose tragic death diminished the joy in the world, Tupwa, and Robina; among many others, both within the Kwongwomboli lineage and throughout the Shui Aimasa clan. Of my many teachers, I acknowledge, above all, Dmoiawan and Gamboromiawan. I also appreciate the erudition of Yambukenandi, Agumoimbange, Henry Wikwarlngawi, Linus Apingari, Biagimbange, Vaimuliawan, Karawusameli, Mendangumeli, and others. You have all taught me well. I hope I have proven to be a worthy student.

Fieldwork support was generously provided in 1988–90 by a Fulbright award and the Institute for Intercultural Studies. My return visit in 1994 was kindly aided by the Wenner-Gren Foundation for Anthropological Research and DePauw University. I received additional support during my graduate studies from the Department of Anthropology and the Graduate School of the University of Minnesota, including a Shevlin Fellowship and a Doctoral Dissertation Fellowship. More recently, DePauw University aided my research and writing through a Fisher Time-Out and various Faculty Development and Presidential

Discretionary grants. In the field, my parents were an extraordinary source of unfaltering support and assistance, and I credit much of my education to them. Only through this generous financial and moral assistance have I been so fortunate to be able to pursue anthropology and the crossing of cultures.

In Papua New Guinea, many people and institutions aided my research and well-being: The East Sepik Provincial Government, the National Museum, Institute of Papua New Guinea Studies, Jan and Peter Barter and the crew of the *Melanesian Discoverer*, Mark Worth and Jim Elmslie, and Lawrie Bragge, all immediately come to mind. Prior to my initial fieldwork, I benefited from conversations with Rhoda Metraux, Douglas Newton (Metropolitan Museum of Art), Anthony Forge (Australian National University), and Meinhard Schuster, Brigitta Hauser-Schäublin, Florence Weiss, Milan Stanek, and Christian Kaufmann (Institute of Ethnology and the Museum of Ethnology, Basel).

Much of what I did, or did not, learn about anthropology occurred in Ford Hall, the former location of the Department of Anthropology at the University of Minnesota. Of my many teachers, I am particularly indebted to Gene Ogan's compassionate morality, theoretical judiciousness, and sweeping knowledge of Pacific anthropology. I continue to draw from John Ingham's psychological and psychoanalytic insights. Above all, I thank David Lipset, who proposed that I conduct fieldwork in the Sepik, suggested Tambunum, introduced me to the work of Bateson, supervised my doctoral dissertation, and aided me during moments of unforeseen difficulties in Wewak, prior to my arrival in the village. Our conversations about Bakhtin and Sepik ethnology have been an ongoing source of inspiration. I also wish to acknowledge dialogue with other Sepik anthropologists who have clarified various aspects of my thinking, or sought to do so, including Kathleen Barlow, Paul Roscoe, Nancy Lutkehaus, and Borut Telban.

Various portions of this manuscript were also enhanced by the opportunities to present papers at the Department of Anthropology, University of Hawaii; Australian National University; numerous classes at DePauw University; and annual meetings of the Association for Social Anthropology in Oceania and the American Anthropological Association. The Department of Anthropology at Brandeis University kindly lent me office space during summer 1995. I am also grateful to Michael Houseman and Carlo Severi for sending me a draft of their 1998 book about the naven rite and to Bernard Juillerat who did likewise with his 1999 article. By discussing my research and, in the case of the former, by differing, both of these publications encouraged me to refine my thinking.

M. Catherine Bateson and the Institute for Intercultural Studies kindly granted me permission to quote from Gregory Bateson's unpublished Iatmul fieldnotes.

Gilbert Herdt read a prior draft of this book and offered helpful advice. So, too, did two anonymous reviewers. I hope they are pleased with the results.

Susan McDowell and Edith Welliver kindly assisted my comprehension of German with their superb translations. I also hail various colleagues at DePauw

University who provided intellectual stimulation and jovial conviviality; you know who you are. John M. Hollingsworth, Staff Cartographer of Indiana University, drew the fine map. The photos are all my own, taken in Tambunum in 1988–1990 and 1994; many of them were kindly developed by the Australian Museum.

At the University of Michigan Press, I acknowledge the patience and advice of Susan Whitlock and especially Ingrid Erickson.

Finally, for the simple reason that no dedication will ever suffice, I want to recognize again the innumerable contributions of Andrea and our two children, Sam and Zoe. They have enhanced this book and my own understanding of the human experience in more ways than they know. Sam and Zoe in particular have taught me that any analysis of culture that is devoid of a sense of its joys and wonders is truly banal. If there is a lesson here, it is you who have shown it to me.

A Note to Readers

The disclosures of anthropology must always tread uneasily between the facades and secrets of human experience. The men of Tambunum who abided my relentless questions with their insights and silences have all consented to my including in this book various descriptions and photos that they themselves conceal from women and youth. In deference to their sensitivities, I admonish readers to exercise prudence when disseminating this material. It is the least I can do.

1

Introduction: The Grotesque and the Moral

In June 1994, I returned briefly to the middle Sepik River. Four years had elapsed since my doctoral fieldwork in the prosperous fishing and horticultural village of Tambunum. At that time, the broad themes of this book were more or less outlined. But I lacked a singular image or event that could frame my study of men, ritual, and maternal representations. I needed what psychoanalysts call the "aha" of recognition, a summarizing flash of perspective. For me, this insight occurred during a fleeting moment of playful interaction between a mother and her son. This was the scene that finally crystallized the relationship between masculinity and motherhood that is my focus.

As I sat on the steps of my house that morning in June, I watched a young boy wandering in his father's courtyard. Like toddlers everywhere, Miwai cheerfully disregarded his mother, Njoula. She playfully called after him: *makparl ndumbwi, kavlay ndumbwi,* "bad sperm, little sperm." Njoula happened to glance at my astonished countenance. We both laughed.

How is it, I wondered, that a mother—someone who embodies the highest ideals of selflessness and nurture in this culture—would mock her young son with such a phrase? Was it a taboo sexual jest? A whimsical idiom of masculine inadequacy? A suggestion that the father's reproductive substances are impotent before the power of uterine fertility and feeding? Was it a maternal face that men rarely encounter, or rarely imagine, at least so abruptly? Or was this statement a comic expression of a more serious side of motherhood, one that is deeply consequential for men and women alike? In this book, I seek to answer these questions by interpreting the psychodynamic and cultural paradoxes that will occupy this mother and her son, indeed, all Eastern Iatmul persons, as they grapple with the passions and expectations of their social universe.

The Argument

My goal is to analyze the relationship between masculinity and motherhood by focusing on two countervailing images of the body that the great literary theorist Mikhail Bakhtin dubbed the "moral" and the "grotesque." Eastern Iatmul men idealize an image of motherhood that is nurturing, sheltering, cleansing, fertile, and chaste, in a word, moral. But men also fear an equally compelling image of motherhood that is defiling, dangerous, orificial, aggressive, and carnal, hence, grotesque. My argument, in short, is that masculinity in Tambunum is a rejoinder to these contrary images of motherhood. Indeed, I understand culture itself, or *herself* as the case so often appears in the middle Sepik, to be an endless conversation between antithetical visions of social order, self, and desire. I say endless because, ultimately, neither the moral nor the grotesque in Bakhtin's view, neither the authoritative nor the rebellious, holds sway. Instead, the colloquy of culture engenders profound emotional ambivalence.

It will not suffice, however, solely to interpret the symbolism of Eastern Iatmul masculinity and motherhood through a dialogical lens. I need also to analyze the psychodynamic motivations of this cultural conversation in order to account for why men and women so often express themselves in terms of the maternal body. In so doing, I anchor the cultural pervasiveness of maternal representations, especially in the imagination of men, to the nostalgia of infancy, the complexity of oedipal desire, and what Margaret Mead (1949) aptly termed male "womb envy." Eastern Iatmul women, while they may aspire to the politicoritual privileges of men and respect greatly the august bearing of manhood, nonetheless evince no yearning to become fathers. Men, however, in ways they do not always wish to admit, define themselves as mothers.

While my focus is on the metaphoric voices of masculinity and motherhood in the middle Sepik, I seek as well to converse with several debates in contemporary anthropology and social thought. Methodologically, I parse culture into dialogical images of the body and morality. But I also synthesize this theory of culture with various psychoanalytic perspectives on masculinity, motherhood, and social life. Ethnographically, the book revises recent notions of Melanesian personhood and gender, and, more significantly, provides new data and interpretations on a ceremonial locus classicus in anthropology, namely, the Iatmul naven rite, which remains at the center of lively debate. Finally, it is my hope that this book will contribute novel conceptual and ethnographic insights to the increasingly urgent discussions about the meanings and misfortunes of masculinity.

An Anthropological Legacy

The relationship between Iatmul masculinity and motherhood is powerfully dramatized by a famous ceremony known as *naven*. This rite was first analyzed by the brilliant, iconoclastic thinker Gregory Bateson in two editions of a book titled after the ceremony itself, *Naven* (1936, 1958). Bateson's study was the first epistemological triumph of anthropology and a pioneering account of ritual, personhood, and gender (Keesing 1982, 1991; Lipset 1982; Houseman and Severi

1998).[1] It is one of only a handful of early-twentieth-century ethnographies that continue to exercise theoretical influence across the spectrum of anthropological and social thought (Marcus 1985; Geertz 1988, 7; Nadar 1988). My own interpretations build on this legacy.[2]

The naven rite celebrates first-time cultural achievements such as spearing fish, wearing spirit masks, trapping prawns, and, formerly, bloodshed. Today, naven also honors the feats of modernity, including airplane travel and the purchase of a 25- or 40-horsepower outboard motor for a dugout canoe. Bateson saw naven as a perplexing rite of transvestism and ridicule. Mothers' brothers, then and now, dress like old hags and lampoon birth while women, adorned with male finery, boastfully prance in a burlesque rendition of masculinity. Especially vexing for Bateson was the culminating gesture, a "sexual salute" (Bateson 1936, 13) known as *nggariik* whereby a maternal uncle honors his nephew by sliding his buttocks down the youth's leg. At the end of the rite, the emotionally exhausted honorees present gifts to their matrikin and other ritual participants.

The bizarre antics of naven, Bateson argued, enable men and women to transgress their emotional norms or ethos, and thereby to achieve a degree of psychological integration.[3] In everyday life, he observed, Iatmul women tend to be cooperative and demure; men are fiercely competitive and flamboyant (Bateson 1936, chaps. 9–10). Women derive joy from the achievements of others yet the norms of daily life provide them with no means of lively, public celebration. By the same token, the self-serving exuberance of men denies them the capacity to derive pleasure from any accomplishment that is not of their own making. During naven, however, women *do* rejoice raucously in public, and men *do* celebrate rather than challenge the achievements of others. Through the nggariik gesture, in this view, the maternal uncle pantomimes birth in order to claim a role in fostering the developing personhood of his niece or nephew. Yet while naven permits each gender to transcend its emotional limitations, the mockery of these transgressions maintains, in the end, normative behavioral and ethological patterns.

Sociologically, naven was equally integrative. Iatmul relationships, Bateson claimed, are beset by a divisive principle he called *schismogenesis*. Bateson (1936, 265; 1935a) defined this cumbersome neologism—developed, like his ethos concept, through legendary fieldwork conversations with Mead and Fortune—as "a process of differentiation in the norms of individual behaviour resulting from cumulative interaction between individuals." Schismogenesis also characterized normative modes of interaction between Iatmul groups. Unless curtailed, the "progressive change" (Bateson 1936, 176–77) of schismogenesis would eventually fracture a community into extinction.[4] The village would simply collapse.

Since the 1890s (Kuper 1988, pt. 1), anthropologists have looked to marriage for the integration of so-called primitive societies. Rules of matrimony, in this view, guarantee that separate groups periodically restore bonds of solidar-

ity by exchanging women and valuables, and by merging their collective interests. Yet Iatmul marriage rules, observed Bateson, were contradictory. What's
more, people tended to ignore them. In the absence of a coherent and binding
marriage system, there seemed to be no provision for Iatmul society to renew
itself. What held the community together? Bateson's answer was the naven rite,
a ceremony that regularly ensured the exchange of gifts and ritual theatrics
between intermarrying patrilines. Naven, not marriage, renewed the moral
relationship between affinal patrilines and thereby counteracted schismogenesis.[5] In sum, Bateson resolved the enigma of naven through a unique combination of functionalism and what later became known as the Culture and Personality school of anthropology.[6] However outlandish naven appeared to be, it
restored society and psyche.

An Anthropological Puzzle

When I set forth for Tambunum in August 1988, I had no intention of studying
the naven rite since Bateson had presumably solved the puzzle. Likewise, I had
little concern with masculinity and motherhood. Shortly after my arrival,
though, I witnessed my first naven. This rite, and the many others that followed, including two for myself, exhibited a different tone and drama than
those reported by Bateson. These ceremonies did not appear to effect any psychological, emotional, or sociological closure—just the opposite. The ritual
seemed to intensify the paradoxes and conflicts of the culture. It especially con-
founded the standards of masculinity and motherhood.

The Eastern Iatmul ceremony does, as Bateson observed, celebrate the
mastery of cultural skill. Yet naven in Tambunum is an elaborate event only on
the occasion of *male* achievement. More significant, the central dramatis per-
sonae of these large-scale performances are mother-figures who beat women
and especially men with palm fronds, embarrass them with bawdy jokes, and
pelt them with substances that symbolize menstrual blood and feces. These
women, despite their maternal associations, contravene the nurturing ideals of
motherhood that are so dear to men—and to which men attribute their
growth, brawn, and cultural successes. The women also, during the rite, regress
men back into infants and thus subvert the stated intent of naven, namely, the
celebration of achievement.

The uncle's nggariik gesture, too, hardly seemed laudatory. It was mortifying! Upon its performance, men often wept tears of shame, not joy. Indeed,
the mother's brother, when he rubs his buttocks down the shin of his nephew,
appears ignominiously to expose, sometimes even before women, all the hidden yearnings and taboo desires of masculinity. Naven is no heroic vision of
manhood. No exemplars of moral mothering appear during the rite. Rather,
naven portrays masculinity as a tragic tale that is scripted through images of
carnivalesque motherhood.

I vividly recall parading down the village after one of my own extemporaneous naven rites. This particular ceremony celebrated a personal as well as cultural achievement: paddling a dugout canoe while standing. I was enthusiastically mocked by elder maternal women whom I ordinarily treated with the deference befitting of stately grandmothers. They ran up the village and thrashed me with sticks and branches. They mouthed ribald jests, smeared handfuls of mud in my face and hair, and spit red betel juice on my head. Other women cheered. The "mothers" next chased after my brothers, some of whom ran inside and hid. When these ritualized aggressions vanished, as quickly as they appeared, men shook their heads with silent bemusement. Somewhat stunned, a bit embarrassed, and filthy beyond belief, I quietly walked to the river to bathe. Later, another group of women hurried to my house with coconut half-shells of mud, only to be stopped by my adopted mother who was concerned for my basic well-being.

Playful thrashings. Filthy defilement. Lewd quips. Fleeing men. Blood-red spittle. All instigated by mother-figures, and directed at men. Despite the singular genius of Bateson's analysis, the puzzle of naven persisted. A clear understanding of the rite, I realized, required a framework that would interpret the bodily semiotics of masculinity and motherhood. I now sketch the three dimensions of that framework: the dialogical, the psychoanalytic, and the gendered.

The Dialogical Perspective

At least since Hobbes, two images of the body have prevailed in Western thought.[7] The *individual* body is natural, appetitive, orificial, unkempt, and transgressive. By contrast, the *social* body is cultural, inhibited, bounded, clean, and obedient. As a symbol for sociopolitical order and legitimate authority, the social body, like Hobbes's anthropomorphic Leviathan ([1651] 1958), encompasses individual bodies within its juridical contours (MacRae 1975; Foucault 1978, 1979). The social body carefully preserves the morphological distinctions male/female, pollution/purity, inside/outside, upper/lower, and so forth. It cautiously regulates feeding, excretion, and sexuality. All told, the social body privileges the maintenance of collective life over the dissonant, individualistic, and concupiscent aspects of human experience.

Anthropologists tend to associate the social body with rules governing sexuality, diet, beauty, and what Mauss ([1935] 1979) termed the everyday "techniques" of the body such as posture (see also Synnott and Howes 1992; Synnott 1993; Strathern 1996). These "collective representations," as the Durkheimians emphasized, are particularly evident during communal ritual when the norms and categories of social order are painted, incised, and otherwise marked on the potentially rebellious bodies of individuals (Durkheim [1912] 1995; Hertz [1909] 1960; Mauss [1925] 1990). Even licentious "rites of reversal," which disfigure the body and disarticulate social divisions, are said to regenerate the social order (van Gennep [1908] 1960; Radcliffe-Brown 1940;

Gluckman 1945, 1956; Turner 1967b, 1969; Geertz 1972). Bateson was no enthusiast of this functionalist, teleological tradition (e.g., 1958, 287–88). Nevertheless, the ritual behaviors of naven, he asserted, which were censored from mundane life, integrated Iatmul society and psychology.

Yet, as we learn from Freud (1913), the triumph of collective morality over bodily passion is ambivalent. Sexuality and violence are forever poised to shatter the conventions of social life. Human discord and woe are integral to culture, not residual. Still, the conflicts of human experience in the Sepik are too complex to be understood solely in terms of the opposition between social morality and individualistic desire. We need a binocular view of culture that recognizes the body as a source of passion *and* a symbol of social order. This perspective, too, must be attuned to the plurality and cacophony of culture. In other words, we need the dialogical framework of Bakhtin.

Bakhtin understood culture to consist of contrary discourses—authoritative and dissident, dominant and submerged, verbal and gestural—that are lent two antithetical human forms. The "moral" body, much as Durkheim and Hobbes theorized, symbolizes the official view of social order. This body is thoughtful, somber, restrained, and sanitized. Its profile is unambiguously defined. It shuns eros. It refuses to open itself to the world unless permitted by the reigning authority. Literally and metaphorically, the moral body keeps its mouth shut.

But, Janus-faced, the moral body has a necessary counterpart that Bakhtin (1984a, 1984b) termed the "grotesque." This carnivalesque body expresses "the hyperbolization and hypertrophization of corporeality" in order to transform the world into oxymoronic ambivalence (Lachmann 1988, 126–30). The grotesque body overwhelms the contemplative voice of authority with laughter, gluttony, and lechery. Here, thoughtful restraint is muted by the sensual, procreative, and defiling excrescences and cavities of what Bakhtin called the "lower bodily stratum." This body trespasses across the boundaries of hierarchy, taste, and gender (Davis 1975). Above all, the grotesque body is dominated by an insatiable, devouring and egesting, carnal maw.

The grotesque body is "never finished, never completed" since it "swallows the world and is itself swallowed by the world" (Bakhtin 1984a, 317). Bakhtin realized that the grotesque is no simple expression or aesthetic of destruction. Grotesque logic is refractory. It combines images of death *and* rebirth, defecation *and* parturition, abuse *and* praise. Hence, cultural dialogism leads neither to Marxian revolution nor to functionalist orthodoxy but, rather, to ambivalence. The dialogical relationship between the moral and the grotesque captures, in Bakhtin's (1984a, 62) felicitous phrase, the "contradictory, double-faced fullness of life."

New Guinea is far afield from the Rabelaisian carnival.[8] Nonetheless, Bakhtin's focus on bodily imagery is especially suitable for Melanesia, a region where ritual and myth are replete with symbols of feeding, sexuality, birth, decay, excretion, phallus, vulva, and breast. Indeed, bodies in Melanesia are subject to innumerable rules and a heightened awareness concerning socioso-matic boundaries, pollution, order, and purity. Yet ritual in Melanesia often violates fantastically this meticulous moral topography. Furthermore, body symbols in this region are rarely stable, unitary, or limited to a single context.

Indeed, epistemic gaps are commonplace in Melanesian cosmologies. Discursive strategies, as Weiner (1995a, 9) writes, tend "more to cut off or obvi-ate explanatory expansion than to facilitate it." Local interpretation and reflexivity are elusive endeavors, more a matter of insinuation than clarity (Weiner 1995b). For me, Bakhtin's "idea of hidden dialogue as a metaphor and a methodology" (Lipset 1997, 4) encourages anthropological analysis to attend to the irreducible polyphony of local thought and experience. Of course, cul-ture also exhibits a degree of systemic coherence, or patterning. We need not rehearse the Boasian arguments against what Lowie once chastised as the "threads and patches" theory of culture. With this in mind, I have tried to dis-cern symbolic connections *as well as* the symbolism of silence, discrepancy, uncertainty, and doubt. There is sense, we might say, to non-sense, to the "con-tradictory, double-faced fullness of life" that is the artifice of culture.

Why artifice? Because, as Lipset (1997, 12) writes for the Murik of the Sepik Estuary, the symbols of culture that Sepik men deploy in validating themselves "foreground what is not the case while backgrounding what is true." In Tam-bunum, the artifice of manhood and culture is best revealed, I argue, through two related discourses of the body and morality. On the one hand, as I have already stated, there is a dialogical relationship between masculinity and moth-erhood. On the other hand, the cultural elaboration of motherhood herself comprises its own double-voiced, and double-bodied, conversation between the moral and the grotesque.[9] Separately, and together, these two dialogues are forever unresolved, and forever ambivalent.

The Psychoanalytic Perspective

After I was established in Tambunum and set about the affairs of fieldwork, I was immediately struck by two seemingly unrelated aspects of marriage and architecture. When Eastern Iatmul describe their ideal form of matrimony, they say that the bridegroom's father "gets his mother back." This idiom, and the rule of marriage it specifies, hints at a yearning by adult men to rejoin their mothers. The vernacular architecture reveals a more ambivalent, even fearful, image of motherhood. Eastern Iatmul explicitly envision their domestic houses to be nurturing mothers. Yet the doorways, which symbolize the genitals of these mothers, are often surrounded by ornamental crocodile teeth. These con-trary symbols of motherhood, I realized, elicit local meanings that are both cul-tural *and* psychodynamic.

I did not enter the Sepik with any expectation of engaging in what Freud termed "applied psychoanalysis." Rather, my adoption of psychoanalysis for the interpretation of cultural symbolism was encouraged solely by the visual, ritual, and conversational idioms of motherhood I encountered, again and again, in contexts that are essential to men. While psychoanalytic analysis in cultural anthropology remains controversial, much of this dissension arises from misunderstanding. Let me explain.

As Paul (1987) observes, the anthropological distrust of psychoanalysis (e.g., Leach 1958) rests on the false belief that culture is entirely distinct from the individual (see also Spiro 1951). To the contrary, Obeyesekere (1981) splendidly analyzes the interrelationship between private and public symbols during the popular Kataragama ceremony in Sri Lanka. Through optional participation in various ceremonial dramas, the "deep motivations" of male and female ecstatics are therapeutically "canalized and objectified in a culturally constituted symbol system" (Obeyesekere 1990, 12). Conversely, the private psychological idiosyncrasies of these men and women provoke behaviors that, while somewhat eccentric, are nonetheless integral to the ceremony. Accordingly, psychodynamic processes are vital for the analysis of cultural symbolism.[10]

Personal symbols, Obeyesekere (1981) emphasizes, originate in and remain tethered to deep motivation. Their primary significance lies in the unconscious and emotional lives of specific individuals. "Psychogenetic" symbols, while they also originate in the unconscious, are detached from deep psychological motivations. These symbols, as in myth and ritual, code for the collective rules, etiquettes, and tenets of culture—social life rather than the lives of individuals. But it is equally true, as I show in this book, that cultural symbols communicate messages of psychodynamic or unconscious importance to groups rather than simply to individuals. Often, these symbols express "psychic problems arising from relations with parents and significant others, themselves conditioned by the nature of socialization under the governance of specific familial structures and values" (Obeyesekere 1990, 25). This is especially so in societies that promote myth and ritual as legitimate modes of everyday action and intellectual activity. In these communities, where the mythic and the mundane intentionally overlap, fantasy is not, as in our own society, consigned to irrational and often devalued realms such as child's play, art, or psychological abnormality. Hence, in Tambunum, mythopoeic fantasy is a fundamental element of the overall worldview.

Myth, ritual, and other highly stylized realms of culture often communicate conscious messages. This is obvious. Less evident, these cultural expressions are also "designed to be deciphered subliminally by the innate mechanisms of symbol formation which typify the unconscious psyche of *homo sapiens*" (Paul 1987, 89). Primary processes such as condensation, inversion, and especially projection[11] are as integral to myth and ritual as they are to dreams. But as Obeyesekere (1990, 51–68) reminds us, a Freudian outlook on myth and ritual does *not* understand cultural symbols to arise from dreams. The "work of culture," according to Obeyesekere (1990, 55–56), entails modes of mentation that are absent from Freud's (1900) "dream-work," especially "the logic of causality, syntax, and temporal sequence." A psychoanalytic interpretation of cultural symbolism is not, therefore, tantamount to saying that culture is psyche. Quite the opposite: so-called Freudian symbols, argues Paul (1987, 89–90), are "out there in the culture to begin with," as a "shared basic template" that pertains to both panhuman and culture-specific patterns of sociality.

Like language, then, psychodynamic structures exist as collective phenomena. Insofar as one can study grammar without scrutinizing the linguistic competence of specific individuals, Paul (1997) argues, one can equally interpret public expressions of fantasy without reference to individual biographies. When fantasies, claims Paul (1987, 91), "express themselves in forms intended for public consumption, such as . . . myth, or ritual, we may be assured that precisely because they are intended for communication, it is possible for us to comprehend them." The matter of verification here is no more occult than in any other anthropological approach to symbolic meaning (Paul 1987).[12] One seeks to demonstrate the presence of patterns and themes in a broad array of social and cultural contexts that may include, as in this book, marriage and myth, childhood and kinship, architecture and canoes, sexuality and ritual.

In exploring Eastern Iatmul masculinity and motherhood, I offer four specific psychodynamic arguments. First, I demonstrate the centrality of the preoedipal mother-child bond in the cultural imagination of men and, to a lesser extent, women (see Klein [1932] 1975; Mahler 1963, 1971; Chodorow 1978). As Mead (1949, 112) noticed, the play of adolescent Iatmul boys turned "phantasy back towards the childhood that they shared with their mothers, not forward towards the splendour and dash of male public life." As a result, at least in the view of classic psychoanalysis, the attainment of manhood requires a traumatic repudiation of preoedipal attachment, what Greenson (1968) terms "disidentifying" from the mother. Thus Iatmul women are aggressively excluded from the male cult. Displays of hypermasculinity and male solidarity, so it is declared, are defenses against a regression to early maternal symbiosis (e.g., Lidz and Lidz 1977, 1989; Herdt 1981, 1982a; Poole 1982; Stoller and Herdt 1982; Gregor 1985; Gilmore 1987a, 1990; Ingham 1996a, 66–70).

But the central dramas of manhood in Tambunum, while they do strive to define masculinity in the absence of women and femininity, also express a profound desire by men *to return* to an ideal, nurturing mother (see also Loewald 1979; Herdt 1987; Juillerat 1999). This is my second psychodynamic argument: masculinization in Tambunum adheres to a broad "maternal schema" (Lipset 1997; Barlow 1995). Indeed, Eastern Iatmul manhood often resembles a great "transitional object" (Winnicott 1953, 1967)—albeit one that, as Juillerat (1988) argues for Yafar, a nonriverine Sepik society, is entirely unsuccessful.

Men in Tambunum also define themselves through oedipal desires and anxieties.[13] This is my third psychodynamic argument. Here, however, the central dimension of oedipality is not punitive fatherhood (see Whiting, Kluckhohn, and Anthony 1958; Burton and Whiting 1961; Kitahara 1974).[14] Rather, oedipal imbroglios such as marriage and inheritance revolve around mother-figures. Even the symbolism of male initiation, where senior men dominate their juniors, privileges the maternal rather than the male or paternal body.

Male envy of female parturition and fertility is my final psychodynamic argument, one inspired by the eminent work of Alan Dundes (e.g., 1962, 1976b, 1979, 1983, 1986, 1993).[15] Hence, while women are barred from the male cult house, the building itself is a mother. In her "belly" men store ritual accoutrements that their primal forefathers allegedly purloined from ancestresses in order, as men say today, to compensate for their inability to give birth.[16] Yet men in Tambunum do not only mirror the female body. Rather, they often displace the procreative potential of women with idioms of anal birth. This aspiration notwithstanding, men scorn the female reproductive tract (see also Loewald 1951; Bloch and Guggenheim 1981, 379–80; Shapiro 1989, 72). At the same time, men carefully disguise their parturient fictions as if the very value of manhood itself would be divested of its meaning should it be truly understood by women. For this reason, among others, the uncle's renowned nggariik gesture during the naven rite, when he slides his buttocks down a youth's leg, is especially embarrassing for men when it is staged, as it often is, before an audience of women.

It must not be supposed, however, that Eastern Iatmul women passively acquiesce to men's psychodynamic encounters with motherhood. On this point, I fuse my psychoanalytic perspective with the contrapuntal imagery of Bakhtin's moral and grotesque (see also Daelemans and Maranhao 1990; Ingham 1996a). During the naven rite, women and mother-figures respond to masculinity with thrashings, ribald jokes, and the hurling of debased substances. Not only do women thus contest the nostalgic yearnings of men and vividly portray men's fear of female sexuality, but they also invert the idealized nurturing capacities of motherhood. In so doing, women during naven doubly disgrace manhood since they call into question both the foundations and fables of male self-worth.

The Gendered Perspective

The symbolism and values of Eastern Iatmul masculinity are also connected to broader notions of personhood and gender. For this reason, I must address Strathern's (1988) wide-ranging thesis that Melanesian persons are divisible and partible rather than indivisible and bounded. At "the heart," writes Weiner (1995a, 13), lies "not some inviolable self-identity but the deposited or introjected traces, both semiological and imagistic, of the others who constitute that person."[17]

Yet personhood in Tambunum is only partially sociocentric, as others have argued for non-Melanesian societies (Shweder and Bourne 1984; Hollan 1992; Spiro 1993).[18] Eastern Iatmul deeply respect the egocentric agency and concealed thoughts of *in*dividuals. Even "an unborn child," wrote Mead (1949, 83), "can hurry or delay as it wishes." The Eastern Iatmul person is no mere "ensemble of personages" as Leenhardt ([1949] 1979, 153) claimed for the Canaque of New Caledonia, a being who "exists only insofar as he acts his role in the course of his relationships . . . an empty space." Not only does identity in Tambunum assume dual forms, sociocentric and egocentric, but each form entails its own desires, emotions, and persuasions.

Gender is equally dual and fluid. According to Strathern (1988), Melanesian gender is "transactional" rather than fixed, inherent, and mutually exclusive. What you *do* with the body is more important than what you *have*. In some settings, usually mundane ones, Melanesian men and women act as same-sex beings who are singularly "male" or "female." But in other contexts, such as myth and ritual, men and women are cross-sexed. They transact substances, personified objects, and body parts that are normally coded as solely male or female.

The truly important diacritics of Eastern Iatmul gender are, as per Strathern, androgynous. Nevertheless, one gender in Tambunum is more androgynous than the other: male. Whereas men model their identity after motherhood, women rarely aspire to be fathers. Whereas the overall thrust of myth and ritual is often the incorporation by men of uterine organs and capacities, women hardly ever seek out male or paternal physiology. In the Eastern Iatmul case, therefore, the theory of "transactional" gender must be redesigned to recognize men's psychodynamic desire for the parturient abilities of women. This yearning, however, is largely silent. It is muted, in fact, by the eager willingness of men to extol the merits of motherhood and to articulate the perceived dangers of the female body. Finding a genuine identity amid this dialogue of contrary values and virtues is the great predicament of Eastern Iatmul masculinity.

Chapter Summaries

I have divided the book into three parts that respectively interpret the cosmological, social, and ritual relationships between masculinity and motherhood. The first part, "Cosmic Masculinity," begins by sketching the social organization, ecology, and history of Tambunum (chap. 2).[19] Far more important, I interpret the myth of Kwianalagwi, an ancestress who transformed the fetid sores that carpeted her aging body into palm trees that, when mixed with coital fluids, enabled the creation of edible sago, the sine qua non of a maternal repast. Kwianalagwi thus represents the predicament of men as they define themselves in terms of inimical visions of motherhood.

Chapter 3 discusses gender as well as the presence of bodily and uterine reproductive symbols in totemism, cosmology, and male initiation. The chapter ends with an interpretation of a mythic snake-child who was killed for his refusal to vacate the shelter of his mother's womb, a fate that symbolically threatens all men in the culture. I next turn to the human body itself (chap. 4) and consider conception, ethnophysiology,[20] sexuality, the bodily referents of personal names, and, odd though it may now seem, the procreative symbolism of male flatulence. Here, I expound on the local acknowledgment by men that, while they alone sit on wooden stools, mothers are the true "stools" or pillars of the culture. Yet motherhood is not merely nurturing and reproductive. She is also a clown, personified by men, who chases and teases children. Chapter 5 expands on this dissonant imagery by analyzing domestic dwellings as symbolic mothers who shelter *and* devour their inhabitants. Houses also exacerbate oedipal tension since fathers build these architectural mothers at great personal travail yet cede them to their sons.

The first two chapters of the second part, "Social Masculinity," detail the relationship between masculinity and motherhood in kinship and marriage. I discuss the contrast between patrilineal trees and feminine water, as well as child-raising and the roles of kin who significantly shape male identity such as fathers, maternal uncles, and mothers (chap. 6). I also inquire, in chapter 7, into the complex entanglement of oedipal desire and preferential marriage since a son's ideal bride is his father's "mother." The last chapter of this part examines masculine incompetence and perilous achievements, two situations that threaten to regress men to a shameful state of childhood defilement (chap. 8). Much of this humiliation arises from the cultural elaboration of feces and maternal care such that men are identified simultaneously as dependent infants and solicitous mothers.

The centerpiece of the book is the last part, "Ritual Masculinity." In chapter 9, I interpret the carnivalesque dramas of the famous naven rite wherein figures of motherhood, as I mentioned earlier, seek to assault, seduce, defile, and embarrass men. Much of this material is entirely new to the ethnographic literature and thus enhances considerably the long-standing debate over the significance of the naven rite (e.g., Rubel and Rosman 1978; D'Amato 1979; Handelman 1979; Gewertz 1983; Karp 1987; Lindenbaum 1987; Houseman and Severi 1998; Juillerat 1999). In my view, naven is a perverse mockery of masculinity and motherhood that exposes the fictions and fragility of manhood.

The differing strands of the book come together in chapter 10 with an interpretation of the enigmatic nggariik pantomime. Why does a maternal uncle during naven feel compelled to wipe his buttocks down a nephew's leg? The answer lies in complex images of excrement and birth, taboo eroticism and male shame, the laughter of women and the tears of men. The nggariik gesture, I will show, uncovers all the earnestness, folly, and pathos of Eastern Iatmul manhood.

Finally, in the Epilogue, I ask, What, if anything, can the cultural construction of manhood in the middle Sepik River tell us about masculinity in general? The answer, I believe, lies somewhere between a young boy who desired to wander from his mother, yet was unable to escape her mocking jest, and adult men who present their buttocks to nephews in a tearful gesture of masculine celebration.

PART 1

Cosmic Masculinity

2

Food and Floods

It was over a generation ago that Margaret Mead (1938, 153–201) offered the first systematic characterization of the Sepik (see also Mead 1978; Harrison 1987). Yet many of her keen insights into regional interactions and local-level social life accurately describe Tambunum today (map 1). The village is acephalous. Its autonomous descent groups are differentiated by hereditary accoutrements such as masks and totemic names, not by material wealth. Despite a hiatus in large-scale male initiation, the male cult and its many other rituals are still vital to masculinity. And gender relations remain complex and problematic.

Tambunum and other Sepik villages, too, continue to maintain regional trade networks that circulate food, material objects, and cultural forms such as magical spells among different language groups, communities, and ecological zones. In the 1930s, regional integration was also ensured by ongoing warfare. Typically, vendettas were launched between communities that were linked by trade. As a result, normative modes of regional interaction were at once those of amity and enmity (Harrison 1989a, 1993a; Knauft 1990). Outright warfare is now extinct yet skirmishes do arise over various sorts of insults, assaults, and challenges to land and water rights. A martial ethos assuredly remains integral to masculine identity. Indeed, notwithstanding the vast changes that have flowed into the Sepik since contact with Europeans in the late nineteenth century, local manhood and cultural configurations display remarkable continuity.

An Aquatic Plentitude

Another enduring cultural theme is the Sepik River.[1] Life begins and ends with the Sepik, a dangerous yet sustaining feminine presence that forever winds through the landscape, relentlessly flowing into the Bismarck Sea. The serpentine river and water are central motifs in Eastern Iatmul culture and cosmology. The birth of the world was aquatic (chap. 3)—as, perhaps, its demise will be. Human destiny is also aqueous since the souls of the deceased travel down the river and out to sea, eventually arriving at the place of the dead.[2] The river

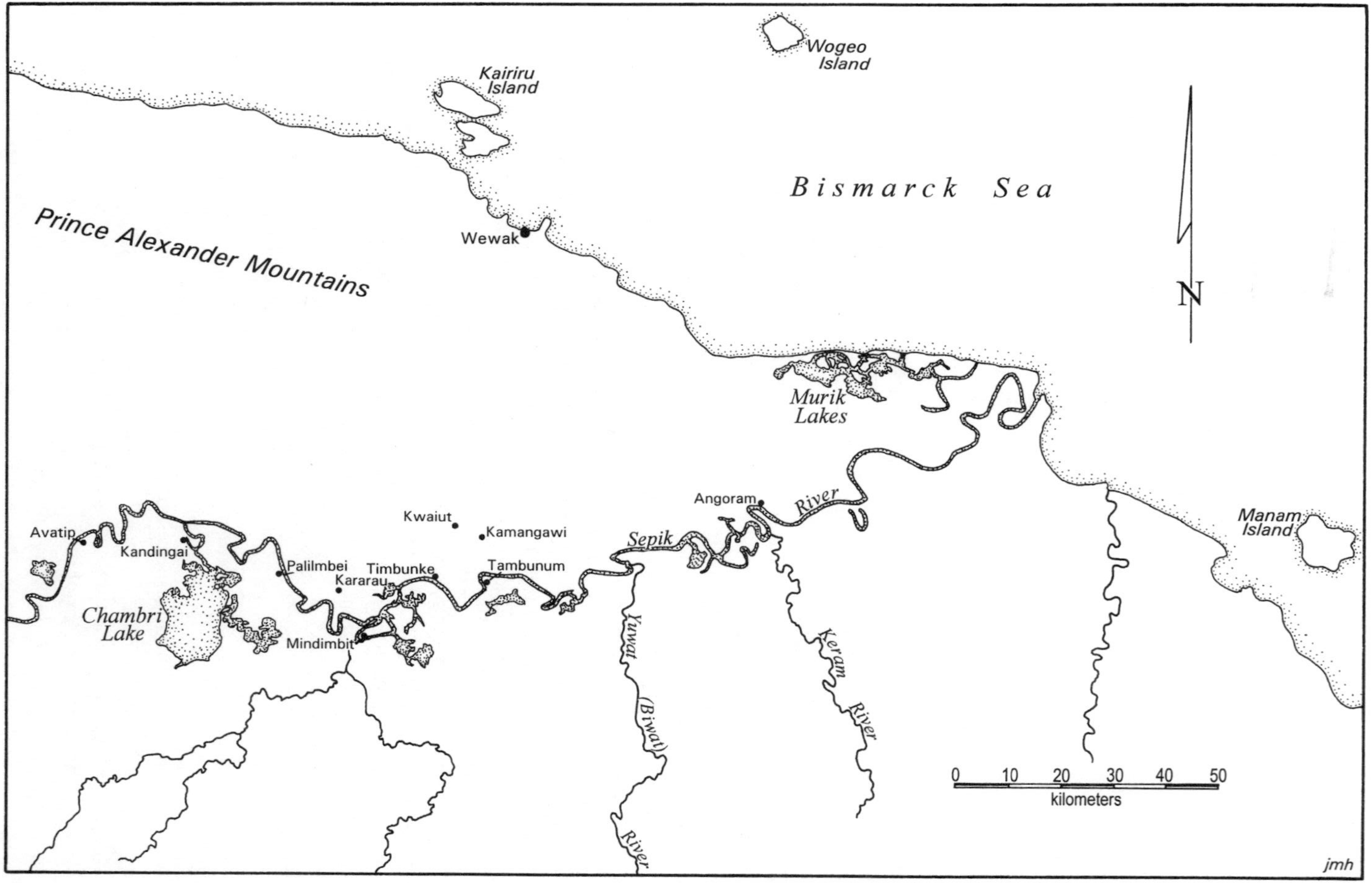

Map 1. Sepik region of Papua New Guinea

also provides two symbols of ethnic identity, namely, the canoe and the crocodile, and thus distinguishes Iatmul speakers from their neighbors who dwell in the bush and other regions of Papua New Guinea.[3]

The river is the source of a pervasive aesthetic that imbues Iatmul music, art, and ritual with a sense of fluid motion and impermanence—*yivut*, which Bateson (1936, 129 n. 1) dubbed "liveliness." Wave motifs decorate nearly all forms of material culture, from baskets to houses. The river is both generative and dissolving, defining and liminal. Above all, the Sepik is a powerful image of motherhood that nourishes life but erodes the works of men: their houses, trees, and villages. In this regard, riverine water is a symbol of femininity against which men and demiurges construct their sense of worth.

The mosaic environment of the middle Sepik, lush with natural resources, sustains large and prosperous villages. The river provides Eastern Iatmul with the bulk of their protein—mainly fish but also prawns, mayflies, and the occasional crocodile. Each family plants gardens of taro, yam, sweet potato, and tobacco. They tend fruit trees such as coconut, banana, breadfruit, citrus, papaya, and mango. Postcontact domesticates include corn, beans, cucumber, pineapple, and watermelon. Various bushes provide greens. The local cuisine also includes chicken, wild fowl, snake, turtle, frog, sago grubs, lotus seeds, bandicoot, cassowary, bat, and, on ritual occasions, pig and sometimes dog. Trade stores stock rice, canned fish and meat, biscuits, and fried flour. In spite of this variety, subsistence still revolves around water: the river, rains, and flooding.

During the rainy season, the river often overflows its muddied banks and dramatically evokes the aquatic genesis of the cosmos and the changing, unforeseeable conditions of existence. In fact, Tambunum today spans both banks of the river since erosion has claimed vast portions of the main village since the early 1990s. During the annual floods, amid the rising waters and treacherous village paths, social life is confined to small islands of culture: domestic and cult houses. These islands are erected exclusively by men (chap. 4). Yet they are motherly spaces of shelter, adorned, as I just noted, with wave motifs. Even culture and social life, despite a terrestrial grounding in the labors of men, are ultimately aquatic.[4]

The Myth of Sago: From Sex to Sustenance

Eastern Iatmul attribute their strong bodies and vigorous culture to the consumption of sago, a starch produced from the palm tree *Metroxylum sagu*. Men chop the pith, which female kin scoop into an apparatus fabricated from various parts of the tree. After ladling water into the pulp and kneading the mixture, women squeeze the cloudy liquid through filters and troughs, where it settles on the bottom and dries (fig. 1). The raw sago is then stored in clay pots or, more commonly today, empty sacks of rice. Whether fried into flat cakes (*nau*) or boiled into a gelatinous soup (*njangwi*), sago is the sine qua non of a

Sepik repast. Men even report a nostalgic yearning for fried sago when they reside outside the region or visit Australia and America. Any type of sago is said to be a source of vitality, courage, and vigor. Yet adults especially value youthful meals of sago cooked by their mothers. Similarly, maternal uncles, in their capacity as male mothers, are associated with gifts of fried sago, garnished with meat. But all such meals must be prepared by women since only they, men say, can properly cook sago. Sago is therefore a culinary idiom of nurturing motherhood. But the mythic origins of sago bespeak a rather different image of motherhood, one considerably more grotesque than moral.

There was a woman named Kwianalagwi, an ancestress of the Mboey Nagusamay patriclan. Her body was covered with fetid boils. The odor was repulsive but the male leaders of the clan allowed Kwianalagwi to remain with the group. The clan ascended Kombrongowi Mountain [the totemic name for all land that lies south of the river]. While the group slept, Kwianalagwi plucked a sore from her left shoulder and threw it on the ground at the edge of the camp. It is called Asamaymbange [a totemic name for sago]. She yanked another sore, this time from her right shoulder, and did the same. It is named Avanau [another totemic name for sago]. The sores became sago palms. The group continued to sleep, while the wind rustled the fronds of these new trees. In the morning, the clan awoke to the sound of fluttering leaves. They saw the trees and named them Naugamburungundu. Kwianalagwi instructed the men to cut down a sago palm, split it open, and chop the pith. Then she told the women to construct an apparatus out of leafstalk, bast tissue, leaf sheath, and limbum palm. The men put the chopped sago into baskets that they gave to the women. In turn, the women processed the pith through the apparatus and produced five baskets of sago starch. At Kwianalagwi's command, the women cleared away the debris, carried the baskets of sago into their houses, and tried to fry it in clay hearths. But nothing happened; the processed sago did not congeal into edible pancakes. Then Kwianalagwi gave instructions for a couple to have sexual intercourse atop the sago-washing apparatus, so that male and female coital fluids would drip into the sago as it was drying in the troughs of water. They followed her advice. Afterward, the women were able to cook the sago into edible pancakes. Since then, we cook and eat proper sago.

As in many Oceanic and Southeast Asian cultures, this myth attributes sago to sexuality, gender, and the body (Ruddle, Johnson, Townsend, and Rees 1978, chap. 4; McDowell 1991, 34; Tuzin 1992a). Yet several specific transformations in the Eastern Iatmul tale merit further attention.

Kwianalagwi, in an act of self-disembodiment, plucked abscesses from her skin and threw them onto the ground. Ordinarily, a woman's procreative powers are embedded inside her womb or belly (*iai*). Kwianalagwi's fertility, how-

Fig. 1.   A young, unmarried woman processes sago for her family

ever, was located on the surface of her body. In the myth, too, sexual intercourse, and the combination of male and female genital fluids, was a necessary moment in the metamorphosis of a natural and raw substance into a cultural, nurturing, and cookable food. But here, procreative fluids dripped downward and outside of the body; they did not migrate upward into its interior. The myth, in other words, inverts processes and distinctions that define the moral topography of the feminine and maternal bodies.

Similarly, heterosexuality in the myth resulted not in a pregnant wife and a mother, as we might expect, but in edible sago. This idea of carnal nurture points to a dialogical relationship between motherhood and masculinity. Sexual relations with women, when viewed from the androcentric perspective of Eastern Iatmul politics and social structure, are necessary for the reproduction of kin groups and society. Men need children. But sexual contact with women, all men say, is debilitating. It imperils men's ritual efficacy, hastens aging, atrophies the body, and renders men vulnerable during warfare (see chap. 3). Indeed, the foul odor of Kwianalagwi's pustules resembles the way village men describe the scent of female genitals and menstrual blood, both of which are antithetical to the ideals of masculinity (see also Lidz and Lidz 1989, 68; Tuzin 1992a, 111–12). In its original state as uncooked and uncookable antifood, sago symbolizes men's perception of female sexuality: raw, wild, dangerous, and repelling, yet necessary and desirable.[5]

Kwianalagwi's body, too, signifies postmenopausal decomposition. Elderly women are normally harmless for men. But they are nonreproductive. They do not imperil a man's virility—but neither do their bodies enable him directly to reproduce his lineage. From this perspective, the transformation of Kwiana-lagwi from an elderly woman into edible sago represents one answer to a central predicament of masculinity: How to reproduce without acknowledging the indispensable roles of women, heterosexuality, and female parturition. Recall that Kwianalagwi lived alone, on the periphery of society. The scent of her decaying body repelled people who might otherwise have enjoyed interacting with her—perhaps even have been fed by Kwianalagwi. This mother was non-nurturing, maybe even dying. Her nurturance was only revitalized through dis-embodiment and sexual intercourse. In this myth, sago is a metaphor for the reproductive process. It makes sexual intercourse and childbirth literally palat-able for men whose erotic desires for women, and potential interests in partici-pating in birth, are dampened by pollution beliefs. Yet, ironically, explicit sexual intercourse is a central element in the myth. Through contrary images—old/new, raw/cooked, parthenogenesis/sexual reproduction, and nature/cul-ture—the myth of Kwianalagwi expresses men's high valuation of moral moth-erhood and their fear of the female body.

There is one final point. Kwianalagwi's body, as the source of sago, was a tree body. Yet all other trees, especially towering and phallic coconut palms, are masculine (chap. 4). In fact, male ancestors planted trees in order to create a solid foundation for culture and social life amid the watery, feminine state of the primal cosmos (chap. 3). Kwianalagwi, as a maternal tree, thus appears to be androgynous. Not only is she a grotesque mother, in the Bakhtinian sense, but she is also a pregnant and phallic mother whose generative potential remained untapped until decay and sexuality rendered her benign and nurtur-ing. Where once Kwianalagwi was an object of male dread, she is now a culi-nary symbol of maternal tenderness and care. But while the uneasiness about Kwianalagwi may have been replaced by the nourishment of food, motherhood herself, in the imagination of men, remains contradictory.

Social Spaces

Tambunum, with a population that hovers around one thousand, is the largest village in the middle Sepik. Three large patriclans define themselves as legiti-mate social and cosmological categories on the basis of unique mythic histories and totemic names. These groups also assert custodial rights over residential wards, gardens, streams, sago palm groves, uncultivated grasslands, forests, spirits, and ritual sacra. Most of these entitlements are justified by reference to names and the mythic events they memorialize. Clans are subdivided into patrilineages (*yarangka*), then branches (*tsai*).[6] Most descent groups are exog-amous and patrilocal.[7] They tend, too, to be arranged hierarchically in accordance with ancestral primogeniture. This ranking, however, confers only minimal politicoritual prerogative, no trading entitlements, and no privileged access to resources.

The three major patriclans in Tambunum are named Shui Aimasa, Mboey Nagusamay, and Mogua. The initial ancestors from each group climbed out of a primordial pit and created the universe along distinct migration routes through the bestowal of totemic names (chap. 3). Shui Aimasa's leading ancestor hero, Tuatmeli, walked across the primal sea. Each step created ground that Tuatmeli named and then tapped with his spear in an evident gesture of phallic fertility. His expanse of land, which stretches north of the Sepik River, is the totemic domain of the Shui Aimasa clan. The ancestor heroes of Mboey Nagusamay and Mogua did likewise, respectively materializing the ground that lies to the south of the river, including the Highlands, and the sea.[8]

Tambunum contains a fourth patriclan, named Wyngwenjap. But this group is so diminutive politically and demographically that I did not even learn of its existence until several weeks into my 1988 village census. Nonetheless, Wyngwenjap corresponds to an important topographic and cosmological feature: the Sepik River. In addition, the group's affiliations illustrate nicely the linkages that often blur the boundaries between descent groups. From the perspective of mythic history, Wyngwenjap unites with the Mboey Nagusamay clan since this group was the source of a bamboo tube of water that Wyngwenjap poured into the Sepik basin, forming the actual river. For most practical and ceremonial purposes, however, Wyngwenjap associates with the Mogua clan, with whom it shares a distant genealogical connection and, broadly speaking, a common aquatic totemism.

Descent, inheritance, and jural obligations are consistently reckoned agnatically. Yet, as in many Melanesian societies, descent is only one of several principles that govern social life. Other factors include residence, affinity, and especially matrifiliation. Actually, matrilateral sentiment often *overshadows* the jural force of patriliny. During disputes, for example, a man is expected to endorse his avunculate rather than his own father and agnatic kin. Still, the emotional force of matrifiliation, which arises from the semiotics of motherhood, is unable to supplant entirely the androcentric structure. Maternal sentiment, we might say, is an ever-present emotion that periodically washes away the fixtures of patriliny, much like the river erodes the trees and houses of men.

Cosmic Spaces

The four patriclans of Tambunum map onto a quadripartite cosmos, complete with four cardinal directions and four seasonal weather patterns (Silverman 1997, 105; Bateson 1932, 254–55; Wassmann 1991, 10–11, 203). These spaces, to repeat, were created largely by male ancestors who formed land, planted trees, and erected villages out of an aquatic void. I will have more to say about this process in chapter 3. For now, I want only to identify the cosmological contrast between a primal, watery feminine formlessness and male beings who shaped the landscape and its distinctions.

Male and female imagery can also be discerned in the mythic geography of the river itself. The sinuous riverbanks are formed by the parallel bodies of a snake and eel, which are totemic ancestors of the Wyngwenjap clan. The two creatures look at each other near the village of Yambun, upriver from Avatip (map 1). Traditionally, this location was a geographical terminus in the local cosmography; it is characterized by river rapids. The tails of two subterranean beasts extend to Manam Island, an active volcano that towers above the sea near the mouth of the Sepik. When the two phallic creatures periodically entangle the tips of their tails, say Eastern Iatmul, the volcano erupts in fiery destruction, a violent conclusion to what may be an image of same-gender coitus.[9] This aside, the mythic topography of the Sepik River represents the masculine containment of feminine water—an enclosure that is annually burst by flooding.

The village itself, like the broader cosmos, is differentiated into gendered spaces. A married woman, unless she is visiting kin elsewhere in the village, tends to remain in her husband's domestic ward, gardens, and riverbank. In the early morning light, just after daybreak, women quietly paddle their small canoes through the cool mist and set fish traps along the shores of the river, which they later retrieve at dusk.[10] Young children also remain within the domestic ward, or with their mothers. Adolescent boys and girls roam throughout the village, seemingly unaffected, at least today, by spatiojural rules (see Leavitt 1998). Men, if they are not occupied by some form of intermittent labor, usually gather in ceremonial houses and related ritual spaces.

The main village corridor, the male path (*ndu yembii*), closely parallels the Sepik. It affords a nice view of the river and thus, in a sense, allows men a privileged gaze. In other Iatmul villages, where river erosion may be minimal, this path leads to the senior cult house and is thus barred to women, girls, and uninitiated boys. The female path (*tagwa yembii*) traverses the middle areas of the community. Ideally, men avoid it. Anybody can walk along the bush path (*muli yembii*) at the rear of the village. But this path borders on danger since it leads to the undifferentiated forest and its menacing denizens: mysterious cassowaries, fierce boars, seductive tree spirits (*winjiimbu*), diaphanous ghosts (*wundumbu*), and, formerly, sorcerers (*kwikwandu*) and sorceresses (*kwikwalagwa*). Narrow footpaths, which link together houses within individual wards, traverse the three gendered walkways. Overall, the spatial layout of the village consists of a lattice arrangement of paths and zones defined according to age, gender, prestige, and even morality.

The three parallel paths of the village roughly correspond to levels of existence. Humans live on the surface (*aiwat*) of reality. Spirits inhabit a concealed (*attndasiikiit*) world. For this reason, they possess powers that exceed the abilities of mortals and other phenomena that merely reside on the "surface" of existence.[11] This stratigraphic metaphor, we will see, also organizes totemic names (chap. 3) and the local ethnophysiology such that masculine bones support a surface of feminine skin (chap. 4). Men would thus seem to be primary in this spatiosomatic ontology. Yet women and *not* men are averred to be the true supports or "stools" of the village, which is a direct result, men say, of feminine fertility and nurture. Since women are associated with interior and hidden, or *attndasiikiit*, powers, the primacy of masculinity is illusory. Appearances to the contrary, the lives and concerns of men pertain to the surfaces and facades of social life.

The Emergence of a Local Modernity

Tambunum today is thriving. As local people tell it, their current renown builds on past military successes and former control of regional exchange routes that circulated shells and other preciosities. In the main, Iatmul speakers dominated the Sepik through superior magic and totemic names in addition to warfare (Harrison 1987, 1990, 1993a; Errington and Gewertz 1987a; but see Hauser-Schäublin 1990). A simplified version of their language was the lingua franca of regional discourse and trade (Mead 1938, 159–60; Foley 1986, 25; Williams 1995). Mead (1938, 163), ever the keen observer, understood well a key reason for the success of Iatmul villages in the precontact Sepik: "an absorptive and retentive ability in excess of their powers of integration." This elasticity enabled these large communities to attune their structures, categories, and symbols to the upheavals of the past century.

The first European to explore the Sepik River was Otto Finsch in 1885, one year following Imperial Germany's annexation of New Guinea, then termed Kaiser Wilhelmsland. By the early twentieth century, labor recruiters were regularly prowling the Sepik, or Kaiserin Augusta Fluss, as well as ethnological expeditions (see Kaufmann 1985). An administrative post, established at Angoram (map 1), tied the middle Sepik into a distant governmental structure that remains in existence today, albeit in the form of a postcolonial nation-state. European steel knives and axes supplanted a neolithic technology; many of these implements are still utilized today and evoke bittersweet stories of culture contact. Recruiters and indentured laborers introduced into the Sepik unprecedented quantities of shell valuables and even porcelain imitations manufactured in Europe. There was pronounced inflation. Exchange networks were disrupted; some faded altogether.[12]

After World War I, the League of Nations transferred the colonial administration of New Guinea to Australia as a Mandated Trust Territory. In the 1920s and 1930s, the river was a principal source for labor recruiting (Firth 1983, 164). Young men who worked on coastal plantations returned to Sepik speaking tokpisin (Neo-Melanesian pidgin), the national language of Papua New Guinea and a creole for many urban dwellers. The Pax Australiana allowed Eastern Iatmul to venture to areas that were previously inaccessible due to warfare. Likewise, men employed as porters on official Australian patrols paddled to the upper reaches of the river and trekked across the Sepik Plains into the Prince Alexander Mountains. Many Eastern Iatmul migrated in the 1930s to the Bulolo gold fields near the modern city of Lae. Most never returned. The localized world was rapidly expanding.[13]

Eastern Iatmul recollect the horrors of World War II in terms of a brutal Japanese occupation and devastating Allied bombing raids. Fear and hunger were widespread; people allegedly fled to caves in the distant hills. Several local men were murdered, including a renowned sorcerer who could apparently transform himself into a parrot; he was the father of Gamboromiawan, one of my principal research assistants. Villagers report that they were forced to feed and labor for the Japanese soldiers, for which they were recompensed with occupation script.[14] Ironically, this currency is now offered for sale to tourists.

During the past one hundred years or so, Sepik societies have increasingly confronted alien social, political, and economic forces (Gewertz and Errington 1991; Smith 1994). Many of these changes were, and remain, disempowering. Yet premodern modes of ideation have not been outright erased (Metraux 1976). Many transformations actually foster novel modes of local creativity and agency—new forms of space and time (Silverman 1997; Smith 1982), for example, a self-conscious awareness of "tradition" and, in tokpisin, "kultur" (Errington and Gewertz 1996a; Silverman 2001a), and innovative aesthetic styles (Silverman 1999). Mead is vindicated: Eastern Iatmul continue to assimilate new cultural ideas and social forms.[15]

Modern Manhood

During World War II, some Eastern Iatmul men served in the Australian army, a common occurrence throughout New Guinea and Papua. In Tambunum, this experience still elicits mixed emotions of pride and bitterness. Villagers rejoice at the bravery and military endeavors of their grandfathers during the war. Yet they resent the trivial trinkets and paltry commendations these men received at the conclusion of the conflict. The war promised a certain degree of equality between Australians and Papua New Guineans—a shared sense of masculine realization. When the soldiers went home, local men were effectively abandoned. Resentful and disillusioned as they were, they were left on their own to re-create a sense of "modern" manhood.

The senior cult house in Tambunum was destroyed by Allied bombers.[16] The conflagration disrupted the annual cycle of full-scale male initiation (see Roscoe and Scaglion 1990). There are minor initiatory events during funerary rituals, and men have constructed a series of modest cult houses adjacent to the former structure. In 1994, too, they cleared space in the jungle behind the village for the construction of a new cult house that will rival in splendor, I am told, the former edifice. Nevertheless, male initiation remains dormant in Tambunum. While this rite will hopefully revive, the related activities of warfare and sorcery are unlikely ever to do so. Indeed, sorcery is an imprisonable offense in Papua New Guinea, and Eastern Iatmul are of one voice in their frank endorsement of its demise.

While the events of modernity have modified and extinguished several traditional arenas in which local men forged their manhood, new institutions have to some extent filled these gaps. These include schooling and literacy, participatory democracy, vocational training, cash employment, capitalist prosperity, familiarity with Western norms, and the acquisition of prestige consumer goods (see Errington and Gewertz 1996b; Knauft 1997). Tourism, too, enables men to express their assertive agency and creativity, especially through art but also through the generation of lore concerning trysts with European women and other intercultural entanglements of sexuality, aggression, and rivalry (Silverman 1999, 2001a, 2001b; relatedly, M. Morgenthaler 1987a; Errington and Gewertz 1989; Schmidt 1990; Gewertz and Errington 1991; Coiffier 1992a). Tourism, in fact, is the single greatest source of cash today. While Eastern Iatmul often comment on the travails of participating in a cash economy, the village, which lacks electricity, of course, contains no shortage of outboard motors, radios, cassette recorders, kerosene lanterns, and bicycles— even the occasional VCR!

The Catholic Church also structures the lives of some Eastern Iatmul men (see also Gewertz and Errington 1991). Early in the last century, German Catholic missionaries proselytizing for the Society of the Divine Word irresponsibly exposed male cult secrets to women and destroyed the men's magical bamboo flutes (see also Bateson 1935b, 164; Hauser-Schäublin 1977, 144). Yet the Christian devaluation of traditional ritual verities was not totalizing. Although many people endorse the Church's emphasis on nonviolence (Tuzin 1997), men continue to comport themselves with an aggressive ethos. Likewise, participation in Church activities does not invalidate naven ceremonies, totemic chanting, and funerary ritual. The involvement of local women in the Church, it is true, exceeds that of men, both in number and fervor. But, in sum, Christianity has not engendered radical transformations of self, gender, and identity in Tambunum.[17]

By contrast, men and women in another Sepik society, Ilahita Arapesh, recently embraced millenarian Christianity as the path to utopian gender equality (Tuzin 1997; relatedly, see Brison 1995). Men divulged ritual esoterica to women and abandoned a long-yam cult that encoded an "abstract, shimmering, metaphysical way that is the mystery of livingness" (Tuzin 1997, 35). Christianity was enthusiastically espoused. But no egalitarian paradise ensued. Instead, men suffered enormous cultural anomie, and social tensions escalated with a devastating increase in domestic violence. The "mystery of livingness" that once defined masculinity simply disintegrated.

The recent history of Tambunum lacks Christian revivals, indigenous annihilations of ritual and religion, and abrupt attempts at reshaping masculine identity. Men who ally themselves too closely with Christianity, in fact, may forfeit their voice and legitimacy in ritual and local politics. Eastern Iatmul enforce no exclusions on the basis of baptism or totemism. Most inhabitants of the village are adherents to both cosmologies. They experience little sense of theological incongruity (see Gewertz and Errington 1991, 156). Tokpisin choral songs to Mama Mary increased in the 1990s, a shift that is befitting of a culture that so deeply values motherhood. But her presence is no more monolithic than that of Papa God and, more significantly, the crocodile spirits.

For most men, biblical beliefs and Catholic rituals seem rather more linked to amorphous notions of the nation-state and modernity than to glimpses of ultimate reality (Errington and Gewertz 1995, chap. 4; Silverman 1999). Eastern Iatmul do not evaluate monetary success and failure in terms of Christian morality, as Smith (1994) powerfully illustrates for Kairiru Island (relatedly, see Brison 1991). Economic distinctions are unrelated to village politics.[18] The vibrant and steady tourist trade has in many respects maintained the village's traditional position as a regional center. Hence, the traditional cosmology is in no need of total reorganization.

Tambunum contains several small trade stores that stock a range of commodities: tobacco and rolling newspaper, warm beer, canned meat and fish, cooking oil, sacks of rice and flour, batteries, kerosene and petrol, aspirin, tea, coffee, powdered milk, cookies, biscuits, soap, and laundry detergent. Intermittent sources of income include the sale of tobacco, betel nut, fruit, fish, chickens, and the occasional dog for ritual exchange. Some men are regularly employed in towns and cities as teachers, merchant ship crewmen, army personnel, lawyers, provincial labor officers, policemen, store clerks, and prison guards. They often provide monetary support for village activities, such as the acquisition of a truck that provides frequent transportation to Wewak, the provincial capital town. But these men and women often return to the village to be, as they say, with their aging mothers.

Capitalism, of course, emphasizes egocentric personhood, individual desire, and the self as a bounded moral unity. Yet these figurations of identity fail to eclipse the force of sociocentric selfhood and the norms of reciprocity that govern gift-exchange and kinship-based morality (Silverman n.d.). With the exception of outboard motors, the status and symbolism of manhood are largely removed from wealth. In fact, the capitalist self in Tambunum draws on a traditional valence of individuated personhood, which I discuss in subsequent chapters.[19] My point here is not to deny changes in selfhood and subjectivity. Instead, I want to suggest that Tambunum today is neither a "fragile Eden," to draw on Errington and Gewertz (1995, 5), nor an "inflexible tradition," but a hybrid of heritage and modernity.

Indeed, Eastern Iatmul men have long-standing experience with contrary moral forces and paradoxical constructions of identity. The tragedies of masculinity in Tambunum are not exclusive to the world system. They pertain, instead, to the myth of sago and the ambiguous body of Kwianalagwi. It is motherhood, and not modernization, that endures as the great enigma for Eastern Iatmul men.

3

Cosmic Bodies and
Mythic Genders

The genesis of the Eastern Iatmul cosmos began with calm water, not chaos. Eventually, a wind started to blow over this vast sea (*melembe*), and land surfaced amid the waves. A chasm opened, called the totemic pit (*tsagi wangu*), out of which emerged five ancestors. These culture heroes radiated outward along migration routes or totemic paths (*yembii*), like spokes on a wheel as John Mban Tubundu once drew in the dirt, and created the universe.

As the originary fathers (*nyait*) trod upon the primal sea, distinct regions of land materialized under their footsteps.[1] Darkness prevailed. With long forked branches, the ancestral quintet thrust upward the opaque sky and separated night from day. They established villages and marriage. Male offspring, individually or as sibling sets, further differentiated the landscape by setting forth on their own migration paths across the larger totemic spaces.[2]

During these mythic-historic perambulations, male ancestor heroes generated the features of the world through the power of toponomy or naming. They conferred names to mountains and streams, stars and weather, flora and fauna, villages and cult houses, even mundane activities such as chopping a sago palm and scraping the pith. The ancestors planted gardens and trees that, along with land, formed a terrestrial realm for human society that complemented and contrasted with the original aquatic state of the cosmos. Indeed, the original ancestors are sometimes envisioned to be trees themselves (see also Wassmann 1991). Every descent group traces its ancestry to one or more of these cosmogonic paths. Eastern Iatmul, drawing on an idiom of patriliny and masculine procreation, refer to totemic names as their fathers and grandfathers (*nyai'nggwail*), or simply grandfathers (*nggwail*). Men, as well as some women, are deeply passionate about names since they represent the history, or roots (*angwanda;* also *ndup-mi, mi-munga*), of the lineage. In my experience, sober Iatmul men weep in public on only two occasions: the final gesture of a naven rite and the ceremonial recitation of names.

My concern in this chapter is not simply to describe the local cosmology (Silverman 1996, 1997).[3] Rather, I want to highlight the preponderance of bodily and reproductive idioms in this totemic system and thus to begin constructing my argument concerning the relationship between masculinity and motherhood.

Totemism and Identity

Descent groups in Tambunum, as I remarked in chapter 2, define themselves as legitimate sociocosmological categories on the basis of unique totemic migrations during which ancestors named the world into existence. The memory of these migrations is encrypted as long chains of paired polysyllabic names called *tsagi*. Any entity that possesses a totemic name is in some sense animate and sentient. The name bestows a numinous quality of beingness, what we commonly label a spirit or soul (*kaiek*).[4] Names are pivotal for male personhood. They specify a man's jural obligations, politicoritual prerogatives, and magical renown. For this reason, all configurations of the totemic system, except for the primal pit and sea, are inevitably contested.[5] The most prestigious men in Tambunum, called *numa ndu* (big men),[6] are not men who can boast the greatest economic wealth or success in material pursuits. Instead, leaders are elder men who possess extensive ritual and totemic knowledge (Metraux 1978).

Totemic names are also personal names. Each patrilineal descent group divides its names into two alternating sets, paths, or "lines" (*mbapma*) that repeat every second generation (Bateson 1936, 244; Wassmann 1991, 277–83). A man's names and those of his father's father, son's son, and so forth, conform to one line; the other would include his son, father, and so on. Or, to phrase this system in a different way, a man inherits one line of names from his paternal grandfather; he confers another line, his father's names, onto his children.[7] Similarly, a woman receives names from her father's father's sister, which her brother will later bestow onto his son's daughter.

Totemic namesakes, human and otherwise, share a consubstantial identity (Harrison 1990, 48; 1985a; 1985b). Persons also, through their names, identify with living, dead, and future agnates in the same totemic line. The identification with paternal grandparents and grandchildren is especially important. This is a common pattern in the Sepik (e.g., Mead 1935b, 203). But in Tambunum, persons may actually adopt characteristics of their deceased namesakes and be held accountable for their misdeeds. This way, names in Tambunum disperse a person's identity and culpability across time and space.

The identification between person and totem is not merely esoteric. It is a real presence in everyday social life. Every mythic entity, for example, has a living human counterpart, someone who possesses the very same totemic name. Subsequently, men recount myths in the present tense and using the first-person pronoun as if they themselves, or their living kin, were the actual primal protagonists (see also Harrison 1983, 14–15; 1990, 161–62). It is not the case, though, that moments in a personal biography may resemble a "lived totemic myth" (Young 1983). Rather, myth may resemble biography. Mead (1964, 75) suggested that this "scrambling" of time, space, and generation created a "broken, discontinuous sense of the self" and that, "in addition, this is a very poor situation into which to introduce new knowledge." But I am inclined to invert Mead's suggestion. Epistemic discontinuity actually enables the ready integration of novel institutions, as Mead herself noted when describing the regional traffic in objects and ideas (see chap. 2). Moreover, the apparent fragmentation of the self, while true on one level, partially arises, at least in the case of names, from the stratigraphic ontology mentioned in chapter 2. Hence, on another level, names ensure that distinct beings possess a common essential identity. This mystical continuity exists "underneath" any "surface" or bodily differences.

I dramatically witnessed the force of totemic consubstantiality during a Christmas dance in 1988. The dance was acquired in the 1950s from the Murik of the Sepik Estuary in exchange for a feast; the transaction occurred near the modern town of Lae, in another province of Papua New Guinea. Today, youth in Tambunum perform the dance in honor of Christmas and New Year's Eve. The accompanying song concerns two fish that are portrayed by embellished wood carvings. Each year a different clan sponsors the celebration. Despite its foreign origin, Eastern Iatmul easily incorporated the dance into their ceremonial repertoire since the totemic heraldry of each clan includes ancestral fish. Prior to the dance, men decorate the wooden sculptures in the bush behind the village and bespell them with love magic to seduce women. During the ceremony, two totemic spirits from the sponsoring clan dwell in the images.

In 1988, a drunken youth slashed one of the fish with an axe. He was immediately beset upon by an outraged sponsor of the dance, Aguotmeli, whose personal name happened to be identical to that of the totemic fish. Notwithstanding the obvious corporeal differences between the man, the wooden image, and the ancestral creature, all three entities embodied the same totemic soul. The assault on the fish was at once an attack on Aguotmeli's sense of self.

Reproduction and the Male Cult

In Tambunum, of course, women give birth. The reproduction of the cosmos and society, by contrast, is the privilege of men. Lacking wombs, they use names and totemic accoutrements. Or, as Hogbin (1970, 101) heard famously on Wogeo Island, "men play flutes, women bear infants."

Conception and gestation, in the local procreation ideology, are essentially egalitarian. Upon birth, this somatic unity ceases and, henceforth, individual qualities are important. Social and politicoritual differences largely result from achievement rather than ascription. The cosmology mirrors this reproductive paradigm. The totemic pit that birthed the world, which is a topographic feature of no uncertain uterine symbolism, was a collective unity.

Creation was the differentiation and separation of entities from the primeval void. For the Iatmul of Kandingei village, the "negatively valued" stage of cosmic creation was characterized by "darkness, aimless roaming, the maternal womb, prenatal time and standstill" (Wassmann 1991, 52). This era was succeeded by "positively valued . . . brightness, postnatal time and movement." These latter traits are associated in Tambunum with ancestor heroes who wandered the primordial sea, naming into existence the features and categories of the natural and social world. Devoid of a totemic name, an entity is essentially nonexistent. It resides outside the lineaments of cosmology, history, and society. Names therefore possess the power to create and, through ritual, re-create the universe.

The male cult in Tambunum lacks fixed age-grades. Nonetheless, descent groups are loosely ranked in accordance with their onomastic regalia. Men from high-status lineages oversee the rituals that enact totemic creation. These men personally identify with those culture heroes who generated the primary paths of the world. As such, they assert themselves as the true fathers who begot the village and surrounding cosmos. A comparison with the Murik (Lipset 1997, chap. 4) may be useful. Senior ritual leaders or *sumon goan* among Murik, who validate their leadership through the possession of shell-and-boar's tusk insignia and plaited baskets, may be either men or women. In actuality, though, they tend to be men. The symbolism of Murik leadership, while it is androgynous, is anchored to a vision of preoedipal motherhood—a mother who gives food and thereby creates indebtedness. In Tambunum, the insignia of leadership are names, not material emblems. Titleholders, such as they are, tend to be men alone. Their power resembles that of a birth mother, not a nourisher. Hence, men in Tambunum respond to the pervasive maternal schema, or their culture herself, by excluding women from the cult and feigning birth. They also, as we will see, give food. Yet the provisioning of nourishment is second to the enactment of parturition.

Totemic birth is a male entitlement. Its creative powers issue from names rather than wombs, and engender differentiation and hierarchy instead of gestational sameness.[8] Somatic bodies, in fact, delivered from women, are overlain with totemic identity, born of men (see also Harrison 1985a). Since men dominate the inheritance and distribution of names, totemism is a male sociopolitical system that resembles a maternal body writ large. Names endow men with the procreative powers responsible for cosmic creation.

The symbolic equivalence between totemism and reproduction was corroborated by a research assistant who claimed that the ultimate determinants of human pregnancy are senior crocodile spirits (*wai wainjiimot*). As a proverb states, *nian wangay, mbandi wangay;* or, the crocodile spirits alone give birth to children (*nian*) and initiated men (*mbandi*). In this idiom, the procreative capacities of women are ultimately administered by numinous crocodiles. Among Murik, conception is administered by humans—yet the "true mother" of the womb is a spirit "bat mother" who lives in the placenta (Lipset 1997, 54).

By contrast, the birth mother in Tambunum has proprietorship over her womb. Yet the crocodile spirits cause the presence or absence of the fetus. These mythic beings are also responsible for the existence of dry ground. In some scenarios, they stirred primal mud into land. In other tales, they float on the primordial sea while supporting the ground on their backs (see also Schuster 1985; Wassmann 1991, 84, 91). Wai wainjiimot crocodile spirits are crucial for cosmological and human reproduction. Yet the crocodile spirits communicate *only* through men since men alone are the current custodians of names, flutes, and ceremonies. Since totemism is central to male ritual and politics— in part, because it symbolizes birth—somatic reproduction is magically consigned to the realm of ancestral crocodile spirits and the male cult.

A younger man named Koski unknowingly confirmed this interpretation. Young boys in Tambunum often play naked. But little girls are almost always clothed below the waist. I asked Koski about this disparity one day, as we milled about aimlessly at the top of the village. He replied in a mixture of tokpisin and vernacular "no gut ol i lukim *tagwa wainjiimot!*" In other words, "men shouldn't see women's [*tagwa*] genitalia!" But instead of speaking *kitnya* (vagina), Koski said *wainjiimot,* the word for spirits and, more importantly, the sacred flutes of the male cult that, as he added, are forbidden to be seen by local women.

Koski is a bright, responsible man, a good father and husband, the son of a noted carver. He has a wonderful disposition and great respect for the totemic and ritual system. Yet Koski is no stranger to humor, and we both chuckled at his statement. Nonetheless, his reply summarized a central theme of the culture, namely, the transformation of female fertility into totemic names and male ritual esoterica. Masculinity, he revealed, is defined in terms of female fertility and motherhood.

But the local imagery of motherhood is dialogical rather than unitary. In Kandingei village, male "clan founders" were responsible mainly for the establishment of society, dry ground, and settlements (Wassmann 1991, 178–81).[9] It was an ancestress, though, who was "the most important bringer of culture," including tools and pottery, "and it was out of her body that some of the useful plants grew." This cosmogony recalls the mythic origins of sago from Kwianalagwi's body (chap. 2).[10] Wassmann also indicates that the first ancestress of each Kandingei clan was a cannibalistic ogress. Like motherhood more generally, at least in Tambunum, the originary ancestress in Kandingei was dangerously orificial yet indispensable for humanity and men. She was, in short, irreducible.

Androgynous Gender and Mythic Beaks

The totemic pit (*tsagi wangu*) was a landed cosmic womb amid a feminine sea of fertile potential (see also Hauser-Schäublin 1977, 124; Wassmann 1991, 182).[11] The term *wangu* or pit is polysemic. In the context of sexuality, it connotes a vagina. But in a play on homophony that forms the basis for a rich repertoire of jokes and comical asides, a uterine *wangu* resembles a phallic *wangi*, or an eel, and thus a penis. This androgyny aside, Eastern Iatmul still use two terms to unambiguously designate man and woman: *ndu* and *tagwa*. How can we make sense of this dual conception of gender, at once discrete and blurred?

For the most part, Western forms of gender are proprietary: "breasts belong to women" and "phalluses are the property of men" (Strathern 1988, 127). Yet Melanesian gender, as I discussed in chapter 1, is "transactional" and mutable rather than fixed and innate (Strathern 1988, 1991; Weiner 1995a). Persons continuously incorporate and detach, or consume and feed, somatic substances and bodily tokens (e.g., Meigs 1984). The body, to echo Leenhardt ([1949] 1979 , 21), "is filled with the world's pulse." Conventional meanings of male and female, writes Strathern (1988, 128), "at best discriminate points in a process." While Melanesians do interact as same-sexed beings who are singularly male and female, the person is also cross-sexed or androgynous. In Melanesia, as Weiner (1995a, 27) writes, "the organs of men and women are always both penile and uterine in our terms."

Eastern Iatmul genders do manifest nonoverlapping and complementary categories (Weiss 1994a; McDowell 1984). Men fish with three-pronged spears while women use nets and traps; men stand in canoes, women sit; men carve, women weave; men have penises and testicles, women have vaginas and wombs; and so forth. Yet the symbolism of local gender expands beyond this dichotomy and "differentiated form through the biological sexing of individuals" (Strathern 1988, 184) to suggest the image of a "common pool."

I am particularly interested here in myth and ritual, since these symbolic forms or metaphoric dialogues communicate messages about the central themes of a culture. In Tambunum, these messages concern fecundity, birth, reproduction, nurture, and aggression. Eastern Iatmul myth and ritual do not, however, divide these vital capacities into two static categories. Instead, maleness and femaleness are defined on the basis of the *same* qualities (see also Stanek 1983b, 166). Yet gender is still dual; differences exist. Each gender emphasizes in a unique way certain elements in the common pool while attenuating others.[12] Hence, as Mead (1940a, 349) observed among the Mountain Arapesh, male urethral bloodletting was likened to female menstruation, while urination among women was equated with men's purificatory bleeding. Furthermore, gendered dispositions in Tambunum are often transacted between the genders—especially, again, in myth and ritual—or associated equally with male and female.

Perhaps the clearest example of transactional gender in Tambunum occurs in a myth about the hornbill. Here is what Gamboromiawan, one of my closest informants and village friends, and a respected totemic scholar in his own right, had to say:

> In the beginning, the hornbill (*tshiibut*) had a narrow and short beak. When he tried to eat fruit, the long-beaked pigeon (*namwiyo*) would force

the hornbill away and eat it himself. One day the hornbill saw a female *yentshuan* bird. She had a small body yet an enormous beak. The hornbill also noticed that all yentshuan birds removed their long beaks, grass skirts, and woven hoods before bathing. The hornbill wanted this beak. But a few yentshuan always stood guard over the detached bills while the others bathed. It was not right, thought the hornbill, that such a small body should have so large a beak whereas I, with my large body, should have only a short beak. So the hornbill magically tricked all the yentshuan birds into bathing together. When they left their beaks unguarded, he stole them. Now yentshuan birds have small beaks but are skillful fliers whereas hornbills have long beaks but are poor fliers. Nevertheless, the hornbill can finally fend off the pigeon.

This myth depicts the partibility and common pool of Eastern Iatmul gender.[13] The long beaks were twice detachable—first, by the bathing female birds and, second, by the male bird's thievery. This doubled transaction poses two related questions that, while seemingly innocent, are actually quite significant. If the beaks were an innate bodily possession of the female birds, then why were they always removed prior to bathing? But if the long beak is an integral part of the male body, then why did the hornbill need to pirate it from his gendered alter?

After telling the myth, Gamboromiawan added that the mournful song of the yentshuan bird today is a call for her lost beak. This avian lament suggests that the beaks are in some sense rightfully feminine rather than masculine. In this myth, I suggest, the long beak is an androgynous appendage of phallic aggression. Both genders identified themselves as uniquely same-sexed (male or female) on the basis of a temporary guardianship over the beak—yet not at the same time. Neither gender, however, can be said to "own" the bill exclusively.

The mythic proboscis is a transactional element in a common pool of gender. But gender in Tambunum is not merely androgynous and transactional. This is a vital point. In this culture, as we just saw with regard to totemism, masculinity mirrors motherhood. No such parallel yearning, however, exists for femininity. Hence, the male bird gained awareness of his somatic limitation only after he gazed at the body of the female bird. He then desired, and stole, what she displayed. True, the female bird today longs for the beak. But she does not aspire to assume a masculine form. She wants only to regain what she lost. Her yearning is restorative; his, mimetic.

The Primal Theft of Masculinity

In the primordial past, women were the sole trustees for ritual sacra such as bamboo flutes. One day, men purloined the ceremonial objects (see Hays 1988). Now men alone blow the flutes (fig. 2). From one perspective, the flutes are androgynous, not unlike the mythic beaks; they are uterine phalli, and

Fig. 2. The intimacy of flute playing in the forest beside the all-male ceremonial house

phallic wombs (see also Lutkehaus 1995a, 216–19; Gillison 1980, 1987, 1994). From another perspective, however, which I now elaborate, the flutes represent the masculinization of maternal reproduction.

Flutes are called *wainjiimot,* a term that refers to a broad category of fecund spirits. Wai wainjiimot (crocodile beings), we have seen, are decisive for human conception (Silverman 1996, 36–37). Yet men and men alone now impersonate these spirits through flute music, other ritual sounds, and various forms of ceremonial costuming. The current era of masculine ritual license, however, was preceded by a time when mythic ancestresses enjoyed the flutes and other sacra such as water-drums, whistles, and masks. Still, men always held one ritual sound-producing object: the bullroarer (*yartwai*). A bullroarer is a narrow, tapered strip of wood that is attached to twine and twirled in the air to produce an eerie low-pitched sound. Primal men, using the din of their bullroarers, frightened away the ancestral women and stole the flutes and ritual objects (see also Dundes 1976b; Hauser-Schäublin 1977, 161–66; Tuzin 1980, 34–35, 55). Now men carefully guard all acoustic paraphernalia lest women, they fear, reclaim their lost sacra and transform men back into figures of cultural impotence and dependence.

The myth of the primal theft is a powerful ideology that justifies men's overall ritual and political prerogatives. But the myth also deconstructs these androcentric claims by asserting the primacy of women and mothers. For example, Eastern Iatmul associate flute tones not only with the voices of crocodile spirits but also with birds (*vabi*). With few exceptions, such as the myth of the hornbill, birds are likened to women and, in this context, flute-playing avian ancestresses (see chap. 4; Wassmann 1991, 181). The musical talents of these bird-women are legendary; they played the flutes with effortless beauty. By contrast, men's instrumental abilities today are barely competent, demanding conscientious and exhausting practice. Men are especially fearful that they will err during a flute performance and arouse the scorn of women.

Hauser-Schäublin (1977, 146), in fact, reports that men in Kararau may secretly dispatch young boys to mingle with women during flute performances in order later to report back on whether or not the women enjoyed the melodies. Men, of course, would never admit to this snooping, at least not to women, lest women learn the "truth" of the numinous voices. Nonetheless, Hauser-Schäublin (1977, 146) also reports that women are not only aware that the voices are male flutists, but that they also know the very identities of the flute players. Further still, women are proud when their husbands can properly blow the melodies. Hence, the male cult, she writes, is "secretive" rather than "secret," that is to say, a cultural artifice of manhood.

If the flutes symbolize male sexuality, then the myth of the primal theft represents one aspect of men's psychosocial development, namely, the emergence from dependence on mothers and the "coronation . . . of masculine domination" (Juillerat 1988, 68).[14] Similarly, Hauser-Schäublin (1977, 166) suggests that the myth of female primal dominance arises, in part, from the close mother-child bond that is the norm of early socialization (see chap. 6). The flutes represent men's dependence on, yet emancipation from, phallic motherhood. Thus, as Hauser-Schäublin (1977, 165–66) writes, *mythic* Iatmul mothers, including the women who once blew the flutes, are understood by men to differ categorically from human mothers and eligible sexual partners, such as wives, since men "honor" and "fear" these mythic mothers. And indeed they should, since these mothers, in one myth (Hauser-Schäublin 1977, 161), killed all male infants and reared only girls.

Murik men once ascended the cosmic hierarchy of their male cult by lending wives, who are classed as "mothers," to cult partners, thus renouncing sexual attachment to mother-figures (Lipset 1997, 210). At the same time, the powerful *kakar* spirits, which are phallic spears, substitute masculine aggression for primary symbiosis. But Murik masculinity does not transfer uterine fertility to the cult house itself since heterosexuality was a part of cult practice. By contrast, the flutes in Tambunum *do* represent female fertility. As reflected in another myth, though, we can discern further symbolism in the image of the flute.

In this tale, women inhabit the hollow interior of bamboo trees (see also Mead 1940a, 377–78). The women were unaware that men existed. Yet men would carefully visit the village when its all-female inhabitants were foraging in the forest or cultivating gardens. Slowly, the women suspected the presence of others. They hid in the trees, saw the men, and seduced them into sexual intercourse and marriage. The bamboo trees, which allude to flutes, are uterine. They resemble everted and self-reproducing wombs that shelter women. But these trees or flutes also represent feminine erotic allure.[15] Likewise, the myth of the primal theft hints at a resolution of the classic Oedipus Complex. Men must learn to divert their libidinal energies away from mother-figures and redirect eros toward female contemporaries and legitimate marriage.[16] Despite the maternal and feminine imagery in the current myth, the flutes are now monopolized by men. The flutes symbolize the phallus. Yet they also define masculinity as a variant of femininity and motherhood. And if men are not careful, women may steal them back.

In fact, the possibility that women might reclaim the flutes and reestablish an epoch of phallic motherhood and feminine ascendancy is a real concern of men. Men in Tambunum tie the efficacy of ritual to the success with which they stage a visual and aural spectacle for women; ceremonies may range in ambience from solemnity to outright flirtation. This is true throughout Melanesia and Aboriginal Australia (e.g., Hiatt 1971; Lattas 1989; Shapiro 1989; Hogbin 1970). Men *must* display sacra to women during ritual. In doing so, however, men might relinquish, should they be careless, their current hegemony over cosmic forces.

From this angle, ritual taunts women. It offers them a glimpse of a possible cultural order that is unlikely to occur, or occur again, memories of which are either unknown to women today, or simply unspoken. In Kararau, writes Hauser-Schäublin (1977, 165), women are not only knowledgeable about men's primal theft of their sacra, but they are proud of their former custodianship over the flutes. I myself, perhaps due to my gender, did not gain a similar understanding from women in Tambunum. Nonetheless, both Hauser-Schäublin and I agree that, while women, at least in Kararau, have no interest in regaining the flutes and therefore restoring a mythic order of feminine ascendence, men themselves are nonetheless fearful that women may try to do so.

At the same time, ritual is as perilous for women as it is for men. Any woman who views "too carefully" the sacred wood carvings during a ceremony, or even glances at the flutes and other sound-producing objects, imperils her reproductive powers. This is explicitly stated by both men and women. Moreover, the husband and male kin of the transgressive woman would be obliged to compensate the cult house with a substantial gift of wealth and food (see also Hauser-Schäublin 1977, 163). For these reasons, men display sacra to women only after they have applied what Mead (1938, 175, 200) called "theatrical" and "disguising" ornamentation to the ceremonial objects. Similarly, men always play the flutes from within some enclosure, well-concealed from the eyes and potential grasp of their original feminine guardians.

What compels Eastern Iatmul men to define themselves to women through these ambivalent ceremonial revelations? These displays, I now want to suggest, disclose in public, *before women,* some essential, dangerous, and taboo facet of masculine identity. During ritual, men dramatize with emotional, intellectual, and aesthetic poignancy the predicament of their masculinity as a failed figuration of motherhood. During ritual, men camouflage yet express their desire for maternal fertility. They deny yet acknowledge their somatic inability to give birth (see also Mead 1949, chap. 4). Ritual is a masculine boast, yet a tragedy of manhood.

After the primal theft, human reproduction remained in the foreground of female identity. Women yielded the flutes but they could still be mothers. Masculinity, however, was dramatically altered since men now defined themselves on the basis of purloined embodiments of female fertility. Men, in other words, could now be mothers, too. But, in a sense, Eastern Iatmul men were *always* mothers. They did, of course, steal the flutes from women. Nevertheless, men already manipulated the bullroarer, which Dundes (1976b) has brilliantly interpreted as the symbolic appropriation of female reproductive powers in the guise of a "flatulent phallus." The bullroarer, in fact, is part of a wider symbolism of male anal birth that will become increasingly important as my analysis unfolds. The flutes, therefore, merely enhanced a preexisting dimension of masculinity, namely, men's desire for the parturient capacities of women.

Dundes (1962) also offers a framework for interpreting the cosmogonic role of mud in Iatmul myth. Primal mud, he argues, like the bullroarer, is often a masculine idiom of anal birth. This suggestion is corroborated by totemic tales that trace the origin of land to earthworm excrement (Bateson 1932, 405) and ancestral feces (Wassmann 1991, 126). Taken together, the parturient symbolism of the bullroarer, primal mud, and ancestral excrement suggests that the flutes are not simply "transactional" tokens of procreative capacity that shifted from women to men. From a psychodynamic framework, these sonorous objects of the male cult represent the masculinization of motherhood (cf. Strathern 1988, 359 n. 9). The anal birthing symbolism of the flutes, bullroarers, totemic feces, and riverine sludge all attest to a yearning by men for the birthing abilities of women. But women exhibit no such comparable desire. For while men purloined the flutes from women, primal women did not steal anything from men.[17] In short, masculinity is androgynous, yet maternal.

Male Initiation: Giant Vulvas and Homoerotic Horseplay

Myth traces the origin of male initiation to men who, wishing to emulate the cosmogonic powers of wai wainjiimot spirit beings, conspired to inscribe crocodile scales into their torsos. This adornment symbolized masculine prerogative since the process of scarification was, and remains today, censored from women. Yet the primal men were frightened of the painful procedure. Would they survive? Would the scars be noticeable and, more important, *admired* by women? Out of fear and uncertainty, the men first tried to "initiate" a dog. It worked. So they killed the dog in order to conceal the undertaking from women. Then they successfully scarified a woman and slew her.[18] The *human* genesis of male initiation, then, occurred on a female body. But the rite was quickly transformed into a male privilege that differentiated masculinity from female identity. Or so it seems.

The myth about initiation and the actual rite itself suggest that men strive to replicate childbirth. They emulate the fortitude of women during delivery with their own ceremonial trauma and blood. The express goal of male initiation is to "grow" boys into men through bodily transformation inside the all-male cult house.[19] Despite the regime of physical brutality and bodily indignities (Tuzin 1982), male initiation in Tambunum and throughout the Sepik is permeated with idioms of parturition and maternal nurture (e.g., Bettelheim 1954; McDowell 1991, 135–37; Telban 1997a; Lipset 1997, 159–62). With raffia umbilical chords strung around their waists, neophytes are smeared with mud that, after Dundes, bespeaks masculine anal parturition. Initiates are fed, toward the end of their seclusion from women, huge meals of sago and pork by their male initiators, who are called mothers (*nyame*) or elder brothers (*nyamun*).[20] Ideally, these meals so strengthen the young bodies of neophytes that their real mothers will no longer recognize them.

Cicatrization is a major component to Iatmul initiation. These cuts, men say, purge from the bodies of neophytes the last drops of maternal blood that, acquired at birth, stymie their full growth into men. Hence, as Hauser-Schäublin (1977, 178) recognizes, this purgative symbolism could not easily transfer to women. The scars themselves provide visible testimony to the consumption and oral rebirth of initiates from the mouth of wai wainjiimot crocodile spirits. The achievement of masculinity, according to this logic, requires men to nullify the maternal fluids of parturition. But male initiation is a rite of rebirth; its expiations are mimetic. Men elicit in a same-sex context what is otherwise the outcome of cross-sexed or male-female relations. Likewise, the famous markings resemble, according to men, the breasts and genitals of women and female crocodile spirits (see also Weiss 1987b, 184). The manifest content of the rite, which is the theme of exclusive manhood, is called into question by the latent symbolism of the patterned scars themselves. In male initiation, men assert themselves as procreative women and aggressive mothers.

Images of birth, growth, and feeding, which men ordinarily associate with tender mothers, are cast during initiation into what Bateson (1936, 130) called "the spirit of irresponsible bullying and swagger." An Australian travel writer who recently underwent initiation himself in Kandingei (Allen 1987, 136) reports that novices crawled through the swaying legs of twenty initiators. When they emerged from this "bruising tunnel," they were forced to consume a choking dollop of coconut, sago, and ancestral bone scrapings. A violent image of parturition, in other words, was followed by an equally aggressive cannibalistic repast. As Bakhtin might have said, the male initiation rite is a grotesque dramatization of moral reproduction and motherhood.

Initiation hardships seem to be modeled directly after the *pain* of parturition (see also Telban 1997a, 318).[21] Neophytes should suffer their travails stoically. Any screams are muffled from the ears of women by men who beat on slit-drums. Similarly, women in Kararau who endure birth silently are a particular source of pride for the village (Hauser-Schäublin 1977, 121–22). In the past, I was told, as in birth, some neophytes actually died. Hauser-Schäublin (1977, 147) contends that the male cult and women's bodies are separate and equivalent systems of value such that the cult, specifically, is unable to transcend the powers of women. To some degree, this is true. But male initiation, and the absence of any such rites for women, suggest just the opposite: uterine powers, which men desire, are ultimately transcendent.

In addition to themes of death, rebirth, and bodily harm, initiation also contains the threat of castration. These torments are not perpetrated by paternal figures but, rather, by the female body itself (see also Mead 1938, 348)—by phallic mothers, as per Juillerat (1999, 162).[22] After scarification, initiators crop the hair of their charges, place the trimmings inside the uterine "belly" of a makeshift wai wainjiimot crocodile spirit, and sink the creature into a swamp. More strikingly, "giant vulvas are clapped down" on the heads of novices by initiators (Mead 1949, 115). The entrance to the ritual enclosure is called a crocodile mouth or "clitoris gate" (Bateson 1932, 432, 439; 1958, 282). This imagery is aggressive, oral, and sexual, as a vaginal maw consumes boys and then disgorges them as men (see also Tuzin 1982, 348–50). These allusions arise from men's fear of engulfment by the maternal body. They are also coupled to men's envy of female fertility, a yearning that is emphatically denied.

The physical ordeals of initiation also, in the past, entailed male sexual aggression and homoeroticism (see also chap. 10). Ritualized homosexuality is common in Papua New Guinea (Herdt 1984a; Knauft 1993; Allen 1998). But it is absent in Iatmul communities (cf. Keesing 1982, 11 n. 6; Herdt 1984a, 43–47, 62; Knauft 1987, 158; Lindenbaum 1987). However, Bateson (1936, 131) did comment that novices, while "being mercilessly bullied and hazed," were called the "wives" of the initiators, "whose penes they are made to handle." In his unpublished fieldnotes, Bateson (Notebook G. IV) reported on other forms of sexualized "play" during the rite.[23] One initiator fell and "insisted on being lifted by penis." Another "dances squatting with anus towards *bandi* [neophytes]." When a third initiator tumbled against a post, neophytes were instructed to tug at his leaf-enwrapped penis. When they finally pulled away this floral sheaf, the initiator feigned death.

This "nonorgasmic homoerotic horseplay" (Knauft 1993, 232) established a dominance hierarchy within the male cult by feminizing novices (see also Creed 1984). Yet homoerotic sexuality during initiation was not solely an idiom of political order. It also flirted with taboo eroticism. Normally, men view any sexual encounters among themselves to be antithetical to the ideals of manhood. I will have more to say on this topic in later chapters. For now, I want only to note that the carnal pranks of male initiation, should they occur in any other setting, would be highly shameful to men, *especially* if seen by women.

Under the auspices of the male cult, these otherwise humiliating gestures of prohibited sexuality are reframed within the religious system and made to symbolize a masculine cosmology. But try as they do, men are unable to erase the erotic tones of these gestures, and the intimacy of the cult house.

One strategy men in Tambunum employ toward denying their homoerotic desires is comedy. This metamessage, to invoke the language of Bateson, also serves to disguise the recognition that masculinity is a rendition of motherhood. During initiation, homoerotic pantomimes are humorous. But this drollery contradicts the very seriousness of men's birthing fictions and therefore calls into question the local value of manhood itself. Comedy, in other words, becomes tragedy.

A Parturient Metaphor for Male Esoterica

The everyday life of men also reveals the presence of uterine symbolism. Hardly a day passed without my hearing the characteristic drumbeat of a totemic recitation (*tshui tsagi*) somewhere in the village.[24] These ubiquitous chants are informal gatherings; men, children, and even women casually come and go. Yet totemic recitations are far from trivial. They summon enormous magical and spiritual power.

Totemic chants initiate large-scale ceremonies, such as funerary rites, and consecrate houses, canoes, and ritual paraphernalia. Today most totemic recitations abate a form of mystical retribution known as *vai* that causes illness and a host of misfortunes. Vai typically results from the violation of a social or ritual norm. It also develops from any willful or inadvertent damage inflicted on totemic entities such as houses, canoes, and masks. Less frequently, vai arises from past homicides and sorcery. The key quality of vai is that it persists long after the original infraction. It has the ability, as local people say, to remain "in the ground." Unless averted by a totemic chant, the vai may eventually "turn back" and afflict the perpetrator's kin.[25]

The sponsor of a totemic recitation must not himself actually chant. Instead, he solicits the aid of ritual specialists who, while they perform the recitations of names, receive food, betel nut, and tobacco. The sponsor must also feed fried sago and cooked chicken to his sister's children (*laua-nyanggu*). This meal of avuncular nurture enables nieces and nephews "to grow and become strong." At the same time, the sister's children eat on behalf of their maternal ancestors, with whom they identify during the event, whose exploits are commemorated by the recitation. These gifts of food are in no way ancillary to the magical efficacy of the chant itself. They may, according to some, be more important than the actual recitation. If a man must enact a chant but he is simply unable, or unwilling, to provide food and betel to the chanters, he can perhaps effect the same outcome merely by feeding his nieces and nephews. In a real sense, then, the act and intention of staging a totemic chant each revitalize four types of bodies that occupy the concerns of men: the cosmic body, the social body, the magical bodies of matri-spirits, and the somatic bodies of sisters' children.

The totemic system is astonishingly complex (Bateson 1932; Wassmann 1991). Each name is binary: a large name (*numa tsa*) or elder brother (*nyamun*) linked to a little name (*mak tsa*) or younger brother (*tshuambo*). Hereditary leaders carefully regulate the disclosure of many little names since they often embody immense mystical power that adversaries could deploy in malevolent magic. Public names can also be termed *aiwat nyangiit,* "external speech," while secret names and knowledge are *attndasiikiit nyangiit,* "underneath speech." The attndasiikiit concept is important. It refers to phenomena that metaphorically exist inside (*aiwula*) of, or hidden (*pagu*) from, the obvious (*kapmba*) elements of human awareness, which reside on top (*yaapmba*) of reality.

Iatmul totemism is Platonic (see also Wassmann 1991, 218). The world of appearances bears little relation to the world of essences. Secret names, which lie beneath the realm of public comprehension, refer to underlying relationships between primal ancestors and events that are known only to a few erudite men.[26] These names, writes Wassmann (1991, 61–62, 170, 222–23), are an elusive shadow of truth that lurks beneath the "non-reality" of the public totemic system. Indeed, totemic pluralism is illusory. In actuality, there are only a few ancestral beings who transform themselves into a diversity of subordinate forms (Wassmann 1991, 169; see also Harrison 1990, 56).[27] These primary spirits merely slip, as it were, into temporary "envelopes" (Wassmann 1991, 170), much as men don costumes for ritual.

Since esoteric names are so concealed, men may resort to magic at the beginning of ritual in order to "raise" these names to consciousness. Totemic memory is often likened to a basket (*kumbi*). By chanting the names of a clan's totemic basket (*tsagi kumbi*), ritual specialists "open" their collective memory and ensure that the proper names and melodies "flow" during the actual ceremony. This way, men avoid the ire of totemic spirits, and the ridicule of women.

The image of a totemic basket resembles cosmic creation. Totemic differentiation resulted from the opening of the totemic pit. Likewise, men during ritual unfold a basket of memory in order to be assured of an accurate outpouring of names. These idioms, as I intimated earlier in this chapter, are not like regal baskets among Murik, which signify the plentiful food offered by a mother (Lipset 1997). Rather, totemism in Tambunum is modeled after the capacity of women to bring forth children. In Melanesia, argues Herdt (1997a, 219), the seclusion of women during birth forms the basis for a broad ontological premise: acts are truly creative when they transform things that are public and visible into things that are secret. Equally creative, however, at least in the middle Sepik, are acts that transform concealed phenomena into public displays. Both dimensions of this process are integral to male ritual. And both are rooted in an image of feminine parturition and fertility.

Debating Mystical Power

A layered, inside/outside concept of reality and numinous esoterica is common in New Guinea (e.g., Jorgensen 1980, 1990; Barth 1975, 1990).[28] The degree of truthfulness attached to any totemic or cosmological assertion thus pertains to its relationship to other details of sacred knowledge. Epistemic certainty is ascribed only to "inside" or secret knowledge. Yet all interior truths, especially those disclosed in public, can be seen as the superficial or outer surfaces of another hidden and therefore more powerful body of knowledge. "The point of social communication," writes Weiner (1995b, 6), is therefore "to release the evidence of knowledge in a controlled and allusive way, to show the proof that it exists rather than the knowledge itself." Concomitantly, prestige often arises from the entitlement to know something rather than the actual information one knows (Simmel 1950, part 4; Lindstrom 1990; Weiner 1995a). This episte-mology is sustained by an "aura of ambiguity"[29] that lends itself to a highly contentious politicoritual structure. Not surprisingly, a great deal of men's life in Tambunum revolves around totemic disputes.

Totemic knowledge is a form of symbolic power. It creates hierarchy and difference in the ritual system and village social organization (see also Lind-strom 1984; Harrison 1989b, 1995a). *Tsagi numba* (totemic persons) are men who command considerable respect. They have studied names through a lengthy and arduous apprenticeship under the tutelage of a clan elder (Metraux 1978). In turn, these ritual teachers receive food, canoes, garden produce, sago, and often a large house. Access to totemic knowledge and mystical reproduc-tion is thus exchanged for worldly productivity.[30]

Formerly, a few women were also totemic specialists; they were called *tsagi tagwa* (see also Hauser-Schäublin 1977, 136).[31] Likewise, I was told that there must always be one woman in the village who knows the truth about the spirit voices—that they are men blowing flutes. She often serves as an intermediary between the male cult and village women since she alone can approach, yet still not enter, all but the senior-most cult house. This woman, called a *wainjiimot tagwa*, must not tell any other women what she knows about the flutes except for one successor, often a daughter, from the next generation.

The last woman to hold both of these putative titles in Tambunum was Mundjiindua, a wonderfully vibrant person and one of my closest confidants in the village. In a private discussion, Mundjiindua confessed to knowing that ancestresses once enjoyed blowing the flutes and staging the ceremonies but that men killed them in order to steal the sacra. For this reason, she volun-teered, women are "senior" in birth rank to "junior" men. It is noteworthy that Mundjiindua said nothing about the bullroarer, even when I tried obliquely to coax this information from her. Clearly, this object is unknown even to the wainjiimot tagwa. In October 1989, Mundjiindua mentioned that another mid-dle-aged woman in the village, Wanmbaymange, wished to inherit this role. Yet Mundjiindua told her to wait, for, as she said, "I am not an old woman yet!"

Tragically, Mundjiindua died in 1990. She never did entrust the secrets to Wan-mbaymange. Most men believe that the office of wainjiinot tagwa will now remain vacant.

The idea and actual presence of wainjiimot tagwa adds another dimension of inside/outside knowledge to the totemic system. It also suggests that totemism is a debate, albeit one that is ideologically loaded in favor of men, concerning the gender of names and sacra. In practice, however, this debate may often put men in a dependent relationship to women and wives. As Hauser-Schäublin (1977, 167–69) discusses, Iatmul women are extremely knowledgeable about myth. True, myths told by women lack the totemic names that are so important to men's tales, and that effect a greater aura of potency than women's legends. Lacking names, however, women's myths also lack the veil of secrecy that surrounds male narratives. As a result, a woman's knowledge of myth may actually exceed that of her husband—she may even need to tell him myths so that he can appear knowledgeable to anthropologists and peers! In this sense, the ideological contention by men that women's tales are "outside" knowledge when compared to their own "inside" myths is, in actuality, often inverted.

Despite the official inclusion of some women into the esoteric body of totemism, and the fact that men must often rely on women for mythic knowl-edge, the totemic system has always been dominated by men. Yet the andro-centrism of totemism does not pertain solely to matters of gendered power. Totemism also encapsulates many dimensions of masculine ethos. Totemic disputes are lively, impassioned events. Men challenge the mythic histories of rival descent groups and deny the existence of competing totemic beings. They argue that adversarial totems are little more than the surface forms of their own hidden and therefore superior ancestors. Some men, too, boldly steal names. Political motivations aside, totemic feuds are inevitable since different mythic histories and migration routes often intersect, thus causing uncertainties over the rightful custodianship of certain names and paths.[32]

Debates are staged inside a men's house or *ngaigo* (fig. 3). An orator's stool (*kawa tugiit*) is placed at the center of the floor. The audience sits along the periphery of the building on clan- and lineage-specific platforms (see chap. 4). Disputants successively approach the orator's stool and present their case. They punctuate their rhetoric by striking the stool with a bundle of ginger leaves (see also Bateson 1936, 125–26). Until a man relinquishes this gavel and returns to his sitting platform, he alone is entitled to speak and stand in the middle of the building. From the physical arrangement of a debate, one might conclude the presence of a clearly definable center and periphery in the society and its cosmology. But the low cacophony of peripheral voices—muted replies and offhand comments, requests for betel nut and outright conversation—challenges any so orderly a sociocosmic structure.

Men mnemonically represent totemic names by inserting wooden pegs into the stems of palm fronds (*tsagi ngau*).[33] Each peg references the first pair

Fig. 3.   A communal meeting of men inside the Wingwariimbiit cult house. Visible, in the absence of the facade, is Vendigarlagwa, the female spirit who spreads her legs across a beam and supports the superstructure

of names along a totemic path. The length of a man's tsagi ngau is proportionate to the size of his stock of names. Hereditary leaders, as the de jure custodians over the entirety of a patriclan's esoterica, may enter a debate with a long baton that hold scores of pegs signifying hundreds, even thousands, of names.[34] They may also highlight their elite status by capping the pegs of their most powerful names with bright fruit. It is tempting, when rival men tote their totemic batons to the cult house, to see an image of phallic competition in these debates—and this image would not be unprecedented. Tuatmeli, the first culture hero and spirit to emerge from the totemic pit at the dawn of mythic history (chap. 2), was the sole owner of a primal spear. He alone, late at night, could hunt pig, much to the bafflement of his rivals in the morning as they dined on his pork. Eventually, Tuatmeli's wife stole one of his spears and gave the prized weapon to her brother. Outraged, he killed her. Thereafter, the original ancestors engaged in ongoing, chaotic warfare. Phallic domination, we might say, having been diffused by women and marriage, resulted in eternal competition.

Totemic orators marshal a variety of rhetorical strategies (Bateson 1936, chap. 9). They recite mythic histories, construct genealogies, recount migrations, and chant paths. Men skillfully mock the claims of rivals while trying to muster support of kin and allied descent groups. Most oratory occurs in the vernacular but it is common for men to code-switch into pidgin and English. Ritual specialists, who "carry in their heads between ten and twenty thousand polysyllabic names" (Bateson 1936, 126, 222), rely on their knowledge. Less erudite men count on panache and even belligerence.

Totemic disputes can last indefinitely. Any resolution is tenuous since authority is largely gerontocratic and consensual (see Tuzin 1974). There are no fixed alliances, agnatic or affinal, during these disputes.[35] Men offer support only to those claims that might further their own political aims. It is said that you can always rely on the support of sisters' sons. But in truth, even this moral duty is conditional. Ultimately, totemic authority draws on the threat of violence. But there is no Hobbesian anarchy here. Aggressive posturing does not lead to brawling since a disputant forfeits his claims should he strike a rival inside the cult house (cf. Bateson 1936, 126–36; see also Harrison 1990, 162). In this respect, Eastern Iatmul totemism is paradoxical. It is highly stable, at least in ideology, yet eternally contentious, and it is a male sociopolitical system that betrays its own gender through idioms of female fertility.[36] Totemism, we might say, is as fragile as masculinity itself.

Desire and Social Life

In the nearby Sepik societies of Chambri (Errington and Gewertz 1987a) and Manambu (Harrison 1989b, 1990), men are hesitant about divulging esoteric wisdom to junior kin. These bestowals are necessary for maintaining the intergenerational viability of descent groups. Yet totemic succession depletes elder men of their mystical powers, thus hastening the onset of old age and death. In the end, however, social morality eclipses selfish desire.

Totemic inheritance in Tambunum also prompts a conflict between self and society. But this inner strife centers on themes of autonomy and dependence rather than somatic and cosmological atrophy. Many men, despite their concerns about totemic continuity, simply decline to reveal their wisdom to sons and agnates.[37] It is, as they say, "their problem." Genuine considerations for the future of the lineage clash with a man's sense of individuality.

Similarly, a descent group's totemic chants and rituals celebrate and secure its vitality. But these tributes, as we saw, are accomplished only through dependent exchanges. Totemic recitations, to repeat, require sponsors to feed their sisters' children. Men maintain warm sentimental ties to these kin—yet uterine nieces and nephews are members of different lineages and clans. The totemic specialists who perform chants, too, are rarely drawn exclusively from the sponsor's lineage. Assertions of totemic autonomy thus acknowledge the importance of social trust.

This predicament was vividly portrayed by a man I will call Vabindu. He is poised to inherit the office of a patriclan "father." One day, while speaking in private, Vabindu commented on the inevitable loss of names to other lineages and clans. He specifically bemoaned the steady erosion of his group's mystical power and autonomy. If the lost names were returned, he fantasized, then his lineage could expel everybody else! They would finally stand alone as the legitimate group of the village! No further diminishment of totemic power and names would ever occur! Alas, he recognized, this could never happen, for then who would his kin marry? Where would his lineage seek alliances? Where would they sleep when mystical retribution infected their dwellings with mysterious illnesses? This private yearning confessed to the presence of an unresolvable dilemma in the local experience of masculinity. Men value autonomy and social independence. Yet this desire clashes with the exigencies of social life that demand reciprocity with rival descent groups and the unavoidable assent to dependence.

Vabindu's quandary parallels the relationship between masculinity and motherhood. In Tambunum, unlike in Avatip (Harrison 1990), men alone attend totemic debates. Women are permanently barred from cult houses, which are spatially separated from the domestic areas of the village by rows of palm trees and earthen ridges. Insofar as totemic disputes concern the emergence and structure of the cosmos and human society, these debates enable men to assert regenerative and parturient capacities in the absence of women.

But the maternal body still has a crucial presence during totemic debates and ritual. In fact, "she" is the cult house itself, which, like domestic houses, is explicitly envisioned by men and women alike to be a nurturing mother (chap. 5). The rituals and ideology of masculinity boast of reproductive autonomy, or monogenesis. The practices of manhood consistently exclude women. Ironically, men envelope themselves in a maternal shelter. Indeed, it is only within this uterine space that men can assert themselves as men and not women. A similar set of paradoxes, I now show, shapes the local understanding of the body and sexuality.

4

Human Bodies

Conception ideologies vary greatly across Melanesia.[1] In the Trobriand Islands, for a famous example, conception occurs through the union of a woman and a spirit child who is reincarnated from a matrilineal *baloma* ancestor (Malinowski 1916; Weiner 1976, 122–23). The father has no role in the actual genesis of the child. He merely contributes to the outer substance and growth of the fetus. Yet these bodily substances are ultimately ephemeral since the soul returns to the matriline after death. Since Trobriand society is matrilineal, the procreative primacy of motherhood corresponds with descent and identity. Elsewhere in Melanesia, however, reproductive substances are unrelated to social structure. Thus the Murik understand nurture and postpartum feeding, rather than corporeality or conception, to determine personhood (Lipset 1997). For Eastern Iatmul, nurture and substance combine.

In Tambunum, conception occurs when paternal semen (*ndumbwi*) mixes with maternal blood (*yerokwayn*). A single act of sexual intercourse is sufficient (compare Bateson 1932, 271–72; Hauser-Schäublin 1977, 76, 117). During gestation, semen congeals into bones while menstrual blood develops into organs, skin, and regular blood. Accordingly, the materiality of the body (*mbange*) is male and female.[2]

The sex of the child is said to be determined by the more powerful gendered substance, semen or menstrual blood. But to ensure a male offspring, one man confided, the husband must penetrate the woman from behind during intercourse, a position termed *kwutmbe wagandii*. The "missionary style," he said derisively, tends to result in the birth of girls. The key issue here seems to be the conjunction of sexuality and power since kwutmbe wagandii allows the man a position of carnal dominance. This is a significant issue for Iatmul men who believe, as Bateson (1936, 132) noted, that "a passive role in sex is shameful." Why shameful? Because, as we will see, passive eroticism is understood by men to feminize their manhood.

In this chapter, I survey the symbolism of the Eastern Iatmul body in order to illuminate the erotic passions and taboos of men, as well as their sexual anxieties and vulnerabilities. More generally, I demonstrate that the cosmological dialogue between manhood and motherhood that I discussed in chapter 3 is not merely consigned to the esoteric realms of mythology and totemism. It also finds voice in the immediacy of bodily experience.

Teeth, Hair, Bones, and Fat

In Eastern Iatmul ethnophysiology, muscle (*wimbu*) develops from either maternal or paternal sexual fluids, and sometimes from a combination of the two. The specific developmental path for a person's musculature is governed by the relative strength of each parent's procreative fluids. (One makes a determination on the basis of facial resemblance.) However, most other bodily organs and features are associated with one or the other gender. They may evidence the person's initial association with motherhood, or a subsequent manifestation of paternity.

Milk teeth or "breast teeth" (*mwunya niimbi*) derive from the mother.[3] Permanent teeth are formed from paternal substance.[4] A child's first locks of hair (*niimbii*) are also maternal in origin while later growth is paternal. While most Eastern Iatmul now regularly trim their hair, long locks once characterized warriors, male leaders, totemic men and women, initiates, and, even today, mourners. Unkempt tresses thus signify hypermasculinity and transitions sanctioned by the religious system. The extensionality of hair symbolizes liminal identity, or the ability of persons in certain categories to extend their bodies and agency through social and magical spaces. In some of these contexts, too, namely, warfare and leadership, hair appears to be a phallic expression of supernatural power and aggression.[5]

The bodily dialogue between motherhood and paternity is especially evident in the vocabulary of blood and bone. After conception, the mother's blood or "thick blood" becomes the regular blood (*yerokwayn*),[6] skin (*tsiimbe*), and fat (*kwiya*) of the child. As the pregnant mother eats, she nourishes the growing fetus; the womb is termed the "child's string bag" (*nian wut*).[7] Healthy persons are said to have "strong fat," a compliment that reflects on the generosity and nurturance of their mothers. In the case of men, this praise also acknowledges the success of male initiators who, as aggressive "mothers," beat and humiliate neophytes but then promote the growth of their undeveloped bodies through meals of sago and pork (chap. 3). In the eyes of many men, these meals even exceed the much-touted, nutritive properties of maternal sago. In this sense, initiation requires men to hyperbolize maternal feeding in order to nourish a part of the male body that is otherwise traced to polluting, maternal fluids.

All bones (*ava*) originate with paternal semen. Two bones in particular mark this association: the spine is the "father's bone" (*nyait ava*) and the pelvis is the "grandfather's bone" (*nggwail ava*). The supporting structure of the human skeleton is thus likened to patrilineal ancestors, men who are similarly called *nyai'nggwail* or "fathers and grandfathers." Iatmul women, Mead (1949, 6, 113) recorded, may taunt men with the phrase "have you no bones?!" In this way, women derisively question a man's masculinity as it is defined in terms of his somatic and ancestral strength.

To summarize, male contributions to the body are modeled after maternal substances, as in the case of fat, or simply mocked by women. Since these substances—bone, semen, fat—are white, it seems prudent to inquire into the cultural symbolism of bodily and culinary whiteness.

The Bodily Paradox of Whiteness

The spine is connected to the brain (*njagula*), which, like the heart (*mauwi*), derives from a combination of paternal and maternal substances. Together, the brain, spine, and testicles (*manda*) form a seminal vascular system. But unlike in other regions of Melanesia (e.g., Herdt 1981, chap. 6; Godelier 1986, 69), semen in the middle Sepik does not metamorphose into breast milk once it is absorbed into the female body through sexual intercourse or fellatio. Breast milk, too, is not classed as a masculine substance (see Weiner 1986), despite its bonelike color. In fact, the prohibition on sexual intercourse during pregnancy is said precisely to prevent semen from combining with breast milk. A violation of this taboo will severely impair the development of a nursing infant.[8]

There is little stated connection between masculine or paternal body parts and white foods such as sago and coconut. But myth, recall from chapter 2, does associate sago with coital fluids. This relationship is problematic for male identity. On the one hand, the origin of sago is traced to an ailing female body and sexual intercourse; the former was repulsive to men, the latter atrophic. On the other hand, men attribute much of their masculine strength to maternal and avuncular meals of sago. While men can augment their supply of semen by consuming sago, they are unable themselves to prepare the cakes or pudding. Instead, they must rely on their mothers and wives to cook this valuable substance. The male cult in Tambunum, too, lacks any rite that replenishes semen; by contrast, Sambia men offset the loss of male fluids by ingesting the "milk sap" of certain trees (Herdt 1981, 100–101). Men in Tambunum have only two solutions to this dilemma: avoid women, or eat maternal sago. To be sure, Eastern Iatmul men often define themselves through the exclusive somatic substance semen. Yet men are dependent on the very same persons who deplete semen for its replacement: women and mothers.

A similar predicament introduces the mythic origin of coconuts. Coconut, of course, like sago, is a white food. The tale opens with a man's head spiraling up an ancestor's fishing spear and closing its jaws on his testicles. The head refuses to release its bite. The ancestor walks up the riverbank and shatters the skull with a stone axe. The brain falls to the ground and sprouts three coconut shoots.[9] This myth attributes the origin of a nourishing and white substance to a potentially dangerous situation that threatened the somatic integrity and strength of men, namely, oral castration and decapitation. The myth clearly identifies coconuts with brains and testicles. In another tale, a cassowary becomes pregnant after consuming a man's brain. Yet, in the current myth, the sequential transformation of testicles into brains, and brains into coconuts, was enacted through a violation of the male body.[10] The white foods of sago and coconut, while they are nourishing for men, are mythically dangerous for masculinity.

In Kararau, pregnancy magic associates coconuts with women, claims Hauser-Schäublin (1977, 119), not men, specifically the womb and children. Hauser-Schäublin (1977, 156–60) also reports several other myths of the origin of coconut. In some tales, the coconut is uterine. Hence, a bride is given a young coconut shoot by her kin; if the shoot breaks, she can no longer bear children (1977, 159). Pregnancy magic, Hauser-Schäublin also mentions, invokes totemic coconuts, and the afterbirth, as I noted in chapter 4, is buried in a coconut half-shell. In yet another myth reported by Hauser-Schäublin (1977, 159), men had intercourse with young coconut shoots prior to the appearance of women. However, coconuts also symbolize during ritual and warfare rites the decapitated heads of enemies, both in Kararau and Tambunum.

I agree with Hauser-Schäublin (1977, 160) that mythic coconuts symbolize male and female fertility, and male and female bodies. But this is only one matrix of meaning. As I just discussed, the symbolism of the coconut biting a man's testicles also conveys an image that threatens masculine virility and procreative potency. This is another level of meaning. And while mythic coconuts, too, as Hauser-Schäublin (1977, 160) concludes, mediate between male and female fertility—another level of meaning—I disagree with her statement that it "would definitely be wrong to draw the conclusion that Iatmul men imitate the fertility of childbearing women." In sum, I understand the mythic and ritual symbolism of coconuts, at least in regard to masculinity, as engendering multiple meanings, rather than a singular semiotic system as per Hauser-Schäublin. The coconut, not unlike sago, sustains and subverts, nourishes and emasculates, manhood.

Another totemic tale associates a third white food, breadfruit, with a transgression of motherhood.

A woman was catching fish in a stream when the skull of an adult man leapt on her breast and began to suckle. It refused to let go. The woman's sister tried to knock the skull away from the breast, but he continued to suckle. The skull told the woman that he would release himself only if she fed him breadfruit. She agreed. The skull remained at the foot of a tree while the woman climbed to pick the breadfruit. Along came Wayndugumbwan, an ancestral pig spirit of the Shui Aimasa patriclan, bedecked in all his regalia. The skull tried to flee but the great pig spirit quickly consumed him. In return, the woman and her descent group presented Wayndugumbwan with gifts of betel nut.

Adult men, this myth seems to admonish, should not regress to infantile suckling and dependence on mothers. The desire for the maternal body should be
sublimated into the oral ingestion of white food. Otherwise, men may become
so polluted by the female and maternal bodies that they will suffer—at least to
their own way of thinking—symbolic castration or decapitation.[11]

Thematically, these myths suggest that white foods are neither exclusively
nurturing nor dangerous but rather paradoxical and ambivalent for men. Sago,
coconut, and breadfruit sustain male bodies and, to some degree, replenish
men's procreative substance. They also enable male aggression since men often
attribute masculine valor to the presence of testicles. Yet each mythic source of
these foods is antithetical to masculinity. Sago derived from an ailing mother-
figure and sexual intercourse; coconuts sprouted from an act of castration; and
breadfruit originated in a deadly return to the maternal breast. In sum, white
foods encode a dialogical relationship between masculinity and motherhood.

Procreative Wind

The expulsions of the male alimentary canal are no less complex than the foods
that enter it. The nearby Chambri infer that the "wind" generated by sexual
intercourse imprints the father's patriclan on the fetus, much like totemic
names sculpt the world (Errington and Gewertz 1987c, 146 n. 8). Eastern Iatmul
also identify wind with conception and creation. At the genesis of the cosmos
(see chap. 3), land surfaced out of the primal sea through the agency of wind. A
phallic gust, we might say, stirred the maternal waters, thus effecting cosmic
birth. In some contexts, breezes are expressly female (see also Wassmann 1991,
72, 200); hence a feminine suffix (-*agwi*) is appended to all anemological
totems. Often, however, as I just noted, wind symbolizes masculine procreation or fertility. This association, I now want to show, is an important clue to
the psychodynamic symbolism of the male body and its evacuations.

In a myth reported by Bateson (1932, 272), "a dog had connection with a
woman, and the wind caused her to conceive." Bateson (1936, 230) also mentioned that the "ghost of the dead is blown as mist by the East Wind up the river
and into the womb of the deceased's son's wife." More recently, Wassmann
(1991, 20, 134) recorded a myth from Kandingei where wind impregnated a primal woman (see also Hauser-Schäublin 1977, 161). Wassmann also suggested
that water spirits (*wainjiimot*) are envisioned to be "breath or movement of the
air." For Eastern Iatmul, the crocodile spirits are both male and female. Yet,
"underneath," as one man said, they are male. At any rate, they clearly have an
overarching association in the cult with masculine procreative powers and
bamboo flutes (chap. 3). In an absolute or acontextual sense, wind is androgynous or devoid of fixed gender, much like the flutes and mythic beaks. But in
the specific context of totemism and male ritual, as I have just shown, wind
symbolizes masculine reproduction.

There is one further, scatological dimension of wind that we need to consider. Men in Tambunum view their flatulence to be a type of wainjiimot croc-odile spirit. Men also assert exclusive authority over human and cosmological reproduction by creating the sounds or "voices" of these beings through the use of flutes, bullroarers, and other aerophones. These objects, like men's flatu-lence and feces, are all hidden from women. Indeed, one mythic woman who carelessly walked into view of her defecating husband was killed. The same penalty is allegedly imposed on women who glance at the flutes or other sound-producing sacra of the male cult. A parallel rule, yet one that is not sanc-tioned by violence, applies to the female body since the pubic area of toddler girls is concealed from the public gaze of men (see chap. 3).

Several questions arise. Why is wind associated with men's flatulence? Why is male defecation related to aural procreative spirits? Why are the flutes and bullroarers, men's feces and flatulence, all camouflaged from women? Why is this concealment violently enforced? Finally, why are these masculine symbols correlated with female genitals? Once again, Dundes (1962, 1976b) offers an answer: Men, in their emulative desire for birth, transform vaginal delivery into a masculine idiom of anal parturition. In turn, this male somatic image is projected outward into the world as a framework for envisioning cos-mic creation.

Furthermore, legend describes fire as originating from the primal flatu-lence of a man. In this regard, it is useful to reflect on the serpentine creatures whose bodies define the riverbanks of the Sepik (chap. 2): when their tails col-lide, the Manam Island volcano erupts. Drawing on Paul (1982, chap. 7), I pro-pose that Eastern Iatmul culture often ties together wind, male flatulence, phal-lic creation, masculinity, and fire, in contrast to uterine images, moral motherhood, and water (see also Freud 1932; Bachelard [1938] 1964). Sub-stances that enter the male body attest to men's dependence on women—sub-stances that exit men's bodies confirm their envy of female fertility.

Names and Bodies

Names reveal a different relationship between the male body and motherhood. Patrinames, we have seen (chap. 3), circulate through a fixed intergenerational system of "lines."[12] Semen thus appears automatically to confer paternal iden-tity since fathers do little in the way of actively bestowing patronymics onto their children; there is no naming ceremony (compare Wassmann 1991, 35). In fact, an infant's patrilineal identity is known prior to birth. By contrast, the avunculate in Tambunum is understood to actively provide matrinames for his nieces and nephews. This postpartum conferral may even be delayed for several months or years. These names, too, are not necessarily known prior to birth. Both paternal and maternal names are predicated on somatic substance. Yet the mother's blood, unlike the father's semen, does not by itself translate into a totemic identity.

While grandparents are the source of a person's names, fathers and mothers' brothers tend to be envisioned as the actual totemic executors. However, there are several important differences in the way Eastern Iatmul speak about and envision these two inheritances. First, the conferral of patrinames emphasizes the person who receives them, and the grandparent who from whom they came, rather than the father who gives them. In this context, the father is passive. Conversely, the inheritance of matrinames foregrounds the avunculate, or the donor, as the active person; the sister's son and his maternal grandfather are the passive participants. Yet the avunculate, of course, is not simply an uncle: he is a mother's brother, which in this culture is tantamount to a mother. The bestowal of names is thus an idiom of oedipality since it diminishes the role of fathers and father-figures in social reproduction and highlights the centrality of mother-figures.

A second difference between the inheritance of paternal and maternal names concerns the issue of mortality. Matrinames are fixed for life, in part, because recent ghosts are "pulled" by these names to the place of the dead (see also Bateson 1936, 42; Harrison 1985b). Advanced age, however, and not death, is the sole prerequisite for the inheritance of patrinames. It is common, in fact, for elder men to bestow their patrinames onto paternal grandchildren. These nameless individuals are then known as *kwoiyen*.[13] They remain full members of society but they have ceded their totemic identity to grandchildren. In a sense, kwoiyen are reflections of their former selves or, as one man said in English, "secondhand" persons. Male kwoiyen, too, may also relinquish their personal regalia such as shell ornaments and cassowary feather headdresses. As an elder man peels away the accoutrements of his masculine achievements, he seemingly regresses his body to its original state of unadorned nakedness. Despite his age, he resembles an infant. The reproduction of the patriline, therefore, requires men to self-sacrifice their masculine identities.

The mother's brother (*wau*) not only actively confers matrinames onto his sister's children (*laua*), but he continuously feeds them throughout the life cycle. He also celebrates their achievements with naven rites. (The father, it is worth noting, is entirely marginal during these honorific ceremonies, much as he is in the local understanding of patrilineal naming.) In return, sisters' children reciprocate with valuables. The uncle, when he feeds cooked meat and fried sago to his nieces and nephews, complements the nurturing role of his sister, who nourishes her children with breast milk, premasticated victuals, and, later, whole cooked food. These ongoing tokens of nourishment, both avuncular and maternal, suggest that the uterine facet of identity is dynamic, reciprocal, and fragile. It requires continuous renewal (see also Tuzin 1976, 148–50). Similarly, flesh is delicate, at least when compared to bones, and so demands constant cleansing, that is to say, ongoing maintenance.

The father's role in conception is singular and momentary. During gestation and childhood, the father, unlike the mother and mother's brother, contributes little else directly to the bodily growth of the fetus and infant. Therefore, the discharge of paternal semen must instantly develop into an enduring somatic substance, or bone, and confer an immediate totemic identity.[14] Expectant fathers of firstborn children, it is true, must abide by a series of prohibitions. If the father cuts vine, the umbilical cord will sever; should he split coconut, the child's skull will crack; and so forth. These interdictions might seem to indicate that the father continuously participates in the bodily growth of firstborn children, much like mothers and mothers' brothers. Yet these prohibitions only protect against bodily harm. The father, in this sense, is no nurturer. He simply deposits, as it were, a seminal foundation for bones and patrinames. Conversely, the mother and avunculate directly, even selflessly some people say, contribute nourishment and substance to the growing child.

Patrinames are the roots (*angwanda*) of a descent group, its totemic and cosmological foundation. These names evoke ancestors, primal migrations, mythic creation, and natal ground. The relationship between maternal and paternal identities, then, like that between skin and bones, would seem to correlate with the epistemic contrast between "surface" and "interior" (chap. 3). Casual conversation with men upholds this analogy. Yet men ironically say that motherhood, not fatherhood, is the true support of masculinity and social life.

Landed Immobility and Aquatic Flow

The relationship between men and women is paralleled by the distinction between male and female patrinames. Any totem can be appended by a gender-specific suffix and used as a personal name. The suffixes for masculine patrinames denote man (*-ndu*), body (*-mbange*), ground (*-andi*), forest (*-muli*), person or child (*-nian*), and sitting platform (*-njambe*). The feminine counterparts are woman (*-tagwa*), body (*-mbo*), floating island (*-agwi*), forest (*-mange*), sea (*-woli*), and fishing net (*-njua*). These seemingly random suffixes actually form three semantic categories (see also Bateson 1932, 409–10). One group refers to bodies. Another set contains important features in the regional cosmography: sea, land, and floating islands. The third category refers to artifacts that discriminate gender into same-sex configurations: fishing nets for women, cult house platforms for men. Together, patri-suffixes connote corporeality, topography, and objects. These concepts coincide with the bone symbolism of patrinames themselves, and the abridged versions of mythic history that simply detail the ancestral creation of trees and ground (chap. 3). In pidgin, patronymics are a person's *nem tru* or true names.[15] They elicit an image of thinglike substantiality. They are metaphoric trees, and, as Leenhardt (1979, 19) wrote for New Caledonia, "the tree confers social and civic authenticity on a man."

The physicality of patrilineal names, however, becomes more complex when we parse the gendered meanings of patri-suffixes. Male suffixes depict stationary terrestrial entities: earth, forest, and sitting platforms. Female suffixes refer to aquatic movement: water, fish, and floating islands. These complementary idioms recall the local view of conception and gestation whereby firm, enduring, and white bones contrast with liquid, impermanent, and red blood. As a nongendered category, patrinames are akin to a fixed core that supports the body, personhood, and social life. But from a gendered perspective, male patrinames evoke the permanence of skeletons and terra firma whereas female patrinames allude to the impermanence of nonseminal body fluids and water.

Men Are Wood, Women Are Masks

Maternal names exhibit a dichotomy similar to that of patrinames. There are two, and only two, matri-suffixes: -*awan* for men, -*yeris* for women. Bateson (1936, 42) translated *yeris*, or *yelishi*, as "old woman" and "old lady," and *awan* as "old man." Eastern Iatmul today are unable to corroborate these translations; for them, the etymologies are mysterious. Instead, they simply associate these two suffixes with the concept of matrifiliation.[16]

The word *awan* also refers to clan-specific dance costumes. Through what logic, it is important to ask, are male matrinames signified by a masked figure? The answer, not surprisingly, is the logic of dialogism, specifically, the paradoxes posed to men by femininity and motherhood. The details of this answer begin with the maternal qualities of the awan figure. These costumes are stored in various cult houses. During ritual, the awan exits this masculine space and dances with women. She may playfully scold, tease, and chase young children (see also chap. 9). Like all spirit costumes, the awan is donned by men alone. These ceremonial raiments entirely disguise the bearer's identity. Quite literally, they enclose male bodies. In the case of the awan, however, this enclosure has uterine significance. Most other costumed spirits of the male cult are associated with a warrior ethos. The awan is uniquely maternal. It is an aesthetic idiom of motherly flesh that enwraps paternal bones. Since men are expected to impersonate their matri-spirits during ritual, mothers' brothers not only feed their nephews, they also present them with the awan as a ceremonial "skin."

The artistic portraits of patrilineal ancestors are hewn from trees. The one cult object that signifies matrifiliation, the awan, is a hollow frame rather than a solid carving. It is fabricated from cane and rattan, not wood.[17] When men bedeck patri-spirits with floral adornment prior to ritual displays (chap. 3), the wooden object itself is compared with paternal bone; the ephemeral ornamentation is maternal skin. Similarly, a man who "carries" an awan costume during ritual is akin to the skeletal support for an outer, epidermal facade. In an idiom of corporeality, therefore, the form, substance, and lexical connotations of the awan all suggest that motherhood is a fragile, even superficial, veneer that covers a stable, essential core of paternity. But, as I intimated earlier, this symbolism is inverted when men attribute to motherhood the real foundation for their masculinity.

The *awan* and other feminine objects such as houses and canoes (chap. 5) are striped with yellow paint. This color is often associated with birds and women. I have already discussed one image of avian femininity, namely, the primal flutists (chap. 3). Relatedly, women are "bird people" (*vabi nyanggu;* see also Bateson 1932, 419 n. 48). If you toss a stick at a resting flock of birds, my friend Linus Apingari remarked, they will scatter and squawk like women. Women, too, resemble birds in marriage since they "fly" between arboreal, or patrilocal, lineages. Yellow color also paints an idea of near-miraculous reproduction. In one legend, primal men were molded from white clay; women and certain birds of paradise were fashioned from yellow clay. These beautiful birds, my interlocutor added, are still presumed to be hatched from yellow soil since their eggs remain undiscovered. From a male perspective, then, yellow associates women with unseen, incomprehensible, and wondrous procreative capacities.

The same face that appears on the awan also adorns domestic and cult houses. These buildings resemble the body of a woman and mother (chap. 5). The identical countenance is depicted on the ceremonial costumes of mythic *agwi,* or floating islands, who, during the cosmogonic ritual known as *tshugukepma mbwanggu,* deposit eggs (*mbuandii*) of dry land atop the primal sea.[18] Memories of this primal event ceaselessly drift down the river today. These floating islands remind men that, while land is envisioned to be male in many totemic scenarios, the ground was also hatched from a female spirit. In another Iatmul village, in fact, floating islands are a placental remnant of an originary cosmic mother (Coiffier 1995, 239). Indeed, all four of these bodies— awan, domestic house, cult house, and agwi—exhibit some maternal, nurturing, or birthing capacity. They have an especially prominent feature: large, attentive eyes. For men, these eyes evoke the vigilance of mothers who watch carefully over their children and the entire village.

My aim in this section was to demonstrate that the awan figure and awan matrinames symbolize motherhood, matrilateral identity, and the maternal body.[19] Now I can address the question Why is the awan a masked costume, all outer surfaces and facade, devoid of wooden substance?

The Mysteries of Motherhood

Bateson (1936, 43) was absolutely correct when he wrote that matrinames "represent a more mysterious aspect of the personality" than paternal names. After all, the female and maternal bodies are themselves mysterious to Iatmul men. These bodies contain gestational and birthing capacities that are entirely unknown to men. They undergo physical changes in the absence of male ritual. What's more, men regard birth, vaginal secretions, the loss of semen during intercourse, and even loitering in the domestic areas of the village to be debilitating. Men are particularly fearful of menstrual blood, a pollutant to which they attribute shortness of breath, wrinkled skin, weight loss, withered strength, and magicoreligious impotence. All these female substances and spaces deplete men of the ritual heat (*kau*) that ensures their success in the masculine pursuits of ritual, fighting, and, formerly, gardening. Men, in other words, are unable to act *as men* if they encounter the carnal, birthing, and maternal bodies of women.

Yet these are the precise bodies men desire. Indeed, adult men wax nostalgic about motherhood. Did not your mother, they will ask rhetorically, feed and cleanse you, carry and shelter you? The sentimental bond that unites a man and his mother—or the ideal of moral motherhood—thus appears as a rejoinder to the menacing qualities of the female body that men otherwise fear. Men also recognize that they continue to be succored by mother-figures in the guise of avuncular meals of cooked food. So powerful are the emotions which men identify with moral motherhood that they strive to "get back" their mothers through marriage (chap. 8) and the construction of houses (chap. 5). Men, too, deploy symbols of female fertility and maternal nurture in the male cult such as flutes. In this regard, masculinity is defined as much in terms of motherhood as it is defined in opposition to her.

Mothers enable the growth of infants through daily nourishment. The very concept of moral motherhood, as I have emphasized, is pivotal for adult men. Nevertheless, children and men frequently circumvent their mothers and interact with the matriline solely through the uncle. This expectation affirms yet denies the centrality of motherhood. Similarly, while the role of the mother's brother is maternal, the uncle remains a man. His very manhood, in fact, requires that he continuously assert this nurturing fiction through gifts of food. As far as the uncle is concerned, his "children" are never too mature or autonomous to benefit from a meal. But these assertions, because they are fictions, are as transparent to Eastern Iatmul as they are real. The maternal uncle, like manhood itself, is a mask, much like the awan.

The awan is an important spirit yet the only cult persona who frolics with humans and youth. Youngsters laugh at the dancing awan, yet she chases toddlers and can reproach children who ignore their mothers. In Palimbei, the awan annually roams the village reprimanding children with a stick for all their transgressions: stealing melons from gardens, failing to look after younger siblings, refusing to gather wood for hearths, and so forth (Stanek 1983c, 159). During full-scale male initiation, the awan is a punishing mother who may scold novices for sexual peccadilloes. Initiates, too, were once forced to rub noses with the awan, who then slapped them (Bateson, unpublished Notebook G.IV). The awan, moreover, lacks any aesthetic and ritual counterpart. There is no paternal spirit-clown, no image of manhood that is equally contrary. For men, patrifiliation and masculinity are embodied in a comprehensible form: their own body. But maternal bodies are a quandary for men, the subject of their nostalgia, desires, envy, and fears. The awan, to summarize, represents the dialogical relationship between masculinity and motherhood.

Two Castrating Bodies

Further features of the awan become evident when we consider the iconography of wooden *mai* masks. These patrilineal spirits represent aggression and warfare (see also Forge 1973, 172). While the nose of the awan is broad and flat, the mai spirit's proboscis is long and tapered. It exemplifies the aesthetic transformation of masculine ferocity into what Bateson (1936, 164) termed a "leptorrhine standard of beauty." Whereas the awan is garbed in a woman's skirt, the mai is surrounded, like a male Medusa, with tassels called *tambointsha.* These long insignia, which swing to and fro, were awarded after victorious homicides and head-hunting raids (see chap. 8; Hauser-Schäublin 1983, 24). Prior to pacification, too, the red and white facial designs on the mai were swabbed with black paint after a successful homicide. Black (*ngi*) is the color of violence and ritual heat (*kau*). By contrast, the awan is never blackened. Nor does it change its appearance on the occasion of masculine triumph. Indeed, the flat-nosed awan represents the antithesis of phallic assertiveness and the hypertrophic male body.

When men perform feminine tasks at the cult house such as sweeping rubbish and preparing food, they may slip on the awan costume. When a man, in other words, intentionally feminizes his masculinity, he can also choose to mask his very identity. Mai spirits pertain to warfare and head-hunting rather than domestic chores. In these contexts, men aggressively negate the masculinity of rivals rather than their own manhood. Since Iatmul equate the skull with testicles (chap. 3), head-hunting can be envisioned as symbolic castration, or the forced feminization of men (see Dundes 1997b). The awan, as I detail in chapter 10, may honor a man during a naven rite; yet her iconography inverts his masculinity. The mai spirit, festooned with flowing homicide tassels, proclaims success in warfare. Yet "he" is a creature born of men's fear of castration, much as Freud (1922) argued for Medusa herself.

It is a poignant commentary on Eastern Iatmul masculinity that two prominent spirits that men impersonate before women are emasculating. The mere fact that men alone create, adorn, store, and shoulder these spirits attests to their ritual and cosmological prerogatives. But the mai spirit is an aggressive figure who symbolically severs men's heads and, by association, their genitals. The awan is not a martial figure but a maternal one. Nevertheless, her appearance and demeanor contest the values of masculinity. Indeed, her watchful eyes imply that it is not men who protect the village and its inhabitants, much as they often contend, but mothers.

Carnal Bodies

The feminine or antiphallic features of the awan also express the linguistic and cultural ideal that women are passive during sexual intercourse. Iatmul can only say "he [active subject] has sex with her [passive object]," or *ndu tagwa-*

gat wangutandii (see also Bateson 1936, 141). The statement "a woman [actively] copulated with a [passive] man" is uproarious.[20] Grammar and ideology aside, women *do* initiate lovemaking (see also Bateson 1936, 142 n. 1; Leavitt 1991). Yet while women often refuse men's sexual advances, men would be ashamed to do likewise since women's flirtations, whether genuine or in jest, challenge their domineering masculinity. I am reminded here of the angry husband reported by Bateson (1936, 149) who remarked "Yes, we copulate with them, but they never retaliate." In point of fact, women do often "retaliate," both in sexuality, as I just mentioned, and in other ways, as we will see.

It is important to distinguish not only between linguistic conventions and actual erotic encounters, but also between the aggressive ideal of manhood and the everyday behavior of women. Ideologically, men are active in sexuality. They are also prone to violence when insulted or slighted. Yet these two statements, which any Iatmul man might offer, are at best a partial glimpse into the society. For example, it is women who are associated with unrestrained, appetitive sexuality whereas men are understood to exercise greater self-control over their libidinal urges (Hauser-Schäublin 1977, 75), and it is women, *not* men (or sober men, at least), who have a much greater vocal presence in the village. Men may have the legitimate political voice in Tambunum, but this voice is largely confined to the cult house. To hear the voice of men, as it were, one must seek it out. By contrast, when one listens to the ambient sounds of the village, one hears women as they talk, laugh, yell to one another, and, most significantly, argue and fight. Likewise, women are far more likely to engage in fisticuffs than men.[21]

As a result, men generally attribute all social cleavages and disturbances to women, and especially to the disruptive effects of female sexuality. In 1988, a brawl erupted at the Wewak courthouse between Tambunum and Masandanai, a modest village that now inhabits a small yet lush stream called Kangrime that flows slightly southeast of Tambunum. The two communities have been feuding over the waterway since the 1940s. During this particular brawl, a Masandanai man was disemboweled and killed. Since men in Tambunum feared retribution, they expended enormous efforts during the following months at forging and maintaining a sense of village, and intervillage, solidarity. Daily, however, some dispute or another threatened to rend this political-military unity. During one such quarrel, which resulted in yet another massive meeting in the cult house, Dominick Maibut argued that the source of male discord was the flirtatious behavior of unmarried women. The solution, claimed Maibut, himself the husband of three wives, was to quickly betroth all unwed women, even if it meant that some husbands would now need to assume the responsibility of additional wives.

There may have been some truth to Maibut's admonishment. As Hauser-Schäublin (1977, 75) observes, women are more readily able and willing than men to approach potential lovers and spouses directly. In matters of the heart, a metaphor that is not entirely alien to Eastern Iatmul ethnopsychology, men tend to be somewhat reticent. In order to muster the resolve to approach a woman, a man often requires the psychological assistance of love magic. Women's desires, by contrast, require no such magical empowerment. Similarly, groups of women often embarrass men publicly with sexual innuendo, but not vice versa (Hauser-Schäublin 1977, 74). Still, as Hauser-Schäublin (1977, 77) continues, a "bad" woman means a neglectful mother rather than a woman who, to use our own idiom, is sexually "loose." Female sexuality, I am suggesting, is problematic for Eastern Iatmul men and, consequently, is placed into contradictory categories: passive, yet also appetitive, dangerous, and divisive. At the same time, men are equally conflicted about their own sexuality, which is linked to martial bravado yet requires magic to become real rather than fanciful.

Underlying these diverse and oftentimes inconsistent views of male and female sexuality is one common theme: aggression. Overall, sexuality among Eastern Iatmul is brusque rather than gentle. Indeed, aggression itself, as Bateson (1941, 352) noted, is "self-rewarding" and pleasurable for Iatmul. A man, for example, will "excite" himself to greater efforts while cutting down a tree by imagining that he is actively assaulting it. Children, when driving away mosquitoes, "will smirch them with violent sexual abuse." A splayed tongue signals either a threat or a sexual advance; when used in joking, it is carnal and malevolent (see chap. 9). In these contexts, sexuality is clearly competitive. Some men report that they silently vie with their partner during heterosexual intercourse to see who can stimulate the other first to reach orgasm (*yimi-yami*). Men and women alike are sexually assertive—especially men who consider any passive role in sexuality to contravene the ideals of masculinity. The cultural erotics of competition is summarized by a mythic era in which men and women regularly competed in tug-of-war games. Regardless of which gender triumphed, the goal was always the same: random copulation.[22]

The adversarial dimensions of coitus are cosmological (see Weiner 1995a; Juillerat 1996, 285–86). In the *tshugukepma* ceremony I mentioned in the previous section, sexual intercourse is dramatized as a cosmogonic encounter between a crocodilian ancestor and a floating island (*agwi*) who deposits eggs of dry land. The paternal reptile pursues the maternal island and tries to swat her with his long canoe paddle. In effect, he seeks to direct her reproductive powers to different areas of the primal sea, thus containing or controlling her ability to birth land. But she persistently flees the reach of his aggressive phallus. (Lest this phallic interpretation seem unjustified, consider that the preferred paddle for this drama is the type that was formerly used by men to deflect spears during canoe warfare.) This cosmological theater resembles the local belief that the sex of a child is determined by the "stronger" procreative substance, paternal semen or maternal blood (chap. 3). By the same token, some women report that they "compete" with men during mortuary ritual over who can produce the loudest sounds: (male) flute music or (female) keening. Yet the ceremonial clash of crocodile and island also suggests the presence of an unresolvable tension in the culture between masculine containment and unfettered feminine fertility.[23]

The sexual act in Tambunum is relatively brief, much like the erotic encounters described by Mead (1935b, 216) for Mundugumor. There is little tender or extended foreplay—perhaps only, as some men describe it, hasty caressing of the woman's breasts. There is no deep mouth-to-mouth kissing. Mouth-to-genital contact, which was unknown prior to the arrival of Europeans, is shunned. Men are especially aghast at the idea of cunnilingus.[24] Women's breasts are an object of men's erotic gaze. But they, too, are neither kissed nor sucked. Instead, "breasts are for children." Consequently, some local men understand European sexuality to confound the moral distinctions between eroticism and motherhood. For Iatmul men, motherhood and sexuality are entirely incompatible concepts (Hauser-Schäublin 1977, 136). Nevertheless, marriage regularly blurs the boundary between eros and agape since the ideal form of matrimony reunites a man with his mother (chap. 7). Transgressive concupiscence is thus an institution of social reproduction. We can discern a similar contradiction, as I discuss in a moment, with regard to same-gender male eroticism.

Men associate masturbation with young boys. They do not exactly deny its occurrence among themselves, at least not for *other* men, but masturbation is clearly shameful for adult men.[25] It is discussed strictly sotto voce. Sexuality is largely a private matter in Tambunum. Little honor, for example, is accorded to female virginity.[26] Nevertheless, sexuality is not consigned to "nature," as among Yafar (Juillerat 1996, 284), where it is banished entirely from the "cultural" spaces of the village. Likewise, heterosexuality is neither humiliating nor alarming for men despite their belief that excessive libidinous contact with women results in somatic atrophy. Moreover, men in Tambunum practice no genital purgations that in some Sepik societies (Tuzin 1997, 164–65; Lipset 1997, 160–61) are understood to expel female impurities from the male body.[27]

Men emphatically deny the occurrence of male homoeroticism or same-gender sexual relations, in either ritual or everyday contexts.[28] (Women do likewise when queried about female homoeroticism.) But men privately mention, more so than in the case of masturbation, other men in the village who do engage in these erotic practices. In this regard, it is surely significant that, as Hauser-Schäublin (1977, 135) remarks, women are not viewed by Iatmul men to be sexual objects—white, European women, yes (Silverman 2001b), but not local women. To some degree, the object of men's erotic gaze is men themselves. Anecdotally, men described the physical characteristics of other men, at least to me, more commonly than they did women's. Still, the public norms of adult personhood condemn homoeroticism as shameful and derogatory. If this mode of sexuality does occur, which appears to be the case, it is thoroughly concealed and erased.[29]

Young men, especially cross-cousins, often hold hands in public and tenderly caress each other. This alone suggests the presence of occasional and clandestine same-gender sexual encounters. No such affectionate displays occur between men and women. Whiting (1941, 50) reported that Kwoma men, like their Eastern Iatmul counterparts, also denied the practice of same-gender sexuality. Even so, Kwoma boys enthusiastically played games with homoerotic themes. Young men "who have not seen one another for some time rush together, throw their arms around each other, and hug and pat one another and rub one another's cheeks with their lime gourds" (Whiting 1941, 50). Boys may also greet elder men with these gestures—yet never women.[30] Male homoerotic desire in Tambunum, as among Kwoma, is strenuously sublimated through the ideology of manhood. Yet this sublimation is not entirely successful.

When same-gender male liaisons do occur, they exist outside the authoritative gaze and discourse of masculine morality.[31] During ritual, however, the moral status of homoeroticism is less clear. Many ritual preparations and ceremonial rehearsals are nocturnal affairs, attended exclusively by men, and colored by an erotic ambience that is recognized by the participants themselves. In the weeks leading up to the mai ritual of 1989, pairs of men nightly retired to a clearing in the bush where they honed their skills at chanting totemic poems through flutelike bamboo voice modulators. Male ritual partnerships, called *kaishe-kaishe,* are associated with flute playing. Broadly speaking, the kin term *kaishe* refers to same-sex cross-cousins,[32] a relationship so intimate that male kaishe may even share the same female lovers. The pidgin term for ritual partnerships, *poroman,* explicitly recognizes the sexual undertones of these relationships since *poroman* also refers to same-gender male sexual partners.[33] If the erotic implications of ritual partnerships and male cross-cousins are not actualized in deed, they are nonetheless salient in the experiences and imagination of men. As a result, two relationships that are central to men's lives both sanction and subvert an ideal of masculinity.

For the most part, serious public allegations of male homoerotic activity are slanderous. These denunciations imply that a man has abandoned the conventions of male personhood. Perhaps he went so far as to expose himself in public—conceivably before the eyes of women.[34] Indeed, it is not homoerotic sexuality per se, I was told, that evokes such strongly negative reactions in men. Instead, it is the profound shame that would result if men were ever discovered in flagrante delicto by women! Curiously, homoerotic displays often climax the honorific naven rite—a ritual that ostensibly celebrates, rather than foils, the norms of masculinity. I refer to the famous nggariik gesture whereby a maternal uncle suggestively presents his buttocks to his younger nephew (chap. 10). Here, again, the sexual morality of manhood is revealed to be an uneasy reconciliation between ideology and desire.

The nggariik pantomime also feminizes the maternal uncle's manhood. I will have much more to say on this topic in chapter 10. But several comments here are in order. For men, same-gender sexuality implies the existence of an unacceptable relationship of complementarity. Normally, as Bateson (1936) argued, the mode of interaction between Iatmul men is expected to be symmetrical, that is to say, competitive, assertive, and aggressive. By contrast, the behavioral norm for cross-sex interaction stresses complementarity: women are passive, men are dominant. According to this logic, same-gender male sexuality transforms one partner into a submissive figure of femininity, not unlike the position of male neophyte "wives" before their initiators. Initiation, however, betokens male personhood. Complementary sexuality does not.

> In the village of Tambunum, when two little boys exhibit what looks to their age mates like homosexual behavior, the others put sticks in their hands and make the two stand up against each other and "fight." Indeed, any suggestion of passive male homosexuality is exceedingly insulting in Iatmul culture and leads to symmetrical brawling. (Bateson 1958, 291; see also Mead 1949, 113; 1952, 419)

This anecdote vividly illustrates the antimasculine and feminine connotations of male homoeroticism. It supports, too, my argument concerning the erotics of Iatmul aggression and, conversely, the presence of aggressive sexuality. The conversion of homoerotic desire into serious violence also informs contemporary men's fears about anal rape, especially in regard to so-called criminal *raskols* who prowl the provincial road system and the urban centers of the country.[35]

To conclude, Iatmul sexuality often emphasizes what Herdt (1997b) terms "doing" rather than "being." The roles specified by any given sexual encounter have greater significance than do permanent categories of sexual identity. Eastern Iatmul lack conceptual equivalents of "homosexuality" and "gay." What men dread in sexuality, no less than in fighting and debating, is passivity. For this reason, men can only display tacit homoerotic desire. It is the translation of this desire into actual carnal activity, and not some associated life-style on par with "being gay," that is so problematic.

The erotic definition of Eastern Iatmul masculinity is complex and often ambiguous. The ideology of sexual manhood is called into question by innuendo and ritual. The truce between desire and personhood is tenuous. Male sexuality, too, is envisioned through a maternal schema, if only as an admonishment against European lust. Hence, it is a superb insult, as once infantilizing and incestuous, to say to a man "You walk under your mother's skirt!" But all men do, at least in this culture, as I now demonstrate with regard to the symbolism of architecture.

5

The Architectural Grotesque

The finest domestic houses in Tambunum are immense, ornate structures (fig. 4). They are a particular source of pride for the village and figure into the touristic allure of the community. The architectural skill in evidence on these dwellings, and their elaborate symbolism, lack parallel in the Sepik and much of Melanesia (see also Coiffier 1992b). Construction requires years of effort and a considerable amassing of resources. Yet these domiciles may stand for a generation or longer as a testimony to the role of motherhood in male identity.

Eastern Iatmul houses offer shelter and sustenance, much like mothers. In fact, the architectural ornamentation of a domestic house resembles the body and jewelry of a woman. But the tender sentiment surrounding houses is hardly univocal. The inheritance of these dwellings exacerbates the oedipal rivalry between fathers and sons, and the orificial countenance of these mothers threatens to devour its inhabitants.

A Sociological Shelter

The village is divided into patrilineal residence wards. Rows of houses, corresponding to lineages and branches, are perpendicular to the Sepik (see also Wassmann 1991, 208–11). The eldest male of the group erects his house closest to the river; juniors follow behind in descending birth order. This arrangement symbolizes the prestige structure of the corporate group, which holds to filial primogeniture. Each lineage also claims a section of riverbank for tethering canoes, cleaning fish, washing plates and clothes, and bathing.[1]

Residence in Tambunum is normatively patrilocal. The standard household consists of an extended patrilineal family, typically an elder man and his wife, their wedded sons and children, and unmarried dependents. Most domestic houses (*ngai*) are owned by an asymmetrical pair of agnates: father and son, or brothers. The senior male inhabits the front half of the house (*ndama-ngai*), which "looks" toward the river.[2] His junior, the eldest son or younger brother, resides in the rear half of the dwelling (*ngumba-ngai*), which

64

Fig. 4. The domestic house "mother" of Yambukenandi, my adoptive village father. Notice the wave pattern, central face, and, just below the mouth, two breasts. On this house, the doorway is her vagina; underneath the awning are sago spathe crocodile teeth

"faces" the jungle behind the village. Additional male siblings and sons occupy intermediary sections of the floor. Wives and daughters are allotted places along the side walls, where they store their cooking hearths, pots, plates, and urns of sago. Evoking Hertz ([1909] 1973), husbands inhabit the right side of the house, wives the left (Hauser-Schäublin 1977, 108). Despite the absence of physical barriers—save for a few discreetly positioned personal items (Hauser-Schäublin 1977, 108) and, today, a web of twine that suspends mosquito nets—these internal spaces are relatively isolated. During the many months I lodged in my village father's dwelling, I rarely saw its occupants walk into the space of another coresident. Likewise, households do not necessarily labor as a single subsistence unit or engage in regular communal dining. Even spouses eat separately (Hauser-Schäublin 1977, 129), in different areas of the house.

Domestic dwellings in Tambunum thus represent society rather than a unified family. More precisely, as Harrison (1990, 32) argues for Manambu houses, the Eastern Iatmul domicile mirrors the gendered spatial organization of the village. Men, arranged according to birth order, occupy the central spaces and foyers. Women, specifically unwed daughters and in-marrying wives, dwell in smaller sections along the periphery. As a result, men form the central axis of the house across which women are exchanged in marriage. By reflecting inheritance, jural organization, and affinal relations, the house symbolizes the moral rules and patrilineal "backbone" of society.[3]

The Architecture of Motherhood

Domestic and cult houses symbolize cosmic motherhood. On the facade is depicted a woman's face, complete with nose ornaments, breasts below the mouth, and earrings at the lower eaves. The same visage appears on ancestral agwi islands that, as I discussed in chapter 4, deposited eggs of dry land during primal creation. The interior of the house is a belly (*iai*), or womb (Mead 1949, 211), which conjures not simply a female body but specifically a mother. Roof thatch is shaped into her woven hood (*yoli*). On new houses, men paint the posts and beams with the yellow color of femininity (chap. 4). Finally, the exterior of the dwelling is decorated with a wave design (*mbimbim nyodnyot*) that recalls the river and primordial ocean, two local idioms of female fertility. These motifs, too, tie the house to the primal agwi islands, and hence to cosmogonic reproduction.

When mythic agwi islands hatched eggs of land, they established a terrestrial foundation for the trees and villages "planted" by men (chap. 4). Motherhood, in this sense, supports the masculine creation of society. The maternal agwi islands, however, were pushed atop the primal sea by male crocodilian ancestors. Cosmological agency was thus masculine, much as I argued for the parturient wind that stirred the primordial ocean (chap. 3) and the wai wainjiimot crocodile spirits who govern human conception (chap. 4). Likewise, men control the doorways, or mouths (*kundia*) and vaginas (*kitnya*), of house mothers. As a representation of the cosmos, the house is a maternal body whose orifices and internal spaces are carefully guarded by men.[4]

The spaces located immediately outside the house are far less secure than her belly. Patrilineage rows are separated by earthen embankments topped with coconut and betel palms. The trees are owned by specific households. But the rows themselves are liminal, even to some degree polluted, since they often serve as refuse and burial mounds. At night, young men raid these mounds for betel nut. Consequently, the moral order of society is regularly contested along the interstitial corridors between patrilineages and groups.

The house itself is a place of refuge and security. Theft from residences is virtually unknown and people rarely enter a domicile without express permission from its owner. Today, some men padlock their dwellings. But outside of anecdotal comments about youthful *raskols* (see Leavitt 1998), this precaution seems unrelated to any real increase in offenses. Men are particularly cautious lest intruders bespell a doorway or house-ladder. I became aware of this anxiety only after witnessing Gamboromiawan, one of my research assistants, erupt into a rare fury when, upon returning to his house, he learned that a distant agnate had momentarily stepped inside. During the former era of sorcery, men would pour water down the ladder upon awaking in the morning, prior to exiting the house, to wash away any magic that was set there by rivals under cover of darkness. But, again, more than the threat of sorcery or thievery is at stake in these trespasses and deterrents.

The personal names of a house are cognate to the patronymics of its male owners. Hence, as Wagner (1986, 46–47) wrote for the Usen Barok of New Ireland, the house "is a very visible sanctum of personal inviolability. . . . Any assertive or aggressive intentions displayed by a nondweller in its vicinity are understood as violations of the inhabitants' personality." Furthermore, Eastern Iatmul houses symbolize the social and cosmic bodies. Thus men, in their concern with protecting the doorways of dwellings, preserve their totemic identities and the sociocosmic distinctions of the world. Men's efforts at shoring up the integrity of houses also reflect the reverence with which they view motherhood since house mothers, like a real mothers, offer shelter, warmth, and food.

The comforting functions of the house were likened by Linus Apingari to a bird's nest (*kwarl*), an idea that resonates with the broader avian imagery of femininity (chap. 4). Mothers are hens, he continued, who spread their wings to protect young chicks from preying hawks. (Like chicks, I might add, Iatmul children trail behind their mothers in a line as they walk through the village.) Two female spirits safeguard the nurturing capacity of each house; they dwell in the pair of central support posts. These spirits are called *ngai agwi*, or "house floating island," which associates the house with the primal islands that gestated and deposited terrestrial eggs during cosmic creation.[5] The personal names of these female spirits derive from the patronymics of the male house owners, appended by a feminine suffix (chap. 4). In many cases, they are the exact names of their sisters.

Other mystical beings may be painted and incised on the external posts and beams. The outstanding characteristic of these spirits is a large pair of eyes, which evokes, as on the awan figure (chap. 4), the watchfulness of mothers. These house spirits may also extrude their tongues in a gesture of aggressive sexuality. Another spirit, called a *wain*, serves as the sentinel for the entire lineage or branch, and inhabits collectively the group's front house-ladders. All of these magical beings, however different in minor respects, exhibit the maternal capacity to safeguard the domestic ward. And like mothers, they will strike if their nurturing dominion is violated.

Mothers and Snakes

The motherly protection offered by house spirits seems decidedly antimaternal, if not masculine, in its wrathful potential. Likewise, house mothers rest on horizontal posts that resemble phalli, specifically, canine penes. Dogs exemplify sexual immodesty rather than chaste nurturance; they are ravenous, not selfless. Other Iatmul villages see a snake skeleton in the undercarriage assembly of posts and beams (Coiffier 1992b, 48). In Tambunum, the victor of a homicide raid was entitled to place a wooden riser beneath his house-ladder, thus supporting his mother with a trophy of murderous aggression. The overtly tender and maternal qualities of the house thus overshadow a symbolism that is rather more lewd, aggressive, and androcentric.

A round plaque called a *tsamboe*, suspended from the ridgepole, represents the brain (*njagula*) of the house. The tsamboe is ornamented with war spirits (*sabi*) and the wai wainjiimot crocodile beings who administer cosmic and human fertility. Here, two defining images of the male cult are united in a display of violence and procreation. The tsamboe and canine phalli, while admittedly far less visible on the house than her maternal face, nonetheless frame this mother with symbols of masculine thoughts, deeds, and genitals. The monologic body of architectural motherhood is really plural. Her moral virtues are disputed by images of male aggression, immoral sexuality, and canine appetitiveness.

The house is ambivalent in another respect, one that is best introduced by a mythic snake-child.

A female snake lived near a swamp on a floating island. The snake laid two eggs that she covered with wild taro leaves. A woman paddled her canoe to the swamp in order to gather greens for sago pudding. She discovered the two eggs and ate them in secret. The next morning she was pregnant. But neither the mother nor her village neighbors realized that she was carrying a male snake-child. It was a painful pregnancy; her belly swelled enormously. Each night, while the mother slept, the snake-child slithered out of her womb and searched for food. He always returned just before dawn. The mother experienced excruciating pain. Everybody now realized that she was pregnant with a snake-child, one who refused to leave the womb permanently, even after nine months. This was not right. The mother asked men to cut down and hollow a large bamboo stalk. Her husband collected sago grubs. One night, when the snake-child was searching for food, the husband trailed sago grubs along the ground, up the house-ladder, and into the bamboo tube, which he concealed in his wife's sleeping net. The snake-child happily ate his way along the trail of grubs and into the bamboo tube, which the husband quickly sealed. In the morning, village men lit a fire and tossed the bamboo tube onto the flames. As the snake-child burned, he cried "mother, I am a man, not a snake!" But it was too late. The village men would not listen to him. The snake-child burned to death.

The psychodynamic symbolism of this myth is striking.[6] The snake represents the yearning by men to escape from maternal dependency. But the snake-child forsook true adult autonomy since he rejected a proper birth. He was unwilling fully to depart from the shelter of his mother's body. Equally troubling, the snake ignored her wishes. By fatally relinquishing all social responsibilities and continuously retreating into a maternal sanctuary, the snake was incapable of attaining the proper balance between desire and morality. His struggle, we might say, represents the predicament of adult men in Tambunum.

In another myth, a solitary culture hero named Migaimeli endeavors to carve a wooden spouse. But his lone, celibate efforts to birth a woman are futile. Migaimeli is unable to gain a wife through independent masculine means. Artistic creativity is no match for intercourse, uterine feeding, and delivery. As a result, Migaimeli is shamed into marrying a woman from another group when a man discovers his wooden carving. One version of the myth tells that Migaimeli was even seen in the disgraceful act of copulating with the wooden mannequin.[7] On their own, this myth implies, men, in the absence of exchange and marriage, lack the ability to reproduce themselves and society (relatedly, see Moore 1964; Dundes 1983). In an ascetic state, men are even unable to eat properly since, as I stated in chapter 2, they admit to being incapable of cooking sago. Migaimeli suffered only shame. The snake-child was condemned to death.

The snake-child also represents an oedipal phallus that threatens paternal authority, violates the chaste asexuality of the maternal body, and trespasses the rule of adult men.[8] Additionally, the snake-child renounced his mother's uterine nourishment since he exited her body specifically to search for food. In leaving the womb, he contravened the fundamental quality of moral motherhood, namely, selfless nurture. But in returning, he refused to grow up. The snake-child's death is a lesson to men who might wish to transgress motherhood, or refuse to sever the maternal bond, or shun the world of their adult peers. This complex tale about separation-individuation and oedipality expresses a great dilemma for Eastern Iatmul masculinity: men desire moral motherhood yet they must flee her body.

Only by forsaking the maternal shelter of domestic houses can men hope to gain maximal male personhood. They must extend their masculine selves in social space and encounter coequals and potential rivals. These movements are dangerous, often antagonistic; the world of social responsibilities is perilous. When a man walks beyond his domestic realm, he places his body and renown in no uncertain jeopardy. The moral qualities of the maternal realm, however, promote somatic growth alone. They permit minimal achieved identity. Adult men retain a lifelong wish to return to maternal safety. They aspire to reckless or juvenile autonomy—as in Vabindu's fantasy of banishing all other groups from the village (chap. 3). Yet moral personhood, as we learned from Mauss ([1925] 1990), entails continuous reliance on others through exchange. Eastern Iatmul must therefore negotiate between individual yearning and social morality. To do otherwise is to risk the fate of the snake-child or, at the very least, the humiliation of Migaimeli.

"Mankind," Lévi-Strauss ([1949] 1969, 497) ironically concluded in his magnum opus on social life, dreams "that the law of exchange could be evaded, that one could gain without losing, enjoy without sharing." We seek the "joys, eternally denied to social man, of a world in which one might keep to oneself." The gender of Lévi-Strauss's claim, while admittedly biased, is fitting for the middle Sepik since Eastern Iatmul men also wish for an ideal world that diminishes the obligations of social life. Alas, they live in society, and so the masculine self cannot return to motherhood. Nor, in one respect, would men necessarily want to do so, for the mothers they idealize, the nurturing bodies for which they yearn, are bodies of dialogical rather than solidary meanings.

A Maw of Ambivalence

The equivocal imagery of architectural motherhood becomes especially evident when we examine the alimentary symbolism of thresholds. The doorway is a gaping maw that swallows (*kuga magna*) its inhabitants at night and disgorges (*krungwiya*) them in the morning. From another perspective, the front entrance is the mouth of an architectural mother while the rear doorway is her buttocks (*mogwi*) and anus (*miiwiit*). Indeed, the house can be viewed as a single body or a dual body, possessing an entire alimentary canal or solely two mouths (*kundi*). When the house is a body devoid of an anus, it becomes a mother who is untainted by feces and who, in turn, is unable to corrupt her inhabitants with excrement.[9] An image of maternal cleanliness, in fact, actually corresponds to the behavior of mothers since they bathe children. Yet the bodies of architectural mothers are not fundamentally modeled after real behavior. Instead, these bodies represent heteroglossic discourses between motherhood and masculinity that are ultimately rooted in cultural values and psychodynamic processes.

Houses permit legitimate sexual relations. Men willingly reside with their wives, albeit usually in different sleeping areas or beds. No shame is attached to marital sexuality. Still, a man who frequently makes love to his wife, like one who tarries about the house, may experience premature somatic degeneration.[10] The house expresses these heterosexual anxieties, no less men's fears about female genitalia. On some dwellings, the doorway is surrounded by ornamented sago spathes cut to resemble crocodile teeth. When the entrance is a mouth, the teeth present a consumptive image of the maternal body that evidences the fear of oral devourment (see Devereux 1966). But on some houses, the door is a vulva, in which case, as one man explicitly stated, the teeth are *vagina dentata*.[11] These houses swallow men, both vaginally and orally, and evacuate them through an ambiguous orifice of expectoration, defecation, and birth. To some degree, as Tuzin (1977) discusses for Ilahita Arapesh, this psychodynamic image is a projection of men's contradictory feelings toward the culturally salient idea, often expressed in myth, of an aggressively sexual and phallic mother.

The architectural juxtaposition of the moral and the grotesque, or feminine carnality and maternal love, is related to the psychoanalytic defense modality known as splitting (Freud 1938; Klein 1975). But the house in Tambunum, while it combines split images into the same body, does not fully integrate them. Indeed, the house violates in numerous ways the ideology of manhood and mothering. The toothed vaginal-oral symbolism allows men's fear of consuming female sexuality to eclipse the nourishing, culinary associations of motherhood. This orificial symbolism also violates the cultural taboo on mouth-to-genital contact (see also Mead 1935b, 75). It does so, however, not with reference to oral sexuality but by inverting mouth and vagina.[12] This way, the doorway confounds the distinction between maternal feeding and female eroticism that is so important in the local definitions of masculinity and motherhood.

Men in Tambunum do not build house mothers in order to control the female body and her labor. Political economy (e.g., Rubin 1975; Whitehead 1987; Allen 1988) has limited utility in this case. Rather, men construct these mothers in order to express, perhaps even to confront, the psychodynamic desires and anxieties that constitute their masculinity. Houses symbolize men's yearning to rejoin the nostalgic ideal of a nurturing and preoedipal mother. But this mother is devouring and excreting, orificial and vaginal, carnivalesque and oedipal. She represents men's fears about female sexuality. Her menacing maw also, in this regard, would seem to encourage men to overcome their libidinal attachment to the ideal of motherhood (see Lidz and Lidz 1989, 15). The house threatens to castrate desire and thus enables men to mature into adulthood. (Yet this message, we will see in chapter 7, is contested by marriage itself.) Similarly, during male initiation, senior crocodile spirits who are fierce and procreative eat boys and orally disgorge them as grown men. Both initiation and houses communicate messages about ambivalence, not resolution, through a lexicon that is overwhelmingly orificial, feminine, maternal, and transgressive.[13]

Gilmore (1996) argues that femininity in the Mediterranean is "split into good and bad halves" (see also Carroll 1986). In New Guinea, he contends, femininity is "feared and rejected." To a large degree, Gilmore's thoughtful thesis pertains to Highland New Guinea (e.g., Meigs 1984). In Tambunum, by contrast, Mediterranean-type splitting is prominent, especially in the symbolism of vernacular architecture. Both Sepik and Spanish men, I suggest, define themselves *in part* through the same desire: to restore male ties to an ideal, nurturing mother. But whereas Spanish men deny the "split-off bad mother" (Gilmore 1996, 43), Eastern Iatmul men encounter her directly (see also Tuzin 1997, 122–23). Indeed, they walk into her very body. It is a body, however, that intensifies rather than resolves the contrary faces of motherhood.

The Architecture of Oedipality

Younger brothers and sons have unrestricted access to the residential spaces of their elder brothers and fathers. (Admittedly, they rarely choose to exercise this entitlement.) The same pattern of privilege, as among Murik to some extent

(Barlow 1990; Lipset 1997, 65–67), extends to a wide range of cultural contexts, from seemingly trivial acts such as reaching into baskets for betel nut to leviratic marriage. But reciprocal claims from elder to younger brother, and father to son, are limited by moral censure. Upon my departure in 1990, I gave my wristwatch to Dmoiawan, one of many final tokens of gratitude for his care, confidence, and ethnographic insights. When I returned in 1994, he remarked that his son had shortly after my departure asked for the watch. Dmoiawan refused. While he slept, his son slipped the timepiece off his arm, and that was that. Dmoiawan felt it impolite, even immoral, to comment to his son on this exercise of filial liberty. I must add, too, that the relationship between Dmoiawan and his son is no more, or less, strained than any other father-son relationship in the village.

Consequently, the emotional ties that sustain the father-son and brother relationships are somewhat equivocal, especially the former.[14] When a boy reaches the age of about five or six, he begins to have increasingly limited contact with his father. Any further trace of paternal intimacy is abhorrent. Many forms of casual conduct, too, as I learned in a moment of personal embarrassment, become just as awkward or anathema. When I offered to walk a matrilateral father to the cult house, I was instantly scolded. "You don't walk with your father!" he barked. "Go walk with your mother!" I was shocked, but gratified of course, for having been lent this local courtesy, such as it was. This "father," Linus Apingari, is one of the most polite, considerate, level-headed men I have met in this or any culture. His knee-jerk response, while it seemed so out of character, attested to the deep entrenchment of father-son hostility.

Youthful and middle-aged fathers should refuse all cooked food from their eldest child (see also Bateson 1936, 40–42). Otherwise, they are in danger of premature aging. While elderly men, because they are no longer susceptible to untimely senescence, accept plates from firstborn daughters, they still decline meals from firstborn sons. To be safe, some men say, fathers should only accept raw food from these children. They should never allow firstborns (nguma-nian) to cook for them. It is equally unsafe for the father to rekindle his hearth with embers from a firstborn's fire.[15] A similar forbiddance applies to canoes. The father steers from the stern; his eldest child sits at the prow. The father may not quench his thirst by dipping into the river until the firstborn has raised his or her paddle. Even then, the canoe must glide past the spot where the child's paddle last touched the water.

The hazards posed to a father's health by his firstborn child parallel the pollution that all men attribute to menstruating women and postpartum mothers. In the case of firstborns, though, men do not seek to mirror the very qualities they fear. Or do they? Firstborns are perilous for fathers, men say, because these children are "closer" than later offspring to their mother's vaginal and birthing fluids. These substances, of course, embody the very qualities that men seek to encompass during cult ritual within the regime of masculinity. But in terms of generational succession and primogeniture, the eldest child, especially a firstborn son, is the greatest and most immediate threat to the father's status.

After the marriage of sons and the birth of children, the father is expected to abandon the domestic house he built and relocate to a modest residence. Not only do sons gain their father's architectural mother, but they consign him to live out his days in a meager, oftentimes dilapidated, shelter. The inheritance of the house underscores the local idiom that sons "replace" their fathers in the legal and ritual structure of society. At the same time, an elderly father may choose to bestow his patrinames and ornaments onto his grandsons (chap. 4). An older man, when divested of his architectural mother and totemic identity, is transformed largely into a somatic being who is animated by only a trace of his former masculine self. Lacking names, regalia, and a house, the father is symbolically regressed to the state of naked infancy.

The building of an architectural mother is an arduous and expensive endeavor. It takes years of effort; the village is dotted with the half-built hulls of these huge residences. The construction of a large house is a lifelong goal for many men. Ironically, while human mothers feed children, the erection of a house mother depletes men of food and money. But the relationship between human and architectural mothers is more subtle than simply one of opposition. A human mother nourishes her son so he can mature into adulthood. When he does so, he builds "her" body by denying his own hunger in order to feed, like a mother himself, other men who drag logs to the village, upright posts, weave thatch, and so forth. This way, the completion of a house, especially a large dwelling, both asserts and denies the nurturing ideal of motherhood.

The inheritance of dwellings is unmistakably oedipal. Houses are not simply buildings. They are maternal bodies built by fathers and ceded to sons. The same is true for canoes, as I detail shortly, which may also comprise a son's patrimony. The interior of the house is a belly, or *iai*. The very same word is a kinship term that refers to women in the father's clan, including a man's ideal bride, specifically, his father's mother's brother's son's daughter (FMBSD).[16] A potential husband calls this woman *iai* but his father actually identifies her as "mother" (*nyame*). Through this matrimonial prescription, as I detail in chapter 7, a man is said to reacquire his mother as his son's bride. Fathers, I am suggesting, yield three symbols of motherhood to their sons: houses, canoes, and iai women as brides. This way, men reproduce the hierarchical and androcentric body of social order through the Oedipus complex.

The oedipal quandary among the Ilahita Arapesh is encapsulated by a tale about a young son who conspires with his mother to avenge the father's theft of her prized feather skin (Tuzin 1997). This variant of the Oedipus complex is absent in Tambunum. Mothers and sons do not plot against the father. Instead, the Eastern Iatmul predicament is akin to the Yafar myth about Wam, a primal son who was unable to upright his house posts. The image of Wam's posts repeatedly toppling to the ground is psychoanalytically significant since the earth is the body of a Great Mother in Yafar mythology (Juillerat 1996, 28–37).[17] Eventually, Wam's own mother asked his father, Tapi, to aid their son's efforts. Tapi excavated a pit, climbed down into it, and told his son to drive the stakes into his back. The posts finally stood erect.[18] In a similar fashion, Eastern Iatmul sons inherit a mother constructed by the backbreaking labors of their father.

Why do fathers in Tambunum suffer the toil and expense to build these monumental houses for their sons? One answer is the sheer force of maternal sentiment in the moral lives of men. Men assemble these houses precisely because they symbolize moral motherhood. At the same time, these dwellings afford men a concrete expression of their anxieties concerning the female body, grotesque motherhood, and father-son succession. Of course, local men themselves do not phrase their commitments to building houses in quite this manner. But they do say that fathers construct and then vacate these dwellings to avoid listening to their sons' lovemaking. This explanation seems to speak to incestuous jealousy. Likewise, men report that a father who fails to build a house for his son may suffer from public ridicule—especially by the son's wife (see also chap. 6). From this angle, houses are feminine bodies that symbolize the precarious role of the daughter-in-law in the relationship between fathers and sons. And this triangular configuration of emotions and roles is assuredly oedipal.

Among the Mountain Arapesh, the "young, springing manhood" of a son can "endanger his father's slackening, sexless hold on life" (Mead 1935b, 78). Once the son enters the male cult, though, all that the father "does is done in his son's name." In Tambunum, male offspring also ensure a paternal legacy. But sons represent their father's aging frailty and death. This is a common pattern in Melanesia (e.g., Brison 1992, 143; Young 1983, 89–91) and beyond (Paul 1982). "The moral regulation of filio-parental relationships," wrote Fortes (1974, 104), must ultimately strike a culture-specific balance "between the compulsion that is dramatized in the Oedipus story . . . and the control that is dramatized in the Isaac story."[19] To this, I need only add that the emotional ambivalence of fatherhood and sonship in Tambunum is symbolized by the maternal body rather than, as per Reik (1946) and orthodox Freudians, male hostility toward other men. For this reason, the inheritance of a house mother is a bittersweet enactment of masculinity that once again attests to the value of motherhood.

Who Are the True Stools of Society?

Through conception, fathers provision their sons with bones and patrilineal identity. If the society lacked this somatic and sociological backbone, it would consist solely of matrifiliation and sentiment—the fragile and emotional ephemera of flesh and blood. Yet the father-son relationship is fraught with tension. Furthermore, the patrilineal structure of society reproduces itself through the very bodies it excludes: women and, more pertinent to this discussion, houses. Another symbol of motherhood supports and supplants masculinity: the stool.

The politicoritual leader or father (*nyait*) of each patriclan is normatively determined on the basis of primogeniture (see also Metraux 1978; Wassmann 1991, 23).[20] In actuality, men must couple this birthright to some acclaim in masculine talent, especially ritual and esoteric wisdom. The leader of each clan is the authorized trustee for the group's totemic insignia, including its secret names and spirit masks. Rarely, of course, is there any uniform agreement within a clan on who exactly is its genuine "father." For that matter, there is little consensus over which lineages are even the legitimate members of the clan. Nevertheless, patriclan fathers and other male leaders are metaphorically likened to central features of the cult house. They are sitting platforms (*njambe*),[21] firewood embers (*yetembuno*), and stools (*tugiit*).

These furnishings delineate the interior space of the cult house. At each end of the building is a fire hearth, adjacent to a central post. Nearby are low stools. The inside walls are lined with platforms, assigned to specific descent groups, on which men sit, recline, and nap.[22] During formal ritual and political events such as totemic disputes, the seating arrangement inside the cult house represents the social structure of a patriclan or the entire village (see also Bateson 1932, 259). In these settings, men should no more sit on another group's platform than they should mix fire from the front and rear hearths of the cult house.

Cult house stools, platforms, and hearths serve as the foci and boundaries for men's political and ritual events. Since only men can enter the cult house and enact its totemic ceremonies,[23] these three expressions of leadership imply that men alone "sit" at the center of sociocosmic order and define its limits. Stools, platforms, and tinder are whittled from wood. Trees complement or contrast with feminine water and symbolize masculine permanence, physicality, and patriliny (see chaps. 3, 4). But the platforms, stools, and fires of male leadership are all located inside the belly (*iai*), or womb, of the cult house. Once again, a maternal body envelops masculinity. This image of motherhood, unlike the domestic house, is sheltering to men rather than dangerously consumptive since men retreat to the cult house for totemic debates, ritual preparations, and the initiation of youth into manhood. Likewise, the cult house offers refuge from women. Still, the cult house represents the encompassment of manhood by maternal primacy.

Bateson (1946, 120) conjured a similar image for Iatmul aesthetics when he wrote that "the masculine assertive art . . . has its locus within a grandiose female matrix." Forge (1973) argued likewise for the potent *nggwalndu* spirits that Abelam men paint on the facades of their own cult houses. Although women view these paintings, they are unable to identify them as the nggwalndu spirits. By concealing this vital knowledge, men appear to eclipse women in Abelam ritual and cosmology. Yet the nggwalndu portraits are surrounded by oval shapes that Forge deciphered as female genitalia. He concluded that male authority among the Abelam is a "cultural" transformation of "natural" female fertility. One could offer a similar interpretation of manhood in Tambunum. Yet a dichotomous view of Sepik gender, and a static nature-culture division,[24] do not sufficiently attend to the meaning of enclosure when masculine symbols such as leadership stools are contained within female forms.

Normally, only men in Tambunum rest on wooden stools. Women sit on the ground, as do male neophytes during the early stages of initiation when they are feminized and infantilized.[25] From this angle, the enstoolment of male leadership simply reflects the dichotomized spatial and vertical domains of everyday social life. However, men say that *women* are the "true" stools of their society since women birth and feed children, and were the original flutists and ritual performers. (Women are also, by the same logic, the elder brothers of men.) From this, quite different angle, stool symbolism reflects not masculine privilege but sociocosmic reproduction within the "common pool" of gender (chap. 3). Both men and women are stools. From yet a third angle, the symbolic stool betrays the ideology of manhood. It attests to men's recognition that moral motherhood alone is the foundation for their culture and masculinity.

Moral motherhood, too, resembles a soothing fire.[26] During the cool evenings and mornings, men may sit on stools inside the cult house, huddled over hearths. But of greater value, at least in moments of male reverie, is the warmth afforded by women and mothers who tend cooking fires underneath domestic houses.[27] Widowers, men say, "have no fire." They sit alone, shivering through dusk and dawn, dining on cold food. As idioms of male leadership, the stool and the ember are not only enclosed by a maternal body—they are transformations of moral motherhood herself. In short, men are mothers.

A Nautical House

Like cult houses, large canoes in Tambunum are dialogical symbols of jural order and masculinity. No single canoe represents the entire village on par with the majestic cult house. Yet each lineage and clan is entitled to chisel a large dugout (*numa vara*) that personifies a senior totem. The spirit's animal form, usually a crocodile but sometimes a pig or bird, is carved into the prow.[28] Formerly, these vessels were used for warfare and trading voyages. Each of the three internal spaces—prow (*ndama vara*), middle (*yinde vara*), and stern (*kayngu vara*)—is reserved for specific descent groups within the lineage or clan. This way, the seating arrangement inside a large or male canoe mirrors village social structure.[29]

Men identify personally with their canoes. In addition to incising a totemic animal in the prow, they may decorate the exterior with engravings and painted motifs, scrawl the name of their lineage or clan along the hull, and affix magical plants on the prow to assure that the vessel glides as swiftly as an eagle flies. The construction of a large canoe, like that of a house, requires considerable craftsmanship, organizational abilities, and generosity. A score of men may spend three days hauling a tree trunk from the bush into the village; after that, the canoe may require several weeks of daily work, from eviscerating the pith to charring the hull, from smoothing the sides to consecrating its spirit. Everybody must be fed. During the labor, which occurs outside the cult house, men often chant totemic poems through bamboo voice modulators that extol the warlike mai spirits (see chap. 4). This encouragement confirms Bateson's (1941, 352) observation that Iatmul tend to envision labor as combat: "they habitually convert their conative efforts into imaginary aggression." It is common, too, for women to dance short honorific naven rites during the work, and for sisters' sons to lay small gifts of betel nut and money into the hull. All told, canoe construction involves a series of activities that are important to masculine identity.

Canoes, again like houses, are mothers. They are associated with maternal food, bodies, and cleanliness.[30] Canoes have a mouth, anus, and belly. Yet female (not just male) identity is bound to canoes. In this respect, a woman's self-worth is dependent on her husband's willingness to carve her a dugout. The canoe thus mediates between spouses and represents, in a sense, the state of their marriage (Weiss 1987a). Most men ensure that female kin have daily access to small dugouts so they can set fish traps and paddle to gardens.[31] Women carefully maintain these vessels; they bail water as diligently as they sweep houses and weed the dirt plazas in front of dwellings. In fact, the canoe appears to be a nautical analogue of the house. Women's hesitancy about allowing others to use their canoes parallels men's proprietary concerns about the doorways of their domiciles. A woman who carelessly secures her canoe so that it drifts down the river at night is morally neglectful. On one such occasion, the shame of my village sister, and the rage of our mother, was palpable for weeks. It is noteworthy, in this regard, that the male cult house during funerary rites is literally tethered to a tree like a canoe. In essence, this lashing prevents the entire architecture of masculinity from accompanying the ghosts on their aquatic journey and floating downstream.

Canoes are also sheltering. Like bridges (*tagu*), they permit safe passage over water. In this respect, dugouts resemble mothers who may throw themselves to the ground during naven rites so their celebrated son can walk over their bodies (chap. 9). The role of the mother's brother during male initiation also bears on the symbolism of canoes (Bateson 1936; relatedly, Gewertz 1982). During this ritual enactment of violent gestation and parturition, mothers' brothers hold and caress their terrified and sometimes screaming nephews as they are scarified. Afterward, the uncle may sooth "the boy's cuts with oil gently applied with a feather" (Bateson 1936, 77). Alternatively, the youth can clutch the keel of a canoe. Eastern Iatmul would surely agree with the Avatip man who remarked to Harrison (1982, 152) "canoes are our mothers; they carry us everywhere."

But canoes signify more than merely moral motherhood. After all, canoes are associated with male identity and the aggressive ethos of masculine labor and warfare spirits. They derive from trees that are cosmological symbols of masculine creation amid feminine or uterine water. Canoes, too, embody the supreme spirits of the lineage. Likewise, canoes enclose a representation of male hierarchy and patriliny. But, again like houses, this enclosure is maternal. Hence, the canoe is a nautical conversation, metaphorically speaking, between the prerogatives of men and the mothers they envy and fear.

Beneath the Legs of an Ancestress

The cult house exhibits the same feminine and maternal attributes as domestic dwellings: breasts, earrings, uterine belly, and so forth. Her spirit is female. Sometimes she is even bordered by a fringe "skirt." The interior posts were once "elaborately carved . . . and the images instead of being of men were all of women or of crocodiles" (Shurcliff 1930, 244). But there is, of course, one key difference: the cult house is barred to women and mothers.

In the previous section, I discussed various ways that the male cult house promotes and rejuvenates masculine personhood, and shelters symbols of male leadership. Yet, however much the cult house allows men to sit upon the stools of political and ritual leadership, it is moral motherhood herself, as an architectural belly and an ethical ideal, that is ultimately primary. Metaphorically, mothers unseat men. The cult house is equivocal for men in other ways. During warfare, "she" may pierce and thereby feminize adversaries since men may shout her spirit name prior to slaying an enemy. Within the village itself, the spirits who dwell in the cult house may inflict upon men who violate her rules of order the various ailments, misfortunes, and fatalities that are associated with mystical retribution (*vai*). Magical forces, akin to invisible spears, may impale and kill the transgressor.

The code of conduct in the cult house environs forbids any sort of joking, rough and tumble play, loud disturbances, and the like, even irreverent language. I recall one instance when a younger man, irate about the censure of his father after a dispute concerning the distribution of money during a ritual, insulted a group of elders inside the cult house by shouting in pidgin, "You stink[ing] cunt!" I was shocked. The elder men were outraged. One of them, my own village father, Yambukenandi, leapt to his feet and unsheathed a knife. He was only restrained by the matter-of-fact announcements uttered by his contemporaries to the slanderer: "You will now die. For having used this type of language, at us, inside the ceremonial house, the cult spirits will kill you." And perhaps they did, in a sense, for some of his peers died a few years later. It remains unclear, however, if his true iniquity was merely to scream at his seniors inside the normally somber belly of the cult house. Perhaps, instead, his impropriety was to recognize in such an overt manner the uterine encompassment of masculinity that men are otherwise loath to admit.

The cult house is also dangerous for women. Its ritual heat (*kau*) is said to imperil female reproductive potential. A woman who enters the building can even be gang-raped and beaten. I have no clear sense as to whether or not men today would actually enforce this vile mode of punishment. The absence of this practice, however, hardly lessens its symbolic force. I received no sense from women that they actually live in daily fear of the male cult house. Nonetheless, I recall no instance when women were willing to test male resolve in this matter. Hence, the cult house is a phallic mother who can genuinely terrorize women (and men) with the threat of violent penetration should they trespass her boundaries.

There is one further aspect of the cult house that requires some attention. An ancestress named Vendigarlagwa supports the attic and towering roof of the cult house.[32] A similar effigy adorns the Tchambuli or Chambri ceremonial structure. According to Mead (1935b, 271), "she is the symbol that controls their [men's] emotions" (see also Errington and Gewertz 1987c, 61). In Tambunum, as men cross the threshold at either end of the cult house, or sprawl atop its front and rear sitting platforms, they pass underneath the legs of Vendigarlagwa, which are spread out along a horizontal roof beam. The Murik cult house, while a "beautiful spirit-man" rather than a mother or woman, also permits a similar transition (Lipset 1997, 179). When men brush through the spirit man's skirt of sago fringe bunting that surrounds his architectural body, they are said to be "crawling underneath the skirts of their mother." In Tambunum, however, the prominent genitals of Vendigarlagwa and the position of her legs speak to a more varied meaning.

Vendigarlagwa resembles the genital-oral maw that is sometimes depicted on the embellished lintels and porches of domestic houses. However much this spirit woman supports the edifice of cultic manhood, her stance threatens to pollute masculinity since she appears simultaneously to be in the act of birth and sexual intercourse. Any contact with vaginal secretions should temporarily bar a man from the cult house. Moreover, juxtapositions of motherhood and sexuality in the same female form are grotesque rather than moral renditions of maternal values, at least in the eyes of men. Vendigarlagwa thus contests the very ideology of the cult house, no less the ideal of moral motherhood, both of which are dear to men. From this perspective, the cult house does not so much shelter the stools, fires, and platforms of masculinity as defile them.

Yet it is only in the shelter of the cult house, again, that men can achieve the goals of manhood. Indeed, the time men spend lounging inside the cult house is analogous, I was told, to the slumber of male crocodile spirits who burrow inside the ancestral floating islands or agwi, which I discussed earlier in this chapter. Men emerge from the belly of the cult house, birthed in essence by Vendigarlagwa, ensorcelled by magical heat (*kau*), and prepared for ritual and, formerly, warfare. Inside this architectural womb, men deliberate their totemic cosmology, relax and chat, resolve political disputes, initiate youth, and assemble for meetings. They also decorate ceremonial objects, prim spirit costumes, and practice flutes, all of which they will partly reveal during ritual to an audience of supposedly awestruck women and children.

Of course, the display of this ritual paraphernalia is somewhat redundant since a powerful woman, the spirit of the cult house herself, no less her associates in the spirit pantheon, are the ever-present witnesses to the rites and powers of these objects and melodies. The very presence of the cult house, we might say, as a woman and mother, authenticates the efficacy and veracity of these male ritual claims. At the same time, the cult house defiles and defies these masculine boasts with her belly, skirt, breasts, and, in the sculpture of Vendigarlagwa, her outstretched legs.

Domestic and cult houses represent cultural dialogues between fathers and sons, and between mothers and men, that concern the "ownership" and "occupation" of maternal bodies. Eastern Iatmul culture undeniably celebrates the male physique. Yet this body and its achievements forever dwell in contrary spaces of motherhood.

PART 2

Social Masculinity

6

A Symbolic Forest of Kin

During the first six months of fieldwork, my efforts at eliciting myths were bedeviled by countless totemic inventories of seemingly innumerable place-names. At these locations, ancestor heroes established villages and especially planted trees. Eventually, I did compile a corpus of myth. I also came to realize the importance of these totemic catalogs: primal arboriculture anchors male identity to land and villages amid the original aquatic, feminine state of the universe. Planting is an external metaphor that transforms the internal birthing capacities of women into the masculine realms of totemism and cosmology.

The kinship system, too, emphasizes vegetative propagation. These concepts of arboreal fertility, and the sentiments and symbols associated with significant relationships, further indicate the dialogical conversation between masculinity and motherhood. If one must condense this kinship debate to a single image, then it would surely be a tree surrounded by water.

A Moral Forest

Eastern Iatmul imagine their society to be a forest.[1] The ancestors, lineages, and branches of a patriclan are likened both to sago palm roots and a type of tree that rises from an extensive root system. In this metaphor (*yerik-mbanj*), patri-lines germinate from apical ancestors much as young shoots grow from rhizomes.[2] When the progenitor dies, too, the group's expansion is seen as analogous to the emergence of new trees from the roots of a fallen palm. Apical ancestors are also said to be giant trees whose seeds (*siik,* the same word used for "penis") drop to the soil and sprout into young plants, or sons. Daughters and daughters-in-law, as I remarked in chapter 4, resemble vines that entangle patrilocal trees into a web of affinal kinship. By the same logic, women are "bird people" who fly through the patrilineal forest; they are also pollinating butterflies that flitter between flowers.

Bateson recorded three comparable metaphors of botanical relatedness. When totemic rivals wished to profess cosmological unity, they exclaimed

"One father, one mother, one root" (Bateson 1936, 236). A proverb stated, "Legs of a *Caryota,* legs of a *Pandanus;* women hither, women thither" (Bateson 1936, 94). These plants are distinguished by "aerial roots diverging downwards to the ground from the trunk," and so "diverse groups are tied together by affinal bonds due to past marriages of past sisters." Last, Bateson (1936, 249) wrote that Iatmul understand their villages to undergo continuous fission, "like the rhizomes of a lotus."

In Tambunum, one botanical image of relatedness mirrors the local epistemic contrast between the surface discontinuities of perceptual reality and the unseen realm of primary connections (chap. 3). Although they rarely need to do so, Eastern Iatmul can explicitly designate classificatory relatives by appending the prefix *maymbange* to a relationship term. This word, which approximates the concept of "side-by-side," is cognate to a *miambange* taro leaf. "When you plant a *miambange* leaf," one man explained, "a wide root system grows, from which other leaves sprout, all "side-by-side." The leaves appear to be separate but they are all linked beneath the surface." Genealogical distance and the limitations of human memory aside, all kin are united by a common relative.

Many botanical metaphors envision men as stationary trees. Society is a forest of male bodies. But is this timberland really so masculine? The answer, like the artistic relationship of figure to ground, is a matter of perspective. Male trees certainly seem to dominate in this arboreal space. Yet the expansiveness of the social forest is enabled by female vines, birds, and butterflies.[3] Likewise, men and *not* women feel compelled to detach themselves from this forested integration and create their own space, namely, the cult house. Yet, just as the cult house is a maternal body (chap. 5), the forest of kinship, however much it celebrates the primacy of patrilineal social structure, is forever at risk of feminine flooding.

Trees amid Water

When totemic chants tally sites of ancestral cultivation, they focus on sago and coconut groves. Since, in the esoteric language of totemism, the word for coconut palm (*tupma*) is synonymous with village (*ngepma;* see also Wassmann 1991, 72), mythic-historic planting is a metaphor for the establishment of communal life. It is no coincidence that lineages are segmented into branches (*tsai*). But only men sowed orchards. As a result, trees (*mi*) symbolize the cosmogonic triumph of masculine sociality over originary, presocialized feminine water.

Upon further reflection, however, the ability of plant metaphors to prevail over aquatic dissolution is inconclusive. Recall that the *wooden* features of male leadership (see chap. 5) sit inside a maternal body that is also the "true" stool of society. Sago is vital for the growth of male bodies and the horticultural creation of land in mythic history. Yet the genesis of sago was doubly defiling for men: disembodied abscesses from an aged woman followed by the consumption of coital fluids (chap. 2). Similarly, the very same word that refers to the branches that assemble into arboreal lineages, *tsai,* also designates small creeks that trickle into the river. In this context, trees and streams are contrary topographic voices, albeit spoken through the same vocabulary, that join a wider conversation about gender and culture.

Ideologically, this topographic discourse privileges land and trees over water. But the botanical vision of authoritative social order, again, is not so overgrown that we and Eastern Iatmul are unable to perceive an aquatic milieu. The culture expressly associates water and the Sepik River with uterine fertility. Water, to borrow from Eliade (1958, 188–215) and Douglas (1966, 161), symbolizes the amorphous and timeless state of the cosmos that preceded masculine creation (see also Jung 1956). Water gave birth to form, nonliquid substance, and temporality, that is to say, humanity and social life. Yet water may also signify the final state of existence when the world and society inexorably dissolve. After all, the swift Sepik is continuously changing and flowing, forever eroding the terrestrial realms of forest and village. The arboreal ascendence of masculine structure and permanence is illusory. The river ultimately prevails. During some rainy seasons, in fact, the flood waters truly seem to regress the world back to the original and undifferentiated state of the primordial feminine sea (see also Schuster 1985).

Unlike the Umeda of the West Sepik hinterlands (Gell 1992a, 38), Eastern Iatmul are not eschatologists. Nevertheless, gendered images of kinship in Tambunum do hint at a sense of aquatic destiny. So, too, do men's resigned and sorrowful responses to the erosion of their village and houses. What trees truly symbolize, therefore, is men's *desire* for patrilineal, social, and cosmological permanence in a world that is forever awash in female contingency. Is there anything men can do to stem the feminine tide of watery encompassment? Yes, they can plant trees—that is to say, men can build houses, chant names, conduct rituals, and sustain the arboreal system of patriliny.

The human life cycle and ethnophysiology parallel the relationship between trees and water.[4] Vegetative idioms of social structure correspond to the spine and pelvis, which are named after fathers and grandfathers (chap. 4). This sturdy paternal skeleton is enwrapped by maternal organs and delicate flesh. The final embodiment of the corpse, as a white skeleton, seems to signify the eventual triumph of paternal substance. Yet the ghost travels down the river, under its matrinames, to an unknown place in the ocean inhabited by maternal ancestors. The funerary rite, too, while it begins with totemic chanting beneath a "father-tree" (*nyait-mi*), actually concludes *in* the river. The final two stages of the ceremony are a collective bath followed by a torching of the deceased's belongings by their sisters, who then sweep the ashes into the current. Likewise, the rigid or skeletal father-son relationship is eclipsed by the tender interactions between maternal uncles and their sisters' sons. Indeed, the kinship system itself, as a forest of patrilineal trees, is nourished by maternal water.

Throughout Papua New Guinea, as an Eastern Iatmul man jested, there are two and only two sources of male strife: land and women. For this reason,

Henry Ngawi confided more seriously, all ground is actually female. In one cosmological scenario, land was hatched from maternal islands (*agwi*). These mythic islands are sometimes understood to rest on male crocodile spirits (see also Wassmann 1991, 98). Nevertheless, these numinous reptiles float atop the feminine sea, thus suggesting, yet again, that water is primary.

Oedipal Flooding

The feminine water of the primal sea, as the original condition of the cosmos, required no oppositional or complementary "other" for its existence. Water, like the female body, is self-referential. But land and trees, or the male body and masculinity, are defined *against* the feminine powers of watery creation and dissolution. However, even manhood itself is sometimes aquatic. In the mythic past, a man unwittingly killed his wife by severing her breast and roasting it with sago and grubs. The fatal recipe was recommended by a duplicitous cross-cousin. The husband, while somewhat leery, was assured by the cross-cousin that no harm would befall his wife. When she died, the enraged husband petitioned Mendangumeli, a senior crocodile spirit, to exact revenge. The powerful spirit flooded the world. The great waters gushed from a long water lily, which, as some men explicitly confirm, symbolizes the crocodile's penis. This genital flood washed away a twofold moral breach: a violation of the female and maternal breast, and a rupture in the intimate and trustworthy cross-cousin relationship. The deluge also enabled a male survivor to repopulate the world in accordance with renewed moral norms. The floodwaters, as Dundes (1986) argues for other such tales, signify male birth envy (see also Tuzin 1976, 1977). The flood casts female fertility and the waters of parturition as a masculine idiom of destructive regeneration.

The meal of breast and sago was a double violation of motherhood. First, the breast was already, prior to its deadly dismemberment, a source of maternal nourishment. Second, men say that only women and mothers can cook edible sago. Not only does Mendangumeli appropriate female fertility but "he," a spirit who also oversees conception (chap. 3), appears to be a phallic mother who violently protects "her" nurturing capacities. This myth, it is worth noting, is mentioned with greater frequency than perhaps any other tale in the culture.

The fabled flood, while signifying a dangerous plentitude of aquatic semen (see also Lipset 1997, 145), might also instance a symbolic projection of the trauma of weaning, such as I discuss below. The severed breast resembles a castrated phallic mother—a mother who, in her architectural embodiment, sometimes displays crocodile teeth in her mouth/vulva (chap. 4).[5] Despite "her" own trauma though, "she" returned in full phallic force to punish male immorality.[6] If the oral consumption of the breast, moreover, can be said to have a sexual meaning, then the ensuing waters also caution men against acting on oedipal desire, much like the tragic tale of the snake-child (chap. 3). Sexuality is incompatible with the ideal of moral motherhood, at least to men. The maternal breast has no place on the erotic body of wives.

Eastern Iatmul seemingly envision their social order as the triumph of masculine land and trees over feminine water. But arboreal metaphors for kinship are less sturdy than they first appear. Likewise, assertions of masculinity often mask the primacy of femininity and motherhood. Even the wrath of Mendangumeli, the fiercest male crocodile spirit in the pantheon, is a transformation of female parturition. "He" is also a mother-figure who usurps the phallic aggression that defines masculinity in order to safeguard "her" own body from the appetites of adult men.

The Ambiguity of Kinship

Anthropologists tend to view kinship as a means of reducing the inherent disorder in social life. Kin terms, for example, precisely specify obligations, behaviors, and expectations, and thereby delineate the social identities of individuals. In the Eastern Iatmul setting, however, kinship both defines and confounds social personhood *and* gender, especially for men.

Eastern Iatmul negotiate their forest of kinship by manipulating three principles: patriliny, affinity, and matrifiliation (see also Bateson 1936, 18 n. 2).[7] The "morphology" of social structure, as Bateson (1932, 289) recognized, is resolutely agnatic. But "the sentiment of the people is preponderantly matrilineal." Or, as Mead (1935b, 307) described Tchambuli, the "institutions and the emphases" of society are "at odds with one another." Both men and women in Tambunum profess to value mothers above fathers. As they say, "my mother, therefore I am," adding that only mothers bore you, fed you, cleansed your body, carried you around the village, and looked after your safety and well-being.[8] For this reason, many Iatmul frankly prefer to determine kinship through matrilateral ties (see also Hauser-Schäublin 1977, 152), thereby allowing maternal affection to eclipse, like skin to bones, or water to trees, the androcentric norms of their society.[9]

The kinship system is equally fluid from the perspective of what Bateson (1936, 35–37), drawing on Radcliffe-Brown, termed "identification." This concept refers to moments when two otherwise separate individuals are treated as a single moral person. Today, we might say that egocentric personhood is superseded by sociocentric or "dividual" personhood. One form of identification links together kin whose patrinames derive from the same generational "line" (chap. 3; Bateson 1936, 35 n. 1). Thus a man identifies with his father's father, brother, and son's son, whereas a women unites with her father's father's sister, sister, and son's daughter. Other salient identifications include husband-wife, father-son, uncle-nephew, and brother-sister.

Identifications, as Bateson recognized, are contingent rather than absolute. In some settings, the two individuals are entirely distinct. In other contexts, people behave toward one person as they would the other. Identifications, then, like the "conversation" between patriliny and matrifiliation, add an element of ambiguity or structured uncertainty to the kinship system. It is never entirely clear, even to actors themselves, what forms of relational logic are currently employed, and by whom, in any given context.

The kinship system also entails another mode of ambiguity, one that creates a linguistic and symbolic sense of diffuse gender identity for men. To begin, I want to return to the brother-sister identification. These kin identify, in part, because they often share the very same patrinames, differentiated only by gender-specific suffixes (chap. 3). Yet there is more to this relationship than the symmetrical logic of identification. In the Trobriand Islands, according to Malinowski (1929, 437), brother-sister avoidance is "the supreme taboo." By contrast, this relationship is informal in Tambunum, devoid of complex interdictions other than immodest joking and outright sexuality (Bateson 1932, 288). Absent from the brother-sister bond is any of the tension that exists between male siblings. A sister is akin to a nurturing mother. She feeds her brothers who, in turn, offer protection. Although these roles are modified after marriage, the close brother-sister relationship endures throughout the life cycle (see also Hauser-Schäublin 1977, 106). It explains, many men say, village endogamy.

The indissolvable cross-sibling bond, however, advances the social goals of brothers more than those of their sisters. It also hints at the dependence of brothers as *men* on their sisters as *mothers.* A sister's marriage transforms her brothers into wife-givers who can now present demands to subordinate male affines. Of far greater importance, however, are the children she will birth since they provide her brothers with the opportunity to fill the important role of male mother or avunculate (*wau*). This role is vital for masculine identity and pivotal for nearly all social institutions. Male personhood is therefore contingent on the sexuality and reproductive powers of women. But the cultural elaboration of female identity, and the social role of the sister in particular, do not exhibit a corresponding dependence on the fertility and sexuality of men.[10] The role of father's sister (*iau*), in fact, is relatively minor for women as well as for their brothers' children. By contrast, many essential dimensions of male life specifically revolve around the ritual and everyday services provided by, and to, mothers' brothers. The same asymmetry, I now detail, accounts for the presence in the kinship system of "feminine husbands."

Submissive men in myth often appeal to the sympathies of superior rivals by calling them "husband" (*lan*). A docile man thereby pacifies and feminizes his masculine identity. Today, men resort to the same form of linguistic androgyny during *naven* rites when, as they are assaulted by women from the father's mother's clan (chap. 9), they shout "*lan nyiin to!*" or "you [feminine pronoun], my husband!" By thus acknowledging their submission to *women,* men in this context can be said to triply reduce their masculinity as it is normally defined on the basis of aggressive assertion (see also Bateson 1936, 82).

Not only do they assert their own passivity and femininity, but they further degrade their masculinity by subordinating themselves to women. The exhortation "*lan nyiin to!*" can also be uttered by a maternal uncle should he slide his buttocks down a nephew's shin during naven. Yet there are no comparable expressions by women during ritual, no parallel enactments of demure femininity, and no corresponding terminological assertions of feminine androgyny.

Another linguistic example of male androgyny is revealed by the kin term for a sister's husband, *lando,* which condenses the words for husband (*lan*) and man (*ndu*). Overtly, as men say, this term implies that a sister's husband is submissive and indebted to his wife's brother. For this reason, it is advantageous to call men *lando* whenever possible. Yet the term insinuates that the wife's brother is actually a woman who is wedded to the sister's husband, and thus subordinate. Similarly, the patrilineal progeny of the sister's husband are also the maternal nieces and nephews of her brother. Thus a wife's brother, while he asserts no uncertain moral claims over his sister's husband in his dominant role as a wife-giver, is nonetheless reliant on his affine for the opportunity to demonstrate his effectiveness as a male mother. Moreover, the sister's husband is both beholden to and superior to his wife's brother since he, the husband, exercises sexual privileges that are denied to his alter. The ambivalence and ambiguity of the brother-in-law relationship, and the manner in which it binds masculine identity to feminine reproduction, would seem to explain the terminological androgyny of the sister's husband.

The reciprocal term, *tawontu* or wife's brother, derives from the vernacular phrase *tagwa-ndu* or wife-man (Bateson 1936, 210). A married woman maintains close somatic and sentimental ties to her brothers. (This bond, by the way, is voiced exclusively as the sharing of maternal and *not* paternal substance.) Yet, ideally, she forges equally enduring bodily and emotional ties to her husband. This role was eloquently summarized by the tokpisin remark "*em i bilong mitupela wantaim,*" that is to say, "she belongs to both of us," husband and brother. By using the term *tawontu,* a husband acknowledges the existence of an indelible relationship between his wife and her brother. He also admits to his marriage to *both* of them, sister and brother. A wife, however, is wedded only to her husband; she is not simultaneously married to his sister.

The brother-in-law relationship, phrased in terms of masculine androgyny, attests to the importance of female sexuality and uterine fertility in the local definition of male personhood. Despite the ideology of manhood, men are sometimes women. But the kinship system fails to define any comparable social roles of "manly women." The gendered identity of women is far more stable than that of men. This recognition requires us to revise a subtle observation by Mead (1941, 53–54). Iatmul social life, she correctly noted, is highly unreliable in the sense that men are continuously subject to competing demands and overlapping alliances. As a result, the society itself is unable to provide men with psychological "integration." Instead, a man "maintains his integration by acting in the same way in all situations." For many men, this is undoubtedly true. But it is also the case that, despite continuity in emotional and behavioral expression, the gender of men, when defined through women in the kinship system, is far less stable. In effect, a man is unable to act "in the same way in all situations" because in many contexts he is also a she.

Kind Grandfathers, Oedipal Fathers, and Preoedipal Uncles

Among all male relationships, the fondness and warmth in evidence between a sister's son and his mother's brother are unsurpassed. No other social bond in the culture so closely approximates the affective qualities of preoedipal motherhood—the feeding, comfort, and emotional reassurance. Yet the avunculate relationship, too, confounds any clear attribution of gender and morality to social roles. Normally, anthropologists contrast the maternal uncle solely with the father. Yet in Tambunum, we need to expand this relational framework to include the paternal grandfather. These three senior men provide a socializing triangle within which we can locate significant dimensions of masculinity.

The kin term for paternal grandfather and grandson, *nggwail,* is reciprocal. It suggests equality. After all, these kin share the same totemic "backbone." The term *nggwail* also, we saw in chapter 3, refers to patriclan spirits, ancestors, totemic names, and sacra. But the grandparent relationship, while it evokes the magical and mythic-historic heritage of the descent group, also conjures a degree of intimacy and tenderness that is never associated by adult men with fathers and elder male siblings. They connote deference alone. Still, the grandfather is unable to provide a man with the symbols of motherhood that he so desires, namely, houses and brides. For this, a man must turn, however reluctantly, to his father.

The father-son relationship, as I have repeatedly emphasized, is emotionally stilted; numerous interdictions frustrate any possible sense of lasting intimacy (relatedly, see Mead 1935b, 50–51, 55–56; Tuzin 1997, 169–72). This is not to say that the father-son relationship is totally devoid of any attachment. If a father is physically abused or verbally insulted by another man, his son will almost always spring into action to defend him, often violently. Still, the father-son relationship is akin to the rivalrous entanglement between Ilahita Arapesh brothers, who vie "for the mother's approval and (sexual) favor, and the idyl of an immortal existence replete with sex and Mother" (Tuzin 1976, 193–96).[11] Eastern Iatmul brothers, it is true, may occasionally scuffle (compare Bateson 1932, 287).[12] Yet oedipal tension in Tambunum is most evident in the interaction between fathers and sons as they "compete" for mother-figures through the inheritance of houses (chap. 5) and in marriage (chap. 7).[13] Furthermore, the birth of children results in the father's banishment from his wife's bed, an "Oedipus situation" to which Whiting (1941, 125–26) attributed Kwoma men's shame at sleeping with their wives. Of course, the father will later return, thus displacing his child, who may also be weaning.

Many elder men gladly bestow their totemic identity and patrinames onto grandsons (chap. 4). By contrast, sons "take the place" of their fathers in the political structure of the society. Both of these bonds enable the totemic continuity of the patriline. But the latter relationship is expressly antagonistic and oedipal since sons are said outright to replace their fathers. This might explain why some men, despite carefully guarding their names, nonetheless refuse to deliver to their sons this magical patrimony.

Father-son tension is exacerbated, I suggest, should the father beat his wife in front of his young children. Although this form of domestic violence was more common in the past (Bateson 1932, 274), it does occur today, often the result of alcohol, and may temporarily traumatize young children. Adult men tend uniformly to disapprove of spousal abuse; yet they are equally adamant that, in some cases, it is wholly appropriate (see also Scaglion 1990). Not once did a man mention any such episodes between his own parents. I recall, however, one anguishing incident when a toddler sobbed for his beaten mother as she lay writhing on the ground. Still, I infrequently witnessed or heard about men who beat their spouses. It was, to be sure, far less in evidence than the vicious brawling that often occurs between cowives (see chap. 8). But, again, spousal abuse is not unknown and would certainly seem to contribute to the awkward ethos of the father-son relationship.

Despite the myriad structural, emotional, physical, and oedipal tensions between fathers and sons, the father's sister (*iau*) has a relaxed relationship with her brother's child (*kauggat*). The amitate provides an emotional counterbalance to the authority of the father. Yet the role of the father's sister does not parallel the position of the mother's brother. The father's sister is neither a feminine father nor a symbol for the relationship between fatherhood and femininity.[14] The avunculate, however, *is* a male mother, one whose identity is singularly expressive of the complex relationship between masculinity and motherhood. It is to his role that I now turn.

Bateson (1936, 36–38) singled out the distinction between the mother's brother and the father as the "one important discrimination" in the culture. Both relationships, to repeat, are somatic, one based on maternal flesh, the other on paternal bones. Whereas sons inherit their father's spirits, which are often wooden, nephews only impersonate maternal totems—they don ancestral costumes, blow flutes, and eat meals during the uncle's totemic chants.[15] Formerly, maternal uncles "hailed" their nephews with matrinames, thus implying that they, rather than the uncle's own sons, were the human embodiments of his clan totems (Bateson 1936, 43–44). Persons also, we have seen, revert to the matriclan in death, and men are symbolically birthed from the uncle's anus during the honorific naven rite (see chap. 10).

The emotional contrast between fathers and maternal uncles is especially striking. As warm feelings between father and son wane, their relationship is increasingly mediated by an architectural personification of motherhood (chap. 5). Furthermore, Mead (1940c, 37) suggested that the mother "is the center of attention and the process of growing up for males may mean transfer of emotional attention from the mother to the male group, with no great importance ever attached to the father-child tie." Boys, we might say, learn the norms of masculinity in the absence of any strong paternal presence. Ties to matrikin, however, remain intimate and direct throughout the life cycle. In contrast to the Manambu of Avatip (Harrison 1984, 398; 1990), this bond is only marginally related to political and economic interests. It is true that, as I noted before, sisters' children are expected to support their mothers' brothers during totemic disputes—even against their own fathers. Nevertheless, the avunculate relationship is anchored to maternal attachment rather than law or structure.

The paternal and avunculate relationships, too, both revolve around a human mother-figure: a wife/mother or a sister/mother. Likewise, both relationships are represented or condensed into an aesthetic mother: the domestic house and the awan costume. But the sentiments and exchanges within the avunculate relationship are preoedipal first—they pertain to themes of nurture and birth—and oedipal second. Conversely, the father-son relationship is in the first instance oedipal, and only secondarily nurturing. Moreover, the relationship between father and son centers on idioms of maternal loss and restoration. Hence, the father "gets back" his mother during his son's marriage, but he then "loses" her again when the son inherits his house. Within the avunculate relationship, the mother is never lost: she, as the uncle, is always there.

The tender emotions associated with the avunculate (*wau*) are superseded only by the mother (*nyame*) herself. In fact, the avunculate can be called *nyame-wau-ndu*, or mother-uncle-man, an attribution that surely speaks to his androgynous and maternal role. "He" promotes the growth of his sisters' children (*laua*) by feeding them sago and meat.[16] "He" protects their health by affixing shell-and-twine talismans to their ankles, wrists, and neck, accompanied by a brief meal (fig. 5). During painful initiation, "he" soothes his nephew and once presented him with token homicide ornaments, thereby promoting, like a mother, the nephew's strength and courage. Finally, the mother's brother celebrates the achievements of his nephews and nieces with naven rites since "he," again like a mother, experiences pride and delight in their successes. So maternal and venerated is the uncle in Tambunum that, whereas other Sepik societies such as Kwoma (Whiting 1941, 12) fear incest as the paramount threat to social order, Eastern Iatmul dread sexual joking with a mother or mother's brother.

Nevertheless, avuncular morality is hardly altruistic and transparent. The uncle expects his sister's children to reciprocate for his gifts of nurture with valuables and small sums of money. While the actual amount of cash is negligible, the symbolism of these transactions is highly important since neither the uncle nor his nephew wishes to appear selfish. Each man, in fact, attempts to appear more generous than his alter.[17] A subtle ethos of competition thus pervades all reciprocal gift-giving between uncle and nephew. From this viewpoint, the maternal uncle is no mother possessed of unconditional love.

Fig. 5. A mother's brother bedecks his sister's children, one of whom is breast-feeding, with shell-and-feather jewelry to ensure their health

In this regard, the death of one of the central figures in mythic history, Tuatmeli, is surely significant. Tuatmeli was the first culture hero to crawl out of the totemic pit (chaps. 2, 3). He also had an exclusive monopoly on spears, at least until he was betrayed by his wife. But her duplicity did not end Tuatmeli's immoral reign of phallic aggression. In its own way, the great spirit's body was a split representation of the moral and the grotesque. His right side was all human—vulnerable flesh and blood, covering bone. His left side, however, was unscathable rock. When Tuatmeli speared a rival, he simply turned to stone, as it were, and was thus rendered impenetrable. Eventually, Tuatmeli's adversaries succeeded in gaining favor with the great spirit's nephew. Under the pretext of grooming, the nephew, having cut the hair on Tuatmeli's head and face, asked his uncle to raise his right arm in order to trim his armpit hair. When he did so, the nephew struck Tuatmeli in the torso with an axe. Tuatmeli died, and so did, we might say, any pretense that the avunculate relationship is devoid of potential antagonism.

The avunculate relationship, then, unlike the mother-son bond, is maintained through a mode of interaction that resembles what Bateson called "symmetrical schismogenesis." In this type of encounter, two individuals or groups interact through the same mode of response. If a Iatmul man boasts, for example, he incites a rival to do likewise, which causes the first man to redouble his efforts, and so forth. Ironically, symmetrical schismogenesis describes norma-tive interaction between all categories of men except for maternal uncles and nephews. Men strenuously censure behaviors that might conspicuously intro-duce this mode of interaction between these kin. Otherwise, the avunculate bond will be eroded of the precise emotional qualities that make this relation-ship so unique in the lives of men.[18] If a maternal nephew initiates any symmet-rical interaction with his uncle, such as boasting, the mother's brother may respond by threatening to perform a naven rite (Bateson 1958, 289–90; see also chap. 9). That is to say, the uncle curtails his nephew's moral lapses with the very same ritual that ostensibly celebrates the advancement of moral personhood.

The avunculate relationship, in sum, is doubly paradoxical. First, it is char-acterized by the simultaneous presence and absence of symmetrical schismo-genesis. Second, the uncle scolds and celebrates his nephew, degrades and hon-ors him, through the same ritual form: naven. No other male relationship among the Iatmul is so complex, or so highly valued. Yet, in actuality, each of the three categories of senior men that are crucial to male identity is in its own way contradictory and complex. The father is a distant figure of oedipality whose emotional attachments to motherhood provide his sons with their own maternal shelters: a house and a wife. The grandfather represents the relaxation of struc-ture yet the root of totemic identity. Finally, the uncle serves in the role of a male mother, yet his mothering taints the ideals of motherhood with male rivalry.

Mothers Moral and Otherwise

If the mother's brother is a figure of such ambiguous and labyrinthine emo-tions, commitments, and representations of manhood, then it stands to reason that the mother herself must evoke contrary rather than solidary values. By now, it is surely evident that Eastern Iatmul men idealize the mother-son rela-tionship. As Weiss (1987b, 185) writes, the unified duality of the mother-child bond is the closest human relationship for the Iatmul, one that is the model for all future relations with any other person. When a man calls a woman "mother" (*nyame*), he implies her direct responsibility for one-half of his somatic existence. The same, of course, is true for fathers (*nyait*). But mother-hood receives far greater symbolic elaboration. Indeed, the designation "mother" implies that a woman birthed, fed, washed, carried, and protected a man when he was a vulnerable infant and child, responsibilities that, according to men, are fulfilled by mothers at great personal travail. No comparable set of cherished qualities is ever associated with fathering.

In this regard, too, mothers contrast with other significant female kin such as wives and daughters-in-law (chap. 7). While men associate wives with material comfort and food, female spouses are a source of antimaternal wealth and sexuality. Men may strike their wives, but never their mothers. Similarly, men call a daughter-in-law the kin term for "mother" but these women are labeled "greedy." Mothers, needless to say, are only generous.

In the nostalgic gaze of men, mothers in the course of their daily activities constantly cradle and carry their infants, rarely laying them to rest far from their watch or grasp (see also Hauser-Schäublin 1977, 136). A mother will promptly, if not always willingly or graciously (see next section), interrupt whatever she is doing in order to console a fussing child with her breast or snack, attend to a toddler, soothe a newborn, or wipe away the tears of child-hood. Mothers, *not* fathers, are reputed to lend unconditional support to their sons during feuds and, formerly, warfare. Mothers, too, and *not* fathers again, encourage a son's bravery. As Linus Apingari said, when a man is young, his mother whispers into his ear "No matter how you die—by warfare, fire, sick-ness, serpent bite, or falling from a tree—you must be strong, and face death like a strong man. You cannot cower and shrink away from death." Mothers, men might say, can do them no harm.

Mothers have primary responsibility for teaching infants to walk. Sym-bolically, motherhood alone enables children to stand on their own two feet and begin mastering the autonomous achievements of adulthood. Mothers are also, we have seen, linked to the cleanliness of houses, canoes, and courtyards. More important, they are responsible for the daily hygiene of children. Human mothers, too, cleanse the architectural mothers hewn by their fathers and hus-bands, which their brothers and sons inherit, and they also bathe children in the river. Toilet training is another task of motherhood. In fact, many men aver that fathers are expressly prohibited from so much as even touching the feces and urine of a child, especially the excrement of firstborns.[19] Some men say that fathers should even refrain from holding these infants. A child who disre-gards his mother may be chided with the words "who cleaned your feces?!"[20] A violation of paternal authority elicits no such exhortation.

Men attribute their strength and health to childhood meals cooked by their mothers, especially a pudding of boiled sago and coconut called *nunjiik.* One man reported that a boy's first spoonfuls of nunjiik remain solidly in his belly until just before death when, after a lifetime of nourishing and sustaining his body, this meal is finally expelled through his last evacuation.[21] Maternal feeding, too, men say, enables the growth of their musculature and ensures the presence of feces (*ndi*) inside their bellies, both of which enhance masculine health, strength, and sexual attractiveness. Likewise, the standard fare offered by mothers' brothers to their sisters' children, fried sago and cooked meat, also contributes to bodily growth. Provisioning of food is a common metaphor for social morality throughout Melanesia (e.g., Strathern 1977a; Kahn 1986; Lipset 1997), as it is in Tambunum. Yet Eastern Iatmul also associate male and female gifts of food specifically with mothering. A childless woman, Weiss (1987b, 151, 153) was told, is little more than the paper label that surrounds an empty food can. In short, feeding is an index of moral personhood, which takes anchor in an ideal vision of motherhood.[22]

Women themselves and not just men eagerly extol the virtues of mother-hood. They often add that fathers are like children for all the daily work they accomplish. As Mead (1949, 180–81) observed, in Tambunum no less, "men must be aroused into working sago even to feed their own families. The village is shrill with the vituperations of wives goading their husbands by insult and invectives to work sago for their households." But mothers, women say, are always cooking, cleaning, caring for children, tending to domestic chores, and working in general. While no man would ever diminish the physical toils involved in constructing houses and chiseling canoes, women suggest that these efforts pale in comparison to their own daily ordeals as mothers. As Mead (1949, 180) observed, "the ability of Iatmul woman to work steadily at unexciting tasks, without boredom or serious disturbances in rhythm" contrasts dramatically with "the disinclination of Iatmul men for any such tasks."[23]

Above all else, three aspects of moral motherhood are paramount in men's nostalgic imagination: feeding, consoling, and cleansing.[24] Few insults in this culture are as heinous as those that attack motherhood: "Go fuck your mother!" (for which one woman was fined in the 1980s), "You eat your mother's cunt!" and, perhaps most viciously, "You bastard!" (literally, "Your mother conceived you on the road"). One of the great slanders of fatherhood, too, refers to a mother, albeit in architectural form. If a man fails to build a large dwelling, his sons may be humiliated with ridicule along the lines of "Your father built you a pig's house!" Few Eastern Iatmul disagree with the local adage "my mother, therefore I am." But the reality and symbolism of motherhood has another visage.

Bateson (1936, 76) summarized the role of the Iatmul mother as a provider of food, a source of comfort, and a person who feels pride in the accomplishments of children. He also claimed that the "Iatmul mother's behaviour towards her offspring is simple, uncomplicated by self-contradictory elements such as characterise the patterns of a father's behaviour" (Bateson 1936, 75). Curiously, these statements seemingly contradict Mead's (1949, 90) own description of Iatmul motherhood:

> As soon as the Iatmul child is a few weeks old, the mother no longer carries it everywhere with her, or sits with it on her lap, but instead places it at some distance on a high bench, where it must cry lustily before it is fed … a baby that has had to cry hard for its food eats more definitely, and the vigour with which the mother thrusts her nipple into its mouth increases.

Mead (1949, 114) also wrote, in a passage that evokes the notoriously aggressive style of Mundugumor parenting (Mead 1935b; McDowell 1991, 183–84), that "the Iatmul mother chases her erring two-year-old with a ten-foot paddle with which she threatens to kill him when she catches him—and never does." How can we account for this ethnographic discrepancy, one that arises between two of anthropology's keenest observers?

In short, Bateson and Mead are both correct. Bateson's comments, I suggest, pertain largely to men's idealization of moral motherhood. Mead, however, was more attuned to the daily interactions between mothers and children, many of which contravene men's fond reminiscences. I never witnessed a

mother pursue a defiant child with a canoe paddle. Still, Eastern Iatmul mothers and *not* fathers regularly discipline children. These scoldings are often
shrill, physical, and downright mean (see also Bateson 1932, 272).[25] Men seem
only to shoo away children from their adult undertakings, effectively sending
them back to their mothers.

Humiliation and embarrassment are common forms of moral censure by
mothers, who frequently yell. More than yelling, I was told, mothers can even
bind their children by the feet and hang them upside down! I myself never witnessed this extraordinary method of chastisement; I do not know if it ever
occurred. I was astonished when it was even mentioned—by one of my most
trusted informants, Dmoiawan, a man who was employed by my predecessor
in the 1960s, Rhoda Metraux, and whose father was *luluai*, or elected village
magistrate, under the Australian colonial administration during the Tambunum fieldwork of Mead and Bateson. His comment was seconded, I might
add, by other men. Regardless of veracity (I have no reason for doubt), this
maternal behavior is salient in the imagination of at least some men—men
who otherwise view motherhood with tenderness and longing. At the very
least, frustration and anger are common experiences in infancy and early childhood. Early disappointments tend to be associated with mothers since they are
the primary adult caretakers (see also M. Morgenthaler 1987b, 223). In this theatrical and boisterous culture, toddlers often vent their discontent through
furious temper tantrums. Ultimately, mothers are held accountable for these
outbursts when the children disturb men, as they often do.

Moral mothering itself can be brusque. As Mead (1940b, 100) put it, "Iatmul mothers treat their children in a matter-of-fact, face-to-face way, acting
almost as if the child were an individual equal to the mother in strength and
definiteness of purpose" (see also Mead 1949, 96, 110).[26] Nonetheless, Iatmul
mothers are continuously engaged with, rather than aloof from, their children.
Mead (1940b, 100) also proposed that the casual style of Iatmul mothering
socializes children "to act like their mothers, to orient themselves towards other
objects . . . instead of being in a dependent, over-stimulated relationship pre-
dominantly oriented towards their mothers."[27] While mothers are a source of
comfort, then, they are not always particularly tender, especially with toddlers.
Bathing is hasty and rough. It is common to see mothers towing their sulking or
sobbing, foot-dragging toddlers by the hand through the village to the river for a
wash. Mothers are also the central figures in weaning, which can be disruptive to
a child. Some children have access to the breast until the age of five or six. Weaning includes light slaps, knocking the child away, yelling, and the smearing of
mud, tree sap, hair, and other distasteful substances onto the nipple.[28]

Mothers promote self-confidence and courage in their sons, in effect, aid
them in battle. But this encouragement is itself somewhat aggressive. According to Mead's (1949, 90) description of a Iatmul mother feeding her child, the
greater the intensity of the child's sobs, which the mother cultivates by waiting
until the infant has cried "lustily" before finally offering it her breast, the

greater the "vigour" with which she shoves her nipple into its hungry mouth. "In this interchange between mother and child," Mead (1949, 90) continues,

> the sense of the mouth is built up as an assertive, demanding organ, taking what it can from a world that is, however, not unduly unwilling to give it. The child learns an attitude towards the world: that if you fight hard enough, something which will treat you as strong as itself will yield—and that anger and self-assertion will be rewarded.

The Iatmul mother does, it is critical to keep in mind, eventually yield food to her children. But her morality often assumes a tone and obstinacy that, when enacted in any other setting by any other person, might be confused with antimaternal aggression. Nonetheless, little boys and male adolescents, wrote Mead (1949, 112), not only play with children, but "they are surprisingly feminine, willowy." Despite moments and styles of aggressive mothering, it is maternal tenderness that nostalgically and psychologically prevails.

To put it another way, the Eastern Iatmul mother virtuously promotes in her children personality traits that ensure their adult successes. In so doing, however, she must to some degree contravene the ideal moral image of motherhood as seen through the nostalgic lens of manhood. Mothers, it may be said, make strong warriors by tolerating and even encouraging childhood tantrums. The mother's brother, too, may clandestinely foster his nephew's warrior temperament with magic. By contrast, among Murik, the mother's food-giving is something that is often seen as hindering, rather than aiding, masculine socialization (Lipset 1997, 58). While the Murik image of "a baby nursing itself to sleep . . . is one of their quintessential images of morality," it is still the case that infants must learn, or be coaxed, into liking "social" foods that, unlike breast milk, are imported from trading partners. These extramural partners are, however, termed trading "mothers." In both contexts, Eastern Iatmul and Murik, the relationship between motherhood and socialization is dialogical. In one, the mother's antimaternal behavior promotes adult qualities that are attributed to maternal succor. In the other, the mother's morality must be superseded by socialized behaviors that, as it turns out, are nothing other than a variant of motherhood herself.

Among Ilahita Arapesh, mothers beat their sons, whom they view to be nonproductive and useless members of the household (Tuzin 1997, 166–67). Consequently, sons may later strike their mothers (173–74). Nothing like this happens in Tambunum. Both Eastern Iatmul and Ilahita Arapesh mothers are associated with nurture. But mothers in Tambunum can, and again do, feed crying children. Ilahita Arapesh mothers may simply yell and hit hungry children, perhaps out of simple frustration since they inhabit a marginal environment that experiences periodic shortages of food (173–74). The disjunction between the reality and ideal of mothering, writes Tuzin, partially explains the local misogyny. In Tambunum, however, the relationship between masculinity and motherhood is best understood in terms of dialogism rather than misogyny. Hence, gentle memories of moral mothering eclipse any recollections of maternal aggression and childhood frustrations that, instead, are projected onto various expressions of grotesque motherhood.

Likewise, while men do not speak about their fathers with marked warmth and fondness, many fathers are quite loving to infants and children (see also Mead 1949, 112). Furthermore, fathers may seek to restrain the brutal hazing of their sons during initiation. In one village household I knew quite well, a young boy would run to his father for consoling after he was scolded by his mother, who was the disciplinarian in the family. The same boy, however, witnessed his father beat his mother one afternoon, and he repeatedly watched his mother fight her cowife, sometimes with knives. Moreover, this young boy had recently been banished from his mother's bed by the birth of a baby girl. For this child, to invoke Bateson, *neither* motherhood *nor* fatherhood is unitary or "uncomplicated by self-contradictory elements." The prevailing image of fatherhood inverts the cultural ideal of mothering. Paternal memories foreground oedipality and background paternal care. By contrast, the culture elaborates the contrary dimensions of motherhood. The symbolism of parenting, we might say, forgives fathers of their love, yet refuses to forget maternal behaviors that diverge from the impossible ideal. As a result, fathers are figures of distant authority, lacking in emotional intimacy, while mothers are either lovingly selfless or dangerous to the bodies and achievements of men.

Menstruating and postpartum women, for example, should refrain from feeding male kin. (Admittedly, these and related taboos are not strictly enforced.) Indeed, the prohibition on fathers cleaning feces and urine from children and especially firstborns arises precisely from the close association of these excreted substances with birth, menstrual blood, and vaginal secretions (see also Hauser-Schäublin 1977, 125).[29] A postpartum woman can *only* access her residential house by climbing a ladder through the window lest she corrupt the doorways and thereby pollute her husband.[30] I was dumbstruck when I witnessed my own brother's wife, scarcely a day after delivery, grunting with pain as she slowly inched her way out of the window and down a bamboo ladder while toting a bucket full of soiled diapers. For men, the idyllic valuation of motherhood is contested by the mother's body itself.

An even more dramatic enactment of transgressive motherhood occurs during the naven rite that celebrates first-time cultural achievements. Elderly women from the father's mother's clan accost their male and female alters with sexual banter, beatings, and substances that represent feces and menstrual blood. These women are called *iai,* a category of female kin that includes a man's preferential spouse. The term *iai,* too, as we have seen, connotes a mother's belly and womb, and the interior cavities of houses and canoes. Iai women, as mother-figures, symbolize moral reproduction and care. Yet they also tarnish the body with "dirt" (Douglas 1966). As Bakhtin might say, iai women turn everyday motherhood inside-out and upside-down. This is the topic of the next chapter.

Oedipus in the Sepik

Anthropologists, certainly since Lévi-Strauss ([1949] 1969), have tended to view marriage as an institution whose primary significance is the reproduction of a moral society. In Tambunum, this view is surely correct. Through marriage, women become affinal vines and birds that entangle patrilineal trees into a unified social order. Through marriage, women and especially men progress from the status of adolescence to adulthood. And through marriage, a young man expands his body and persona beyond the safe embrace of idealized motherhood and asserts his autonomy and competence in the intricate realm of affinal relations. But marriage in Tambunum is far more than simply a matter of sociological integration and moral personhood. The cultural symbolism of marriage, as I demonstrate in this chapter, reveals a deep existential quandary for manhood that pivots on the position of motherhood in men's imagination.

Affinal Relations

The intent to marry is publicly revealed by some form of coresidence.[1] Usually, the woman sleeps the night in the house of her potential husband.[2] Later, the bride's male kin, typically brothers, may formally accompany their sister to her new residence, laden with her domestic possessions: clay fire hearth, ceramic bowls, enamel plates, cooking utensils, kerosene lantern, suitcase of clothes, foam mattress, pillow. This procession announces the legitimacy of the union.

Bateson (1936, 310) noted that the Iatmul bride was adorned with shell valuables that constituted a gift to the husband's descent group. This wealth is called *nggwat keranda*, a phrase that in Tambunum refers to a bygone conciliatory gesture whereby men smeared tree sap (*nggwat*) down the legs of their opponents. This courtesy was enacted during the resolution of conflict and warfare, and the purchase of land from nearby and often inhospitable Sawos villages. In the context of marriage, the reference to nggwat is a symbolic attempt at subduing affinal tension (see also Bateson 1936, 147).[3] Still, affinal asymmetry is moderate in Tambunum, at least when compared to other

Melanesian societies, more a matter of sentiment than economic indebtedness (see Forge 1972; Gewertz 1983; Strathern 1984; Errington and Gewertz 1987b, 1987c; Lindenbaum 1987).

Nevertheless, one image of affinal conflict points to the maternal dimensions of Eastern Iatmul marriage. When the bride's agnatic kin choose to parade their sister to her husband's house, they often assume a menacing tone. These men may actually enter the house of the groom, *uninvited,* and demand some final confirmation of the marriage or an immediate token of bridewealth. In so doing, potential affines violate the chaste integrity of a man's dwelling as a symbol of moral motherhood.

Marriage is also expressive of nonmaternal female identity. Wives are a nexus between potentially belligerent lineages. The aphorism *tambe iaman, siik iaman* (hand spear, penis spear) cautions men against seeking both their spouses and victims from the same group (see also Hauser-Schäublin 1977, 135). The failure to separate marriage and homicides will assuredly result in injurious, perhaps fatal, mystical retribution (*vai*).[4] Although this aphorism clearly ties male sexuality to aggression, it also suggests that women precariously separate love and sociality from hate and violence, at least for men.

It is masculine personhood, however, that is most directly affected by marriage. Eastern Iatmul understand bridewealth (*waingga*) to constitute "payment" for a woman's reproductive potential and sexuality (Bateson 1936, 79; Gell 1992b, 166). These gifts, too, "compensate" the bride's parents and patrilineage for the difficulties incurred during her child-raising. Formerly, they also discouraged affinal sorcery.[5] Yet bridewealth itself has little role in maintaining affinal alliances (see also Bowden 1983b, 1988; McDowell 1990). Today, bridewealth consists of two gifts. The first presentation is often assembled as a public display: a pig, crowned with some banknotes attached to a cluster of betel nuts, is placed before the house-ladder of the bride's residence, which is usually the house of her father or brothers. This gift may also include a few cartons of beer. Later, the groom's kin will present to their new affines a considerable sum of cash—yet not so exorbitant that, as Bateson (1932, 280–81) claimed, men are "ruined" by bridewealth indebtedness. In fact, village endogamy tempers these affinal demands, as does the high value men place on brideservice.[6]

A son-in-law (*nondu*) is expected to perform a wide range of labors for his father-in-law. He should construct canoes and houses, chop sago, and tend gardens. Nevertheless, the relationship between a daughter's husband and his wife's father, like that between fathers and sons, is one of avoidance. They are especially proscribed from sharing meals and dipping into the same lime gourd while chewing betel nut. Since lime gourds evoke the phallus, and food is often a metaphor for sexuality, these taboos mediate the tense relationship that inevitably arises when two men in a small kinship network assert opposite sexual and moral claims over the same woman.

Both men and women are active in courtship. However, as Hauser-

Schäublin (1977, 75) writes for Kararau, men are generally less willing and able by themselves to initiate amorous contact than are women. While women directly approach potential husbands and lovers, as we saw in chapter 4, men often resort to intermediaries and love magic. To some degree, as I stated then, this shyness, as it were, arises from the cultural attribution of sexual appetitiveness to women, and sexual modesty to men. However, it is also the case, as I elaborate in chapter 8, that the conventions of adult male personhood largely forbid unmediated assertions in many contexts. Consequently, potential male affines often enlist their sisters' children (and other nonlineal kin) to negotiate, present, and accept bridewealth. This way, nephews assume the collective voice and agency of their matrikin. Although marriage enables men to reach adulthood, the roles assigned to sisters' children in the context of bridewealth actually deny or disperse the assertive identities of male affines.

Bridewealth also exacerbates father-son tension. A father, in raising a son's bridewealth, will commonly request contributions from various agnatic, affinal, and matrilateral kin. But a refusal, as an affirmation of individual autonomy, is everyone's prerogative. In the end, the financial burden of a son's marriage is his father's alone. Indeed, when men think about marriage, they unequivocally prefer daughters instead of sons. An ideal son-in-law will tirelessly work on behalf of his father-in-law. By contrast, the marriage of a son introduces a "greedy" woman into the household, namely, the daughter-in-law. Furthermore, married sons are said to be so busy with fulfilling brideservice obligations that they are simply unable to look after the welfare of their own parents. Yet sons, of course, reproduce their father's patriline and provide grandchildren on which the father can bestow his names and ornaments. The affinal dimensions of marriage, then, while rather moderate economically, nonetheless entail a complex symbolism for men and women alike.

Nurturing Daughters, Greedy Daughters-in-Law

The relationship between marriage and female identity requires further discussion. A daughter and her husband, motivated respectively by sentiment and obligation, will allegedly feed and care for *her* elderly parents (see also Tuzin 1976, 94–97). No such conventions compel a son and daughter-in-law to provision *his* parents.[7] They are, instead, greedy (*kokwat*), an immoral quality that is also attributed to carnivorous and ravenous animals, especially dogs and rats. If daughters thus represent moral motherhood, then daughters-in-law evoke a contrary image of consumptive, neglectful selfishness.

A woman can only attain the formal status of a daughter-in-law if the father of her potential husband is successful in raising her bridewealth. In so doing, the father-in-law depletes himself of his own wealth. He becomes, in this sense, hungry. The daughter-in-law continues to "eat" at his expense, and she fails to reciprocate him directly for her new status. True, she births and nurtures her father-in-law's lineal grandchildren and thus reproduces his patriline. But a daughter-in-law does not feed her father-in-law, at least not in ideology, despite the fact that he continuously feeds her. Indeed, a man and his wife are always committed to feeding and assisting their sons' families out of consideration for the well-being of their grandchildren. Furthermore, a father fears the gossip of a daughter-in-law should his generosity fail to meet her expectations.[8] In her dual role as a nurturing mother and a consuming woman, the daughter-in-law, like the domestic house, presents men with conflicting images of womanhood.

The contrast between a daughter and daughter-in-law contributes to male ambivalence toward women. After all, any married woman will symbolize to men maternal love as well as feminine rapaciousness.[9] This paradox, together with men's envious fear of female sexuality, is "the problem of men's double and divided claims over women" (Meeker, Barlow, and Lipset 1986, 25). The juxtaposition of daughter and daughter-in-law might seem to parallel the opposition between son-in-law and son. To some degree, this is accurate. But no cultural symbolism elaborates the conflicting dimensions of male identity to either men or women in such a pithy manner as the common statement by men that "women are greedy but never mothers."

The Precariousness of Wives: Wealth, Birth, Killing

In contrast to generous daughters and avaricious daughters-in-law, men associate wives with wealth (Bateson 1936, 147; compare Roscoe 1995a, 80).[10] Wives, of course, birth sons and thus make certain the intergenerational continuity of their husbands' patrilines. Yet men value especially the labor of their spouses. Wives tend food and tobacco gardens, weave baskets and touristic figurines, and contribute to various commercial projects such as trade stores and the sale of crafts (e.g., wooden carvings and net bags) in town markets. They also feed visiting trading partners. Formerly, wives raised pigs and plaited reed sleeping bags that husbands, after conferring with their spouses, exchanged for shell valuables and magic. Today, men continue to rely on female labor products for acquiring, again with consent, prestige goods and signs of "modern" identity. In fact, a common explanation offered by men for polygyny is the association of wives with wealth, renown, and work.[11]

Marital tensions are common (see also Hauser-Schäublin 1977, 127–29). Frustration can lead to blows, in some instances inflicting bodily pain on *both* spouses; some husbands are even dominated by their wives. Marital conflicts often arise over sexuality, including the postpartum suspension of intercourse, as well as cowives (see chap. 8). In addition, husbands complain when their wives do not adequately prepare meals, and wives protest when their husbands are lax in their subsistence duties. Both spouses assume domestic responsibilities. Both men and women value husbands who labor in gardens, carve or purchase canoes for their wives, and provide for their family in general. Both men and women prize hard-working wives who tend carefully to home, hearth, and children. Yet, as Hauser-Schäublin (1977, 77, 134) recognizes, the main goal of men is to participate in the esoteric affairs of the cult and manhood while wives aspire to maintain a sense of domestic harmony and efficiency. When the household is unsettled, women are often blamed.

Wives pose even more direct perils to their husbands. They can restrict a husband's reputation and affluence simply by refusing to work, cook, or lavish generosity onto visitors (see also Bateson 1936, 149). These strategies prove wrong the irate husband mentioned in chapter 4 who, as reported by Bateson (1936, 14), growled "yes, we copulate with them, but they never retaliate!" As we have seen, a wife's body, in addition to her agency, can imperil her husband. Postpartum and menstruating women are subject to numerous restrictions (see also Hauser-Schäublin 1977, 124–27). They should refrain from sexual intercourse, cooking food, serving meals to men, bathing in the river, and crossing architectural thresholds. Likewise, all categories of women should take care lest they step over the limbs and possessions of men.[12] One research assistant noted that, when a couple shares the same mosquito net, the woman must sleep near the opening so she will not inadvertently crawl over the man should she need to urinate during the night. Feminine sexuality and conjugal relations compromise the reputations and bodies of men. But in the absence of birthing mothers, of course, and the very ideal of motherhood herself, men lack not only children and grandsons, but also the very schema of manhood.

The relationship between wives and the male cult is equally paradoxical. The flutes that produce the best tones, men say, are fashioned from bamboo that is cut by wives. (Of course, this dictum does not apply to those flutes made today from plastic PVC pipes and, in one ingenious instance, the exhaust pipes from a Japanese aircraft that was downed during World War II.) But this is no simple matter. In some cases, it involves outright theft. If, instead, a man seeks to convince his spouse to chop him bamboo, he must be careful not to divulge the reason for his request. If he breaches this deception, then the magical efficacy of the flute and ritual vanishes. But if men are unable to do this, then their ceremonies and the senior crocodile spirits are denied their finest voices. Either way, by thievery or subterfuge, men today reenact the primal theft of sacra from ancestresses by obtaining flutes from women.

The somewhat antiquated belief system that once surrounded warfare and head-hunting also attests to the complex relationship between the ideals of manhood and marital sexuality. Homicides once guaranteed the general prosperity of the village: "plenty of children, health, dances and fine ceremonial houses" (Bateson 1936, 140–41).[13] The procreative function of killing was especially vivid at Kararau (Hauser-Schäublin 1977, 154, 160). When the "soul" of a dreaming warrior magically killed men in an enemy village that was targeted for a raid the night before the actual vendetta, the warrior's wife felt "the penetration of an ancestor's penis at that moment." Notice the direction of causality: sexual intercourse and procreation did not secure a man's success in head-hunting but, rather, killing guaranteed ancestral procreation and human pregnancy.[14]

In a related way, the safety and success of men during warfare and less for-malized fighting is contingent on the behavior of their spouses (see also Meeker, Barlow, and Lipset 1986, 53–55; Hauser-Schäublin 1977, 155–56). If a wife sweeps rubbish, then her husband will be "swept away" in battle. If she rolls rope, he will trip; if she weaves, his legs will become entangled; if she snips plants, he will be "cut down." Accordingly, women are empowered both to facilitate and inhibit masculinity. Men exercise a similar influence over women since ritual displays of sacra can either ensure or disable female procreative capacities (chap. 4). Likewise, fathers-to-be must abide by an array of prohibi-tions during the pregnancies of their spouses (chap. 4). These interdictions, when situated in the broader context of masculinity, evidence men's envy of female fertility. But there is little evidence to suggest that female restraints dur-ing warfare reflect a corresponding jealousy of male prerogative.

Marriage presents men with contrary images of femininity. Mothers are nurturing, daughters-in-law are greedy, and wives, while they enhance a hus-band's wealth, prestige, and patrilineal continuity, can also reduce his somatic vitality and masculine competence. Indeed, a wife's reproductive potential, as we just saw, is directly tied to her husband's success in combat. Nonetheless, any lapse in her own moral conduct with regard to bodily exudations can kill him.

Rules, Options, and the Tragedy of Names

There is one stated matrimonial preference in the society: the union of a man and his father's mother's brother's son's daughter (FMBSD), a woman termed *iai*.[15] Iai marriage, as I will call it, is asymmetrical. As Eastern Iatmul themselves recognize, this rule fails to specify a reciprocal union. Yet men and women actively seek to balance and disperse their matrimonial relationships. For this reason, the preference for iai marriage is not universal. Two other marriage options exist: sister-exchange and elective marriage.[16]

Sister-exchange and elective marriage are fully legitimate modes of matri-mony. Yet they are contingent practices, suitable under certain circumstances, rather than acontextual or global rules. All things being equal, Eastern Iatmul aver only iai marriage. But all things are rarely equal in this disputatious com-munity. Hence, the ideal of iai marriage is often eclipsed by social exigencies. Sister-exchange, which comprises approximately 18 percent of all unions, tends to address the goal of balanced reciprocity. It also resolves long-simmering feuds. Elective marriage is far more prevalent, accounting for one-half of all contemporary unions. It is particularly appropriate when iai marriage is unsuit-able—say, when previous such unions exist within a male sibling set—or when men and women wish to pursue their own political and economic strategies. Elective marriage, in fact, attests to the ability of individual autonomy and voli-tion to resist the force of collective will or abstract rules (see also Bateson 1936, 107). Iai marriage, we will shortly see, arises from desire rather than coercion.

In contrast to elective marriage, which emphasizes egocentric ambition and situational contingency, iai marriage exemplifies sociocentric personhood. It requires potential spouses to suppress their individual wills and agencies in order to act on behalf of their respective grandparents. While the kinship category designated by the term *iai* includes all women from the father's mother's descent group, the preferred iai spouse is the precise or biological FMBSD.[17] Since a "line" of personal names repeats every second generation (chap. 3), FMBSD iai marriage replicates exactly the union that took place between the paternal grandparents of the bride and groom (fig. 6). In iai marriage, the bride is a *ngaybe yembii tagwa,* "a woman who walks the same house path" as her paternal grandmother.[18] Ideally, this form of matrimony replicates itself indefinitely, both in structure and names. Since a man has the same patronymics as his paternal grandfather, men often say, he should wed the very same bride.[19]

For men, names are a central motivation behind iai marriage. But this sentiment and pattern creates equally persuasive risks. Iatmul villages are highly fissile. Brawls and disputes are almost daily occurrences. Formerly, sorcery and homicides were equally commonplace. These ruptures, as I mentioned in chapter 3, often result in vai, a type of magical or mystical retribution that eventually "turns back" onto the original perpetrators. Vai exacts revenge by afflicting innocent people on the basis of kinship identifications, common names, agnatic and affinal bonds, and coresidence. When the moral relationship between two groups is severely rent, any prescription for marriage is at once a prescription for disaster. For this reason, every patrilineage and some branches should permit only one or, at most, a few iai marriages in each generation, often in accordance with primogeniture.[20] The repetitive structure of iai marriage thus predisposes these unions to tragedy.

Marriage and Maternal Longing

The dangerous desire for iai marriage not only pertains to names and generations. It also results from oedipality. Eastern Iatmul explain iai marriage in two ways.[21] Both formulations, while somewhat complex in translation, are nonetheless rooted in a single kinship term: a father refers to his son's iai bride as "mother" (*nyame*). However, the simple logic of this kinship designation is misleading since the relationship between men and motherhood that iai marriage reveals is profound and subtle.

The first vernacular phrasing of iai marriage begins with the acknowledgment of long-term exchanges between a mother's brother and his sister's son. These transactions, we have seen, are overtly motivated by tender sentiments. The maternal uncle feeds his nephew, promotes his health with gifts of jewelry, and celebrates his achievements with naven rites. The nephew reciprocates with valuables and, to a lesser extent, ritual services. Although the uncle usually initiates these exchanges, men report that the nephew's role is more burdensome since he offers wealth rather than food. As a result, the mother's brother

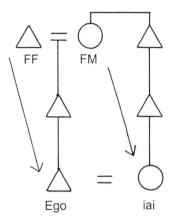

Fig. 6.   Iai marriage and the repetition of names

feels an emotional debt toward his nephew. The uncle redresses this inferiority by telling his own son, who is the nephew's cross-cousin (MBS), to give the nephew a woman whom the nephew calls "mother" (fig. 7). In turn, the nephew's son will marry her.[22]

The second formulation of iai marriage has two variants and centers on the relationship between male cross-cousins (see figs. 6, 7). The first phrasing is from the perspective of the groom: his father's cross-cousin (MBS) gives a "mother" to his father as his, the groom's, bride.[23] The second phrasing is from the perspective of the groom's father: he is plainly said to "get back his mother" from his cross-cousin so that his own son may marry her.[24]

The local understandings of iai marriage clearly emphasize the maternal designation of a son's iai spouse. These idioms testify to the existence of adult male attachment to their mothers since they specify that a man "gets his mother back" as his son's bride.[25] Indeed, fathers are passionate about iai marriage precisely because the maternal bride evokes the nurturing ideals of motherhood, which include feeding and selfless care. The iai woman embodies the proverb "My mother, therefore I am." Moreover, the word iai itself connotes the maternal body since it refers to the belly, including the stomach and womb. Unquestionably, Eastern Iatmul men envision iai marriage through a longing for nurturant motherhood and a sentimental nostalgia for early childhood.

The promise of iai marriage alone will prompt a man to initiate bridewealth years prior to the actual union, thus guaranteeing that a "mother" will return as a son's wife.[26] If the prospective bride fails to return to her "son," as I once witnessed, the spurned father-in-law may seek monetary compensation in a village moot. So strong is the maternal sentiment associated with iai marriage that any obstacle to its consummation is invariably answered with violence. As Gamboromiawan, my informant-friend and father of my own vil-

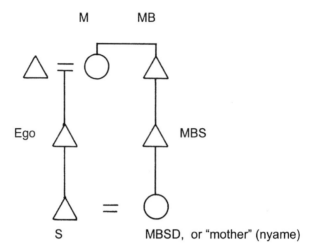

Fig. 7.   The oedipal triangulation of iai marriage

lage brother's iai bride, insisted, "if someone other than your son tries to marry your mother, you must fight him!"

Significantly, men *and* women are passionate about iai marriage. On one memorable occasion, I watched several women surround their domestic ward with an impromptu bamboo fence. This barrier was intended to protect a younger brother from the nighttime seductions of women who were not his prospective iai brides (relatedly, see Bateson 1936, 142 n. 1). Their efforts were successful: no unauthorized lust trespassed this boundary and obstructed the matrimonial reunion between a man and his mother.

Maternal sentiments also explain why groomwealth is obligatory in iai marriage but optional for other types of unions, at least in Tambunum (compare Hauser-Schäublin 1977, 83). These gifts, ordinarily termed *pasiinu kumbi* or "basket of firewood," consist largely of domestic implements such as clay pots, fire hearths, and clothing—items, it is worth noting, that are acquired from non-Iatmul villages. During iai marriage, however, groomwealth (now called *numbun*) must include cash and should equal in value bridewealth. Since these assets figure into the inheritance of the newlywed's future children, it would appear that the fathers of both groom and bride have a keen interest in contributing to the prosperity of a family that is formed through iai marriage.[27] The sociological structure of iai marriage is nonreciprocal and asymmetrical, yet the maternal sentiment and names that motivate these unions are equally forceful to both sets of in-laws.

According to the kinship system, the male term for daughter-in-law is "mother" (*nyame*). This designation uniformly applies to all categories of women, regardless of antecedent kinship ties to the groom and his father, and all forms of marriage. Only in the case of iai marriage, however, was the bride conceptualized as a mother, and called such by her husband's father, *prior* to the actual union. For men, to repeat, the kin term for MBSD (a son's prospective iai bride) is *nyame,* or "mother" (fig. 7). This is a crucial point. The maternal associations of the iai bride not only preceded the marriage—they motivated the union. Furthermore, the iai is the sole category of daughter-in-law understood by men to be maternal in deed as well as in label. In all likelihood, she fed her husband's parents during the years leading up to the formal marriage, and she is expected to continue feeding them for the rest of their lives. From the father's perspective, a son's iai bride is a "true" nurturing mother.

By contrast, any other daughter-in-law acquires the terminological status of "mother" only *after* her marriage to the son. This association is largely superficial. It rarely translates into practice. Not only do the non-iai spouses of a son regularly fail to feed his parents, but they are said to "eat" their father-in-law's wealth and food. Despite their newfound classification as "mother," these daughters-in-law are forced into the unenviable role of immoral motherhood and antimaternal greediness. They invert the emotional qualities and nurturing deeds of iai brides.

Marriage and Oedipality

Ironically, the position of the iai wife in the social structure compromises her moral persona through an unresolved Oedipus complex. To men, the iai woman represents three contradictory relational and emotional experiences: the sexuality of a wife, the nurture of a mother, and the ambiguity of a sister who is a nonsexual intimate and potential namesake. From a man's perspective, too, iai marriage is the final stage in an intergenerational unfolding of triangular relationships. These oedipal configurations consist of two men, one senior to the other, who interact in terms of a pivotal woman.

The first oedipal triangle manifest in iai marriage occurs during brideservice since the groom is said to labor specifically for his father-in-law. This way, the groom clears his debt for the wife-daughter figure. When children are born, this woman becomes a mother-sister figure across which her son and brother forge an avunculate relationship. At this point, what "moves" across her social role is no longer wealth and toil but, rather, tender sentiments, gifts, ritual obligations, and naven gestures. While the mother-sister figure is central to this new relationship, she herself does not participate in these exchanges. In the next and final stage of the cycle, the avunculate relationship is transformed into iai marriage. This three-tiered, intergenerational process then repeats in perpetuity.

The normative interaction between any two male principals in iai marriage is structurally and morally antagonistic. They assert contrasting and often competing claims over a central, if prismatic, feminine figure. The iai, again, simultaneously assumes three contrary feminine roles: wife, mother, sister. As a result, she is one source and expression of male ambivalence toward women. As

previously mentioned, men increase their renown by mobilizing the productivity and hospitality of their spouses. Yet a wife's sexuality and strategies can
deflate her husband's fame. Iai marriage intensifies this predicament since the
iai spouse represents, more than any other wife, the nurturing ideals of motherhood. A iai wife, too, is the object of desire to her husband's father. Consequently, she exacerbates the emotional rupture between fathers and sons. Moreover, elder iai women during naven ceremonies contravene the moral maternal
qualities they might otherwise signify when they thrash, taunt, and defile their
alters (chap. 9). Finally, iai marriage displays the triangular structure of the classic Oedipus complex since two men from different generations symbolically
compete for a woman who signifies the nurture of mothers and the sexuality of
wives. "Women are only mothers," Linus Apingari said with some exasperation,
"that is all . . . Men go from one mother to the other!" Iai women exemplify the
ambivalent transformation of motherhood into matrimony.

Marriage also expresses thwarted desire and motherhood among the
Gebusi of the New Guinea South Coast (Knauft 1985, 1987). During spirit
séances, "voluptuous, beautiful and seductive spirit women" recount sexual
trysts with young men, "including child-lovers, who can transform themselves
fluidly from suckling male infants into adult men and back again" (Knauft
1987, 173). Here, too, as my Eastern Iatmul friend might say, men simply shift
from one kind of mother to another. Gebusi men also fantasize about incestuous liaisons with spirit lover-mothers (Knauft 1987, 173). Eventually, though,
they repudiate, repress, or abandon these oedipal longings and strive instead
for sister-exchange marriage.[28] Yet many of these unions are unreciprocated.
Men are frequently incapable of realizing their dreams of marital passion.
Accordingly, Gebusi society is plagued by an exceptionally high rate of violent
death (Knauft 1985). The ultimate source of these homicides, writes Knauft
(1987, 175), is "the fundamental childhood crisis" of maternal rejection.

Eastern Iatmul iai marriage is equally entangled with incestuous yearnings, at least in the realm of cultural symbolism. The groom's father "gets his
mother back." When he does so, however, he immediately loses the mother to
his son, who then consummates this paternal fantasy since sons, we have seen,
identify with and replace their fathers (chap. 6; Bateson 1936, 38–42). Symbolically, sons kill their father's persona when they assume his jural office. They kill
his body when they assist in transferring his patrinames to lineal grandsons.
And they displace their fathers from architectural mothers. At the same time,
the son's marriage is the only approved route for a father to act on his culturally sanctioned oedipal urges yet remain within the moral order of society. In
short, iai marriage offers an ambiguous solution to the aggression and eroticism of the Oedipus complex.

Hauser-Schäublin (1977, 106) reports one instance of a mother actually
caressing the genitals of her young, not infant, son in order to soothe him to
sleep. Rather different images of oedipal motherhood occur in two Eastern Iat-

mul myths. In one tale, a human mother named Yabarimange births two pigs, Shuigumbwan and Wayndugumbwan. She plants banana trees, a common phallic symbol in myth and proverb, which she later tells her shoats to cut down with their tusks. They easily do so. Yabarimange then turns her sons' tusks inward and tells them to slice down a few more banana trees. They are, of course, unable to do so. In their frustration and rage, they attack their mother, and thereafter terrorize the human inhabitants of a region of the Sepik until they are finally killed by a man. Significantly, the two pigs are the seniormost totems of a patriclan, a group whose moral authority, we might say, arises from an immoral tale of mythic oedipality and incest.

The second myth is more directly tied to marriage. This tale, which I abbreviate here, goes as follows.

> A female cassowary eats the fruit from a man's garden. The man snares the cassowary, but she runs through the bush, trailing him behind her. His body breaks apart, and the cassowary [as I mentioned in chap. 4] eats his brain, an act that leads to her pregnancy. She births a boy. After he matures, she tells her son to pluck out two of her feathers, place them inside his house, and sleep. In the morning, the feathers have transmogrified into two young women. The mother tells her son that they are his wives. Next, she tells the son to hunt wild pigs who are eating the sago she has planted. She secretly hides in the bush and intentionally steps in front of one of her son's spears which was intended for a pig. As she dies, she again tells her son to pluck out her feathers, this time all of them. After her death, the feathers transform into men and women.

Whatever this myth signifies—and it surely encodes multiple levels of meaning—it clearly refers to the ambiguous status of oedipal desire. The son effectively marries his mother or, at the very least, his sisters. Yet this immorality, like the death of the mother herself, is instigated by the mother, not her son. Still, the fatal force of maternal attachment is unmistakable. The son, we might say, is a passive participant in this tragedy, one whose acquiescence is nonetheless vital for the eventual population of the region. In this tale, marriage and reproduction are directly linked to oedipality.

The same can be said, as I have done, for real or nonmythic marriage in Tambunum. Iai marriage pacifies male agency since it requires the groom to replicate a previous union. At the same time, the force of maternal attachment is the precise emotion that motivates iai marriage. Indeed, Eastern Iatmul men, like their Gebusi counterparts, are prone to violence when adversaries disrupt their incestuous fantasies. If rivals in Tambunum hinder the matrimonial return of a man's "mother," the response is often a brawl. The morality of motherhood, as it is revealed in iai marriage as well as in mythic matrimony, is tainted by the violent passion and the foiled desire of oedipality (see also

Knauft 1989b; Herdt 1981, 275). Iai marriage is no mere triumph of social ethics over libidinous turmoil (see also Freud 1913, 1930). Instead, iai marriage is a "social tragedy" (Frye 1957, 218–19, as cited in Paul 1982).

> In comedy the erotic and social affinities of the hero are combined and unified in the final scene; tragedy usually makes love and the social structure irreconcilable and contending forces. . . . Comedy works out the proper relations of its characters and prevents heroes from marrying their sisters or mothers; tragedy presents the disaster of Oedipus or the incest of Siegmund.

Iai marriage threatens the edifice of social structure by introducing filial discord into patrilineal solidarity. This tragedy, too, endangers the moral order of society by juxtaposing contrary images of motherhood in the matrimonial aspirations of men and women.

Lacan's psychoanalytic concept of desire (e.g., [1956] 1968), as interpreted by Trawick (1990, 142–48) in an analysis of Tamil Nadu social life in South India, offers another insightful perspective onto iai marriage. For Lacanians, human existence begins with a tender, sensory, and affective sense of wholeness: the mother-child dyad. This blissful unification—and it is largely idealized as such by Eastern Iatmul men—is ruptured by an alien, distant cultural order. Lacanians variously label the source of this separation Language, Culture, Father, and Phallus. The androcentrism of Lacan's framework is contentious, as it should be (e.g., Rubin 1975; Gallop 1982; Flax 1990). Nonetheless, the daily interactions between mother and son in Tambunum *are* eventually shattered by the youth's assimilation into the masculine norms of collective life.

The shattering of primary unity, however traumatic it may be, enables the development of self-awareness and subjectivity. With some irony, Lacan theorized that the primary yearning that defines individual selfhood is the desire to *regain* symbiotic wholeness. Toward this psychodynamic aim, the self "reaches out" to cultural symbols and localized social goals in order to feel satisfied and fulfilled. Alas, the originary sense of wholeness is merely an illusion—the result of Lacan's famous mirror stage—and so is the promise of redemptive unity. Still,

> the self keeps reaching for this illusory ideal. As long as it has this desire . . . it builds the human world. If its desire were fulfilled, if there actually were closure—a perfect culture—and if the self felt itself to become whole, then human life would end, everything would stop. (Trawick 1992, 144)

Trawick's Lacanian framework is suitable not only for India (see also Nuckolls 1996) but also for Melanesia. This, after all, is a region where the fabric of social life, as Weiner (1995a) emphasizes, is woven from exchanges that are imagined as bodily detachment and incorporation. Indeed, the Melanesian self, writes

Weiner (1995a, 4), drawing on Freud (1917, 243–58), develops from "attachments that are established and then abandoned." In iai marriage, as in so many masculine endeavors, men "reach out" to motherhood in the hopes that they will become complete. But this ideal is never realized.

The tragedy of iai marriage, however, assumes a particular and Freudian form: the Oedipus complex. By blurring the distinctions between sexuality, motherhood, and aggression, iai marriage jeopardizes the foundations of society and manhood. At the same time, iai marriage *does* reproduce men and groups. It neither completes nor negates oedipal desire. No father is killed, no incest actually accomplished. As Trawick (1992, 152) might suggest, the continuation of iai marriage "may be posited, not upon its fulfillment of some function or set of functions, but upon the fact that it creates longings that can *never* be fulfilled."[29]

The Maternal Jester

Bawdy banter frequently erupts between iai women and their ianan alters. This is the only sanctioned joking relationship in the culture (compare Hauser-Schäublin 1977, 107–8). Some men and women insist that *all* interactions that occur between these categories of kin are ribald. (The only woman who is exempt from these antics is a man's genealogical FMBSD iai.) This sexual joking (*kasa nyangiit; tsuay mbwito*) is significant for two reasons. First, the drollery is primarily enacted by women who otherwise symbolize the ideals of maternal nurture, and, second, the unwilling objects of their jests are usually men.

The repartee is almost exclusively verbal and often plays on the theme of erotic aggression as in "I will cut off your head!" There is no physical contact; the immorality of these travesties, in this respect, remains decorous since the relationship is figured largely in idioms of motherhood.[30] The iai women frequently taunt men with a protruded tongue (chap. 4) that signals erotic fierceness throughout the Sepik (Bowden 1984). They may also pun with domestic idioms. The quip "Give me sago!" as a thematic inversion of the myth of sago (chap. 2), transforms maternal nurture into teasing seduction. The barbs can also be quite explicit: "You have a small penis—what can it do?," "Come here! Grab my genitals!" and "Tonight, I will finally visit your mosquito net!" Yet, for the most part, this "grotesque symposium," as Lipset (1997, 143–50) terms Murik joking, is coy and euphemistic rather than unabashedly blatant and physical.

Iai-ianan jesting can pepper any setting, mundane or sacrosanct. I once overheard wisecracks during a male cult performance of bamboo flute music, a time when men may angrily silence mischievous women and children. Yet the joking was permitted! In this setting, the iai's comedy resembled the incestuous desires manifest in iai marriage. Not only did she ridicule the authority of the totemic spirits, but she mocked the moral foundations of masculinity, motherhood, and social order. It is critical, in this regard, to underscore the fact that sexual joking in Tambunum *only* occurs between mother-figures and their "children." Strikingly absent is *any* sexual joking on this order between men.

Authorized joking, Radcliffe-Brown (1940) argued in a famous functionalist thesis, calms the oftentimes tense relationship between affines. But while the symbolism of the iai-ianan relationship does include marriage, their joking pertains to motherhood rather than affinity. The jesting, too, only marginally mediates social boundaries (Lipset 1990), vents sexual tensions (Whiting 1941, 95–96), and eases the transformation of a relationship distinguished by the incest taboo into one of marriage (McDowell 1991, 195–96).[31] While the banter is usually initiated by the iai, it does not appear to give women unusual license to comment on the restrictions of their social roles (Barlow 1992; Counts and Counts 1992). Rather, iai-ianan joking arises from "the irrepressible play of urges and appetites that inspire and threaten the moral order" (Barlow 1992, 81). When iai women jest, they confound the moral and bodily distinctions between maternal care and conjugal sexuality. They also become masculine mothers who, by driving away their ianan, repudiate the virtuous qualities that men attribute to motherhood. This humor, we might say, concerns ambivalent love.

A clowning iai, however, does not solely comment on the fragile consignment of "urges and appetites" to different realms of culture and social life. The iai's quips, like architectural *vagina dentata* (chap. 5), hint at male anxiety about female sexuality and the role of motherhood in masculine identity. In this regard, the iai's jesting is surely tied to the oedipal issues that figure so prominently in iai marriage itself. The iai's lewd brashness, as a result of the father-son identification, is directed at both her potential husband *and* his father, a man she calls "son." This son, recall, is the very same man whose desire to "get back his mother" is expected to evolve into the iai marriage itself. In consequence, the aggressively humorous flirtations of a joking iai both encourage and deter incest.

Finally, iai-ianan joking is the antithesis of the comforting yet sober avunculate relationship. Like the mother-son and father-son dyads, the interaction between maternal uncles and their sisters' sons is entirely devoid of erotic innuendo and licentious raillery. From this perspective, the iai is a phallic mother whose assertive sexuality inverts the tender sentiments that the avunculate, as a parturient male mother, displays toward his nieces and nephews. The relationship between a mother's brother and his sister's son is openly maternal and complementary, and only mutedly competitive and masculine. Conversely, the joking relationship between iai and ianan, which lampoons men's veneration of motherhood, is expressly competitive and only implicitly complementary. Iai-ianan joking, I am suggesting, is a spirited dialogue between carnivalesque female mothers and modest male mothers.

For men, the Eastern Iatmul universe is a riverine world of feminine water, erosion, and dissolution. In this changing topography of landscape and culture, iai marriage ensures intergenerational continuity and thus corresponds to the arboreal imagery for genealogy. Whereas trees appear to be solid men amid the flowing river, iai marriage offers an equally stationary mooring in a society characterized by uncertain fluidity. But iai marriage is an anchor of dialogical rather than solidary meanings. It offers men a moral image of motherhood that validates their existence. But iai marriage also present men with a contrary image of motherhood against which they continuously struggle.

8

The Shame of Masculinity

Among the many activities that exemplify the cultural ideals of manhood, several stand apart as particularly paradoxical. Success in ritual, oratory, marriage, and, formerly, warfare, as well as basic everyday agility and bodily purity, all attest to masculine competence. Yet each of these endeavors requires men to enlist the aid of hereditary partnerships called *tshambela* that, as I argue in this chapter, actually confound and negate, as much as they encourage, the conventions of masculinity.

Generally speaking, tshambela partnerships link together different lineages through a system of reciprocal ceremonial duties.[1] As such, the tshambela institution integrates patrilines that might otherwise feud through the logic of schismogenesis. But the tshambela relationship, like marriage, is far too significant to be relegated merely to Durkheimian sociology. On the one hand, tshambela partnerships enable men to pursue the assertive goals of masculinity. On the other hand, tshambela disperse a man's identity, mask his agency, assume his voice, and accept responsibility for his actions. Tshambela, too, in the event of shameful male incompetence, set in motion a series of dramas that regress men back to infancy, a stage of life that in this context is associated with excrement and dependence. At the same time, these ordeals transform men into mothers and evoke the passive and feminine role in anal sexuality. In many respects, the tshambela relationship, while it seemingly upholds the virtues of masculinity, is an embarrassment for men since it dramatizes the maternal and feminine themes of manhood.

The Diffuse Achievement of Murderous Reproduction

In the past, homicides were a prestigious element of masculine identity that elevated a warrior's social status, renown, and name. For this reason, head-hunting would seem to have emphasized an individualized mode of male personhood. To some degree, this was true. Yet a warrior's tshambela complicated any notion of egocentric masculinity. They also, on these violent occasions, blurred the distinctions between the everyday capacities of men and women.

After a successful homicide, a warrior's tshambela boiled and cleansed the victim's severed skull. Later, they remodeled the head with clay, paint, hair, and shells in a human likeness. For these efforts, the victor recompensed his tshambela with food, betel nut, and valuables. Credit for a homicide was solely the killer's. He alone received a *tambointsha* homicide tassel from his initiators. Formerly, men proudly affixed these feathered insignia to cassowary bone spatulas that they dipped into gourds of lime powder when chewing betel nut (Bateson 1936, 46 n. 1, and plate XXIVA; see also chap. 3).[2] Yet the killer's tshambela, by tending to the victim's skull, symbolically assumed responsibility for the violence. In fact, tshambela performed these ceremonial duties only *after* they first ritually rekilled, or "purified" (Bateson 1931, 49), the victim inside the cult house. (The base of the skull was struck again while it sat atop the wooden representation of a female turtle spirit named Kwomkwombarlagwa.) The tambointsha tassel signified the successful homicide, but the real trophy, the head, was denied to the victor. Instead, it was awarded to his tshambela partners—but with the tacit proviso that they attend to the skull "under the name" of the victorious warrior. In this arena of masculinity, the male self was both egocentric and sociocentric. A man was honored as an individual yet his bounded identity was dispersed by the celebrants themselves.

The ritual reconstruction of a human portrait on the victim's skull must also be seen as the attempt by men to assert reproductive capacities that are normally associated with women, pregnancy, and parturition. Here, as in male initiation, men collectively assert procreative prerogatives by killing or sacrificing (Jay 1992) a person born from woman. Men, by ornamenting the skull with red and white swirls of paint that signify maternal blood and paternal semen, symbolically transferred physical gestation from the female body to the all-male cult house. This ritualized act of male reproduction, predicated on killing, guaranteed human and cultural prosperity (chap. 7). Moreover, this transformation of murderous aggression into a mimetic dramatization of female reproduction occurred in the "belly" of the cult house—an internal space from which women, of course, are violently excluded.

External warfare was not only procreative for the community. It was also dangerous. Even today, I am told, when men return to the village from a fight during which they inflict a mortal wound, they must sleep in the cult house and participate in rites of cleansing. The same rules apply to their weapons. In the morning, it is safe to reenter the residential houses and the domestic spaces of the village. By the same logic, a group of men who are carving a large canoe must conclude the workday by tapping their axes in unison against the hull. This hasty formality allows them to return home without fear of polluting and harming women and children. A similar rite occurs when men use awls to stitch together roof thatch (see also Coiffier 1992b, 48). In each of these instances, men wield weaponlike tools to hack, pierce, or slaughter totemic bodies (e.g., human, canoe, house). In each of these instances, too, men must dissipate the unpredictable power or toxic charisma that ensues from their collective action. This ethereal malignancy resembles the unhealthy power that emanates from newlyweds who are actively trying to conceive their first child—a poisonous "scent," as it is imagined in Tambunum, that drives away fish and wilts gardens (see also Hauser-Schäublin 1977, 117). Early conjugal sexuality, like collective male aggression, is exceptionally potent. It is a mode of fertility that ironically endangers all living things, human and otherwise, except for the principals themselves. Significantly, in the cases of warfare and certain types of labor, these principals are men.

Warfare precautions delineate same-sex male and female activities. From men's perspective, these decrees prevent women from interfering in their masculine endeavors. However, this boundary is permeable, if not paradoxical, since male aggression once empowered female fertility as expressed in birth, horticulture, and fishing. What's more, the martial prerogatives of men are largely housed within the architectural "belly" of the cult. The sequence of events that unfolded from a successful vendetta—the actual slaying, the cleansing and remodeling of the victim's skull by tshambela, and the resulting fertility—was a grotesque transformation of moral motherhood. This process defined manhood on the basis of reproductive murder.

After a homicidal achievement, the warrior fed his tshambela so they, in turn, could promote his renown. The victor's success in warfare attested to his hypermasculinity. Yet upon this achievement in the brutal enterprise of head-hunting, the conventions of the male cult essentially transformed the warrior into a female figure of docile nurture. Like a mother, his role was now to feed others, and thus to promote their own murderous agency, which they enacted by symbolically slaying the victim atop the wooden turtle spirit. For the most part, the killer remained on the periphery of cult activity. In addition, as Bateson reported in his unpublished fieldnotes, "it is terribly costly to be a killer" since the victor was required to feast not only his tshambela but also various shamans and all other clans of the village. Having taken a life, the triumphant warrior's task was to sustain the bodies of rival men who, having partaken of this meal, would themselves presumably seek to kill.

Head-hunting was once a signal accomplishment of manhood. Yet in the context of warfare and homicidal vendettas, the tshambela relationship was uncannily poised to invert many of the conventions of masculinity. It blurred male and female identities, called into question the everyday associations of manliness and motherhood, dispersed egocentric personhood, and reduced a warrior's wealth.

The Psychology of Concealment

We can also interpret the tshambela relationship in terms of the psychology and phenomenology of killing, much as Harrison (1989a; 1993a, chap. 6) has perceptively discussed for Manambu warfare. Any moral order established through continuous and omnipresent violence requires ego defense mecha-

nisms that confront and perhaps overcome the trauma of individual accountability (relatedly, see Schwartz 1973). Warriors in Tambunum resorted to a
range of homicide practices that diffused their responsibility, agency, and identity. These rites, as Harrison argues, generally depersonalized the killer himself
rather than victims. It was not the identity of a man's enemy that was alien and
problematic: it was his very own sense of self.

The deliberations inside the cult house that preceded an actual raid evidenced one psychological defense modality. During totemic debating, we have
seen (chap. 3), men accentuate their oratory by rhythmically slapping bundles
of ginger leaves on a wooden stool. Physically and metaphorically, this lectern
centers the debate on the speaker and his discourse, a feat of no uncertain consequence in an acephalous society that delights in schismogenic interaction.
The debating stool, while taller than normal sitting stools, is equally
unadorned. It is also devoid of a totemic name and hence a *kaiek* spirit or soul
(see chap. 3). When men discussed killing, however, they orated from a different and magically potent stool that is named and carved to resemble Tuatmeli,
the culture hero who first surfaced from the totemic pit at the beginnings of
cosmic creation. Homicide debaters stood behind the tall figure of Tuatmeli.
The spirit's buttocks receded into the flat wooden surface on which orators
slapped their leaves. The overall effect during homicide deliberations was one
of Tuatmeli himself speaking rather than the human discussants. At the very
least, the great spirit sanctioned the dialogue while decentering the debate away
from living men. Either way, Tuatmeli effectively assumed responsibility for
any eventual homicide.[3]

A related example of dispersed culpability occurred during the actual raid
itself. Warriors, as Tuzin (1976, 51–52) discusses for Ilahita Arapesh, often
shouted the name of the cult house while delivering the fatal blow. Here, again,
individual men were simply agents for nonhuman forces and beings. Final
responsibility resided in the realm of the numinous (see also Tuzin 1982, 339).
The tableau of victims' skulls displayed on the facade of the ceremonial house
also suggested that the body of the cult herself, a phallic mother who represented the male collectivity, was ultimately accountable for these deaths.

Spears, shields, and warfare ornaments are incised with the features of *sabi*
spirits who ensorcell warriors and their weaponry. These spirits are best known
from the masks that adorn the center of Iatmul canoe shields. Nautical sabi are
phallic regardless of gender. Whereas a female sabi sticks out her tongue, a long
red fringe is stuffed into the mouth of a male sabi, a type of homicide ornament
(see below) that sways to the motion of the canoe in battle. This symbolism
aside, sabi ensure that killers and their murderous appurtenances exist in a
state of exceptional and dangerous ritual power (see also Harrison 1989a, 1993a,
1995b; Tuzin 1976, 51–52). Magical charms and spells, while they bewitched
rivals, more importantly endowed warriors with an abnormal, heightened
degree of aggression and strength that eclipsed rational thought, speech, and
hearing. The verbal execution of these hexes and most other types of spells

includes the oral expulsion of blood-red spittle that consists of chewed betel nut, ginger, and croton. Eastern Iatmul associate these plants, which are also interwoven into magical amulets, with ritual "heat" (*kau*), dubbed *kik* in tokpisin, and mild dissociative states. During one of these trancelike episodes, a man's actions are not evaluated according to the moral standards that govern mundane social life. Essentially, he is forgiven transgressions and violence that would otherwise be censured and avenged.

After a homicide, the warrior staged a pig feast inside the cult house in order to elude the wrath of his victim's ghost (*wundumbu*). The victor was specifically obligated to feed men from other descent groups. The warrior himself was unable to partake of the repast lest he suffer from mystical retribution (*vai*). As Harrison (1993a, 89) writes, these pseudocannibalistic meals established a bond of complicity, "a shared experience of transgressing norms, and a kind of exciting and, for some men, frightening, collective culpability."[4] By transforming a univocal achievement into a sociocentric event, the feast transferred the responsibility for murder from an individual to the entire village and its numinous pantheon.

Eastern Iatmul men also masked their everyday identities during homicide raids and fighting with an array of facial and body ornamentation. This adornment, like the magical spells, empowered warriors with an unnatural intensity of "heat" that is attributed to powerful ego-alien spirits. It also stunned the intended audience with feelings of fear and awe (Harrison 1993a, 124; 1993b, 111–25; Roscoe 1995c). The aesthetics of warfare ornamentation enabled violence to be tied to the transformational qualities of ritual magic, paint, and ornaments rather than to individuals possessed of common rationality. At the same time, this visual embellishment prevented the ghosts of the victims from recognizing the killers.[5] (I offered a similar interpretation for ceremonial displays of masks and other sacra in chapter 3.) A successful warrior, too, would sprinkle lime powder on his retreating tracks to make sure that the murdered person's ghost would not follow him back to Tambunum and exact revenge.

Formerly, male leaders owned personified scepters called *tshumbuk* that allegedly flew under the cover of darkness and killed rivals by piercing their bodies with fatal magic (see also Bateson 1936, 60, 72).[6] As partible appendages of the male body, tshumbuk allowed men a supernatural means of safely bridging the dangerous interpersonal zones between descent groups and male opponents, albeit for nefarious purposes. These aerial phalli, too, pacified adversaries with an image of sexual dominance (see chap. 4). The scepters performed the same function as warfare magic and adornment: they made it possible for men to kill without incurring the psychological toll of direct accountability.

Eastern Iatmul ethnopsychology does permit extreme feelings of rage and melancholy to "swell" from "within" the body and to overcome a person's normal faculties. But the homicidal aggression associated with the male cult, to draw again on Harrison (1989a, 1993a), which was a daily part of men's lives, was entirely different. These capacities are not innate. They are unable simply to arise from within the person as the result of prosaic hatred and anger. Since most men are not born with this level of malevolence, it was acquired through magic. The ability to kill was also beaten into men during the ignominious ordeals of male initiation, when neophytes ingested a small morsel of an enemy's brain, spinal column, or jawbone. (If cannibalism was impractical, initiates, I was told, ate sago pudding mixed with a minute amount of feces from a noted village warrior.) The purpose of this horrible repast, men say, was to embody the ferocity and courage of the deceased. But as Harrison (1993a) argues for Manambu, the cannibalistic meal also enabled young men to confront directly the terror of killing—and to inure themselves to its psychic trauma.

Tshambela partners and warfare practices both affirmed and deflected the assertive ideals of manhood. These conventions dispersed accountability, mediated the body's movements in social space, and dramatized the tension between egocentric and sociocentric personhood. We are now in a position to offer a second interpretation for why feathered homicide insignia took the very specific form of swinging tassels. In chapter 4, I suggested that these ornaments resembled the phallus. To this, I now want to add that these tassels visually expressed the fluidity of masculine identity and the difficulty in fixing responsibility for aggression and other decisive acts of manhood.

The Problem of Individual Will

Polygynous marriage is no less problematic for male personhood than warfare and head-hunting. Since men understand wives to enhance their wealth and renown (chap. 7), polygyny is a common aspiration. Nevertheless, this matrimonial practice is highly contentious. Fathers and brothers prefer their daughters and sisters to wed men who are unencumbered by prior affinal obligations. For the same reason, a woman's agnates will not take kindly to any attempt by her husband to gain another spouse.

Cowives may be an additional source of polygynous discord if they habitually quarrel, as they so often do, and assail each other with knives and shovels. Ironically, Hauser-Schäublin (1977, 132) suggests that households with multiple wives may actually be managed with greater effectiveness since the usual tension manifest between husband and wife is eclipsed by the rivalry between cowives. Neither woman wants to antagonize the husband and thus become subordinated by her adversary. At the same time, the two women rarely unite against their common spouse. Indeed, Hauser-Schäublin argues that the husband's position in the household is most secure with the presence of cowives since they are more likely to feud with each other than their husband. For the same reason, men are less likely to strike a cowife than a single spouse, and there are fewer divorces. Nonetheless, men in Tambunum view single spousal marriages to be less burdensome than cowives. When asked why they do not marry a second spouse, they inevitably answer, "Too much trouble."

The difficulties with polygyny are often phrased in terms of the opposition a husband may confront when he walks to the house of another man in order "to take" an additional wife. Should her brothers oppose the union, the response could be downright belligerent. Consequently, the suitor may send tshambela partners as his proxy. This way, it is said, neither the new bride's agnates nor the husband's existing affines and wives may legitimately contest the polygynous union.[7] In polygyny, as in warfare, tshambela exempt a man of all accountability by assuming his identity. They also, in the case of multiple marriages, mediate the uneasy encounter between a husband's individualistic resolve and the strategies of rivals.

In many contexts such as iai marriage (chap. 7), men and women effectively waive their right to act on their independent resolve. Nevertheless, Eastern Iatmul profoundly respect the autonomy and privacy of another person's thoughts and desires.[8] As Bateson (1936, 91) wrote, "It was nobody's business to say him nay in this individualistic culture." Men are hesitant, therefore, to contest elective marriages, or even to speculate on the spouses' motivations. Polygyny, poised between egocentric and sociocentric modes of personhood, is a volatile endeavor in which individual male agency often opposes the collective will of others. Like head-hunting, polygyny once expanded a man's names, repute, and social interaction. Today, polygyny is less tied to masculine renown. But it persists as a viable aspiration, albeit a goal that many men are simply unable to attain on their own. Instead, they must rely on tshambela partners.

Tuzin (1976, 245–47) discusses a similar convention among Ilahita Arapesh. When a man feels slighted by a rival, he initiates a cycle of competitive yam exchanges designed to shame his adversary. The insulted man himself, however, does not actually participate in these transactions. Rather, he enlists the aid of "ritual friends" who act on his behalf. They also ensure his anonymity. The recipient never learns the identity of the man he insulted. As in the case of tshambela, these ritual friendships disguise responsibility, eclipse individualism with displays of partible personhood, and mute the assertive ideal of Sepik masculinity.

The tshambela partnership is also related to local notions of shame. The avoidance of humiliation is a prominent feature of Melanesian social life (e.g., Strathern 1977c; Fajans 1983, 1985; Schieffelin 1983, 1985; Epstein 1984, 1992, 212–32; Poole 1985; Battaglia 1990, chap. 7).[9] In Tambunum, moral persons shun explicit forms of self-aggrandizement and self-assertion. Men and women who conspicuously draw attention to their achievements, and thereby situate themselves at the center of social activity, are shameless. Needless to say, the Highland "big man" model of political authority is inappropriate for Tambunum where men rarely arise in public and praise their own exploits.[10] Instead, the oratorical elevation of the self is the responsibility of others, especially one's sister's children and tshambela. A man's tshambela and nephews will also speak on his behalf at public events, including legal proceedings in the provincial courthouse. The very same partners and kin, too, as we have seen, impersonate a man's spirits by donning his ritual costumes and blowing his flutes.

Direct solicitations are also onerous. Eastern Iatmul are uneasy and hesitant about asking to borrow even the most ordinary of household objects, much less food. These petitions diminish the self by attesting to one's dependency and inadequacy—the precise opposite of adult status or maximal personhood. Yet it is perfectly appropriate for *someone else,* especially tshambela, to voice your request. It is not dependency per se that is shaming but, rather, its unmediated public admission. In the early months of my fieldwork, I was befuddled by the many pairs of men and women who, separately and together, meekly approached me prior to my visits to the town of Wewak. With shifting feet and lowered eyes, they quietly initiated idle chatter about some trivial happening. Clearly, another matter was at hand, but it took some time before my interlocutors would broach it: they simply needed something from town. One person wanted me to purchase a relatively inconsequential item, say, aspirin or fish hooks. But he or she remained entirely mute while the *other* person actually stated the request. Men and women were palpably uncomfortable when they asked me directly for insignificant favors. In most instances, I was offered cash or some other remuneration on the spot; these were not the pleas of impoverishment. Likewise, the awkwardness of these encounters was largely unrelated to matters of race and colonialism. Something else was at stake: the shame of admitting dependency.

Ironically, persons incur no feelings of shame when they directly ask tshambela to act in their interests. In this sense, the tshambela relationship circumscribes a social space in which Eastern Iatmul can safely utter their desires, display unmediated assertions of autonomy, and speak their "hearts" (*mauwi*). Once outside this space, however, persons must conceal some partible element of their identity. If the face is seen, then the voice of desire is mediated and muted; if the voice is heard, then the face belongs to others.[11]

Ambiguous Responsibility

If a man drops his lime gourd, tumbles down a house-ladder, or encounters any other physical mishap in his tshambela's residence ward, dwelling, or men's house, the entire tshambela group immediately mimes his clumsiness. Should a man stumble, for example, his tshambela are said to throw themselves to the ground and remain in the dirt until they are recompensed by their maladroit alter with gifts of food, betel nut, and tobacco (see also Lipset 1997, 152–53). Afterward, wrote Bateson (1932, 271), tshambela trim the man's hair and ornament his body. Men are always careful, therefore, to see to it that visiting tshambela sit on sturdy stools and platforms, and (for me, at least) find secure footing along village paths.

Eastern Iatmul state that tshambela, by mimicking misfortune, "help" and "share" a man's shame (*wup*). This way, again, tshambela effectively assume responsibility for the actions of their partners. Here, however, they do so by accepting the contrary roles of sufferer and perpetrator. But tshambela do not simply mirror misfortune: they transform it into a tragic-comic theater of empathy, schadenfreude (Nachman 1986, 1982), and self-mockery (Bakhtin 1984a, 12). These theatrics disperse and reduce shame in order to preserve, but also to ridicule, the ideals of masculinity and, we will see, moral motherhood.

The logic of this tshambela action is complex. In its imagery, we can discern an inarticulate mode of reflexivity that comments on the individualism of misfortune and the infantilism of clumsiness. When a man slips, he transgresses an accepted tenet of social comportment. But he also performs a unilateral and selfish act. By asserting himself as a unique agent, if a blundering one, a man forswears the social expectation that tshambela will serve as his alter ego and function on his behalf. As a result, tshambela transform this individualistic and egocentric mishap into a collective drama that satirizes yet upholds the force of sociocentric personhood.

This drama also expresses the ambivalence of social morality and reciprocity. It is an example of what Trompf (1994) terms "retributive logic." Tshambela, like mothers' brothers, seemingly encourage their alters to act with virtue and humility. They deter men from shamefully engaging in vulgar displays of self-importance and remind their partners to avoid carelessness. In ways both allegorical and real, tshambela assist their alters in walking as proper adults. However, a fine and often indiscernible boundary separates comfort from animosity. By collectively falling, the tshambela group dramatically proclaims its innocence from causing a man's misfortune. Yet their response implies guilt.

When tshambela drop to the ground, too, they are unable to elevate themselves until the man who originally slipped offers them an appropriate gift. In effect, the blundering man must now accept responsibility for his own conduct *as well as* that of his tshambela. As the near-schismogenic drama unfolds, tshambela partners reciprocally defer, to invoke Derrida ([1966] 1978), all attributions of agency, self-other distinctions, and accountability. Likewise, they unseat the center of morality.[12]

A similar yet horrific blurring of identity and culpability was observed by Thurnwald (1916, 261) during a nuptial rite among the nearby Banaro. The groom's father "really ought" to deflorate his son's bride. But he was "shamed" and so asked "his sib friend, his *mundu*, to initiate her into the mysteries of married life in his place."

> The bridegroom's father takes her to the goblin-hall and bids her enter. His *mundu* has already gone into the goblin-hall, and awaits her within. When she come in, he, in the role of the goblin, takes her by the hand and leads her to the place where the big bamboo-pipes (three to six meters long) are hidden. . . . Before these hidden gods the couple unite. Afterwards the girl is led out of the goblin-hall, where her bridegroom's father

awaits her and brings her back to her mother. The *mundu* returns home in a roundabout way, for he is "ashamed" to meet anybody on his way back. (Thurnwald 1916, 261)

In this terrifying context, Banaro mundu resembled Eastern Iatmul tshambela: they accepted the identity, responsibility, and shame of their partners. Yet the mundu "sib friend" could only copulate with his partner's daughter-in-law after he was masqueraded as a cult spirit. The action of one man, the groom's father, required the assistance of two other masculine roles, one human, the other spirit: a mundu alter ego and the "goblin."

The Banaro despoliation rite surely communicated a forceful and humiliating message to women about the authority of the male cult as it was revealed through, and guarded by, aggressive sexuality. The ceremony also exemplified the dialectic between bounded and collective, or egocentric and sociocentric, masculine personhood. The ritual especially emphasized the issue of accountability. Yet the rite was flawed. It did not conclude with masculine triumph. Instead, it led to abject shame.

Shameful Feces, Bewitched Excrement, and Anal Sexuality

Nothing like the Banaro defloration rite occurs in Tambunum. But the tshambela relationship does humiliate men by alluding to sexuality and, in a related fashion, infancy. A man who drops his lime gourd or slips in the mud is socially inept. He is unable competently to stand, walk, and hold onto the paraphernalia of adult masculinity. As Weiss (1987a, 23) remarks, physical maladroitness is particularly humorous to Iatmul. A clumsy man is a joke. He may also soil his body with mud and dirt, perhaps even feces. Unlike adults who may bathe repeatedly throughout the day, this man appears incapable of cleansing himself. By contrast, the ability to wash unaided in the Sepik is a step toward childhood autonomy. It signals self-awareness, responsibility, and mastery over the river.[13]

The phallic implications of dropping one's lime gourd at the feet of potential rivals hardly needs saying. This symbolism is as local as it is Freudian. As warriors once strode through the village, cradling their gourds of lime powder, the long fringes of their homicide tassels would sway as a silent flaunt of bravery and aggression. In Mindimbit village, wrote Bateson (1936, 142 n. 1), men would "scratch onto their gourds tallies of their successful love affairs." When a man topples his gourd, he appears to surrender his prowess in the contiguous arenas of warfare and sexuality. He becomes, as it were, a child—passive and asexual.

Similarly, a man who stumbles regresses his adult personhood to the state of infancy. Who but dependent children would allow their bodies to become so besmirched with mud and feces? Yet the careless man also becomes a mother-figure who feeds others and enables them to arise and bathe. When tshambela partners parody incompetence and throw themselves to the ground, they remain in the dirt until the man who initially tumbled offers them food. Only then can they stand and wash. This gift also cleanses the tarnished moral status of their incompetent partner. An egocentric act of ineptitude, then, not only occasions a display of sociocentric personhood, but it also initiates behavior that shifts a man's identity from mature autonomy to childish dependence, then to nurturing motherhood, and, finally, back to the unsullied and erect posture of masculine adulthood. Two themes are especially prominent in this theater of shameful degradation and sociosomatic renewal: feeding and hygiene, or food and feces. After all, men associate mothering, *not* their own manhood or fathering, with nutritive meals and the cleansing of excrement from children. Hence, this tshambela behavior is another dimension of male experience that defines masculinity in terms of motherhood.

Eastern Iatmul are not excessively fastidious about defecation. Toilet training is lax, as it is among Kwoma (Whiting 1941, 32). Nevertheless, Eastern Iatmul are scornful of children who defecate in the river, along village walkways, and on the dirt plazas in front of domestic houses that women so assiduously sweep each morning and evening.[14] They also remove feces from public view and are particularly careful to avoid stepping on the excrement of chickens and dogs. For this very reason, an untold number of flashlight batteries were expended by one of my own village fathers, and a key research assistant, as he illuminated footpaths at night before my floundering steps.

A person who slips to the ground is thus polluted by dirt or, figuratively speaking, feces. This is an especially acute situation for men since they are deeply ashamed when women hear their flatulence. It is equally demoralizing, we saw in chapter 4, for a man to expose his anus to women. Men carefully conceal visual and aural glances of their buttocks, feces, and flatulence since anything associated with this region of the alimentary canal is understood by men to be a procreative wainjiimot spirit. A man who slips symbolically exposes the bodily fictions of masculinity—perhaps even to women.

The same scatological idiom of clumsiness also opens a man to witchcraft. A common method of this nepharious craft is exuvial: witches burn the feces of their victim and then bespell the ashes. Both men and women, as Hauser-Schäublin (1977, 139–40) notes, are witches. Yet this malignant art is especially associated with women. Most witches are female, most witchcraft is transmitted from mother to daughter, and menstruating women are prone to ensorcelling men. Why? The answer, reasons Hauser-Schäublin, is that Iatmul in some sense equate menstrual blood with the death of an infant. Hence, women possess the innate bodily ability to kill—and, for the most part, they demonstrate monthly this intrinsic, antimaternal immorality.[15] For a man to become a witch, he must assume the body of a woman: essentially, he menstruates. A man who falls to the feces-like mud, then, renders himself vulnerable to the innate cultural toxicities of the female body, the very body that, in both its moral and corrupt forms, he desires.

This incompetence is also sexual. When a man tumbles before his tshambela, he disrupts an otherwise balanced relationship by lying prone at the feet of his alter. Thus he conjures the passive role in sexual penetration, which is particularly humiliating for Iatmul men (Bateson 1958, 291; see also Chasseguet-Smirgel 1985, 158–59).[16] A similar shame is tied to Iatmul men's fantasy of the so-called anal clitoris (Bateson 1932, 278–79). This image, I suggest, has three psychodynamic sources. First, it transforms female concupiscence into a male bodily idiom, and vice versa, since the clitoris in myth originated with a man who inserted the head of a fish into a woman's vagina. Ever since, the stream of urine expelled by women resembles that of men.[17] Second, the anal clitoris pertains to the ritualized fictions of anal parturition that are so vital to the male cult and male initiation. Finally, the anal clitoris is a projection of men's repressed desire for same-gender sexuality (see chap. 4). By slipping, a man not only associates himself in public with childhood defilement and carelessly opens his body to the dangers of witchcraft, but he also displays men's envy of birth and their desire for same-gender eroticism.[18]

The anal clitoris was dramatically symbolized during one naven rite witnessed by Bateson (1936, 20) when a mother's brother inserted a Malay apple into his buttocks. This gesture, even when enacted during the celebratory naven, is dishonorable rather than laudatory and festive (see chap. 10). It symbolizes a "passive female" activity, according to Mead (1952, 419), which can only mean anal intercourse. In Tambunum, a similar pantomime can be used to humble a nephew who profanes the avunculate relationship by uttering lewd jokes before his uncle. When this occurs, the mother's brother may be trussed naked like a pig to his nephew's house-ladder. To intensify the disgrace, a Malay apple or large leaf is inserted into the uncle's anus. There is no more humiliating gesture for men—no gesture, that is, other than the uncle sliding his buttocks down the leg of his celebrated nephew during naven.

These scatological pantomimes are mortifying for men precisely because they uncover before their peers and women a variety of ordinarily displaced desires—sexual, procreative, cosmological, and existential—that define manhood. Yet men who admit to these yearnings, or act directly on them, transgress the ideals of masculinity. A man who slips before his tshambela, in sum, is clumsy and childish, implicates his alters in treachery, besmirches his manhood with a feminine persona, and unveils the fictions that sustain masculinity.

Piles of Food

Mature men are productive gardeners and skillful hunters. They are proficient in carving canoes and paddles, and they fulfill marital obligations. In short, a mature man is regularly fed. By definition, then, only an immature man must request food. He regresses to a shameful state of infantile dependency that denies his own adult personhood and autonomy.[19]

Pleas for food, if voiced to tshambela, are even insulting. A man should never complain of hunger to these ceremonial partners lest they respond with an excessive meal or, as I once experienced it, a massive sack of sweet potatoes. Any such exclamations or appeals cast into doubt the moral status of the tshambela. This partnership, like the relationship between mother's brothers and sister's children, is reciprocally considerate and compassionate. Each looks after the welfare of the other. Consequently, an uncle or tshambela appears remiss in his role as a selfless male nurturer if his alter is so hungry that his only recourse is to solicit food. Indeed, tshambela should only passively receive gifts, and actively give them; they must never ask. The only appropriate response, according to the logic of manhood, is for the seemingly derelict tshambela to humble his ravenous partner with a hyperbolic gesture of motherhood.

Yet this overcompensatory response of "humiliating generosity" (Lipset 1997) actually shames *both* partners. Similarly, a sister's child who naively asks his mother's brother "even for a single yam" (Bateson 1936, 76) will be served, "with exaggerated anxiety," a meal of enormously irreverent magnitude.[20] For Bateson, the avunculate's behavior combines feminine self-abnegation with male competitiveness. A deficient mother's brother, like a lax tshambela partner, restores his moral personhood by overstating the local value ascribed to motherhood. He corrects lapses in moral manhood with grotesque gestures of mothering. Hints of maternal selflessness aside, the lavish beneficence of mothers' brothers and tshambela is also self-serving. After all, men silently compete in these two relationships for renown and moral status. This antagonism, of course, lies beneath the surface of public sentiment. Nonetheless, it colors the two relationships with moral ambiguity.

Men stage equivalent displays of maternal hyperbole during large-scale competitive exchanges of food. These tournaments, called *wolibunaut,* conclude funerary rites and redress cult house violations. In sheer quantity, they are insignificant when compared to the giant ceremonial exchanges of pigs and valuables that take place throughout the Highlands of New Guinea. By their own standards, however, Eastern Iatmul envision wolibunaut to entail a massive amount of food. Ritual moieties named Mboey Wai and Nganga Wai compete to amass the largest pile of coconuts, tubers, bananas, rice, sugar, coffee, tea, tinned fish, dog, and so forth.[21] Both women and men add to these piles. Yet only men swap them. The group that gives away the more plentiful mound of food thus shames its foe with unsurpassed generosity.[22] This way, again, men vie for moral prominence through competitive enactments of maternal nurture.

Curiously, wolibunaut competitions exclude fish, a food that is expressly connected with motherhood and femininity. Indeed, riverine food is conspicuously absent from almost all forms of male exchange. This practice parallels the banishment of women from the cult house. In both instances, men bar female bodies both real and symbolic from male endeavors that, ironically, define masculinity on the basis of motherhood.

Wolibunaut exchanges, as I suggested a moment ago, avert the vengeance of spirits when men violate the rules of decorum that govern the cult house. Men must never toss betel nut and tobacco inside the building, and all forms of banter and roughhouse are strictly prohibited. The mere verbal threat of wolibunaut is sufficient to quell any potential breach. Men, too, are forbidden from walking past the cult house while hauling objects on their shoulders. This rule, however, in an apparent allusion to the privileged status of motherhood, is relaxed for women who carry children and food. Ironically, while moral motherhood is the sole exception to this masculine ordinance, any violation of the rule is redressed by a dramatization of grotesque mothering, namely, a competitive exchange of food. In effect, the ideal values of motherhood safeguard the norms of masculine behavior and the sanctity of the male cult.

Wolibunaut exchanges are not, as in the legacy of Mauss and Durkheim (e.g., McDowell 1980), institutions that merely maintain social solidarity and moral personhood. Like the famous naven ceremony, the periodic interaction between adversarial groups and the resulting reduction of symmetrical schismogenesis that allegedly occurs is a minor element of these rites. Psychodynamic themes are equally important. Feeding becomes an idiom of warfare (see also Young 1971; Barlow 1995, 97). This culinary aggression is phallic and excremental since men strive to exhibit the tallest and largest pile that they dump before their rivals.

The tshambela relationship and wolibunaut exchanges further corroborate my argument that masculinity in Tambunum is an uneasy truce between contrary, psychodynamic images of grotesque and moral motherhood. I also demonstrated in this chapter that masculine expressions of defilement, incompetence, and hunger reveal a dialectic of accountability and humiliation that reduces men to the contradictory roles of shamed and shamer, passive and active, adult and infant. The very same processes, I will now show in the final section of the book, which lead to the very same contradictions, animate the famous and enigmatic ritual known as *naven*. These ceremonies of celebration and woe, laughter and tears, exemplify the complex relationship between Eastern Iatmul masculinity and motherhood. In naven, even more than in the theatrics of the tshambela relationship, men confront the pathos and folly of their own masculinity.

PART 3

Ritual Masculinity

9

Men and the Maternal
Dialogics of Naven

Throughout the life cycle, first-time cultural acts among the Iatmul are celebrated with a naven performance of dance, song, and gesture. Mothers' brothers attire themselves in filthy grass skirts, prance around their sisters' children,
and frantically wave women's mosquito fans. They parody birth and the proto-
cols of motherhood. At the same time, female kin adorn themselves with male
finery such as cassowary feather headdresses. They affect an exaggerated pout
that caricatures the brooding countenance of men and comedically dramatize
the histrionic mannerisms and vain pretenses of masculine swagger. The ceremony formally concludes when sisters' children later remunerate ritual participants with gifts of cash, baskets, clothing, fish traps, and canoe paddles (fig. 8).

All this is known from Bateson (1936, 1958). But in Tambunum, the rite
permits extraordinary emotions and theatrics that have yet to be fully reported,
much less interpreted. Mother-figures feverishly pelt women but especially
men with mud, thrash them with leaves and sticks, and spit red betel nut juice
into their faces. They lewdly protrude their buttocks, taunt men with erotic
quips, and dance with a masked costume. Actual mothers cascade to the
ground so their children can walk over their prostrate bodies. Frequently, the
rite dissolves into near-pandemonium. But, just as often, naven climaxes by
recomposing a communal circle around a classificatory mother's brother who
performs the nggariik gesture by sliding his buttocks down the leg of his
nephew. Out of pity, men weep.

What is the significance of this peculiar rite? How can we make sense of a
ritual that so delights in perverting the emotions and behaviors of everyday life?
Naven, I will show, is a celebratory degradation. It honors, defies, and defiles
masculinity with contrary images of moral and grotesque motherhood. In the
end, the naven ritual expresses and intensifies, but never resolves, the paradoxes of manhood.

Fig. 8.   With festive grass skirt and shell ornaments, her younger child in tow, a mother totes fish traps to present to her son's patrikin after his naven ceremony

Back to Bateson . . .

In Bateson's framework, as I reviewed in chapter 1, naven is largely a ritual of reversal that curtails schismogenesis by renewing affinal alliances. Additionally, the rite allows men and women to experience vicariously the ethos of the opposite gender. Yet this transvestism is satiric, and thus naven reinforces the appropriateness of everyday emotions. Ever since Bateson, many anthropologists have similarly tied naven to the integration of society and psyche (e.g., Clay 1977, 142–46; Rubel and Rosman 1978; but see Karp 1987). A brief survey of the more extensive of these efforts will frame my own perspective and arguments.

Gewertz (1978), in a complex historical ethnography of the nearby Chambri, argues that naven marks the ambiguous relationship between intermarrying clans (see also Lindenbaum 1987). Chambri wife-takers are indebted to their wife-givers. Yet these groups nonetheless compete as equals to forge client-patron relationships with other clans who seek assistance when raising bridewealth. Naven, asserts Gewertz, mediates the clash between affinal inequality and an egalitarian political ideology. In Tambunum, however, unlike among Chambri, the naven rite does not redress affinal inequality any more than it curtails schismogenesis. Indeed, the rite actually intensifies sociological discord.

The next significant analyses of naven were those of Handelman (1979) and D'Amato (1979). In parallel essays, they suggest that naven is a cybernetic governor. The ritual restores normative interaction between uncles and nephews when a sister's son foolishly boasts before his mother's brother. In so doing, the nephew taints this uniquely tender male relationship with hints of masculine rivalry. Should the uncle respond with his own braggadocio, as he would do to any other man's boasting, he would challenge his nephew's emerging identity and contravene his own role as a nurturing mother-figure. But if the uncle remains passive, he diminishes both his manhood and his authority as a male socializer. The uncle escapes this "double bind" with a cursory naven, or the threat of a naven, as Bateson (1936, 8) noted briefly in the early pages of his book and later stressed in the new Epilogue to the second edition (Bateson 1958, 289–90). In this view, the ritual buffoonery of the rite adheres to the logic of a double negative through symmetrical and complementary modes of interaction: the uncle asserts, and then ridicules, a feminine identity. Here, naven reestablishes the morality of the avunculate relationship without compromising the masculine identity of either uncle or nephew.

The central shortcomings with Handelman (1979) and D'Amato (1979) are their near-exclusive focus on Bateson's 1958 Epilogue. They foreground Bateson's post-Sepik concerns with communication theory, mathematical logic, and cybernetics (see Houseman and Severi 1998, chap. 2; Juillerat 1999, 154) and background almost entirely the ethnography of Iatmul. In addition, this perspective fails to capture the emotions and behaviors of the rite and overlooks the crucial fact that the ritual consists largely of actions initiated by women and directed against men. I am not denying that naven can be used by uncles to reprimand nephews. But the corrective function of the rite is entirely insignificant. Had I myself not mentioned it to Eastern Iatmul men, it is unlikely that it would have even received mention. Needless to say, I never witnessed this threat. Moreover, the logic of this reprimand, as I suggested in chapter 6, is that of dialogism, not cybernetics. As I see it, then, naven is no reproof of immodest juniors by senior men. Rather, the rite is a reprimand of culture herself, especially the ideals of masculinity and motherhood.

Most recently, Houseman and Severi (1994, 1998) analyze naven through the concept of "ritual condensation," or the simultaneous occurrence and inversion of two inimical modes of interaction. This detailed, complex, and far-reaching theoretical project draws on recent ethnographies (e.g., Stanek 1983b; Weiss 1987b), including some of my own material (Silverman 1993). Houseman and Severi's specific analysis of naven contains three components. First, they attribute the source of the rite to the cultural premise that a person's immediate identity is his (or her) father and mother. Therefore, all Iatmul kinship relationships are in some sense condensed to, or expanded from, "the postulate of sexual reproduction" (Houseman and Severi 1998, 222) and "the elementary realm of parenthood" (1998, 263). Second, as a result, naven opens up this biological construct in order to define the identity of the honorees in a broad matrix of patrilineal and matrilateral ties that extend well beyond the narrow bonds of parentage. Third, naven is an opportunity for celebrants to assert kinship ties to the honorees that will henceforth serve as the foundation for future political and affinal alliances. The cultural meanings of naven—and presumably the psychoanalytic ones as well, which Houseman and Severi abstain from considering—are therefore subordinated to a pragmatism of social structure and marriage.

For example, Houseman and Severi (1998, chap. 4) contend that two different classes of mothers' brothers participate in naven on the basis of two equally distinct motivations. On the one hand, the rite includes agnatic mothers' brothers who already enjoy a close relationship with the celebrated sisters' children. They join naven in order to affirm and renew, as per Bateson, an existing social bond. On the other hand, the rite also includes uterine and agnatic uncles who were heretofore peripheral to the kin network of the honored sister's children. They enter the ceremony in the hopes of establishing themselves as significant uncles—yet uncles who nonetheless retain an adequate genealogical distance that permits them later to contract future marriages with the honorees.[1]

There are sound ethnographic reasons, as Juillerat (1999) recognizes in some of my own material (Silverman 1993), for rejecting this thesis. A woman's actual father, brothers, and maternal uncles, as least in Tambunum, are largely prohibited from participating in her marriage negotiations and the subsequent dispersal of bride-price. Instead, as we have seen (chap. 7), affines-to-be tend to interact through their respective sisters' children and other classes of kin. In this way, marriage itself often enmeshes numerous categories of "distant" relatives. In turn, these kin can claim a relevant tie to the spouses and their children. Marriage, in other words, fulfills the very sociological function that Houseman and Severi attribute to naven. Likewise, the peripheral uncles who participate in naven are often classed as part of the mother's own lineage or clan. Therefore, Juillerat (1999, 168–71) argues that the concept of genealogical *distance* that is central to Houseman and Severi's (1998) analysis pertains to psychological rather than sociological issues, specifically, incest. Indeed, Juillerat (1999, 171) succinctly writes that naven is a rite of filiation, not alliance.

Bateson (e.g., 1958, 282) himself was suspicious about psychoanalytic interpretations of naven. Freudian concepts, he wrote, "would have distracted me from the more important problems of interpersonal and intergroup process." Houseman and Severi agree. Like Bateson, they seek to model the essence of ritual in terms of a relational morphology and a logic of communication. This is no trivial task. At the same time, the enduring avoidance of psychoanalysis in the interpretation of naven has reached the limit of its fruition.[2] A psychoanalytic perspective is now required, one that can build on, rather than erase or replicate, the ethnographic and theoretical legacy of Bateson.

. . . and Beyond

I want to return in some detail to Juillerat (1999) who, by applying Winnicott (e.g., 1953, 1967) to dialogue reported by Weiss (1987b) from Palimbei village, proposes that naven dramatizes the indissolvable bond between mother and son. As Weiss's female interlocutor said, naven occurs when someone *returns* to their mother, not when they leave. In Juillerat's (1999, 155–57) formulation, naven celebrates moments when men *glance back* to motherhood after successfully completing important, socializing steps toward adulthood. In effect, naven honors autonomy *and* regression.

Juillerat recalls from Bateson (1936, 6) that one of the central events in a man's life, an achievement that singularly marked his maximal male identity, was his premier homicide. This feat occasioned an elaborate naven rite. Yet, in a myth reported by Stanek (1983a) and translated into French by Juillerat (1999, 158–59), the first naven celebrated the indelible force of maternal attachment rather than the emancipation of the ego from primary, mother-child unity. I summarize and paraphrase this myth:

> In the past, there were two eagle brothers. The relationship between them was akin to that of father and son. The younger brother was "soft," feminine, and inexperienced. He clung to his elder brother, who was a fierce warrior that terrorized and consumed the local human population. The

elder sibling wished to tutor his junior in the ways of masculine bravery and ferocity. This way, too, the elder brother could place an emotional distance between himself and his still-too-dependent younger brother.

Out of compassion, the human mother of the two eagles begged them to stop swooping down on the inhabitants of her village. The two brothers agreed to their mother's request, but on the condition that the local people inter the human bones that were littered below their cannibalistic nest. The two brothers departed for a long voyage, the bones were buried, and their nest destroyed. The other villages of the region still feared the two eagles but tranquillity now reigned in their mother's community.

Eventually, the two eagles journeyed back to their mother and her village. They looked down on the serene setting and built a new nest. By this time, the younger brother, who still lacked a homicide to his credit, was weary of dwelling in the shadow of his senior's dominance; he wanted to exercise his own independent will. "When my elder brother sleeps," he decided, "I will fly away and kill many people. Then my brother will know that I am finally somebody! He will be proud of me!" The younger brother takes flight, and rests on a tree. As the sun rises, he pounces on a man who is gardening and finally achieves his solo homicide. He severs the man's head, yet is unsure how to proceed next, and so ascends to his perch. Despite this hesitation, the younger brother exclaims "Me! Only me! I have killed!"

The elder brother, seeing his junior coated in blood and grasping the head in his talons, is overjoyed: "Ah, my little one has killed! Now you are big! This is it! How many times did I tease you? Now you are complete, and our mother will dance for you!" They wrap up the head, fly back to their mother, and present to her the trophy. "What is this," she asks, "breadfruit?" When she opens the parcel and beholds the head, the mother leaps to her feet and immediately dances a naven for her youngest son.

Juillerat's (1999, 159–60) brilliant analysis of this tale begins with a representation of breast-feeding: like suckling infants, the two eagles dine on the bodies of humans from their mother's village. Weaning, initiated here by the mother herself, occurs when the two siblings, especially the youngest, embark on a liminal period of socialization that takes them away from their mother. The avian brothers then forge an intimate yet hierarchical relationship that allows the elder to teach his junior the skills of masculine adulthood and autonomy. This phase of the myth corresponds to the movement of Iatmul boys from the maternal dwelling to the men's house, under the tutelage of senior initiators. The two eagle brothers, by requesting the burial of their skeletal food scraps, effectively renounce maternal attachment.

When the siblings return to their mother, they behold a scene of pastoral tranquillity. Juillerat interprets this pleasant spectacle as a sign that the sons' desire to reunite with motherhood will result in serenity rather than immorality and distress. Autonomy is no longer gained at the price of maternal disidentification. Next, the younger brother severs his bond with the father-figure, whose contributions to his own personhood are subsequently effaced by maternal joy and attachment. Unlike classical oedipal theory, however, it is the father's own initiative that allows his son to reunite with the mother. She, and *not* the father, is then presented with the decapitated trophy. Of course, headhunting and other exploits that are celebrated by naven actually promote separation-individuation. Ironically, the symbolic origins of the rite enable sons to reidentify with their mothers and thus to regress to primary symbiosis. This ambiguity, Juillerat (1999) perceptively recognizes, is the underlying theme of naven, a theme that my own analysis will corroborate and enlarge.

A psychodynamic perspective is also useful for interpreting the broad transformations of gender that occur during the rite. Bateson (1936, 12) claimed that the "outstanding feature" of naven is its "transvestism." Many naven rites do include moments when men and women assume the attributes and genitals of their alters (e.g., Bateson 1936, 17; Weiss 1987b, 170). But the meaning of these caricatured behaviors has remained opaque due to the absence of psychoanalytic considerations from previous analyses. Thus Houseman and Severi (1998, 217) insist that naven transvestism "forcefully confirms the existence of certain inescapable sex-linked qualities" (see also Weiss 1994a). This claim and the logic behind it are not quite correct.

Ritualized transvestism and the prior assumption of dichotomous gender are ubiquitous notions in Melanesian anthropology (e.g., Forge 1973; Tuzin 1980; Bowden 1983b; McDowell 1984; Schwimmer 1984). Following Strathern (1988, 1991) and Weiner (1995a), though, I have advanced three arguments in this book that undermine these two suppositions and the thesis of naven transvestism. First, Eastern Iatmul gender, especially in myth and ritual, is unable to be understood in terms of discrete, immutable, and intrinsic somatic categories. Instead, persons shift between same-sex and androgynous configurations. Second, many of the key diacritics of local gender are partible and transactional. Third, and most important, I argued that masculinity is defined on the basis of a pervasive maternal and especially uterine schema. But femininity lacks any such parallel. The meaning of naven, then, is unrelated to transvestism and its putative messages about absolute sexual dimorphism, matrimonial alliances, and social structure.[3] Rather, the overwhelming imagery of naven concerns the dialogical and psychoanalytic relationship between masculinity and motherhood.

One further ethnographic point undermines the transvestism argument. As Hauser-Schäublin (1977, 130) observed, Iatmul women chastise male kin who neglect to uphold the facade of masculine bravado in public. What's more, women tend proudly to emulate men's ethos in everyday contexts, say, when initiating sexual liaisons (chap. 4). But men *never* emulate women in public—outside of naven, that is—and they *never* admit to female modes of sexuality.

Hence, the so-called transvestism enacted during naven is far more consequential for men than for women. Why? Because men expose before the entire
community, women included, a psychodynamic yearning that they ordinarily
confess to, or act on, only in private.

In sum, the experiential dimensions of the Eastern Iatmul naven are unrelated to the explanations offered by previous analyses, with the exception of
Juillerat (1999). These dramas do not lay the foundation for future political and
matrimonial alliances, redress affinal inequality, curtail schismogenesis,
reproach boastful nephews, highlight biological sex through gender reversals,
or differentiate the moral roles of genealogically ambiguous kin and clans. The
Eastern Iatmul naven resolves *none* of the paradoxes and contradictions that
beset manhood and society. But if the Eastern Iatmul rite is *not* harnessed to
the preservation of social order, what is its significance?

To begin, I need to outline the three different types of naven that occur in
Tambunum. The most common form of naven, which is usually extemporaneous, consists *exclusively* of female participants, especially iai women from the
father's mother's clan, who thrash, spit on, and degrade the honorees and other
celebrants, principally men. I myself not only witnessed innumerable instances
of this type of naven, but I was twice its recipient: once after spearing my first
fish, and again when I paddled a canoe across the river while standing. Eastern
Iatmul themselves, it is crucial to note, tend to describe naven solely in terms of
the iai women who assault men.

The second type of naven in Tambunum consists of male participants
alone: maternal uncles who shoulder their sisters' sons and then perform the
nggariik gesture. This ceremonial form usually develops during another ritual
and celebrates the inaugural cult activities of young men, for example, blowing
flutes or carrying spirit costumes. These small naven rites, too, tend to occur
spontaneously, usually behind some type of fence, and away from the eyes of
women. The third and final variant of the rite is a large-scale ceremony that
involves both male and female participants, especially mothers' brothers and
iai women. These rites often last for several hours, encompass hundreds of people, and conclude with enormous exchanges of goods and valuables.[4] Like the
smaller all-male rites, these naven ceremonies typically conclude with the
uncle's nggariik gesture, which is a humiliating pantomime, we will see, that
combines birth, defecation, and sexuality.

In summary, the central figures in the prototypical Eastern Iatmul naven
are, first, iai women, and, second, mothers' brothers. Both of these figures, as
we have seen, represent dialogical motherhood. Both, too, evoke contrary
emotions in men. It is also important to indicate that most naven rites in Tambunum are occasioned by male rather than female achievements. All told, any
thorough analysis of the Eastern Iatmul rite must focus on the fourfold symbolism of motherhood, iai marriage, masculinity, and the famous nggariik gesture. With this in mind, we can now turn to the honorific humiliation of men.

Mothers Who Beat, Spit, Joke, and Dance

During an Eastern Iatmul naven, women spit betel nut juice into the faces of male kin who are their current or potential affines. These women also beat men about the head and torso with palm fronds and, occasionally, small hand-held brooms that are used to swat mosquitoes. This playful aggression only takes place during naven. It is often the sole activity that occurs during the small impromptu rites.[5]

The iai women, too, may loudly grate men's cassowary bone spatulas in and out of lime powder gourds (Bateson 1932, 279). Formerly, as I discussed in chapter 8, warriors proudly affixed homicide tassels to these spatulas. Bateson (1936, 15) remarked that one husband "complained sorrowfully that his wife had worn away all the serrations on his lime stick so that it would no longer make a sound." Symbolically, the husband was emasculated by his wife's phallic promenade. Similarly, iai women in Tambunum stick out their tongues during naven in a humorous gesture of aggressive sexuality that is normally directed at men. The same flirtatious provocation is communicated when they extrude their tongues through a circle made with the thumb and forefinger.[6]

These naven actions are accompanied by bawdy banter and laughter, such as I discussed in chapter 7. A iai might shout to her male alters, "Are you pregnant with my child!" or "I will spear your house [or ass] tonight!" She might pun with the word *wiliigandi,* which loosely translates as "to swell up." As the only truly authorized joking relationship in the culture, Eastern Iatmul often contrast this repartee with the strong taboo on any such jesting between the maternal uncle and his nephew. Yet iai women are themselves, in their prismatic identity, conceptualized partly as moral mothers. They represent, at least from this facet, values that are antithetical to brazen sexuality, aggression, and joking. During naven, however, these mother-figures confound the boundary between conjugal sexuality and chaste maternal nurture, a distinction that is crucial for the emotional life of men. A ripe banana, say, which mothers might feed to their children, becomes during naven the object of much joking. Likewise, the iai women's quips, gestures, and playful beatings, like the symbolism of doorways in the vernacular architecture (chap. 4), contest men's veneration of motherhood.

Women almost always initiate these naven actions, which they aim at men who serve as their passive and begrudging victims. Men, who are ordinarily assertive, thus become docile prey. Of course, this social role is one that men are generally loath to assume. Women, too, by publicly instigating sexual aggression during naven, contradict their own everyday roles as moral wives, mothers, sisters, and daughters, to which their male victims often utter "*lan nyiin to!*" or "husband thou [fem.] indeed!" This way, as I suggested in chapter 6, men acknowledge their submissiveness to masculine women—to phallic mothers who feminize their manhood.[7]

The expulsion of betel nut by the iai women during naven also makes men symbolically impotent. For the most part, men activate totemic magic by silently uttering cryptic spells and then noisily egesting betel nut spittle. Iai women during naven mock this magical procedure by spitting on men and delivering loud insults. In effect, they publicly hex the magical arsenal of masculinity. This interpretation gains credence from the fact that, as Dmoiawan said, only a few women traditionally chewed betel, except during naven, when all women did so in order to spit.

At the same time, the iai women's expectorations ridicule mothers' brothers who may spray their nephews out of joy with a cloud of lime powder. The white color of this substance suggests the generative properties of semen and thus signals the uncle's contributions to the growth, strength, and bones of the youth. Yet the uncle is mimicking the nurturing capacities of his sister, the mother, since the white powder also evokes breast milk. This laudatory gesture illustrates the uncle's role as a male mother. During naven, however, iai women spray their alters with a substance whose blood-red color appears to invert the moral qualities associated with semen, breast milk, and the uncle's celebratory shower of white powder.

The iai women also perform a dance that burlesques motherhood with seductive allure. They hop and protrude their buttocks. For men, this sashay conjures the image of a robust, plump maternal body, a mother who features well-rounded hips. It also sets in motion the women's colorful grass skirts. The fringes flirtatiously sway to and fro, enticing men with erotic innuendo. A similar image of carnal motherhood was spectacularly performed during a huge naven that celebrated a man's purchase of an outboard canoe motor. During the rite, a score of iai and other women climbed into his large dugout and sped to the middle of the river (fig. 9). As the vessel circled in the current, the mothers—all standing, not sitting as women normally do in canoes—danced and pranced. Their multicolored skirts waved back and forth across the sides of the canoe; an occasional rear end was thrust into the air. The crowd on shore, women in particular, roared with glee. One iai woman even writhed atop the prow, which was carved as a wainjiimot crocodile spirit—the very same being who is said by men to determine human pregnancy. Under ordinary circumstances, this lewd behavior, on the part of mother-figures no less, is virtually unthinkable. During naven, however, iai women are lent license to burlesque motherhood as well as men's authority over cosmological and human fertility.

Elsewhere in the Iatmul-speaking middle Sepik, iai women during naven celebrate manhood and assail the sanctity of men's canoes by splashing dugouts (Bateson 1936, 15–16; Hauser-Schäublin 1977, 96). Mothers' brothers once honored their nephews' first homicides with a similar display. The uncle stripped off his garments and, along with his naked wife, plunged into the water while embracing the youth (Bateson 1932, 277). Eastern Iatmul no longer soak men and canoes during naven. They do, however, connect these former

Fig. 9.   Mothers frolicking in a man's canoe during a naven rite that honors his purchase of an outboard motor

antics with the iai women who ritually beat men.[8] In each of these ceremonial instances, women and mother-figures contest the warrior identity of men. They also challenge a man's adult status by implying that, like a helpless child, he is unable to keep a canoe upright and remain dry. He is even incapable of bathing himself; he must be forcefully washed by mothers. By assaulting the masculine honor of canoes, too, the iai women equally dishonor their own moral symbolism since dugouts, we saw in chapter 4, represent motherhood.

Houseman and Severi (1998, 268–70) contend that the issue at stake here is the perpetuation of affinal alliances. Moreover, "in the *iai's naven,* in which the consanguineal and affinal relations between the protagonists are one and the same, Ego's becoming a procreator is directly linked to the conditions of his own procreation, and vice-versa." But iai are not merely signs of kinship relations. They are, it is true, a man's potential brides, and women his father calls "mother." Yet the word *iai* connotes the maternal body and thus the ideals and ideas, both moral and otherwise, of motherhood. In the ritual setting of naven, these uterine mothers attack men. They reverse the semiotic progression that is encoded in the myth of sago (chap. 2). Whereas Kwianalagwi transformed grotesque motherhood through the mediation of sexuality into nutritive food, iai women during naven de-nurture motherhood through sexuality and threaten masculine achievement. Nevertheless, iai marriage is like sago: both are vital for men. Accordingly, the naven antics of the iai women dramatize the equivocal relationship between masculinity and motherhood.

Mothers Affinal and Oedipal

We can discern additional meanings to naven when we consider the relationship between marriage and personhood. For men, marriage entails a successful negotiation between descent groups and the fulfillment of bridewealth and brideservice obligations. Marriage also results in the reproduction of children and lineages, the inheritance of house mothers, and the creation of an avunculate relationship. In short, marriage is vital for masculine identity and the sociological integration of the society.

But the thrashings by iai women during the Eastern Iatmul naven appear to attack affinal alliances. From this perspective, the rite intensifies, not dampens, schismogenesis. These assaults also, of course, negate the tenderness that men attribute to motherhood. By the same token, the beatings contravene the reproductive and nurturing functions of the iai woman in marriage. They also communicate a contradictory cognitive or eidological message: the iai women are both "potential affine" and "not potential affine" to the men they beat. Taken together, these playful lashings imperil rather than preserve the role of marriage and moral motherhood in social life and masculine adulthood.[9]

Naven also dramatizes the unresolved oedipal issues that are integral to iai marriage. This matrimonial pattern, as we saw in chapter 7, allows a father to "get his mother back" as his son's bride. It also permits an uncle to redress his shameful inferiority to his nephew by relinquishing a "mother" to the sister's son. Structurally, iai marriage pivots on a woman who represents maternal succor to a senior man yet matrimonial sexuality to his junior. Normally, the movement of women in iai marriage would seem to resolve these oedipal tensions. But during naven, once again, iai women suspend their solidary function and collapse the masculine order of society.

As Juillerat (1999, 168) argues, iai marriage and the iai's participation in naven both adhere to the same psychodynamic process: a return *to* the affirming and affective mother yet, at other times, a return *of* or *from* the negative and phallic mother. The ritual travesties of the iai women are likewise tied to the aggressive component of the Oedipus complex, but deflected through an unusual transformation. In this setting, oedipal animosity is not manifest between father and son as they compete over a female figure. Instead, the aggressor is the object of desire herself, namely, the iai woman, who is both mother and wife. Sometimes she assaults her "son," who is the potential groom's father. These beatings ward off the possibility of incest by overpowering his desire. At the same time, she flails the very man or "son" she might otherwise want to feed and nourish. More commonly, the iai attacks her potential lover. But this man, recall from chapter 6, identifies with his father. Hence, the iai during naven dramatizes what we would expect the father to feel about his son: ambivalent love and hostility.[10]

Menstrual Nurture

In their moral embodiment, Eastern Iatmul mothers nurse and feed children with nutritive substances that promote bodily growth. The idealization of this preoedipal relationship explains a father's emotional and economic investment in securing his son's iai marriage (chap. 7). During naven, however, iai women forcefully expel betel nut juice at men who flee from, rather than long for, these "mothers."

Women cannot simply spit during naven; they must expel chewed betel nut.[11] The ritual symbolism of this substance must therefore be significant. The red color of the fluid evokes menstrual blood and feminine reproductive fluids.[12] This is my extrapolation—but male research assistants did concur. While Iatmul men, as Mead (1949, 180) noted, "take menstruation lightly," the symbolic expulsion of this substance onto men's heads is still an extraordinary act of masculine negation.[13] In substance and odor, menstrual blood cools the fiery magic (*kau*) that ensures male successes in ritual and martial endeavors.[14] Vitalized by kau, for example, men do not balk from a fight but actively pursue it. Yet men retreat from the aggressive iai women during naven. Afterward, they may be teased for their childish flight.

Expelling a fluid onto the exterior of a retreating adult body creates an image that is the antithesis of infancy, when dependent and passive children hungrily suckle fluid into their bodies. Mother's milk is smooth and white. The naven expectorant is red and contains small chunks of chewed betel. Breast milk is an upper bodily substance that is the object of maternal attachment; menstrual blood issues from what Bakhtin called the "lower bodily stratum." While this blood repulses men, it is symbolically applied onto their upper bodies during naven. The expectorant does, to some extent, resemble the premasticated food that mothers feed infants. But this ritual substance, like excessive sexual intercourse, is defiling rather than nourishing. It withers men's bodies and stymies masculine achievement. These inversions recall the doorways of domestic houses (chap. 5), which disrupt the moral physiology of motherhood by uniting mouth and vagina, as well as ingestion and elimination.

The ritual transformation of breast milk into menstrual blood, and the symbolic inversion of infantile dependence, might seem to promote maturity by counteracting men's yearning for the preoedipal mother. At the same time, the iai women's betel expulsions seem to reverse a central goal of male initiation, namely, the discharge of unhealthy maternal blood from the bodies of novices. Similarly, mothers may lightly abrade the skin of ill children with nettled leaves in the hopes of eliminating "bad blood." From this angle, iai "mothers" during naven regress men to infancy and afflict them with ailments in order to diminish the quintessential values of masculinity that the ceremony, like moral motherhood herself, is meant to praise.

Muddying the Waters of Motherhood

The iai women who beat, dance, and spit also smear mud (*kaki*) into the faces and hair of women but especially men (fig. 10). Since the rite minimally requires the participation of matrikin or iai women from the father's mother's clan, Bateson's thesis is at one level substantiated: naven does integrate different patrilines and thereby renew the social order. The rite, too, marks the cultural achievements of specific persons. In effect, naven has a dual function, at once collective and biographical. But the mud smearing, like many tshambela behaviors (chap. 5), symbolically dissolves social categories and conceals individual identities. This filthy anonymity, however, is no variant of Turner's (1969) neo-utopian communitas (cf. Ross 1982). Naven reversals, enacted by mother-figures, fail to regenerate society. Instead, they paint the cultural ideals of motherhood and masculinity with profound doubt.

Weiss (1987b, 169–75) reached a similar conclusion. One of her female interlocutors in Palimbei, Magendaua, told a myth about an old couple who refuse to feed two young men who reside in the same dwelling. The old woman nets many fish but is unwilling to part with any of her catch. For revenge, the two youth at night slip a bamboo reed into the anus of one their aged, "anal" coresidents, whose flatulence awakens the other spouse. They alternate recipients; one night it is the man, the next night it is the woman, and so forth. Eventually, the old woman discovers the reed and informs her husband. That night, as two youth themselves fart while sleeping, the old man seals their anuses with wood. They awaken in pain and plot another round of vengeance. This time, they capture a crocodile and guard the reptile's corpse until it rots. Then they consume a grotesque amount of the rancid meat. The two youths return to the house and, during the night, defecate throughout the dwelling, down the ladder, and all over the plaza. In the morning, the old couple find themselves up to their ankles in shit. The fish that they were storing in their canoe die, and shortly they do likewise. Immediately after telling this tale about antimaternal stinginess and anal incontinence, Magendaua, Weiss's raconteur, pantomimes a naven rite. The image of anal dissolution and destruction, as Weiss recognizes, pertains in part to the annual flooding of the river. Yet it also, she continues, refers to naven since the ritual, as Magendaua herself says, dissolves the sexual identifies of its participants through joking, gender blurring, and licentiousness—and, I would add, at least in Tambunum, the smudging of mud.

The mud smearing during naven, like the betel nut expulsions and palm frond beatings, also evokes the helplessness of early childhood.[15] Sometimes the mud is even mixed with feces (*ndi*). (One woman during a brief, impromptu naven joked that she would defecate on the head of another participant.) These actions reduce men to a presocialized state in which they are

Fig. 10.   A iai woman smears mud down the face and torso of her alter during naven

unable to remain clean and wash off the dirt, or excrement, of infancy. The mud contests rather than confirms the values of achievement and maximal personhood that the rite manifestly celebrates. This symbolism parallels the filth on tshambela who may throw themselves to the ground when their partner stumbles (chap. 8). The muddied annointing during naven also, in the case of men, violates a norm of fatherhood since men are ordinarily loath to touch children's feces. The refractory logic of naven distorts normative manhood by subverting the everyday standard of clean autonomy with idioms of sullied dependence and feminine domesticity. Likewise, the mud smearing transforms maternal guardianship into antimaternal and even hypermasculine aggression.

The audible expulsions of the semisolid betel liquid suggest flatulence. Drawing on my prior suggestion in this chapter that the betel spittle inverts the nourishment associated with childhood nursing, I now propose that the betel nut expulsions also juxtapose the pollution of feces with the healthiness of mother's milk. If one side of this complex imagery debases the reproductive organs as excretory, the other side transforms defiling substances into sources of regeneration. A related metamorphosis, to which I alluded in chapter 7, is noted by men who state approvingly "when your mother [or wife] feeds you, you have a strong belly that is full of shit!" Here, filth is fortifying, not polluting. A similar conversion of maternal nurture into excrement that encourages autonomy is practiced by Arapesh mothers who wean children by smearing mud on their nipples. They tell the child, "with every strongly pantomimed expression of disgust," that the mud is feces (Mead 1935b, 38). But naven mud smearing has the *opposite* effect. It emphasizes dependence rather than autonomy, and it counteracts the processes of growth that are sustained by maternal care. Men, as they themselves say, become children again during naven— what's more, in the patois of tokpisin, they are *bagarap* by the mud and betel nut, all "messed up."[16]

Women during naven can also blot the faces of participants and spectators with dark ashes (*kwip*), white soot (*mbau*), and white clay pigments (*kupma*). During male initiation, the latter two substances are therapeutically daubed on the scars of neophytes by mothers' brothers. Mothers themselves apply these salves to the bodies of ill children. But during naven, once again, women transform their wholesome qualities into antimaternal gestures that repudiate manhood and their own identities as comforters.

Defiling the male body with feces, literally and symbolically, is not only an act of regression. It also violates the acoustic taboo on women's knowledge of male flatulence (*kabubu;* chap. 4). In one myth, two cannibalistic eagles pursue a man through the landscape. He finally seeks refuge inside a hollow log; the birds alight for a rest. When the man hears the eagles pass gas, he is confident that they are sleeping and so he quietly climbs out of the log and strikes. Thus betrayed by their own flatulence, the two eagles are killed in their sleep. In another tale, a wife is murdered by her husband after she inadvertently heard him in the act of defecation. Women, I was told, should have no direct knowledge that adult men possess an anus since this orifice and its emanations are important wainjiimot spirits. These numinals, we have seen, are identified with bamboo flutes whose voices "speak" and "cry out" (*wakundi*) during ritual, thus attesting to men's control over human and cosmic reproduction.[17]

The prohibition on women hearing male flatulence may also be related to a cosmological image of androgenesis. Men in Ambonwari, another Sepik society, deny that they defecate in order to assert a bodily image of the cosmos that is not only male, argues Telban (1996b), but closed and self-sustaining. The idea of somatic impermeability nullifies men's dependence on women for food and sexuality. Since this ideal male body lacks cavities, moreover, Ambonwari men are unable to model reproduction after birth. Telban's thesis does help explain why, for some labors such as carving a large wooden slit-drum that is beaten during male initiation, men in Tambunum must refrain from eating food, chewing betel nut, spitting, excreting, smoking, and so forth. But, in Tambunum, men *do* ritually emulate birth; they also associate their flatulence with cosmogonic wind and life-giving breath (chap. 3). Nevertheless, Telban's analysis suggests that iai women, when they expel betel nut spittle and smear mud during naven, respond to the cosmological body of the male cult. These actions, too, in concert with the fact that mothers obviously do see the anuses of their young sons, imply that women in Tambunum are very much cognizant of the zealously guarded fictions of masculinity.

To be more precise, iai women during the Eastern Iatmul naven publicly defile men's bodies with the same exuvial substances that the male cult secretly invests with procreative significance: feces and flatulence. From this angle, women's ceremonial mud smudging and betel nut expulsions ridicule a central desire of masculinity: the displacement of uterine fertility by anal fecundity. In this framework, the oral sound of the betel expulsions parallels and inverts the anal din of the bullroarers. At the same time, the aggressive handfuls of mud that iai women seek to smear on men and other women during naven taunt and mock male initiation, when senior men wipe "feces" on the bodies of novices in order to re-create the process of birth (Bettelheim 1954; Dundes 1962, 1976b; Herdt 1981, 151; Tuzin 1982, 340–41; see also chap. 4).[18] Needless to say, the iai women also displace their own nurturing powers with the aggressive naven inversions and degradations.

The ritual use of betel expectorant and mud during naven also symbolizes the substitution of filth for food (see also Panoff 1970; Lipset 1990). On Goodenough Island, as originally reported by Young (e.g., 1971), competitive exchanges of rotting yams combine "both oral and anal elements . . . by forcing one's enemies to eat excrement" (Epstein 1984, 45–46). This interpretation is corroborated by local scatological obscenities such as "Eat my shit!" and "I shit in your mouth!" A similar message, I suggest, is enacted by iai women during naven. These women become antimothers who symbolically feed nonfood to their alters by covering the heads of men and women with substances that represent feces and menstrual blood.

The aggressions, bodily iniquities, and seductions performed by iai women during the Eastern Iatmul naven are instead performed in Palimbei village by women who are directly classed as "mothers" (Weiss 1987b, 1987c; Houseman and Severi 1998, chap. 5). These mothers scowl with the lasciviousness of anthropophagous witches; they crawl like animals and lick the convalescing scars on their newly initiated sons (Weiss 1987c, 267). The bewitched mothers in Palimbei also impersonate frightening totemic ancestresses—the same spirits that are carved into the wooden posts that line the cult house ceremonial plaza in Palimbei. The alert visage of these spirits and their wrathful response to trespass recall maternal vigilance (chap. 4). Additionally, the Palimbei mothers during naven portray incestuous ancestresses who birthed culture yet cannibalized men (see chap. 3). Clearly, these theatrics play with the everyday distinctions between motherhood and wild sexuality.

For Houseman and Severi (1998, chap. 5), the simultaneous occurrence of these ordinarily contrary identities—incestuous mother, lover, cannibalistic ogress, nurturer, witch—comments on a dualism inherent in Iatmul parentage and kinship. Normally, the mother is understood to be her son's genetrix. Yet the son is also envisioned as a direct descendant of his mythic maternal ancestors—creatures he impersonates, as we have seen, in rituals other than naven (e.g., during the uncle's totemic chants; chap. 3). The mother, by calling into question her own everyday identity as a mother, dramatizes the important yet antithetical relationship between human procreation and totemic ancestry (Houseman and Severi 1998, 208–10). Similarly, other types of naven rites communicate messages about the links and differences between matrilateral and patrilateral filiation.[19]

I see the ritual chimeras in Palimbei to effect a different communication. They are analogous to the aggressively playful iai women in Tambunum. During naven, both witches and iai women threaten men with dangers that repeatedly surface throughout the culture—from myth and initiation to vernacular architecture and postpartum taboos. These figures, which cannot be reduced to social relationships, personify men's anxieties about depleting, carnal, devouring, and oedipal motherhood. As discussed in chapter 8 and Hauser-Schäublin (1977), Iatmul witches—male and female—assume a feminine form since witchcraft is innately connected to menstruation.[20] These anxieties tend to arise from the paradoxical definition of manhood as a form of identity that is different from yet envious of motherhood. Since men struggle to define themselves in the absence of women, the witches and iai women during naven aid this process by repelling men. But they also confirm the cultural reality of male fear.[21] In sum, the ritualized witches and iai women attest to men's unconscious recognition that the values of manhood are maternal in origin.

These figures, as Juillerat (1999, 168) recognizes, participate in naven as part of a broader enactment of split motherhood. The rite dramatizes the classic, Kleinian division of "good" and "bad" maternal imagos. The former, in Tambunum, is exemplified by the sheer joy exhibited by mothers when they stroke their sons' beards (see below). The latter are the grimacing mothers in Palimbei. Naven imagery, too, splits the phallic mother into sacred-fantastic representations, as in the totemic and cannibalistic Palimbei mothers, and those that are ludic, such as the Eastern Iatmul iai.

At the same time, the naven witches and iai women appear to be one response, or metaphoric voice, that women and mothers contribute to the broader conversation concerning masculinity and motherhood. It is a voice, however, that is decidedly ambiguous, even ambivalent, for men and women alike. In a brute sense, Iatmul women are physically vulnerable to men. Nonetheless, men believe that their own bodies and psyches are somewhat defenseless against the powers and exudations of women. As a result, men protect themselves with elaborate defenses such as pollution beliefs and the pervasive ideology of sexual and aggressive dominance. From this perspective, the Palimbei witch, and to some degree the Tambunum iai, are "projective inversions" (Dundes 1976a) of manhood: during naven, they are menacing, belligerent, and cannibalistic. They enable men to avoid feelings of remorse or shame when they attribute negative qualities to women and mothers.

To review, iai women during naven scorn all that is basic to Eastern Iatmul masculinity and motherhood. In no uncertain terms, they throw back into the faces of men the very same symbols that men otherwise use to sustain their ritual prerogatives and cosmological triumphs. Likewise, they confirm and answer men's anxieties about the female body. At the same time, these women muddy, as it were, their own cleansing qualities. And how do men react to these ceremonial aggressions? As I now show, they run.

The Cost of Male Flight

Men flee naven and hide. They try to escape the aggressive iai women who defy moral motherhood and befoul masculinity. They do not want to recompense these women with wealth. But, having been degraded, men must do so since all persons who receive any sort of naven gesture must repay the perpetrators with valuables, money, and store-bought food. This way, naven resembles the spectacle that follows a display of gross incompetence before tshambela partners (chap. 8). In both settings, a man is defiled and infantilized by the very same kin who otherwise elevate his personhood. In both settings, the "victim" restores normative social relations by paying his alters. In so doing, he resembles a moral mother who feeds others. Yet this gesture of maternal nourishment is selfish since it enables iai and tshambela to renew their efforts at caring for, rather than sullying, the "victim." In the specific case of naven, we could say, iai women dispense shit and shame in return for money.

Dundes (1979) offers a similar analysis of the well-known potlatch exchanges that occur along the Northwest Coast of North America. These gifts of copper and food are cast in terms of alimentary, anal, and birthing metaphors, but especially feces. They aggressively shame recipients and place the male donors in a maternal position of ambivalent superiority.[22] If feces, as Freud (1918) claimed, are truly an infant's early gifts to his parents, then the grotesque mothers of naven, much like potlatch competitors, return this present in exchange for wealth. Among the Tolai of New Britain, according to Epstein (1979; 1992, 194–97), after Freud (1908, 1918), shell money is excremental. While Eastern Iatmul do not explicitly liken wealth to feces, an indirect connection nonetheless exists during naven when the mud-smearing iai women are recompensed with wealth (see also chap. 8, n. 14). While moral mothers wipe away filth, the naven actions of these women, as Dundes (1979) might say, wipe it back on the adult person.

Perhaps, too, the symbolic exchange of wealth for feces that characterizes the Eastern Iatmul naven pertains to men's evident dread in this culture of female engulfment. I refer to the *vagina dentata* ornamentation on domestic houses and men's general anxieties about female sexuality. Shapiro (1989) argues that, in societies characterized by prolonged mother-son interaction and an absent father/husband, mothers inevitably yet unknowingly direct emotional and libidinal energies onto their sons. As a result, adult men fear the female body and its substances. From this perspective, the aggressive iai during naven act as if, having swallowed or reincorporated their alters (see also

Juillerat 1999, 168), they evacuate them orally, anally, and vaginally. Lest this interpretation seem unwarranted, remember that these women actually cover participants and especially men with spittle and symbols of excrement and menstrual blood.[23] Moreover, a man's iai kin are idealized by his father for their maternal qualities. Yet, during naven, this culture-specific archetype of hygienic and healthy mothering virtually explodes into a mess of matter that represents the antithesis of maternal nourishment. In fact, naven participants who have succumbed to these assaults appear to be covered with two bodily substances that issue during birth along with the actual infant: feces and blood. But this is no misogynistic image. Rather, naven enables women to confront men directly with the very bodily emissions that justify men's exclusion of women from ritual and public spaces.

By turning the world upside down and inside out, the carnivalesque imagery of naven combines idioms of death and birth, atrophy and rejuvenation, defecation and copulation, desiccation and nurture. Mud smearing and betel nut expulsions evoke both the polluting and generative capacities of the "lower bodily stratum." The ambiguity of these gestures is enhanced by the expectation that persons who are degraded during naven will pay the perpetrators since, as Bakhtin (1984a, 21) wrote, "To degrade an object does not imply merely hurling it into the void of nonexistence, into absolute destruction, but to hurl it down to the reproductive lower stratum, the zone in which conception and a new birth take place."

The Laughter of Motherhood

During many naven rites in Tambunum, the maternal awan figure that I discussed in chapter 4 exits the men's house and, accompanied by children, dances with the celebrating women and teases its youthful entourage (fig. 11). When children creep behind the awan and attempt to touch it, the jocular spirit suddenly reels around and scatters the youngsters amid cries of delight and, from the youngest ones, near panic.

The hollow rattan body of the awan, as we saw, contrasts with the wooden representations of patrilineal spirits. She seems, therefore, to communicate the message that matrifiliation is merely a fragile facade to personhood rather than an integral core—skin as opposed to bones. On this point, her participation during naven is contradictory since the ritual allegedly demonstrates the importance of matrikin for achieved identity. Since most occurrences of the rite, too, celebrate the feats of masculinity, it seems odd that a female rather than male spirit should join the celebration.[24]

The awan during naven is also a jester of ambivalent emotions. Yet the awan differs from many other ritual clowns and tricksters. She neither violates social rules nor amuses spectators with sexual, scatological, or oral puns (see Apte 1985, chap. 5). She is unlike the Rotuman female clown who reinforces everyday forms of gender through comical inversions (Hereniko 1994, 1995).

Fig. 11.   Women, following behind an awan spirit costume, dance a naven in the half-finished hull of a man's canoe

The awan does not mediate conflict between the individual and society (Markarius 1970), effect catharsis (Charles 1945), translate ethereal concepts into "common experience" (Honigman 1942), or generate and resolve cognitive dissonance (Crumrine 1969). Finally, the masked costume fails to portray and then shatter a vision of utopia in order to validate normative social patterns (Hieb 1972). Rather, the awan engenders the ambivalent laughter of Bakhtin's carnival.[25]

But the laughter of the awan is also tied to motherhood since she, like a iai woman, is classed by men as a type of mother. In this regard, two psychological theories of ritual clowns are helpful. Tarachow (1951) proposed that clowning humor pertains to pregenital anxieties concerning sexual differentiation and maturity. Levine (1961) argued that clowning satisfies and subserves "primary process drives" and represents ambivalent feelings toward parents. Does the awan therefore express aspects of early childhood? I believe it does. Specifically, the naven clown expresses the disjuncture between the nostalgic idealization of motherhood by men and the actual experiences of mothering and childhood (chap. 6). Yet the awan's ritual malevolence toward children is playful and halfhearted, hence, again, ambivalent. When she dashes at youngsters during naven, she quickly halts, never actually catching a child, and resumes dancing along the village path.

The awan also, as Barlow (1992) argues for women's clowning among Murik, publicly ritualizes the eternal tension between desire and morality.[26] The awan's grass skirt, like those worn by iai women, theatrically sways when she dances in a wry mockery of female seduction and virtuous motherhood. Both female figures, awan and iai, call into question moral motherhood as well as masculinity during naven by parodying male aggression. But while the iai women physically degrade and regress men with symbols of filth, the awan, who is impersonated by men, politely mocks only herself and children. Her spoofing, moreover, unlike that of the iai women, is noncathartic. During naven, I submit, the awan figure and the iai women dramatize two complementary visions of grotesque motherhood.

A Chaotic Flirtation with Incest

Naven begins with participants dancing around the celebrated sister's children and often singing clan-specific totemic songs. At this moment, in the view of classic sociology (e.g., Shils 1972), society assembles around a literal center. But as the dancing gains momentum, the ceremony expands outward, omnidirectionally, dissolving the distinction between center and periphery (see also Bateson 1936, 14–17; Weiss 1987b, 172). The focus of the rite on the celebrated sister's children disappears amid the chaos of a disassembling society.

Naven transforms the honored nephew or niece from an active agent into a mute and immobile focal point for the actions of others. The heroes of the rite become passive "signs" (Lévi-Strauss [1949] 1969, 495–96).[27] Likewise, at the end of the ritual, a still-quiescent nephew may await the buttocks of his uncle (chap. 10). As the ceremony unfolds, moreover, the honorers are themselves eligible to receive a perfunctory naven from other revelers solely by virtue of their own participation. Celebrant quickly becomes celebrated.[28] A rite that seems to highlight the achievements of one or a few selves gradually encompasses the entire community, thus collapsing social categories and unsettling any fixed location of morality and authority. Sometimes, during a large naven, a tall pole will be thrust in the ground in order to counteract the centrifugal force of the rite. But this gesture is no more successful than are men's efforts at planting trees and chanting totemic names to stem the tide of riverine erosion.

From this perspective, again, naven undermines its own honorific intent since collective life, rather than celebrating the achievement of personhood, obscures the self and social order. This process and predicament, however, is not unique to naven. In varying degrees, as we have seen, men repeatedly dissent from the assertive ideal of manhood. This is true for tshambela reciprocity and notions of shame, former warfare, and contemporary ideas about social accountability. Even the roles assumed by the spouses in iai marriage are largely those of docile silence. The logic of naven and the expressions to which it gives rise expand far beyond the rite itself and any putative reduction to "atoms" of kinship and social structure. They concern and contest, instead, the basic values, emotions, and desires of the culture.

The chaos of naven, too, blurs what Heritier (1982, 176), after Lévi-Strauss ([1949] 1969), terms "the symbolics of incest," namely, "the solid pillars of the identical and the different." The grotesque feeding and ribald joking of the iai women, as Bakhtin would surely have recognized, efface the distinctions between upper and lower body. When the iai direct these actions at their "sons," as I discussed earlier in this chapter, they distort the morphological and moral boundaries that divide motherhood from carnality. Likewise, a mother's brother enacts an image of incestuous insemination when he sprays his nephew with white lime powder. He also flirts with taboo eroticism should he present his buttocks to the nephew during the nggariik gesture (see chap. 10). In each instance, the ambiguity of social roles during naven bluffs at mother-son incest.[29]

Girard (1987, 126–27) writes that "the disorderly phase of rituals . . . makes a good deal of sense if interpreted as the deliberate reenactment of a mimetic crisis culminating in unanimous victimage." By muddling the distinctions necessary for morality, society, and personhood, and by wooing incest, the naven rite enables participants to experience the artifice of culture. They peer through, and shatter, the thin veneer of law, broadly construed, that seeks to deny and enclose desire.

Stepping over Mothers

During the Eastern Iatmul naven rite, mothers may throw themselves to the ground so their celebrated children may walk over them.[30] Although virtually any woman may fall to the ground, Eastern Iatmul associate this drama particularly with mothers. The symbolism of their supine bodies, too, as we will see momentarily, points to birth. The fallen column of mothers is akin to a bridge (*tagu*), or canoe (chap. 5), that provides for safe passage over water. In this sense, the mothers dramatize maternal care and their own exalted role as the foundational "stools" that support men, the village, and the entire cultural edifice (chap. 5). During naven, mothers often caress the cheeks of their children who are at the "center" of the rite and, if the honorees are male, stroke the beards of their sons. These gestures extol the maturity of children. In the case of men, the mothers specifically pay tribute to their sons' growth into manhood. The facial caressing also praises the nurturing capacities of motherhood.

But the mothers, when they cascade to the ground during naven, besmirch themselves with dirt. As their son steps over them, he feels pity (*miwi*) for his mothers as well as sadness (*magen*) for himself since he actively participates in this desecration. Ironically, it is only upon the defiled bodies of mothers that children during the naven rite can securely walk from one state of personhood to a more elevated social position. The mothers who plummet to the ground resemble maternal uncles during naven who may first shoulder their nephews and then appear briefly to squat in the dirt after performing the nggariik gesture (chap. 10). In both cases, the self-abnegating mother, whether "she" is male or female, is recompensed for this degradation with valuables. These exchanges of filth for money recall the tshambela relationship and, more pertinently, the actions of the iai women. Here, again, naven both upholds and degrades the ideals of motherhood and humiliates the very "children" the rite supposedly honors.

The fallen mothers during naven, however, complement, rather than simply replicate, the lewd conduct of the iai women. Whereas the iai pelt men with symbols of feces and menstrual blood, the prostrate mothers pollute only their own bodies. Whereas the iai drive their ritual prey into hiding, the mothers only embarrass men. This difference aside, both the iai and the mothers defile adult "children," especially men, and their own idealized maternal qualities. The same is true for the female awan spirit whose presence during naven, as I discussed earlier in this chapter, devalues the role of matrikin for personhood and taunts young children. Furthermore, the physical form and mundane behavior of this spirit counteract phallic masculinity (chap. 5). The maternal polyphony composed by these three figures during naven—iai, mother, awan—is linked to three equally powerful images: male flight, ashamed sons, and apprehensive children.

Unlike the other naven actions that humiliate the honorees, men actively participate in the ceremonial procession over their mothers. Here, I suggest, is one rejoinder by men to the carnivalesque portraits of motherhood that so often seem to arrest their desires to return to the preoedipal shelter of their nostalgia. By treading atop their mothers, sons appear to triumph over those maternal and feminine likenesses that in other settings are poised to endanger them. In short, the parade enables men to master their fears.

It also appears to demean women's genitals and their birthing capacities. When sons marched over their mothers, reported Bateson (1936, 10; 1932, 278), other women remarked "that so small a place out of which this big man came." This verbal aside seems to be a straightforward assessment of the relationship between masculinity and the maternal grotesque. Freud, however, would have recognized another, more ambivalent message in this naven drama: the debasement of the object of male love (1910, 1912). The procession also inverts parturition. Instead of women squatting over their sons in childbirth, the sons stride over their mothers. In their role as adult men, the sons appear to birth the women. But in the role of sons, they also appear on the brink of enacting incest.[31]

The naven parade by men atop their dirtied mothers evinces one further inversion. Women, we have seen, must never step over men, food, tools, or weapons lest, as men say, they "pollute" masculinity with vaginal fluids. During naven, however, men do to women precisely what they fear women might do to themselves: diminish their personhood with impolite displays of genitals and splayed legs. As such, naven provides men with a ceremonial response to their *own* projections of grotesque motherhood as well as to the iai women who smear them with mud and feces.

Why, then, do men during naven not mock the iai women themselves? Why do they turn their symbolic ire against their genitrixes rather than women whose maternal qualities are more metaphoric? The answer, I suggest, is that the iai women during the rite assume a self-imposed role whose antimaternal and carnivalesque imagery reaches the limits of sacrilege allowed in the culture. What, in short, could men possibly do to the iai during naven that they have not already done to themselves? Any greater desecration of the iai would only further disgrace men! They have only one recourse: to threaten parturient motherhood herself. In other words, the iai women debase masculinity during naven with symbols of male parturition that are normally concealed from women. In turn, men return this profane gift by stepping over mothers, thus enacting a burlesque and public rendition of the single most important female prerogative that is never seen by men: birth. At the same time, men pollute women with masculine or anal procreative substances—substances that, in this context, symbolically invert the vaginal fluids that contaminate men.[32]

Formerly, the supine mothers and other female kin were unclad (Bateson 1936, 20).[33] Out of shame, the parading male youth averted his eyes. But his sister, who often accompanied him and continues to do so today, displayed no such modesty. She attacked the women's genitals while exclaiming "A vulva!" Her horizontal alter replied, "No! A penis!" During this repartee, the sister became her brother's ritual double and assumed a hypermasculine role that affirmed men's ideological and linguistic prerogative in sexual intercourse. She forcibly ensured that the prostrate women remained in a doubly feminine position, both supine and passive. But the mother-figures responded with an equally vehement, if solely verbal, exclamation of phallic denial. This dialogue both transacted and mocked bodily tokens of gender.

But it did far more. It was only on the basis of the sister's identification with her brother, the hero, that she could tread atop the naked women and assail their genitals. Her assault was at once his own. Could it have represented men's unconscious feelings toward female sexuality and motherhood? Bateson (1936, 216) seemed to think so: the sister's attack expressed "with exaggerated dramatisation what we (or she) may suppose to be the repressed desires of the hero." I agree. And for this reason, as throughout the naven rite, the "hero" is repeatedly denied his heroism. The women who begat him and nourished his body also forsake their own dignity. The "hero" of naven not only sacrifices his agency in order to participate in his own honorific ceremony. He is further obligated to communicate and receive ambiguous messages that resolve nothing and leave participants in a state of profound ambivalence about themselves.

"Going on View"

The word *naven*, according to Milan Stanek and Florence Weiss, means "going on view" (Houseman and Severi 1998, 40). How true! Through contrary assertions and retorts, naven allows Iatmul to glimpse the unresolvable paradoxes of masculinity and motherhood in their humanity. While Bateson himself never analyzed the rite in quite this way, he did report on a brief ritual episode that summarizes my argument.

The occasion for this particular naven was a man's first kill (Bateson 1932, 279). The wife of the warrior's elder brother, having stepped across the prostrate mother-figures, climbed to the doorway of a dwelling and tempted the killer with a "comic song" to spear a fish trap that she had placed at the top of the ladder. The hero complied. With this thrust of sexual aggression, he repudiated a feminine castrative taunt (see also Juillerat 1999, 165) and restored his heroic masculinity. By impaling the fish trap, however, the killer also violated the sanctity of moral motherhood by driving a spear into the mouth of a domestic house. At the same time, of course, the killer triumphed over the fearful imagery of grotesque motherhood that besets Iatmul masculinity.

"Freudians," Bateson (1932, 279) wrote, "may be tempted to see in the trap a symbol of the vagina" of the elder brother's wife, with whom, through his spear, the killer copulated. While I agree with Bateson that this interpretation is too narrow, I nonetheless see it as an impoverished example of psychoanalytic interpretation. It does not deprecate the idea of a Freudian analysis of naven. Indeed, Juillerat (1999, 166), drawing on the myth of the two eagles discussed earlier in this chapter, suggests convincingly that, since the elder/younger brother relationship often doubles for the father-son bond, the naven gesture of the youth spearing the fish trap was none other than one of incest. Further support for this interpretation can be seen in the very placement of the trap in the ambiguous maw of the maternal house, which could hardly have been accidental.

Did this architectural mother, and the woman standing before her, seek to nourish or to threaten the hero's manhood? Did the killer pierce the fish trap, or was his spear encompassed within it? The sexual, phallic-uterine imagery is manifest: spears are a euphemism for the penis, and the vernacular word for fish trap, *namwoi*, is a common woman's name. In this setting, however, framed by the doorway of the house, intercourse yielded incest. But as Juillerat (1999, 166) also notes, the symbolic murder of the phallic mother here sustains the incest taboo, and thus allows the youth to build, rather than merely to destroy, society. Of course, at the end of naven, the youth may very well sob, thus suggesting that some great moral transgression has indeed occurred. And perhaps it did, as the murder of the phallic mother can also be seen, after Juillerat (1999, 167), to be the murder of a man: the father.

If, then, as Bateson intimated, naven is a drama about Iatmul heroism, then it is surely a tale of *tragic* heroism. And no part of naven, I will now show in the final chapter, is as tragic as its climax, a moment when, above all else, it is masculine pathos that is ultimately "put on view."

10

Conclusion: Naven and the Pathos of Masculinity

"Masculinity," writes Tuzin (1997, 181), "is a thing of ideology and ontology . . . the symbolic resource members of a culture use to contemplate, understand, idealize, demonize, stereotype, place expectations upon, and otherwise identify men." The ideology and ontology of Eastern Iatmul masculinity are, as I have argued, established through an unresolvable dialogue with motherhood. Indeed, manhood in this culture often appears to be nothing other than a complex rejoinder to the playful mother who taunted her toddler son with the jest that began this book: "bad sperm, little sperm!"

Images of motherhood both virtuous and carnivalesque appear, as we have seen, throughout the entire spectrum of men's experience—their achievements and disgraces, dreams and fears, ritual prerogatives and mythological lessons. In sexuality, architecture, shame, initiation, myth, marriage, and, of course, the naven ceremony, men define themselves in terms of moral and grotesque visions of mothering. I now conclude my account of Eastern Iatmul masculinity by focusing on the nggariik gesture that culminates many naven rites and exemplifies the irreducible cultural conversation between male self-worth and motherhood.

Tragic Emotions

The emotional climax of nggariik begins when the ceremonial singing of naven halts and the dancing women, having dispersed outward, recompose the ritual circle. Men, too, join this perimeter, which centers on a classificatory mother's brother and his nephew. The men quietly stomp their feet and mutter a slow chant: tsh, tsh, tsh, tsh. The uncle nimbly dances around his nephew, who is standing in silent embarrassment, shuffles backward, and quickly performs nggariik by sliding his buttocks down the nephew's leg, from thigh to ankle, before rapidly leaping to his feet (fig. 12).

159

Fig. 12.   The performance of nggariik amid the shadows of a male cult enclosure

Nggariik is an unparalleled moment in men's emotional lives.[1] The overall tone of naven is one of happiness (*wobun tiiga*). Many of its ritual behaviors
are humorous—the bawdy repartee by the iai women, for example, and the
dancing awan costume. Some of the avunculate's antics, too, are ludic. But
nggariik evokes a profoundly different emotional ambience. This gesture, con-
tra Handelman (1979), is no form of ritual comedy. It fails to provoke the
laughter of carnival. Instead, when men behold nggariik, they feel an acute
sense of pity (*miwi*) for the mother's brother and his sister's son. For his own
part, as the performer of nggariik, the uncle himself, some men submit, may be
shamed by his participation in this public exhibition. And the sister's son, dur-

ing the full course of a naven that culminates with nggariik, experiences an emotional slide from sheer elation to ineffable despair.

Indeed, nggariik often reduces the nephew and uncle to tears. At no other time do men so regularly sob. But the tears of nggariik are those of humiliation rather than sweet joy. Instead of celebrating manhood, nggariik evokes the inarticulate woe that Frye (1957, 38–39) ascribed to "low mimetic mode" in fiction. This narrative style "presents its hero as isolated by a weakness which appeals to our sympathy because it is on our own level of experience." Nggariik is a moment of pathos that presents its mute heroes, the mother's brother and sister's son, as deeply ashamed of their masculinity. So tragic is nggariik that it is permitted only of classificatory maternal uncles. If a real mother's brother were to perform nggariik, men say, the emotional impact would be too over-whelming for the sister's son. As far as I know, this has never happened. Even mentioning the possibility is met with dismay. In this regard, the moral fence that excludes real uncles and nephews from joining together in nggariik also prevents them from joking. The significance of nggariik, then, as Juillerat (1999, 168–71) understands, is *not* that it is performed by a classificatory relative as per Houseman and Severi (1998, 207) but, rather, that it is emotionally unthinkable for a real mother's brother to do it.

The flustered facial expressions of men during nggariik clearly reveal an inner turmoil. Still, obligation and sentiment, perhaps even guilt, compel men to repeat this humiliation. Feelings of shame and remorse surely explain why the nephew, who must remunerate all kin for their naven actions (chap. 9), reserves his finest gifts for the mother's brother who performed nggariik. In all respects, the emotions associated with nggariik seem thoroughly alien to the honorific intent of naven. Instead of catharsis and elation, the ceremony con-cludes with tearful humiliation and pity. Why? What does nggariik so tragically reveal about masculinity?

The Painful Ecstasy of Birth

An uncle in Tambunum is prohibited from performing nggariik on his nieces. He can only do so down the legs of his sisters' sons.[2] From this perspective, the Eastern Iatmul nggariik would seem to arise from the gendered logic of inter-action between men. Iatmul mothers, we have seen, are celebrated for their ability to engage in selfless, subordinate, and nurturing relationships. Iatmul men, however, are normally unable to applaud the achievements of others—they can only boast themselves. But an uncle who reacts to his nephew's suc-cesses with his own bluster would violate the manifestly tender ethos of their relationship. A mother's brother who wishes to celebrate his sister's son must therefore adopt a *maternal* mode of interaction. For this reason, nggariik is coded as female since it transforms the reaction to a nephew's success from potential competition into praise.

But while nggariik does reveal the limitations of normative male comportment, this explanation alone will not account for the power and form of the gesture. After all, women during naven also transcend the restrictions of their own gendered norms. Specifically, women exaggerate the demeanor of men and are thus permitted a raucous celebration in public. Yet no female performance during naven effects quite the same emotional tenor as the uncle's nggariik. Hence, the significance of nggariik must expand beyond the everyday inability of men to rejoice at others. And indeed it does, as evidenced by the fact that, while men abstain from burlesquing women's naven actions during the rite, women *do*, quite merrily, feign nggariik on other women during naven.[3] This asymmetry is important. Naven allows both men and women to spoof their gendered alters. But whereas women find the naven behaviors of men to be worthy in their own right of ritual mockery, men are not extended the same satirical courtesy. Men's response to the conduct of women during naven is not to ridicule or parrot these skits but rather to flee them and, in the case of the honored nephew, to step over his mothers. The reaction of women may be quite different since they are entitled to belittle whatever message men seek so solemnly, and even dishonorably, to communicate through nggariik. What, then, is this message?

Before I can answer this question, it is important to add one final point. Not only may women caricature nggariik, but their very presence during a naven significantly alters men's emotional experience of the gesture as it is performed by the uncle.[4] Men react to nggariik with the greatest intensity of emotion, they say, and with heightened compassion for the avunculate and his nephew, when it occurs before women. Now we are in a position to begin untangling the significance of nggariik.

Most apparently, nggariik signifies birth, in particular, anal parturition. The uncle not only admires his sister for having birthed the honoree (Stanek 1983b, 167), but he also seeks during the ritual to mirror her ability to do so. This is not, of course, the sole instance when men transform their envy of the maternal body into ritual mimesis. But it is the only time they so directly pantomime childbirth before women. While performing the gesture, I was told, the uncle may even say to his nephew *wuna mogwimbe kwuka nian-miin*, or "I give anal birth to you, my son." Sometimes, before nggariik, a mother's brother may parade with his nephew on his shoulders, thus mirroring mothers as they carry their children. This promenade, like that of the sons who tread over their mothers (chap. 9), also inverts parturition. In this instance, however, men again seek to emulate, rather than to devalue or ridicule, motherhood and birth. While performing nggariik, the uncle actually resembles a woman who squats during delivery.[5]

In no way is nggariik a mockery of female parturition, women's identity, or motherhood. But while the mother's brother is attempting through nggariik to birth his sister's son, the gesture itself, especially its enactment in public before women (see Bettelheim 1954), also confesses to the uncle's inability to do so. Women convey no such message during the rite. They surely call into question, as we saw in chapter 9, the moral value of motherhood. But women during naven do not, as nggariik does to manhood, "put on view" their femininity as the tragedy of an impossible yearning. This unsettling, somewhat melancholy role is reserved exclusively for men. Nggariik, then, both proclaims and, more profoundly, subverts the central desire of Iatmul masculinity: the reproductive prerogative of motherhood.

The mother's brother, according to Bateson, who births his nephew during the rite, was appareled like an old hag. In Tambunum, "he" may don a tattered skirt. This way, the avunculate appears both to envy and scorn youthful, fertile femininity, and even to impersonate a ludic version of Kwianalagwi, the ancestral embodiment of sago (chap. 2). Recall that Kwianalagwi metamorphosed from an aging and macabre woman into a nutritive symbol of motherhood. By contrast, the maternal uncle during naven transforms the nurturance associated with matrikin into an elderly and seemingly postmenopausal figure of motherhood. In a similar fashion, women burlesque the everyday norms of men during naven. Of course, the mother's brother, costumed as a crone, nonetheless remains parturient since nggariik is, first and foremost, a dramatization of birth. The uncle's sarcastic feminine garb is unable to mask the seriousness and the magnitude of the message that he communicates through the gesture: men's unconscious desire for female fertility.

Nggariik thus appears to be simply one further expression in a rich repertoire of male procreative assertions. As we have seen, this treasury of sacred and often esoteric symbols includes bullroarers, bamboo flutes, cosmogonic wind and mud, flatulence, and totemic names. A similar message is conveyed when the avunculate drops a stone from his stomach after his nephew emerges from the seclusion of male initiation (see also Bateson 1931; 1936, 81 n. 1). In this setting, men report, there is little confusion: the mother's brother is birthing his nephew as an adult man.[6] The same interpretation holds true for nggariik. Yet nggariik is the *only* ritual affirmation of parturient masculinity that occurs before women *and* results in men's tears and shame. Of all the ritual boasts that designate the privileges of manhood, nggariik alone is recognized by men themselves to be expressly fictitious, deficient, and perhaps downright disastrous.

If nggariik instances a humiliating fantasy of parturition for men, then the gesture also, according to Muensterberger (1962, 179), expresses men's "identification with the body image belonging to the omnipotent (phallic) mother." This mother, as we have seen, commonly menaces men in the guise of architectural *vagina dentata*, expectorating iai women, and an overall fear that the female body can diminish masculine potency.[7] Yet nggariik, as Muensterberger appreciated, is not in this respect solely expressive of male dread. Rather, the gesture enables men to identify with the imagined source of their anxieties since nggariik and naven, like male initiation (chap. 3), reveal castration anxieties that are directed at mothers, not fathers.

Muensterberger's suggestion points to another meaning of nggariik. Both figures of parental androgyny revealed by the gesture, birthing man and phallic mother, are enacted by men. Nggariik does *not* empower women with masculine potency. It does *not* enable women to express their own desires or to overcome their own anxieties. The psychodynamic androgyny of nggariik, I am suggesting, still attests to men's recognition that the primary "stools" of their culture are women and mothers. Nggariik is a fiction of birth that, when dramatized before women, reveals in a moment of singular intensity the fragile futility in this culture of defining masculinity as a response to motherhood. Through nggariik, men proclaim their exclusive entitlements and thus validate themselves as men. Yet nggariik is an ambivalent celebration by men of their own masculinity. It threatens to shatter the entire "ideology and ontology" of manhood. For this reason, men sob.

The same equivocal emotions were "put on view" by a mother's brother during a naven performance in Palimbei (Stanek 1983b, 178–86; Houseman and Severi 1998, 50–61). An uncle, assuming the maternal role of his sister, wielded a multipronged fishing spear and histrionically searched for his celebrated nephew. The uncle exclaimed to the youth's paternal aunt, in her ritual persona as the father, "I am the mother! I brought him into the world! I suffered a thousand pains so your clan could gain a beautiful and healthy child! I gave the blood which became his flesh!" She, as the "father," promptly replied: "Yes, yes! But first I had to impregnate you! I took the trouble to give you, again and again, my sperm which became his bones!" The uncle then threw himself to the ground, seized his nephew's feet, and announced that he had finally located the "fish" that he was seeking—a fish so large that it threatened to rend his net! Finally, the maternal uncle began to weep—at first with theatrical flair but, shortly thereafter, with genuine emotional feeling. At this point, the comedic ethos of this particular naven was startlingly recast as pathos. Participants and audience alike gaped in silent astonishment at the sobbing mother's brother. When his tears dried, the maternal uncle regained his somber composure, loosened his grass skirt, and stood naked before the audience.

According to Stanek (1983b, 186), the weeping uncle dramatized the "painful ecstasy" of birth. And indeed he did. This naven, like nggariik in Tambunum and male cult initiation, portrayed a central theme of masculinity, namely, the enactment of, and bittersweet triumph over, the pain of childbirth. Yet the uncle in Palimbei did not simply assert masculine procreative and nurturing capacities—he did so through a fishing idiom of phallic aggression. A similar message is communicated by nggariik, albeit in terms of anal birth rather than the provisioning of food. Both idioms, however, are maternal. Finally, the Palimbei uncle's boastful celebration was linked to an act of defiling self-abnegation that resembles in Tambunum filthy children, tshambela behavior, the mothers who plummet to the ground during naven so their "children" can walk over them, and nggariik. Like these displays, too, the uncle's theatrics evoked conflicting emotions. In sum, it was not the "painful ecstasy" of birth alone that moved the Palimbei uncle to tears. He also sobbed at the recognition that male claims to procreation and maternal powers are, when dramatized in public before an audience of women, a confession of failure. In the end, "she" was a man who could no longer sustain the fictions of masculinity. The uncle, having thus betrayed manhood, removed his garments and wept.

The uncle's tears in Palimbei, like those that flow in the aftermath of the Eastern Iatmul nggariik, were the tears of manhood more generally. They recall Migaimeli, the culture hero I discussed in chapter 5 who was shamefully caught in the act of copulating with a wooden effigy that, despite his best efforts, remained mute, motionless, and barren. Male weeping during naven resembles the sobbing snake-child as he was killed for incestuously denouncing maternal nurture by refusing to vacate the shelter of his mother's womb (chap. 5). These tears, too, symbolize the recognition by Eastern Iatmul men that the wooden emblems of their masculinity ultimately rest on a stool hewn from maternal nurture, and are enclosed by the ability of women to birth children. Finally, the tears of naven express the sentiments of men who must watch the Sepik River forever erode their trees, houses, and villages. The mother's brother in Palimbei, like men who behold nggariik in Tambunum, sobbed during naven because he powerfully expressed the tragedies of manhood.

Scatological Nurture

It must not be supposed that the symbolism and emotions of nggariik pertain only to moral motherhood. There is much about this gesture that would strike Bakhtin as decidedly grotesque. Bateson translated nggariik as "to groove" or "grooving," such as one might "groove" a log while chiseling a new canoe. Eastern Iatmul did not refute Bateson's translation. Yet they tend to use the term exclusively in connection with cleansing the buttocks along a sapling after defecation—and, of course, naven. The performance of nggariik during ritual, however, is a scatological insult rather than a gesture of moral and physical hygiene. The mother's brother does not cleanse "dirt" off his sister's son. Instead, he besmirches his nephew by symbolically wiping excrement down the youth's leg. Insofar as nggariik substitutes anal for vaginal parturition, the gesture appears to birth *and* contaminate the nephew. This type of excrement does not age a man's body on analogy with the blood of menstruation and childbirth. But it does, as we have seen in other contexts, regress the nephew to the status of an incontinent and incompetent infant. This regression is doubly demoralizing since it occurs at the very moment when the uncle is supposedly celebrating his nephew's achievements.

Normally, maternal uncles affix salutary jewelry on the necks, wrists, and ankles of their nieces and nephews (chap. 6). They also feed them "strong" foods such as cooked sago and meat that promote a youth's health, vitality, and growth. In fact, men often say that these avuncular meals exceed the nutritive value of dishes cooked by the mother herself since she tends to serve only fish with sago, which, when compared to "strong" meat, is classed as a "weak" food. During naven, however, the uncle fails to provision his nephew with healthy talismans and nourishment. Quite the opposite: he offers the lad his buttocks. By reversing mouth and anus, food and filth, purity and pollution, the uncle becomes a grotesque rather than moral mother. As an abject repast, to invoke Kristeva (1982), nggariik resembles the many other somatic and social inversions occasioned by naven (chap. 9), especially the mud smearing and betel nut expulsions performed by iai women.[8] In this regard, the meaning of nggariik also refers to an entirely different context (chap. 8): competitive exchanges whereby men heap "phallic turds" and then feed them to their rivals.[9]

The nggariik gesture, too, through a vocabulary of dominance and submission, dramatizes the subtle and unstated competition that permeates the avunculate relationship (chap. 6; see also D'Amato 1979; Handelman 1979; Houseman and Severi 1998, 42–44). Recall from the previous section the uncle's naven in Palimbei: so effective was his nurturance that his nephew the "fish" almost burst the limits of the uncle's socializing "net." This image of uterine rupture signals the unstated competitiveness of the avunculate relationship that underlies its overt feelings of warmth. After all, the uncle in Palimbei did not merely seek to ensnare his nephew: he aimed to spear him. Similarly, nggariik pantomimes birth through images of dirt, defilement, and dominance.

I must now clarify my earlier claim that nggariik is a maternal mode of interaction that enables the uncle to celebrate his nephew *without* launching a sequence of rivalrous schismogenesis that is a hallmark of everyday masculine conduct. The uncle's message to his nephew, communicated through nggariik, is one of ambivalence. The uncle, as we just saw, births his nephew yet also smears him with feces. At the same time, the uncle lowers himself during nggariik until he is virtually squatting in the dirt and resting upon the feet of his nephew. Ordinarily, only women and children sit on the ground; men are seated on wooden stools. The nephew, despite his passivity, appears to gain in stature at the expense of his uncle, who becomes smaller, submissive, feminine, dirty, and infantile at the feet of his towering sister's son. Yet the nephew's elevated status is more than offset by feelings of pity that, evoked by the uncle's ritual deprecation, may cause him to sob. Neither man, uncle or nephew, emerges from naven euphoric.

There is one further symbolic dimension to the uncle's brief pose in the dirt. Nggariik is an attempt by men to recant their own refutation that women alone are the true stools of the culture. During naven, men birth in public the bodies and achievements of other adult men. Women, by contrast, deliver infants, and then only in private. Through nggariik, we might say, the maternal uncle seeks to enthrone masculinity by usurping, replacing, or toppling the maternal supports of human existence. Do not mothers themselves fall to the ground during naven? But that is where women seemingly belong in this culture, at least according to normative behavior, since women sit in the dirt and not upon wooden stools. A mother who drops to the ground is not, therefore, morally defiled in the same way and to the same extent as an uncle who performs nggariik—indeed, the uncle's enthronement lasts but an instant. Ironically, it is a filthy one at that. When mothers arise after their children step over them, which is a humiliation to be sure, they nonetheless can resume their jubilation. This action, too, is a part of the unfolding of naven; it does not effectively halt the rite. When the uncle stands up from nggariik, he cries and then often walks home. His defilement is far more profound and absolute than that of the mother. For this reason, the nephew must remunerate an uncle who has performed nggariik with greater wealth than any mother who dropped to the dirt.

Nggariik is a male sacrifice of masculinity. In most sacrifices, argues Jay (1992), men purge all things feminine from collective representations of society. Nggariik, while it entails no bodily death, is still an all-male gesture of solemn consequence that seeks to expunge, at this moment, femininity from the values of manhood and social reproduction. But by substituting masculine anal birth for feminine vaginal delivery, and then by *denying* the efficacy of this substitution through the very same gesture, men ultimately sacrifice their own sense of cultural worth. Not only does nggariik debase the cultural regime of male procreation, but it also assents to men's dependence on the very maternal body that is banned from any serious rendition of the gesture.[10] In sum, the grotesque logic of nggariik degrades manhood through excremental regeneration. While this dialogical trope might seem, in the end, to celebrate masculinity, it is still the case that nggariik reduces the uncle and his nephew to tears. When women and mothers depart from the rite, they always seem elated, or vindicated. Men, however, often seem rather demoralized.

The Shame of Women's Laughter

When women in Tambunum discuss the naven rite, at least with me, they often laugh about the uncle's nggariik. Men broach the subject quite differently. They speak about nggariik with hushed voices that convey a sense of gravity and revelation. So profoundly do men associate the gesture with the fragile essence of their masculinity that the mother's brother, I was informed, would *never* actually touch his nephew's legs while he performs nggariik if women were present at the rite. Otherwise, women might inadvertently glimpse the "true" nggariik. This is not the first time I have spoken about the cautions and concealments of men with regard to women. We have seen that men display similar concerns about their feces, flatulence, anus, and flutes, all of which they camouflage from the inquisitive and, in the case of the flutes, reacquisitive gaze of femininity. Nonetheless, even a cursory exhibition of nggariik discloses enough about manhood that, when it takes place before women, men may sob.

Later, women may laugh. While the avunculate's nggariik leads men to sorrowful self-understanding, women respond during and after the rite with derisive caricature and glee. In fact, iai women may even tease men about nggariik. "Go defecate and nggariik on this tree!" they may shout during naven and everyday joking, or "I will shit and nggariik on you!" Men, needless to say, engage in no such banter. Not only are they hesitant about performing nggariik before women, but men are also shamed when the iai women joke about it. Ironically, nggariik becomes a complete emotional and semiotic experience for men *only* when the gesture is performed before a female audience.

The complex web of gender, secrecy, and travesty that surrounds nggariik was shockingly confirmed for me during a conversation about the naven rite with a small gathering of women. No other men were present. When I mentioned the avunculate's nggariik, the women giggled. Some even refuted it. The mother's brother, they explained, *does* carry his sister's son on his shoulders during naven. He *does* feed his nephew sago and chicken. In return, the nephew *does* present his mother's brother with money and baskets. But the uncle, they said with absolute conviction, most certainly *does not* rub his buttocks down the nephew's leg! Indeed, these women associated nggariik exclusively with the ritual frolics of the iai women.

Equally astounding was the extent to which my female conversationalists seemed entirely uninterested in men's nggariik! They were not reticent about discussing the gesture as they often appeared to be when I queried them about ritual sounds, that is, flutes. They did not refer my questions about nggariik to elder men as in the matters of myth and esoterica. Rather, men's performance of nggariik was simply marginal to their concerns. The incomparable emotional power of nggariik for men bears absolutely no relation to women's experience of naven. What is so important to men, it turns out, is irrelevant for women.[11]

Then, much to my surprise, one woman leapt to her feet and hilariously pantomimed nggariik on another woman's legs. She also wiggled her buttocks and contorted her face in the melodramatic pout that women often flaunt when they lampoon the austere ritual and political demeanor of men. Unlike a mother's brother who feels self-pity and shame while performing nggariik, she was in the throes of gaiety! I agree with Tuzin (1995) that men in many Sepik societies are bereft of the semantic and conceptual vocabulary that would allow them to articulate the significance of the male cult in such a way that women would not simply laugh. But here, in regard to naven, women *did* laugh! This ribald display of a female nggariik, coupled to the utter lack of interest by women in the gesture as performed by men, strikingly differs from men's sober reflections on nggariik. A greater antithesis between Eastern Iatmul women and men I can hardly recall. When enacted by men, nggariik is a tragic rendition of masculinity that is scripted in terms of motherhood. When performed by women, nggariik is a mockery of manhood. Yet both dramatic modalities, tragedy and comedy, result in the same denouement: the humiliation of men.

Erotic Taboo

Nggariik is similar to the flutes, bullroarers, and other appurtenances of the male cult in one further respect. Ritual demands that men breach, however circumspectly, the veil of secrecy that conceals these objects and musical instruments from women. The same combination of subterfuge and divulgence frames the staging of nggariik. It is the one emotionally charged moment when men symbolically admit to women that they possess an anus, feces, and flatulence. It is the one moment when men so obviously enact before women their parturient yearnings. And it is the one moment when men, again before women, tantalize with taboo homoerotic desire. This message, however, is equally directed at men themselves.

The mother's brother, as noted above, is forbidden in Tambunum from performing nggariik on his nieces. This masculine fiction of birth can only be portrayed when the "newborn" is male. Why? Because men alone, as per Tuzin (1995), fully appreciate the seriousness of the drama. Likewise, a man who presents his buttocks to a woman flirts with pure folly since she can *never,* in the idioms of this culture, actively copulate with him. Yet a man who performs the same "sexual salute" (Bateson 1936, 13) on another man does flirt with carnal desire that *can* potentially lead to consummation. Yet the ideology and morality of manhood are unable to concede or yield to this yearning.

In one naven viewed by Bateson (1936, 20), a mother's brother inserted an orange-colored Malay apple into his anus. The uncle prominently displayed this floral fantasy as he climbed a house-ladder to feign intercourse with his wife, who was attired in male garb. As we have seen, any such public display by men is shaming rather than laudatory. Hence, a nephew who jokes with his maternal uncle may be humiliated into obedience when the uncle is trussed naked like a pig to the nephew's house-ladder. What's more, a bright leaf (*moay*) may protrude from the uncle's buttocks. In both of these contexts, moral discipline and naven, men associate the red color of the fruit or leaf, when it is inserted into the uncle's buttocks, with the inside of the vagina. In both settings, as one man remarked, the red hue conveys the message "My ass is red as if I just gave birth to you."

Eastern Iatmul men also associate these floral insertions with the anal clitoris. As I discussed in chapter 8, this anatomical fantasy expresses several desires of men that are normally taboo, repressed, and unspoken, including same-gender sexual relations and birth. These yearnings are expressed, moreover, in an idiom of the female body and women's sexuality.[12] The public display of this fantastic organ, precisely because it exposes male desire and envy, is horrifically shameful for men. It is no less humiliating even during a celebration of manhood.

Normally, Iatmul men channel same-gender libidinal energies into aggressive competitions such as totemic oratory and, formerly, warfare (see also chap. 4). Naven, however, suspends the sexual norms of masculinity. The mother's brother, through nggariik, offers to become both the nephew's "mother" and "wife" (Bateson 1936, 81–82, 203).[13] In this dual feminine role, the uncle births his nephew *and* offers himself to the youth as a passive and willing female sexual partner. But the uncle during nggariik retains his identity as a man. This way, nggariik is a sign of anal intercourse. Consequently, for men, nggariik evokes culture-specific nuances of submission and degradation. In conformity with so many of their peers elsewhere, men in Tambunum do occasionally utter the ambiguous male threat "*ya wungat mogwimbe wangii,*" or "fuck me up the ass!" And, indeed, this is precisely what the uncle communicates during naven.

Nggariik therefore diminishes the social identities of the uncle and his nephew by associating them with a mode of sexuality that men are normally loath to admit. The uncle seduces his nephew (see also F. Morgenthaler 1987, 128–32). The sacrificial aspects of nggariik, about which I spoke earlier in this chapter, must now also be tied to prohibited eroticism (relatedly, see Bataille 1986, 1992; De Vos and Suarez-Orozco 1987; Irwin 1993). Men rarely insinuate, let alone discuss, homoeroticism unless they intend to joke or disparage. But the status of same-gender male sexuality is not adequately conveyed by notions of naive humor or caustic insult. Bateson, in an unpublished lecture on the naven rite that is housed in the U.S. Library of Congress, remarked that, despite public contempt, "there is actually a good deal of h.s. [homosexuality] among the men and the boys and it is not regarded with disapproval, but as a rather unsatisfactory substitute for het.sex [heterosexual] activities." These comments were scrawled in the margin of Bateson's address, adjacent to a passage that discusses nggariik. Curiously, Bateson also wrote "omit" above this aside; there are no comparable comments in his published writings. These marginalia corroborate my contention that same-gender sexual encounters among Iatmul men do occur in private (chap. 3). Now we can discern another level of shame to nggariik. The passive sexual pose struck by the mother's brother violates the reigning ideology of manhood by exposing the facts and fictions of manhood. The gesture implies that the uncle and nephew are unable to make love to women—or that they simply prefer not to do so.

Nggariik might, in this respect, seem to be little different from the homoerotic horseplay that characterizes male initiation (chap. 3). Both events, as Paul (1991) might say, create solidarity among men through erotic yet aim-inhibited or nonorgasmic activity. Both naven and initiation, too, assert the existence of a hierarchy among men at the same time that these two rites symbolically eliminate generational and individual differences through "a fantasy whereby matter is reduced to the primordial stuff" such as feces (Paul 1996b, 66).[14] But there is a key difference. Male initiation is staged in the absence of women; its goal is the creation of masculinity. The uncle's naven dramatics, by contrast, often take place before women. When they do so, the uncle may resort to the gestural language of homoerotic desire in order to shame himself and thus to annihilate masculinity.

The Incest of Oedipus

In the past, conjectured Lindenbaum (1987), Iatmul men practiced sister-exchange marriage in conjunction with ritualized homosexuality. As village populations increased, these reciprocal exchanges of sisters and semen became impractical (see also Gewertz 1983). Eventually, they were replaced by delayed and asymmetrical bridewealth marriages. The transition between these two systems, Lindenbaum continued, was resolved by nggariik. The superior uncle presents himself as a subordinate female by offering his buttocks; yet the ludic phrasing of this already contradictory statement implies that the two men are really equal.

The historical orientation of Lindenbaum's thesis is doubtful. Nggariik is no vague memory of a prior sociocultural order. Far more serious is Lindenbaum's false premise that the uncle's nggariik is humorous. Nonetheless, the suggestion that naven links homoeroticism and marriage is intriguing. In my view, however, nggariik is a gesture of erotic taboo that confounds rather than resolves moral dilemmas and problems of social order. Much like the aggressive iai women during naven, the nggariik gesture blurs the distinction between maternal love and conjugal intercourse, and it violates the standards of proper affinal relations.

The uncle's provocative, quasi-seductive advance onto his nephew during nggariik reveals the uneasy foundations of marriage. Here I draw on Devereux's ([1965] 1978) addendum to Lévi-Strauss ([1949] 1969). The "elementary" structures of marriage, argues Devereux, are rooted in symmetrical homoeroticism rather than, as per Lévi-Strauss, symmetrical exchanges of women (see also Gillison 1994). Brothers-in-law are vicarious lovers who act on forbidden homoerotic and often sexually competitive yearnings through legitimate matrimonial relations. Along similar lines, Herdt (1981, 294) comments that Sambia men fear that women may discover the "secret" of masculinity: that men forgo pleasurable same-gender sexuality in order to become husbands, fathers, and cult leaders. "Marriage is sacred," wrote Devereux (1978, 201), and "dangerous, precisely because it permits what is forbidden; it consecrates a sacrilege." Nggariik acknowledges this sacrilegious consecration. From the perspective of Iatmul men, to invert Lévi-Strauss, nggariik threatens the rules of culture with natural urges.

In bringing together the uncle and nephew during naven for a sexual encounter, nggariik is also incestuous in addition to homoerotic. Bateson (1936, 81) remarked on "a casual mention in mythology of a man who rubbed his buttocks on the leg of a man who was marrying his sister." For Bateson, this mythic scene was affinal. For Layard (1959, 107), however, it suggested "near incest," a concept that refers to the ability of the brother-in-law relationship to fulfill incestuous desires (see also Knauft 1989b; Tuzin 1997, 117).[15] Men never perform nggariik on a wife's brother or sister's husband. Nevertheless, the theme of incest is altogether present in the gesture. Through the brother-sister kinship identification, the uncle plays the part of his nephew's "mother" during nggariik. He also, as we have seen, becomes at this moment the "wife" of the nephew's father. The nephew, of course, symmetrically identifies with his father. But if we view the nephew as retaining his normal social role while his uncle shifts his own identity to that of the mother, then nggariik, in a parallel inversion of iai marriage, enables a mother to initiate sexual intercourse with her son.

In another myth reported by Bateson (1936, 36–37), a brother and sister return home after an outing of spearing fish and processing sago. Shockingly, their parents immediately disrobe and dance. The two siblings are so humiliated that they paddle to the house of their maternal uncle—but he and his wife, too, strip off their garments and dance. Here, though, the siblings apparently feel no embarrassment, for they dine and later remunerate their uncle with valuables. In actuality, needless to say, the sight of a mother's brother cavorting in the nude would be nothing less than mortifying. Far more devastating, however, at least in this tale, is a parent who does likewise. The shame of incest, I suggest, can thus be linked to the role of the maternal uncle in naven on the basis of myth in addition to the uncle's kinship identifications during nggariik.

After receiving nggariik, the standard gift bestowed by the nephew onto his mother's brother is a spear decorated with dangling shell valuables or, today, cash. This present combines wealth with a phallic image of aggression, a penetrative symbol that resembles the nephew's statuesque appearance during the "sexual salute" of nggariik. For Bateson, the nephew's ornamental spear was a token of bridewealth since the youth during naven was the "husband" of his uncle. But since younger nephews often had few assets of their own, observed Bateson (1936, 81), these gifts were in actuality given by the nephew's father to the father's brother-in-law. As a result, nggariik, like bridewealth (chap. 7), exacerbates father-son tensions. Indeed, some men say that the father during naven unhappily stands aside and merely calculates the wealth he will later need to present to his son's uncle.[16]

During nggariik, as I just noted, the nephew, when viewed as a *son*, symbolically consummates oedipal desire by identifying with his father and ritually sleeping with his "mother" the uncle. Nggariik, then, complements that facet of iai marriage that allows the father to fulfill his *own* oedipal yearnings (chap. 7). The moral and social ambiguity of nggariik, and the impure sexuality it implies, is evidenced by the symbolism of the gift that the nephew offers to his uncle. This gift resembles the valuables given to the mud-smearing iai women after naven (chap. 9) and the food and wealth extended to tshambela partners after they mime male incompetence (chap. 8). In all three contexts, a man exchanges money for feces.

In sum, as a boy grows up and masters the skills of adulthood, he becomes an asset to his patrilineage. Naven, insofar as it celebrates achievement, recognizes this fact of social structure. However, the youth still maintains intimate ties to his matrikin—somatic, onomastic, emotional, and ritual—which the nggariik gesture affirms. Actually, nggariik effectively denies the father's role as genitor and sexually active husband. The uncle not only births the youth, but the youth, in place of his father, copulates with the father's wife. The uncle's nggariik, and the nephew's willing if unhappy reception of it, threaten many of the father's moral, sexual, paternal, and familial prerogatives (see also Juillerat 1999, 171–74). As such, nggariik intensifies oedipality and heightens the structural and psychological conflict between patrilines and men.

Indeed, from another perspective, one that is also reminiscent of iai marriage, the nggariik gesture and its resultant gift exchange express another oedipal rivalry. Here, uncle and nephew appear to compete for the pivotal sister/mother. By offering himself sexually to his nephew, the uncle appears to desire his sister. At the same time, as I just observed, the nephew, having symbolically penetrated his uncle, fornicates with his mother. The nephew's incest is further aided by the conspicuous exclusion of his father from nggariik and naven more generally (Juillerat 1999). For all intents and purposes, the father is a nonactor in this drama. More than that, the father contributes to the erasure of his own moral status by paying for his son's incest. One would be hard pressed to imagine a more tragic, and more oedipal, ritual. Any misgivings about this interpretation are laid to rest when one considers, yet again, the emotional response by the two central thespians in this tragedy, uncle and nephew: tears of shame.

Naven and the End of Culture

The sudden appearance of nggariik in a ritual that seemingly celebrates the mastery of manhood and the moral renewal of society seems truly misplaced. Coming at the climax of naven, nggariik should enable the mother's brother to honor his sister's son: but it fails. Both uncle and nephew are shamed. If that is not enough, the uncle is regressed to a dirty infant, diminished to a squatting woman, and feminized as a passive and sexually receptive man. Nggariik, too, exacerbates oedipal tensions, confounds generational hierarchy, expresses taboo homoerotic desire, and flirts with incest. It corrupts moral motherhood with phallic aggression, and it debases the idea of birth through an image of defecation. Finally, nggariik lays bare men's envy of female parturition. By reducing men to tears, the nggariik gesture, far from renewing society and manhood, signals the end of culture as Eastern Iatmul imagine it.

But nggariik is a misplaced gesture only when viewed through functionalist, teleological, and structuralist frameworks. We cannot understand nggariik if we assume that the primary task of ritual is to construct society and personhood and to solve the riddles of culture. Rather, from a dialogical and psychoanalytic perspective, naven is revealed for what it really is: a ritual that plays on desire and teases taboo in order to effect emotional and semiotic ambivalence rather than a sociological and moral rejuvenation. Naven indeed resembles classic tragedy. It confronts the hidden, repressed yearnings of men and women, and enters these unstated thoughts into wider, ongoing dialogue. Naven, to conclude, enshrines the pathos of culture and rehearses the eternally unresolvable dimensions of masculinity, motherhood, and human experience.

Epilogue: Masculinity
beyond the Sepik

It seems that Freud was right. Culture does repress and sublimate desire. This is not, of course, all that culture does. There is much more to what Obeyesekere (1990) calls the "work of culture" than psychological defense. Still, the human predicament is, at some level, undeniably tragic. The search for meaning frequently leads to emotional ambivalence, existential contradiction, and behaviors that, even though they adhere to the norms for proper comportment, nonetheless bespeak the chaos of primary process.

Perhaps Obeyesekere (1990, 288) said it best:

> The great social theorists, like great philosophers and poets, were centrally concerned with human suffering, impermanence, and death. Current anthropology, however, is like the modern funeral parlor or, better still, like a bourgeois bathroom: everything is tidy, everything smells clean, and the shit is flushed into the dark, rat-infested sewers that line the belly of the city. Like the id, it is the lower part separated by a barrier from the clean life in middle-class households. What is hidden is dung and death. And like dung and death, pain and human suffering are also confined to sanitized environments. There are, however, the few who will be attracted to such forms of experience in which they live, because they have searched, as Freud did, the dark recesses of their own lives and from there have had a vision of the dark side of life in general. The moment you label this vision as pessimistic and oppose it to "optimism," you miss the point of it all. Neither Freud nor the Buddha gave way to gloom or nihilism by his recognition that the purpose of all life is death.

I have not spoken much about death in this book. But what, after all, are the nggariik gesture and the naven rite if not the death and rebirth of masculinity and motherhood as these two ideals are imagined and then destroyed, again and again, by Eastern Iatmul? These bittersweet enactments of celebration and pathos are not, to be sure, traumatic in any true sense of the term. Yet they do result in tears and woe. The pain of being a man, as it were, no less a mother in the eyes of men (and perhaps women), is at the heart of the naven rite and culture more generally in this small life-world in the middle Sepik River of Papua New Guinea.

By focusing on the cultural and psychodynamic symbolism of masculinity in Tambunum, I argued that manhood is largely defined in accordance with two countervailing images of the maternal body, the "grotesque" and the "moral." I also proposed that the semiotic conversation between motherhood and masculinity culminates in a drama of longing and taboo, degradation and regeneration, that is the naven rite. I now want to suggest briefly that this account of masculinity and motherhood is by no means unrelated to other regions of Papua New Guinea, and beyond.

A West Sepik Predicament

Bernard Juillerat (1992) has brilliantly interpreted a rich series of psychodynamic images that unfold during the *yangis* rite among the West Sepik Yafar. After the originary cosmic mother perished in childbirth, her body was cut into pieces. Belly became "rotting" earth; a breast was pulled into the sky as the sun (Juillerat 1992, 28, 58–60). At the end of yangis, a pair of "just-born" male spirits called *ifege* are poised to shoot phallic arrows into the decaying yet fertile, uterine ground. With their arrows cocked, these figures signify "the pre-incestuous instinct of the return to the womb" (Juillerat 1992, 60). But the "just-born" ifege are counseled by their maternal uncles to release their arrows toward the solar breast, and thus they differentiate between the "mother's two successive but antagonistic functions, namely, sexuality and motherhood" (Juillerat 1992, 60–61; see also 1996, 355–56). Yangis concludes with

> a happy ending, leaving the spectator to imagine the future emancipation of the heroes through the next stages of their destiny . . . or it may, on the contrary, be perceived as the implicit recognition of that indelible tie, of that lifelong persistent nostalgia. (Juillerat 1992, 107)

For Yafar and Eastern Iatmul men alike, culture discriminates yet blurs, thwarts yet consummates, two antithetical forms of desire: sexual and maternal (Juillerat 1996, 418–19). The yangis and naven rites both socialize the preoedipal and oedipal yearnings of men into adulthood. Yet both rites confirm the unresolvable relationship between masculinity and contrary images of motherhood.[1]

Yangis and naven both conclude with ambivalence rather than moral restoration. Both rites confirm and subvert the ideals of masculinity and motherhood. Both rites consist of a complex interplay between collective symbolism and psychodynamic process. Finally, both rites define manhood through a set of themes—sexuality and aggression, fear and desire—that are directed at women in general, and mothers in particular.

There is, of course, another side to all this: women. Alas, no rites in these two societies permit women the same symbolic flourish with which to confront their own "anxious pleasures," to borrow from Gregor (1985), as men so often mobilize for their psychic needs. Why?

The Problem of Manhood

The asymmetry between Eastern Iatmul men and women with regard to socially sanctioned vehicles for exercising Obeyesekere's (1970) "work of culture" is frankly disconcerting. It is tempting to embrace classic psychoanalysis and explain this difference in terms of a singular path of psychosocial development that provides men everywhere with their masculine identity. In this view, men progress from infantile mother-son symbiosis to collective manhood. Hence, a man's initial feminine identity must be dramatically, if not violently, "snapped" so his body and psyche can be reshaped anew in accordance with an exclusive, nonfemale set of values. Yet, however much men fear a regression to an infantile feminine state (one need only reflect on the ubiquitous, cross-cultural admonishment to "be a man!"), men nonetheless forge their identity as men through indelible traces, to invoke Juillerat, of maternal nurture.

The problem of masculinity is often attributed to some variant of this psychodynamic predicament. Many would echo the historian Barbara Ehrenreich's warning in her Foreword to Klaus Theweleit's (1987) disturbing account of male fantasies among the officers of the Freikorps, many of whom were instrumental in the rise of Nazism. These men categorized women in three exclusive ways: chaste mothers and nurses who offered nourishment alone, wives whose legitimate sexuality was nonetheless to be shunned, and carnal harpies such as Jews and communists who posed such dangers to masculine identity that they were suitable only for murderous obliteration. Ehrenreich (1987, xv) alerts us:

> For if the fascist fantasy—which was of course no fantasy for the millions of victims—springs from a dread that (perhaps) lies in the hearts of all men, a dread of engulfment by the "other," which is the mother, the sea or even the moist embrace of love . . . if so, then we are in deep trouble.

And indeed we are, at least as evidenced by the proliferating abundance of books and movements, both popular and scholarly, that bemoan the failures of contemporary masculinities.[2]

Not surprisingly, current debates over manhood in the human sciences often revolve around the time-honored dichotomy of universalism and constructivism. Are there global features of masculinity? Or is manhood everywhere a wholly localized construct? Perhaps the very idea of an essential masculinity is little more than a Western, hegemonic premise that ultimately mutes differences? Or, rather, have the heteroglossic premises of postmodernism, the search for radical alterity, and the rising political legitimacy of diverse voices simply inured scholars and anthropologists to the notion that it is impossible, never mind undesirable, to discern any common humanity?

These are far from trivial questions. My own position, centered here as it is on a single village in Papua New Guinea, is one of temperance and reservation. Right now, I believe, we simply know *too little* about masculinity and masculinit*ies* to contrive grand pronouncements. I agree with Connell (1995) that any vision of masculinity is necessarily embedded in specific historical and cultural practices. Nevertheless, the psychodynamic imagery that surfaces again and again in localized masculinities exhibits a striking, cross-cultural similarity (see Gregor 1985; Gilmore 1990). I would not go so far as to suggest the presence of a Universal Male. Anthropological accounts of masculinity, after all, ensure that we do not unknowingly or unjustifiably generalize from any one context to all of humanity (see Gutmann 1997). At the same time, anthropologists who study masculinity too readily abandon psychodynamic perspectives.

My interpretation of the relationship in the middle Sepik between masculinity and the imagination of motherhood lends support to Gilmore's (1990, 223) notion of a universal sense of manhood which he dubs "Ubiquitous Male." But the Eastern Iatmul case highlights a different sense of masculine ubiquity than Gilmore's tripartite scheme of procreation, protection, and provisioning. In Tambunum, men bar real mothers from many of the central rites of masculinity. Yet men also seek to embody the procreative qualities and powers of motherhood. While men, too, strive to escape the maternal embrace, they yearn for her shelter and nourishment. And despite men waxing eloquent about the ideal of mothering, the norms of everyday masculinity reveal the presence of complex anxieties concerning her body and its substances.

In Tambunum, to evoke Winnicott, there is no such thing as a man. Instead, there is a multilayered, irreducible, and persisting dialogue between masculinity and motherhood. This relationship, I want to propose in closing, has sufficient cross-cultural validity to justify its own tentative claim to Ubiquitous Male. I offer this suggestion, and the theoretical synthesis of psychoanalysis and cultural dialogics on which it is based, in the hopes of enhancing the current debate over what, if anything, masculinity is.

Notes

Chapter 1

1. Anthropological assessments of Bateson's book include Malinowski (1936), Haddon (1937), Radcliffe-Brown (1937), Nadel (1937, 1938), Elkin (1938), Powdermaker (1940), Wolff (1944), Lipset (1982), Kuper (1983), and Kuklick (1991). *Naven* was also reviewed by psychologists and psychoanalysts (Dollard 1937; Bakwin 1940) and a variety of popular serials such as the *Times Literary Supplement, Listener, Time and Tide, New Statesman and Nation, Criterion,* and *The Oxford Magazine.*

2. Although I never met Bateson, my work among the Iatmul owes much of its existence to his intellectual accomplishments—all the more so since I studied in graduate school with David Lipset who, in the 1980s, was Bateson's biographer (Lipset 1982). The anthropological predicament of being an "ethnographic double" to a distinguished yet unknowable predecessor, with whom one conducts a silent dialogue, is nicely discussed by Lutkehaus (1995a, 17). In my case, this doubled identity was itself doubled by the equally powerful ethnographic presence of Margaret Mead.

3. Bateson developed the ethos concept during impromptu fieldwork conversations in 1933 with Reo Fortune and especially Margaret Mead (Bateson 1936, x, 258; Lipset 1982, 138; Boon 1984, 1985). Mead introduced Bateson to Ruth Benedict's (1934) novel idea of cultural "configuration," which approximates the zeitgeist notion of German romanticism (see also Wolff 1944, 66; Nuckolls 1995). Interestingly, Mead (1940a, 334) later identified parallels between the Benedict-Batesonian ethological orientation and the early psychoanalytic anthropologist Geza Róheim's concept of cultural "plot" (1932, 1934, 1943; but see Mead 1935a). Yet neither Benedict nor Bateson ever enthusiastically embraced psychoanalysis. Curiously, Bateson's shining ethnographic and theoretical successes among Iatmul were preceded by a failed, frustrating study of the Baining of New Britain (see Lipset 1982, 127–30; Fajans 1997).

4. Bateson's elusive concept of schismogenesis, like the naven rite, has itself become legendary in anthropology and social thought. For Gorer (1936), schismogenesis recalled "the Hegelian-Marxist" notion of "internal contradictions," while Powdermaker (1940) associated it with Harry Stack Sullivan's theory of interpersonal relations. More poetically, Trawick (1990, 246) writes that schismogenesis "is the creation of no human agent, it arise spontaneously, as when I spill blue paint and you spill yellow, nei-

ther of us sees the other, and the green paint that is formed is the consequence of no one's plan."

5. Bateson also argued that the naven rite unfolds in accordance with the cognitive structure or eidos of Iatmul culture. This was a minor aspect of the book yet perhaps its most enduring idea since the eidos notion shaped the influential double-bind theory of schizophrenia (Bateson, Jackson, Haley, and Weakland 1956; see also Rieber and Vetter 1995). Outside of anthropology, the implications of eidos, ethos, and Bateson's epistemological concerns, all of which he first broached in his Iatmul work, continue to enthrall (e.g., Wilden 1972; Berman 1981; Inger 1983; Bateson and Bateson 1987; Hodge 1989; Rieber 1989; Bowers 1990; Etchegoyen and Ahumada 1990; McCall and Green 1991; Krause 1993; Weakland 1994; Harries-Jones 1995; Rapport 1997). Much of twentieth-century social thought is rooted in the book and the rite called *naven*.

6. One of the culminations of Culture and Personality was Bateson and Mead's (1942) now-controversial study of Balinese character (Geertz 1966a; Pollmann 1990; Wikan 1990; Jensen and Suryani 1992). In a number of underappreciated works, Mead and Bateson often contrasted Iatmul and Bali (Mead 1937, 1940b, 1941, 1943, 1947, 1954, 1972; Bateson 1949; Mead and Bateson [ca. 1954] 1991).

7. Scholars from many disciplines have argued that the body is a "natural" basis for human thought (e.g., Onians 1951; Douglas 1966, 1970; Turner 1967a; Csordas 1990; Sheets-Johnson 1990; Johnson 1992). Anthropologists will readily identify this claim with Hertz's ([1909] 1973) analysis of the left-hand/right-hand dichotomy.

8. Other anthropologists and theorists who draw on Bakhtin include Parker (1981), Da Matta (1983), Stallybrass and White (1986), Karp (1987), Trawick (1988), Gottlieb (1989), Limon (1989), W. Weiss (1990), Briggs (1993), Hereniko (1994), and especially Lipset (1997).

9. I hasten to add, although it hardly needs saying, that my use of Bakhtin's concept of the "grotesque" does *not* imply that Eastern Iatmul mothers are in any way inadequate or malicious. Similarly, the "moral" is unrelated to notions of justice. In this regard, I might also add that anthropological interpretation implies neither endorsement nor censure.

10. Fine ethnographic examples of psychoanalytic anthropology include Tuzin (1975, 1977), Kakar (1978), Kracke (1978), Crapanzano (1980), Parin, Morgenthaler, and Parin-Matthey (1980), Obeyesekere (1981, 1990), Herdt (1982a, 1987), Paul (1982), Spiro (1982a), Juillerat (1992), Kurtz (1992), Weiner (1995a), and Dundes (1997a); for broad reviews, see Paul (1989) and Ingham (1996a).

11. The theoretical literature in anthropology on the projective dimensions of myth and ritual is considerable (e.g., Dundes 1963, 1976a; Spiro 1965, 1982b; Paul 1987).

12. Here, Paul (1987) somewhat ironically borrows from the methodology of structuralism—this, despite Lévi-Strauss's ([1985] 1988) critique of Freud and the commitment of orthodox structuralism to expunging bodily experience and sensuousness from cultural analysis, thereby privileging mind over body (Doniger 1989; relatedly, see Mimica 1993; Weiner 1991, 1993, 1995a). By contrast, psychoanalysis attends to the logic of mentation in order to understand the force of passion in human life.

13. The extensive cross-cultural literature on the Oedipus complex includes Spiro (1973), Edmunds and Dundes (1983), Edmunds (1985), Obeyesekere (1990), Cohler (1992), Juillerat (1992), Spain (1992), Ingham (1996a, 73–83), Johnson and Price-Williams (1996), Paul (1996a), and continuing debate over Malinowski's (e.g., 1927,

1929) well-known claim that the Oedipus complex is entirely absent in the matrilineal Trobriand Islands (Spiro 1982a, 1992; Kurtz 1991, 1992, 1993; Ingham 1996b).

14. The term *oedipality,* coined by David H. Spain and cited by Ingham (1996a, 255 n. 1), refers to normal rather than pathological oedipal processes.

15. Bettelheim's (1954) important book *Symbolic Wounds* remains the first, and in some respects the most persuasive, anthropological-psychoanalytic argument concerning the uterine symbolism of male ritual (see also Paul 1990; Kittay 1995; relatedly, Jaffe 1968).

16. Despite my focus on the lives and imagination of men, the primacy of maternal imagery in Tambunum can be seen as lending ethnographic support to nonanthropological efforts at curtailing so-called phallic monism from psychoanalysis (Chasseguet-Smirgel [1964] 1970; Irigaray [1977] 1985; Doane and Hodges 1992; Breen 1993).

17. Melanesian personhood, as recently discussed by Busby (1997), resembles identity in India, e.g., Marriott's (1976, 111) "dividual" and O'Flaherty's (1980) androgynous fluids.

18. The literature on Melanesian identity is vast. Select references include McDowell (1980), Herdt (1981), Gewertz (1984), Harrison (1985a, 1990, 1993a), Clay (1986), Meeker, Barlow, and Lipset (1986), Battaglia (1990), Gewertz and Errington (1991), Godelier and Strathern (1991), Epstein (1992), Juillerat (1992), Telban (1993, 1997a), Smith (1994), Goodale (1995), Stephen (1995), Lipset (1997), and Tuzin (1997).

19. Since Bateson and Mead, anthropologists have studied Iatmul totemism (Wassmann 1991), social organization (Stanek 1983a, 1990), women (Hauser-Schäublin 1977), leadership (Metraux 1978), and children (Weiss 1981, 1990), among other topics.

20. For differing conceptions of the body across Melanesia, see Read (1955), Strathern and Strathern (1971), Gell (1975), A. Strathern (1977a, 1977b, 1977c, 1996), M. Strathern (1979), Herdt (1981, 1982b, 1984b), Meigs (1987), Poole (1987), Wagner (1987), Knauft (1989a), O'Hanlon (1989), Battaglia (1990), Bonnemere (1990), Biersack (1996, 1998), Lipset (1997), Telban (1997b), and additional citations in chapter 4.

Chapter 2

1. The vernacular word for the Sepik River is *Avusett,* which may derive from the terms for bone (*ava*), or large (*numa*), and lake (*tset*). One local origin tale about the actual name *Sepik* is as follows. A European explorer visited the Sepik Coast aboard the sailing ship named *Windjammer* (which, incidentally or otherwise, was the former name of a popular beach hotel in Wewak, the coastal capital town of the East Sepik Province; see map 1, chap. 2). When he visited Kairiru Island, he asked about the trees and grass that washed ashore on the beaches. Is there a river? The flotsam and jetsam, they replied, came "from the wind," or *sipik* in the local tongue. Another account derives the word *Sepik* from the pidgin term for "little," or liklik, since Eastern Iatmul repeatedly asked German explorers in the late eighteenth century for a "little" bit of salt.

2. Notwithstanding the association of water and death, Eastern Iatmul, in contrast to the nearby Mundugumor of the Yuwat or Biwat River (Mead 1935b, 168–69), do not fear the river.

3. Iatmul is a non-Austronesian, or Papuan, Ndu language (Staalsen 1966, 1969, 1972; Laycock 1965; Foley 1986).

4. I am not suggesting an environmental determinism here. The ecological fact of periodic inundation in no way "causes" the symbolic meanings of land. Murik vil-

lages provide a nice counterpart. Contrary to what one might think, land in these land-less intertidal communities "does not present itself as a metaphor of perpetuity, fertility or identity" (Lipset 1997, 34).

5. Young women are likened to moist, freshly cooked sago pancakes, called *ngu-viarpma*, while aged widows are *luganau*, or stale and dry sago.

6. My "patrilineage," referring to what Eastern Iatmul call a *yarangka*, presum-ably corresponds to Bateson's (1936, 4) "phratry" and Wassmann's (1991) "patriclan"; the latter two terms were coined in upper-river, or Nyaura, Iatmul villages. Likewise, my use of the literal translation "branch" (*tsai*) would seem to coincide with Bateson's (1932, 257) "clan," which Nyaura Iatmul call *ngaiva*, after the word for house (*ngai*). These terminological inconsistencies reflect the existence of historical and sociological variation among the twenty-five or so Iatmul-speaking villages.

7. Patriclans are bifurcated into two categories. But this division is far-removed from daily life and even, for many people, entirely unknown. There are *no* totemic moi-eties (cf. Bateson 1932, 256–57; Rubel and Rosman 1978; Lindenbaum 1987; Tuzin 1989). In fact, the Woli-kumbwi and Tshai-iambonai moieties that Bateson (1932, 250) observed in nearby Mindimbit are merely descent groups in Tambunum, nearly extinct.

8. Ethnohistorically, two clans in the late seventeenth century abandoned the nearby village of Timbunke after an altercation concerning marriage and established Tambunum (relatedly, see Newton 1997). For this reason, Timbunke is "elder brother" to Tambunum; today, it is home to a mission station. Similarly, a late-eighteenth-cen-tury dispute in Tambunum resulted in the founding of Wombun, a small community located about a half-kilometer upriver. Bateson's concept of schismogenesis, needless to say, is no mere conjecture.

9. In the traditional cosmography of the Murik, the boundaries of the premod-ern trading system were marked by two large boulders, the petrified testicles of a giant ogre (Lipset 1997, 28).

10. This visual tableau is enhanced by a pleasant sound. Men carve female canoe paddles with a slight angle that lends a sharp and melodious "ca-chunk, ca-chunk, ca-chunk" to women's paddling.

11. Bateson (1936, 237) recognized a related ontology when he wrote that Iatmul believe in separate "roads" or "planes of existence" for humans, witches, tree spirits, and other numinous beings (see also Silverman 1997, 109).

12. Men and women still attend weekly markets in the bush between Tambunum and the Sawos-speaking villages of Kwaiut and Kamangawi (map 1, chap. 2). Yet mone-tary transactions have entirely replaced the former sago-for-fish exchanges (Schindl-beck 1980; Gewertz 1983).

13. The 1930s was also a time of intensive anthropological fieldwork in the Sepik region, e.g., Mead, Fortune, Bateson, Whiting, Hogbin, and Wedgwood. Bateson him-self, in fact, first coined the term *Iatmul*; it was derived from the phrase *Iatmul-Iambonai* that in Mindimbit village denoted "the whole of the linguistic group, 100 miles in length" (1932, 249 n. 2). In Tambunum, where the corresponding phrase is *Iat-moi-Iambonai*, the linguistic group is known as *Iatmoi*. Nevertheless, I retain Bateson's now-standardized nomenclature. Rarely, however, do local people class all these villages as a single, unified ethnic group. The names of many other Sepik cultures, it is worth noting, have shifted over the past century (e.g., McDowell 1991, 5–6).

14. In Timbunke, Japanese troops orchestrated a massacre of nearly 100 men and

women in vengeance for local assistance to an Australian military unit (see also Gewertz 1983, 137).

15. In the words of a former Australian district officer: "They were determined to continue their old ways. I was determined to stop them. So it developed into a game, the rules of which they understood very quickly and as quickly turned to their own advantage" (Townsend 1968, 152–53).

16. For photographs of the building, see Townsend (1968, chap. 9) and Mead (1977, 236–37). Bomb craters still dot the area.

17. In many Papua New Guinean villages, female opposition to men's consumption of beverage alcohol is fueled by Christian dogma. In Tambunum, this association is minimal since, for the most part, alcohol consumption has been relatively moderate. Nonetheless, excessive drinking has at times been responsible for a number of tragic deaths. For the social context of beverage alcohol elsewhere in Papua New Guinea, see Ogan (1966, 1986), Marshall (1982), Smith (1994, 179–86), and Tuzin (1997).

18. The middle Sepik thus contrasts with those regions of Papua New Guinea that are experiencing emergent forms of economic stratification (Connell 1979; Brown 1987; Curtain 1988; Wesley-Smith and Ogan 1992).

19. Because Eastern Iatmul valued a premodern notion of individuality (chap. 8), the modern institutions of citizenship, voting, and moot courts have not proven to be overly problematic in Tambunum (see Gewertz and Errington 1991, chap. 6).

Chapter 3

1. Prehistorically, the Sepik basin was an inland sea (Swadling 1990).

2. For a related discussion of indigenous cartographies in Papua New Guinea, see Silverman (1998).

3. Bateson (1932, 1936), Stanek (1983a), and Wassmann (1990, 1991) discuss totemism in other Iatmul villages. So potent was the regional mystique of Iatmul names that other groups such as Manambu and Chambri would import them to enhance their own cosmological systems (Harrison 1987, 1989b, 1990; Errington and Gewertz 1987a).

4. Harrison's (1985a; 1990, 88–90) discussion of the Manambu "Spirit" resembles closely the Eastern Iatmul *kaiek.*

5. The original tract of ground that surfaced in the primal sea is called *Mayviim-biit.* It was the foundation for the totemic domain of the Shui Aimasa clan, which, as noted in chapter 1, stretches north from the river.

6. Strictly speaking, leaders in Tambunum are "great men" whose prestige arises from ritual and esoteric erudition rather than, as in classic "big man" societies, material wealth and large-scale distributions of pork (see Godelier 1986; Godelier and Strathern 1991).

7. Sepik and Melanesian naming systems vary greatly; compare Tuzin (1976, 135–48), Eyre (1992), Wormsley (1981), Strathern (1977a, 1982), and Wagner (1991, 163–64).

8. This is why, in part, Eastern Iatmul prefer to use kinship terms rather than personal names, despite any true avoidance rules. To address someone by their name is to imply that you have created them. For an intriguing essay on the hostility inherent in bestowing names, see Feldman (1959).

9. Among the Kwanga, a nonriverine Sepik society, ground is an idiom for "the ways of the ancestors" and the male cult (Brison 1992, 112).

10. Despite this maternal imagery, Eastern Iatmul cosmology lacks two mythic elements that are prominent among the West Sepik Yafar: a Great Mother and divine couplings (Juillerat 1992, 1996).

11. This and other references to material from Hauser-Schäublin (1977, 116–27) that discuss pregnancy and birth are from a translation by Townsend (1984).

12. In an exquisite essay, Losche (1995, 54) suggests that the nongendered source of gender among the Abelam of the Prince Alexander Mountains is a "container whose inside is invisible but from within which objects seem to be intrinsically produced . . . a container which gives, and that which is given forth from this container."

13. This type of myth is not unique to the middle Sepik. A common tale in seaboard Melanesia credits primal women with beards, and ancestors with milk-producing breasts; eventually they switched (Young 1987, 229; Lutkehaus 1995a, 218). For Amazonian counterparts to these Melanesian myths, see Gregor (1988).

14. Since the primal theft of the avian flutes resembles the myth of the hornbill, perhaps flute tones evoke the mournful melodies sung by yentshuan birds as they yearn for their lost beaks?

15. For the eroticism of flutes in another Sepik society, see Lutkehaus (1995a, 217). It is worth noting that Eastern Iatmul flutes are not associated with breast milk as among the Sambia of the southeastern Highlands (Herdt 1982a).

16. Some of this symbolism also pertains to the bullroarer. The vernacular word for bullroarer, *yartwai,* is a compound noun that literally translates as sword-crocodile. The bullroarer is thus a double phallus since wooden swords were a common weapon, used only by men, and crocodiles, regardless of their gender, are associated with the masculine role in sexual intercourse; the vagina is likened, in this context, to the river water through which the crocodile swims.

17. Material expressions of motherhood in Tambunum far outnumber those of fatherhood. As a result, to draw on Green (1992, 164–65) and Manenti (1992), masculinity is encountered as a distant concept whereas motherhood lies in the foreground of immediate experience.

18. Women in some Iatmul villages, but not in Tambunum, were initiated along with boys (see Bateson 1936, 10; Schmid and Kocher-Schmidt 1991, 171–73; Weiss 1994b, 243–49; Hauser-Schäublin 1977, 169–78; 1995, 50–52). Men in Tambunum did formerly pacify women who seemed especially domineering or masculine by showing them the flutes. This way, men sought to encompass unusual female aggression within the male cult.

19. The patrilineal initiation moieties in Tambunum are Miwat ("tops of trees") and Kiisiik ("floral detritus"). They are unrelated to marriage and totemic moieties (which do not exist in the village) and lack named age-grades (compare Bateson 1932, 264–65, 432; 1936, 245; Wassmann 1991, 32–33). During initiation and other rituals, each group divides into smaller units termed elder/younger brother, father/son, or grandfather/grandson (see also Bateson 1932, 432). Men from the same initiation cohort are called *tambinien.*

20. For the relationship between male initiation, sexuality, and meat-eating in another Sepik society, see Tuzin (1978).

21. Guidance about adult behavior and esoteric affairs is minimal during Eastern Iatmul initiation (see also Gewertz 1982, 293). While the rite, too, emphasizes the body and somatic fluids, it does not include the drinking of "good" blood (Mead 1938, 348–49), vomiting, nose-bleeding, urethral incision, licking armpit sweat (Roscoe 1995a,

61), and genital laceration (compare Herdt 1981, 1982b). Nor is there emphasis on growing the penis (Whiting 1941, 67).

22. Among Sambia, by contrast, male initiators threaten to castrate novices if they violate sexual taboos (Herdt 1981, 233).

23. Bateson's fieldnotes also suggest that Iatmul initiation was particularly concerned with the nose and mouth. A "man enters with croc[odile]'s upper jaw and giant cigarette . . . pushes each *bandi* [initiate] into building with nose of croc and makes him smoke. Should dance while smoking." The initiates rubbed noses with a female spirit costume called an *awan* (see chap. 5), who slapped them, yelled, and drew blood from their mouths (see also Bateson 1936, 130–31).

24. The Eastern Iatmul use of the term *tshui tsagi* differs from that reported by Bateson (1932, 407).

25. *Vai,* or *kastom trabel* in tokpisin, is akin to the central Iatmul concept of *ngglambi,* which Bateson (1936, 54) glossed as "dangerous and infectious guilt" (see also Mead 1938, 197; Wassmann 1991, 39, 80). The odor of vai evokes the scent of a dead snake (Bateson 1936, 54), or burning stone. The latter recalls in Tambunum the tall stones planted in front of the cult house, beneath which men once interred enemy bones. While vai might seem to resemble the Christian concept of sin (see Turner 1991), Eastern Iatmul themselves do not make this association.

26. The occult quality of totemism is akin to the "veiled speech" in other Melanesian societies such as Kwanga (Brison 1992).

27. According to Bateson (1936, 235), monism and pluralism structured the whole of Iatmul thought.

28. See Silverman (2001a) for a comparison between Eastern Iatmul and Australian Aboriginal systems of knowledge.

29. This phrase refers to Geertz's (1966b) influential notion that religion creates an "aura of factuality."

30. Somewhat analogously, since Yafar class esoteric knowledge as a form of cosmological fertility that is incompatible with blood, ritual leaders are prohibited from hunting (Juillerat 1996, 446).

31. Although these women are sometimes called "big women" in the vernacular (*numa tagwa*), this locution appears to be a derivation from pidgin. At any rate, these women lack the prestige or authority that is normally associated with so-called big women societies (e.g., Nash 1978).

32. Elsewhere in the Sepik, debates arise when rival men bestow the same name onto different children (Bateson 1936, 127–28; Gewertz 1977a; Harrison 1990, 140–46).

33. Upper-river Iatmul villages represent totemic names with knotted twine chords (Wassmann 1990, 1991). Manambu use displays of ornamented spears, arrows, and sticks (Harrison 1990, 160–61).

34. Occasionally, hereditary leaders distribute unclaimed names to men within the patriclan in an effort to avert internecine feuds.

35. Manambu structure their debates with fixed affinal alliances (Harrison 1990, 154–55; see also Silverman 1996, 41).

36. In a myth from Kararau (Hauser-Schäublin 1977, 123–24), the eponymous ancestors of each clan were born from an orator's stool when a man struck it with a bundle of leaves.

37. Chambri men fear that, while asleep, they will inadvertently divulge names to

wives and other intimates, who will then betray them to rivals (Errington and Gewertz 1987a, 111 n. 11; 1987c, 75, chap. 5).

Chapter 4

1. Contrast, for example, Gnau (Lewis 1980, 174–82), Sambia (Herdt 1981), Bimin-Kuskusmin (Poole 1982, 1984), Paiela (Biersack 1983), Kwoma (Williamson 1983), Mundugumor (McDowell 1991, 121–22), Yafar (Juillerat 1996, 246–48), and Murik (Lipset 1997, 55–57). Regional surveys include Jorgensen (1983a, 1983b), Hauser-Schäublin (1989), Knauft (1989a, 204–6), and Weiner (1995a).

2. Bateson (1936, 42) reported that "the afterbirth, lacking bones, is therefore the child of the mother only."

3. When youthful deciduous teeth fall out, they may be thrown to rats in a gesture of "sympathetic magic" since the fangs of these rodents are strong and sharp. Adults, needless to say, desire these very same qualities in their own dentition. On a related note, men also admire the aggression and stealth of rats. Nevertheless, rats represent the antithesis of moral adulthood: they are selfish, steal food, insatiably gnaw through all boundaries, and incarnate ghosts.

4. Not all of these associations are universal in the culture today; it is unclear if they ever were. Thus, some men report that teeth derive from both parents.

5. For hair symbolism in other Melanesian societies, see Serpenti (1984), Van Baal (1984), Strathern (1977b), and Lutkehaus (1995a, 302–3). Ever since Berg (1951), the cross-cultural psychoanalytic interpretation of hair and hair-cutting has been famously contentious (Leach 1958; Hallpike 1969; Hershman 1974; Andresen 1980; Cixous 1981; Obeyesekere 1981; Eilberg-Schwartz and Doniger 1995; Hiltebeitel and Miller 1998; and, of course, Freud 1922).

6. While *yerokwayn* refers to all forms of blood, strictly speaking, menstrual blood is *mbop tagwa yerokwayn*, or "moon woman blood" (see also Forge 1969). Conception is simply termed blood-semen (*yerokwayn-ndumbwi*).

7. The womb is also called a *mi aw* or wooden bowl, in reference to its shape. Among Sambia, for an interesting contrast, the testes and not the womb are called a "net-string bag" (Herdt 1981, 38 n. 9; see also MacKenzie 1991).

8. Difficult pregnancies and late miscarriages in Kararau are blamed on husbands who forced themselves onto their wives after conception (Hauser-Schäublin 1977, part 2). The Eastern Iatmul taboo on mixing semen and breast milk is mirrored by men in another Sepik society, Kwoma, where men refuse to eat food cooked by women with whom they have recently copulated for fear of ingesting their own semen and taking ill (Whiting 1941, 68). Kwoma also abhor the consumption of blood. They class all non-potable liquids as "blood," including urine and, for weaning children, breast milk or "breast blood" (Whiting 1941, 208–9).

9. If you look at the surface of any dry coconut, you will see a pattern that resembles a mouth and two eyes; this face is a remnant of the three original coconut shoots.

10. Newton (1973, 43) recites a similar myth from the Upper Sepik.

11. This fear may have been a real possibility for unskilled warriors prior to Australian pacification since head-hunting was common in the region. In another Sepik society, the testicles of vanquished enemies were strung above the ceremonial ground in front of the cult house and later "pounded to pulp" (Forge 1966, 27).

12. Hence, Bateson's (1936, 42) reference to paternal "reincarnation" makes sense

in Tambunum only with regard to those attributes that are associated with a grandparent's names.

13. Children fathered by a widower's second husband are also called *kwoiyen.*

14. See Harrison (1990, 60–61) for "bone names" among Manambu.

15. Eastern Iatmul allege that patrinames alone were used in sorcery (compare Bateson 1936, 43; Harrison 1985b, 140–41).

16. Perhaps Bateson deduced his translation of -*awan* from the phrase *avut ndu,* which literally means "old man."

17. Intriguingly, Eastern Iatmul wives are likened to "vines" that creep between patrilocal "trees" (chap. 5).

18. These original land forms, which correspond to the totemic domains of the first ancestors who emerged from the primal pit (chap. 3), are themselves floating islands whose names end with the suffix -*agwi* (Silverman 1997, 105).

19. The interpretations of the awan figure and matrinames by Handelman (1979, 179–80) and Houseman and Severi (1998, chap. 3), while insightful, are too narrowly anchored to social structure and eidos.

20. While a Mountain Arapesh "woman who wishes to conceive must be as passive as possible" (Mead 1935b, 31), the vernacular verb "to copulate" can accommodate either a male or female object (105). By contrast, Tchambuli or Chambri women are aggressively sexed (271), and Kwoma women initiate intercourse (Whiting 1941, 126).

21. I do not, however, want to diminish the tragic truth of Hauser-Schäublin's (1977, 128–39) claim that, when pushed to the limits of their ability to withstand frustration, Iatmul men may kill the source of their frustration whereas women may kill themselves.

22. Sexuality for Iatmul men, according to Hauser-Schäublin (1977, 135), but not women, is often a form of violence: it is used to manipulate others. Similarly, Mead (1949, 208) wrote that Iatmul men "day-dream of situations in which a woman's exposed helplessness will give a setting for rape, but in actuality they have to call in their entire age-grade to discipline—by rape—women whose husbands have utterly failed to bring them to order."

23. The *tshugukepma* ceremony, much as Weiner (1984; 1988a; 1991; 1995a, chap. 3) explores for the Highland Foi, also entangles sexuality and space.

24. This sexual practice does occur in another Sepik society, Ilahita Arapesh (Tuzin 1997, 165).

25. Kwoma men associate masturbation with boys who must regularly expel blood from their penises (Whiting 1941, 64).

26. By contrast, Kwoma brothers have a keen interest in maintaining a sister's virginity so they can demand high brideprice (Whiting 1941, 87).

27. Among the Mountain Arapesh, first-time fathers perform an elaborate postpartum rite that includes seclusion and the capture of a shell-valuable "eel" from a water pool (Mead 1935b, 35).

28. Herdt (1997b, 5) advocates the phrase "same-gender sexual relations" as a way to avoid conjuring practices and ideologies now current in Western societies (see also Elliston 1995).

29. Some men report that homosexuality was introduced into the Sepik by colonial Europeans (see also Mead 1949, 113).

30. "Such an embrace is permitted between the sexes only when they are both aged and related" (Whiting 1941, 50).

31. For adolescent homoerotic insults that are linked with overall sexual curiosity, see M. Morgenthaler (1987a).

32. In this setting, the kin term *kaishe* refers specifically to a father's sister's son; the reciprocal term, mother's brother's son, is *na* or *mbuambu*. (In actuality, these three terms encompass wide classes of kin; see Silverman 1993, chap. 6.) The word *kaishe* may be cognate to *kasa,* which refers to laughter, play, and ritual celebrations; the tokpisin equivalent is *pilai.*

33. *Kaishe* is also a reciprocal term for spouses' parents who, in some Iatmul villages, practice an avoidance relationship (Bateson 1932, 256; see also 1936, 309). This category of kaishe should not, of course, be confused with the ritual partnership. Note, too, that the tokpisin term *poroman* also refers to pairs of objects.

34. Adults never display their genitals in public. (The only exception I witnessed was an extremely drunken man.) Yet little boys, unlike girls, may disrobe innocently (chap. 3). Quite the opposite reaction was reported by Whiting (1941, 49) for Kwoma where, if a boy has an erection in the presence of female kin, one of the women, usually his sister, was "expected to beat the member with a stick."

35. Mead (1949, 113) wrote, "the slightest show of weakness or of receptivity is regarded as a temptation, and men walk about, often comically carrying their small round wooden stools fixed firmly against their buttocks" (see also Mead 1952, 419).

Chapter 5

1. Both men and women moor their canoes and bathe at the patrilineal riverbank. Yet only women gut fish, scrub dishes, and launder clothing. To avoid this feminine presence, many men bathe in the river outside a cult house.

2. Male leaders in Tambunum were once called the "eye of the house" (Metraux 1978, 52).

3. The web of interior house lashings, writes Coiffier (1992b, 48), represents communal cohesion. Whole segments of cane are the umbilical chords of demiurgical beings. Bark strips and pith respectively symbolize agnatic and uterine lineages.

4. House symbolism in the Pacific and beyond is anthologized by Fox (1993) and Carson and Hugh-Jones (1995).

5. Among the Abelam, the sides of a towering cult house are the wings of a giant spirit bird named Kwatbil (Losche 1997, 43). According to myth, the bellies of pregnant women were once sliced open and their infants cannibalized. Birth was impossible until Kwatbil swooped down on a mother and created the first birth canal. The specific transformation that ensued beneath the great bird's wings, however, remain a mystery.

6. For snake myths elsewhere in Melanesia, see Mead (1940a, 371–73), Wagner (1972, 18–24), Young (1983, chap. 2; 1987), and Lutkehaus (1995a, 54).

7. Gewertz (1982, 310–19) also reports on a Sepik myth about the ordeals of affinal relations.

8. Mead (1940a, 346) reached a similar conclusion for an Arapesh snake myth: it "expresses . . . women's fear of the men's too great sexuality, which may invade even the realm of suckling a child and render it repulsive."

9. Feasting bowls along the Northwest Coast of North America also feature two-headed bodies. This way, writes Dundes (1979), neither host nor guest partakes from the rear end (see also Walens 1981; Kan 1989). For a different interpretation of "split representation," see Lévi-Strauss (1963a).

10. Formerly, some male leaders slept in cult houses. In the late 1980s, only one man—elderly, mute, never married—continued to do so. He has since died.

11. The vernacular phrase is *ngai kitnya yembii*, or *ngwanya kitnya. Vagina dentata* occur in other Sepik mythologies, e.g., Mundugumor (Mead, reported by McDowell 1991, 152) and Ilahita Arapesh (Tuzin 1972, 243; 1976, 194; 1997, 81), and in Amazonian Mehinaku tales (Gregor 1985).

12. The "clitoris gate" in male initiation enclosures (chap. 3) can also refer to house doorways.

13. Orificial symbolism is prominent in other Melanesian cultures such as Gimi (Gillison 1987) and Ilahita Arapesh (Tuzin 1978).

14. Breast-feeding may also cause sibling rivalry since, as one man said, the elder child, once he sees his younger sibling nursing, will want to do the same.

15. This prohibition confirms Bateson's (1936, 83) comment about "fire and food being closely analogous in Iatmul thought." The corresponding restrictions Bateson (1936, 83) observed in the avunculate relationship are absent in Tambunum.

16. In anthropological jargon, F = father, M = mother, B = brother, S = son, D = daughter, Z = sister, and so forth. In this book, I will occasionally use abbreviations such as FMBS, MBS, MB, and ZS; the meaning of these acronyms should be clear.

17. Somewhat analogously, the Iatmul of Kararau village believe that a man who chops down trees near the mythic totemic pit (chap. 3) will bleed the "primal mother" whose vagina forms this cosmogonic crater (Hauser-Schäublin 1977, 124).

18. In another Yafar myth (Juillerat 1996, 183–84), a father entombs his sons in the earth when they challenge his monopoly on hunting. The brothers are rescued by their mother.

19. Having evoked, through Fortes, the biblical myth of Abraham's near-sacrifice of Isaac, I want also to mention Delaney's (1998) powerful analyses of gender, fatherhood, and paternity in the tale.

20. Ritual and secular hierarchies in other Sepik societies are discussed by Harrison (1985c, 1987, 1990), Hogbin (1970, 190–91), Lipset (1990, 1997), Lutkehaus (1990), and Telban (1996a).

21. Meiser (1955) discusses the political and moral symbolism of platforms in a north-coast New Guinea society. Anthropologists will immediately associate furniture and leadership with the famous Golden Stool of the Ashanti of West Africa, a "palladium of the nation; it is also the palladium of politico-jural office" (Fortes 1969, 142).

22. Men's houses vary in size, membership, and sacredness. As of my last visit to Tambunum, one lineage branch maintains a small shelter; it has minimal ritual significance. Two clans, Mboey Nagusamay and Mogua, have large cult houses that serve as the ritual centers of these groups. Finally, there is one senior, villagewide ceremonial house, under the auspices of the Shui Aimasa patriclan. My use of the term *cult house* refers to the latter two types. Additionally, men may pitch temporary lean-tos for particular ceremonies.

23. In Kandingei, male leaders are called *kwali*, or the "central posts" of the cult house (Wassmann 1991, 236). A similar idiom occurs among the Kalauna of Goodenough Island (Young 1983, 135).

24. Ortner's (1974) classic question "Is Female to Male as Nature Is to Culture?" continues to generate lively debate (e.g., MacCormack and Strathern 1980; Strathern 1988; Ortner 1997).

25. In his unpublished fieldnotes, Bateson reported that initiated men sat on

stools with distinct legs; stools that lacked legs were reserved for noninitiated boys. Only adult men, this contrast implies, possess the competence to stand up to the rigors and honors of manhood.

26. In this context, fire is associated with motherhood rather than, as I suggested in chapter 4, a broader masculine symbolism. Nonetheless, postpartum women are forbidden to kindle fires in domestic hearths (Hauser-Schäublin 1977, 144).

27. A Murik house is centered on its "mother's" hearth. Likewise, the feminine house spirit "is the shadow who peers over a woman's shoulder as she sits cooking by her hearthfire" (Lipset 1997, 35–37).

28. Any man may own a large canoe but each descent group can formally name only one dugout after their senior spirit.

29. When the members of a clan perceive themselves to become "too endogamous," wrote Bateson (1936, 92), they "proceed to formulate a statement that one half of the clan belongs to the bows of the clan war canoe and the other half belongs to the stern." Thereafter, clan endogamy is rephrased as exogamy.

30. For the symbolism of canoes in other Sepik societies, see Lutkehaus (1995a, 162–66) and Barlow and Lipset (1997).

31. Female identity is also, with regard to self-worth and the ability to feed a family, represented by fishing nets (Weiss 1987b, 149) and fish-traps (Hauser-Schäublin 1977, 94). For this very reason, claims Hauser-Schäublin, the inclusion of fish-traps in brideprice effectively symbolizes a mutual exchange of women (see also chap. 7).

32. In truth, only one cult house in Tambunum today incorporates Vendigarlagwa. But this has more to do with the whims of construction than anything else. Female imagery also adorns male cult houses in Amazonia (Jackson 1996).

Chapter 6

1. Most analyses of Iatmul kinship privilege the genealogical grid and alliance theory (e.g., Korn 1971; Ackerman 1976; Kessel 1971; Rubel and Rosman 1978; Lindenbaum 1987; Houseman and Severi 1998). By contrast, I follow here an interpretivist tradition (e.g., Forge 1971; Wagner 1977; Schneider 1984; Collier and Yanagisako 1987; relatedly, Bourdieu 1977).

2. The tree is called *mbanj* (*Hibiscus tileaceus*?); *yerik* connotes the palm roots. Botanical metaphors for kinship, as in Mead's (1935b) famous Mundugumor "rope" (McDowell 1977; 1991, 266–87), are common throughout Papua New Guinea (e.g., Thurnwald 1934, 351; Gell 1975; Herdt 1981, chap. 4; Gewertz 1982, 318–19; Bowdon 1988, 278–79; Juillerat 1992, 26–27; 1996, 241–46; Weiner 1995a; Lipset 1997, 61–63) and Indonesia (Fox 1971).

3. Among Ilahita Arapesh, "good men, like proud, stationary coconut palms, remain in their ancestral place to follow the work of their fathers. Women, by their nature, are the 'vines' of the forest, prone to wander about and climb coconut palms with giddy promiscuousness" (Tuzin 1976, 94–95; 1992a).

4. The cosmological interplay between water and trees in Tambunum also alludes to gendered time, a notion that is found throughout Aboriginal Australia and Melanesia (Silverman 2001a; 1997, 114–17).

5. This interpretation follows somewhat Obeyesekere (1990, 28–40), who cites Starcke (1921), Flugel (1924), and Lewis (1928); relatedly, see Carroll (1987). The mythic motif of the maternal breast, severed or denied, occurs in other Melanesian societies,

e.g., Yafar (Juillerat 1992), Foi (Weiner 1995a, chap. 5), and Ilahita Arapesh (Tuzin 1997, 115–16), as well as in Tibetan Buddhism (Paul 1982). See Tuzin (1997), too, for a phallic mother in another Sepik mythology.

6. Mendangumeli is a Sepik counterpart to the Amazon maiden in Greek mythology. The crocodile sacrificed the phallus in order to kill a man who violated the maternal body. By contrast, the Amazon sacrificed one of her breasts in order to sling phallic arrows at masculine rivals and, I would argue, to withhold her nurturing milk from male infants while forswearing the sexuality of men.

7. For examples of pluralistic kinship elsewhere in the Sepik, see Mead (1935b, 206) and McDowell (1991, 179; 1978).

8. The vernacular phrase is *wuna nyame tiirii, wun tiigaon.* Among Yafar (Juillerat 1996, 73), a similar exhortation is "Where did I come from? I didn't come from nothing: I came from my mother who suckled me."

9. As Bateson might have put it, the ethos of motherhood is transposed into the eidos of sociology.

10. A man's sister and wife, however, are rivals (Hauser-Schäublin 1977, 107).

11. Kwoma brothers clash over sexual jealousy and spousal trysts (Whiting 1941, 145). Mundugumor brothers, according to McDowell (1991, 191), compete for wives in sister-exchange marriage; yet Mead (1935b, 176–81) attributed this rivalry to fathers and sons.

12. The elder/younger brother relationship is a cognitive framework that orga- nizes nearly all serial relations in the culture, from flute melodies to lineage "branches" (see also Bateson 1935b; 1936, 235–48; Metraux 1978, 1990; Spearritt 1982; Wassmann 1991, 225). Interestingly, the Banaro of the middle Keram River apparently organized things as if they were floating downstream (Thurnwald 1934, 350).

13. Herskovits and Herskovits (1958), drawing on West African myth, suggest that sibling rivalry is later "reactivated" as the father's hostility toward his own sons. More famously, Devereux (1953, 1960) provocatively argued from the original Greek tales that the classic Oedipus complex is a reaction to paternal hostility, and *not* vice versa.

14. The brother-sister identification, to put it another way, is not equally decisive for the respective social roles of the avunculate and amitate. In the Mundugumor "rope," by contrast, these two kin manifested considerable symmetry (McDowell 1991, 124, 259–62).

15. Bateson (1936, 45) labeled these meals a "clan sacrifice." He also reported on another culinary rite partaken by sister's children, called *pwivu* (1936, 46–47), which is absent in Tambunum.

16. These meals are prepared by the uncle's wife (*mbora;* reciprocal term *nasa*). She, like all women, transforms the raw into the cooked.

17. Among Chambri, the avunculate bond is "one of the few non-competitive relationships possible" between men (Errington and Gewertz 1987c, 94).

18. "Complementary schismogenesis" refers to individuals or groups who interact through opposed yet interdependent modes of response—say, when an Iatmul man's assertiveness causes a woman or initiate to act submissively, which encourages further masculine zeal, thus leading to increased feminine passivity, and so forth.

19. Ilahita Arapesh men, who associate the feces and urine of infants with breast milk, are also exempt from these parental chores (Tuzin 1982, 337–38).

20. Other bodily substances can be substituted for feces, such as tears (*miningu*), phlegm (*ndamangwi*), and urine (*wutnya*).

21. Among Murik, infant meals of sago pudding dipped in water or fish broth are called "the bones of the ancestors" (Barlow 1985, 144).

22. The Murik also tie food to maternal nurture—to the extent that recruitment into descent groups is based on feeding rather than birth itself (Barlow 1985). In Murik adoption, a woman who feeds a child "cuts the breast" of the birth mother (Lipset 1997, 59–61). Gifts of food thereby erase permanently all biological ties. No amount of feeding, by contrast, can annul the traces of conception in Tambunum. Eastern Iatmul do adopt. But, to draw on the Murik idiom, the maternal "breast" can never be cut.

23. Apropos of Mead, Hauser-Schäublin (1977, 148) argues that the *collective* life of Iatmul men balances the *individual* labor of women, and that, furthermore, men value greatly women who are economically self-reliant.

24. It is shameful for a man to be seen publicly trying to cook himself a meal of sago. Likewise, my efforts during one week to wash my own plates and pans in the river were politely protested by my then-unmarried village sister, who indicated in no uncertain terms that she would suffer some humiliation by the village for being lazy.

25. Bateson (1932, 274) reported that fathers could reprimand sons who were between the ages of toddlerhood and initiation. Both of us, however, failed to witness these scoldings.

26. Not only do Iatmul mothers and fathers treat their children as willful peers, argued Mead (1950, 369–70), but they do so "as if the only means of control which the adult could exercise was not praise or blame, love or punishment, or the invocation of the opinion or possible reward or punishment of outside groups, but only actual physical force, exercised in false pantomime." Therefore, Mead continued, Iatmul individuals lack "hierarchical moral control," as does the society in general, which can only maintain a semblance of order through the threat of violence between equal groups. Here, personality mirrors culture.

27. Similarly, Weiss (1981) was struck by the independence of Iatmul children, which she explains on the basis of their necessary contributions to "work" and child care.

28. A Kwoma mother might tell a weaning child that a swamp spirit "has taken the place of her milk, sometimes emphasizing this story by placing a leech on her breast" (Whiting 1941, 31, 35–37). Kwoma "weaning greatly increases a child's experience of anxiety" since "in the realm of prestige, the Kwoma child during the period of weaning plunges from the very top to the very bottom of the social hierarchy." Among Yafar, the mother may touch "a skull to her breasts in front of the child [who] associates weaning with the idea of death, which is conjured up by separation from the mother" (Juillerat 1996, 397).

29. The placenta in Tambunum, as well as in Kararau (Hauser-Schäublin 1977, 125), is buried in a coconut halfshell.

30. Eastern Iatmul women are assuredly denied the pleasant experience of their Murik counterparts, who inhabit a comfortable birth house, "built by the husband as a further sign that he cares for his wife and their new child" (Barlow 1985, 143). Eastern Iatmul men, too, offer their wives no additional love, food, or support—the first sign of care that a Murik husband bestows onto his expectant spouse.

Chapter 7

1. In Kararau and Kandingei, unlike in Tambunum, marriage and sexuality for men are regulated by the male cult (Hauser-Schäublin 1977, 73; Wassmann 1991, 36). Iat-

mul marriage today occurs in late teen years. While child-betrothals may have occurred in Tambunum, the bride-to-be did not reside with her future husband as his "sister." Among Mountain Arapesh, this type of marriage pattern has generated some controversy in regard to the incest taboo (Roscoe 1995b).

2. Sexual intercourse alone does not constitute a juridical union as it does for Murik (Lipset 1997, 147).

3. Unlike the Arapesh (Fortune 1939; Mead 1935b, 23–24), Torembi (Aitken 1983), and Mundugumor (McDowell 1991, 42, 47), Eastern Iatmul did not abduct wives during warfare or practice bride-theft.

4. Once a groom has satisfied his bridewealth obligations, however, he is said to be licensed to kill his wife (see also Bateson 1936, 139).

5. A married woman, after her bridewealth is fully transacted, is *yuwa-ngamba* or "payment completed"; *yuwa* is a premodern shell valuable.

6. Early in the twentieth century, bridewealth was greatly inflated due to an unprecedented influx of shell valuables into the region (chap. 2). In the long run, and despite the rise of capitalism, the economic value of bridewealth largely faded; to my knowledge, these payments have yet to exceed 1,000 kina, which in 1988–90 was about an equal sum in U.S. dollars (see also Hauser-Schäublin 1977, 84). Elsewhere in Melanesia, exorbitant bridewealth is becoming the norm (see Marksbury 1993).

7. Among Mountain Arapesh, a son "will stay with his parents and be the joy and comfort of their old age" (Mead 1935b, 33).

8. A Mundugumor man "could not ask his son's wife for food or firewood because that might indicate his immaturity or dependence" (McDowell 1991, 208).

9. For the prismatic construction of feminine identity in other Melanesian societies, see Herdt (1981, 162), Williamson (1985), Chowning (1987), Errington and Gewertz (1987c, chap. 5), Lutkehaus (1995a, 159), and Lipset (1997). An apt comparison is the role of Hindu women in Nepal and India (e.g., Bennett 1983; Kurtz 1992).

10. The connection between wives and wealth might explain why Chambri label shell valuables after female breasts, genitals, and skirts (Errington and Gewertz 1987c, 59).

11. There are approximately forty polygynous unions in the village (17 percent); six men have three or more wives.

12. A former prohibition on intercourse during the growing season also ensured that men would not poison their gardens with the fluids or odor of women. This restriction is especially prominent in yam-growing Sepik societies where men competitively exchange long tubers as symbols of the male body (e.g., Tuzin 1972; Scaglion 1986).

13. Fertile connotations of ritual killing, especially head-hunting, were common in Melanesia (e.g., van Baal 1966, 702, 706–8; Whitehead 1987; Juillerat 1996, chap. 9; Harrison 1993a, 86; see also Hoskins 1996, 18–23).

14. Many anthropologists explain the ritualized association of aggression and fertility in terms of exchange and political economy (e.g., Collier and Rosaldo 1981; Whitehead 1987; Harrison 1993a, 86–87; Knauft 1993). But this perspective offers limited insight for Tambunum (see also Weiner 1988b).

15. For an ongoing debate over Iatmul and Sepik marriage, see Forge (1971), Korn (1971), Ackerman (1976), Rubel and Rosman (1978), Williamson (1980), Bowden (1983a, 1991), Gewertz (1983, 1991), Lindenbaum (1987), Silverman (1993), and Houseman and Severi (1998). Most of the analyses, which can range from the picayune to the abstruse, concern the utility of anthropological models, especially Lévi-Strauss's ([1949] 1969) alliance theory, and privilege (largely with the exception of Forge and myself) the

genealogical grid. One of my goals in this chapter is to rephrase this debate in terms of local concepts and experiences.

16. Bateson (1936, 89), hearing the statement "the daughter goes as payment for the mother," reported the presence of another Iatmul marriage rule: a man should wed his father's sister's daughter, a patrilateral cross-cousin called *na*. Most subsequent middle Sepik ethnographers, myself included, have been unable to corroborate the existence of this rule (Gewertz 1977b; Hauser-Schäublin 1977, 83; Rubel and Rosman 1978; Bowden 1991). Men in Tambunum not only deny the practice, but they also interpret Bateson's statement to express the ideal of balanced reciprocity.

17. In iai marriage, the distinction between real and classificatory kin is often fluid; sometimes even elective unions are later refigured as iai marriages (see Williamson 1980; Williamson and Wagner 1990). In Tambunum, the father's mother's brother's daughter (FMBD), while classed as a iai, is not a valid spouse for reasons of age and generational difference (compare Bateson 1936, 89 n. 1). While this union is permissible, it is viewed to be eccentric and impractical. Needless to say, the marriage between a man and his father's mother iai is wholly inappropriate on account of her age, too, but also the fact that she is ideally married to the groom's paternal grandfather.

18. This phrase is equivalent to the Central Iatmul idiom that "a woman should climb the same [house] ladder that her father's father's sister climbed" (Bateson 1936, 88).

19. Eastern Iatmul contend that iai marriage is the original form of matrimony. For evidence, they point to its correspondence with the naming system. Local knowledge thus contravenes anthropological suggestions that iai marriage developed from restricted exchange (e.g., Rubel and Rosman 1978; Gewertz 1983; Lindenbaum 1987, 233–37; see also Bowden 1982, 1991).

20. One-quarter of all marriages are classed as iai; three-fourths of them unite a man with his real FMBSD. Most iai marriages adhere to patriclan exogamy. While these unions are figured into the overall pattern of balanced reciprocity, iai marriage cannot occur with a corresponding sister-exchange. If a potential spouse is too young to wed his iai, the sister's son of his father (who is the father's matrilateral cross-cousin) may do so instead (relatedly, see McDowell 1991, 213).

21. Hereafter, the term *iai* will refer to the FMBSD unless otherwise noted; likewise, the reciprocal term *ianan* will indicate a woman's FFZSS. For kinship abbreviations, see chap. 5 n. 16.

22. In many Sepik societies, long-term bridewealth obligations ensure the periodic renewal of affinal bonds, and various forms of funerary gifts culminate the avunculate relationship (e.g., Mead 1940a, 430; Williamson 1980, 537; Bowden 1983a, 752; Harrison 1984, 396; see also Rubel and Rosman 1978, 43). In Tambunum, these two functions are fulfilled instead by the intergenerational structure of iai marriage (see also Bowden 1988; McDowell 1990).

23. The groom calls his father's matrilateral cross-cousin (FMBS) *warangka*, a kin term whose importance arises specifically from iai marriage.

24. This phrasing of iai marriage instances the intimate and trusting relationship between a man and his uterine male cross-cousin (*mbuambu*).

25. As Bateson (1936, 92) noted, men can marry women directly classed as "mother" (relatedly, see Mead 1935b, 251). Yet these women have a maternal designation only through distant kin ties, and hence they are not placed in the same emotional category as birth mothers or iai women.

26. Among the Mountain Arapesh, a boy was said to "grow" his wife by feeding her food that he himself had cultivated. "In later years, this is the greatest claim that he has upon her" (Mead 1935b, 80).

27. The iai has the greatest prestige among cowives in ideology but not always in practice (compare Bateson 1932, 285–86; Hauser-Schäublin 1977, 131–34). While a husband is forbidden from divorcing his iai, he can still banish her from his household.

28. Gebusi men also channel oedipal desires into nonritualized, same-gender sexual encounters (Knauft 1985, 264–65).

29. Mead (1935b, 132–33) seemed to have understood this point well in her discussion of Arapesh marriage: "Nowhere in Arapesh culture is their lack of structure, their lack of strict and formal ways of dealing with the interrelations between human beings, more vividly illustrated than in their marriage arrangements. Instead of structure they rely upon the creation of an emotional state of such beatitude and such tenuousness that accidents continually threaten its existence."

30. Joking among Murik (Lipset 1990, 1997) and Chambri (Errington and Gewertz 1987c, 109) is rather more physical—grabbing breasts, poking genitals, and so forth.

31. Drawing on the unpublished Mundugumor fieldnotes of Mead and Fortune, McDowell (1991, 196) proposes intriguingly that intergenerational joking was asexual while sibling jests were sexual—genital for same-sex siblings and anal for brother-sister pairs.

Chapter 8

1. The term *tshambela* refers to groups and individuals. Sociologically, these relationships reveal no singular logic. While many tshambela associations unite lineages in the same clan, just as many are cross-cutting. Some lineages possess only one tshambela group; others have three or more. These pairings, too, are asymmetrical: Group A, while it might be the sole tshambela for Group B, is likely to pair with several other lineages. (Demography, I might add, at least today, provides no explanation.) Similar ritual partnerships are found across the Sepik region, including Abelam (Kaberry 1940–41, 256; Forge 1972, 535), Wogeo (Hogbin 1970), Banaro (Thurnwald 1916), Ilahita Arapesh (Tuzin 1976, chaps. 8–9), Manambu (Harrison 1990), Kwanga (Brison 1992, 126–38), Ambonwari (Telban 1996a), Mundugumor (Mead 1935b, 169; McDowell 1976), and Mountain Arapesh (Mead 1935b, 22).

2. In some Iatmul villages (Bateson 1932, 1936; Rubel and Rosman 1978, 44–50; Wassmann 1991, 23), tshambela partners (1) formally participate in male initiation and naven rites, (2) are forbidden from quarreling and making brideprice demands, and (3) conduct food exchanges that explicitly differ from those that occur between men in the same initiation cohort (men called *tambinien*). None of these three characteristics applies to tshambela in Tambunum.

3. These debates were a grotesque commentary on everyday speech. Orators seemingly slapped their ideas into Tuatmeli's anus and out of the spirit's mouth. Here, as it were, men spoke from the bowels rather than their "hearts," which is the bodily locus of rational choice.

4. Harrison also claims for Avatip that these cannibalistic meals were ideological assertions that the village could act as a unified political unit when in practice the polity was little more than a loose confederation of ever-feuding descent groups (see also Harrison 1985a).

5. By contrast, personal adornment on Manam Island (Lutkehaus 1995a, 222) and among the Highland Waghi (O'Hanlon 1989, 8) is said to expose rather than to mask the body.

6. Among Manambu, the cognate term *simbuk* refers to a hereditary officeholder (Harrison 1990, 106–12).

7. By the same logic, a man can ask his tshambela to retrieve disgruntled wives who have fled. In Kararau, in lieu of a formal divorce, a husband may hold aloft a net bag filled with betel and tobacco and call out the name of his primary tshambela (Hauser-Schäublin 1977, 133).

8. Melanesians commonly state that they are unable to apprehend or intuit the motivations of others (see Herdt 1989, 33–35).

9. There are two broad anthropological approaches to shame. The classic Culture and Personality views of Mead (1937) and Benedict (1946) focused on the relationship between shame and social control. Contemporary psychological anthropologists, however, like many clinical psychoanalysts, tend to emphasize shame as a component in the early socialization of gender identity, sexuality, and bodily functions (e.g., Piers and Singer 1953; Spiro 1965; Anthony 1981; Wurmser 1981; Obeyesekere 1981, 1984; Broucek 1982; Coleman 1985; Kinston 1987; Lewis 1987; Creighton 1990).

10. While men *do* comport themselves with an aggressive swagger, they do *not* ordinarily engage in competitive bravado unless prompted by the unusual boasting of a rival. This explains the immorality of excessive drinking: drunkenness can lead to unprovoked, obstreperous, and intimidating assertions of self-importance.

11. Nonverbal swagger can be equally dishonorable: a man who walks through the entire length of the cult house appears to "lay claim to the whole building as his personal property" (Bateson 1936, 123).

12. To borrow from Girard ([1972] 1977), tshambela behavior initiates, enacts, and finally resolves a "sacrificial crisis" that arises from "mimetic desire."

13. Eastern Iatmul are contemptuous of their bush-dwelling neighbors who lack regular baths and neither swim nor paddle canoes.

14. With regard to toilet training, Bateson (1936, 254) offered a suggestive observation that remains true: "Currency and trade and the accumulation of wealth could never be described as the major pre-occupations of the Iatmul. It might be worth enquiring into the relationship between cultural emphasis upon economic aspects of behaviour and the type of personality called anal in psychoanalytic jargon." Anthropological explorations of this relationship outside the Sepik include Dundes (1979, 1984, 1997a), Epstein (1979), Parin, Morgenthaler, and Parin-Matthey (1980), Weiner (1995a), and Clark (1995); see also Borneman (1976) and, for a contrary view, Lévi-Strauss ([1985] 1988).

15. The antimaternal inflection of witchcraft is heightened when the witch conceals her victim's feces behind the cooking hearth of another woman. Her unknowing cooking thus produces nutritive meals as well as fatal magic.

16. Mediterranean men also associate shame with passive homosexuality and feminization (Gilmore 1987a, 1987b, 1987c)—as well as with erotic honor. Eastern Iatmul men do not, however, unlike iai women, insult the sexual skills of their same-gendered rivals. In the Mediterranean, too, shame is related to the "evil eye" (Gilmore 1987a, 162–66; Dundes 1992). This concept is also absent in the Sepik despite the widespread importance of visual concealment for Melanesian gender relations (see Herdt 1981, 284–87; Tuzin 1995).

17. In the Murik village of Darapap, a small door at the rear of the cult house is called the "anal penis" (Lipset 1997, 188). Through this door enter women who must sexually oblige their husbands' cult partners.

18. Eastern Iatmul are not alone in tying feces and anal symbolism to male shame (e.g., Valentine 1963, 451; Obeyesekere 1984, 505).

19. Among Kwoma, by contrast, "no stigma is attached to begging for food" (Whiting 1941, 42).

20. A similar logic may explain why tshambela in Kandingei do not "offer each other food already broken such as half flat cakes of sago" (Wassmann 1991, 23).

21. Rubel and Rosman (1978, 46) claim that Iatmul initiation moieties "feast each other and exchange big yams, sago, live pigs, chickens, ducks, and coconuts." In Tambunum, this characterization applies instead to the Mboey Wai and Nganga Wai moieties. The names of these groups refer respectively to the maxilla and mandible of a crocodile spirit. Mboey Wai, the elder brother or large group (*numa angke*), exceeds in membership Nganga Wai, the younger brother or small group (*mak angke*). These patrilineal divisions cross-cut clans and lineages, as well as the initiation moieties. However, many men today confuse the crocodile and initiation groups; during many ceremonies there is no consensus concerning which of the two systems is in operation.

22. Each moiety is prohibited from bathing at the riverbank gardens of the other. The point of this enigmatic rule may be to prevent the two groups from laying waste to each other's gardens through magic or outright destruction.

Chapter 9

1. Houseman and Severi (1998, 60–63, 132) also propose a relational template for naven that hinges on the symmetry between father's sister (*iau*) and mother's brother (*wau*). But the amitate is an entirely minor figure in the Eastern Iatmul naven.

2. Houseman and Severi (1998, 96. n 22) dismiss in a mere footnote the efforts of Forge (1971) and myself (chap. 7) at interpreting the symbolism and cultural meanings of Iatmul marriage. For them, as for Lévi-Strauss, the kinship system is always primary. They also disregard the oedipal dimensions of iai marriage (Houseman and Severi 1998, 114). Both omissions are unwarranted.

3. Although we remain in disagreement on gender and naven (see Houseman and Severi 1998, 215–18), I am grateful to Houseman and Severi for providing me with a pre-publication draft of their book which enabled me, I hope, to clarify my thinking on this topic.

4. Large-scale naven rites are carefully planned so participants can assemble cash, pigs, food, beer, clothing, baskets, and fishing spears for the concluding exchanges. In Kandingei (Wassmann 1991, 36), there is a distinction between naven such as Bateson described and *sorak*, a rite that has the same honorific intent but entails a slightly different repertoire of behaviors. In Tambunum, this distinction is unmarked; all such rites are simply classed as *naven* or *sola naven* (*sola* roughly translates as happy).

5. Weiss (1987b, 174) also noticed, further upriver, that naven was a ritual largely defined by the actions of women. In Tambunum, it is useful to note, both real and classificatory iai women participate in naven. But this genealogical distinction is unimportant during the rite. Most of the iai who do participate, though, are elder women. On the "smallest possible" unit for a naven in Palimbei, see Stanek (1983b, 170) and Weiss (1987b, 185).

6. Despite female licentiousness during naven, women do not display large penises as per female initiation rites among Yangoru Boiken (Roscoe 1995a, 67) and Murik (Barlow 1995, 105).

7. In one myth, when a woman detects her husband snooping on her magical feathered cloak, she slips on the garment and, hovering in the air, threatens to leave him. The husband replies "*lan nyiin to!* Please come back!"

8. Similar honorific gestures occurred among Manambu (Harrison (1993a, 82) and especially the Mundugumor (McDowell 1991, 69, 121, 125, 143, 262); for a non-Sepik example, see Battaglia (1990, 97).

9. When I asked women if, in the role of the iai, their naven antics were fueled by the discrepancy between their own daily chores and the more sporadic labors of men, the answer was "no."

10. During the rites observed by Bateson (1936, 21–22, 215–16), the father's sister, who again is a minimal figure in the Eastern Iatmul naven, identified with her brother and aggressively beat his son. Thus she seemingly magnified, but did not mock, masculinity and fatherhood. Perhaps, too, she dramatized her brother's oedipal aggression which he himself cannot directly express lest he threaten the reproduction of patriliny.

11. Van Gennep's ([1909] 1960) global survey of "rites of passage" reports that Bulgarians spat on newborns and their mothers in "rites of incorporation" (45); spitting down the throat had the same meaning for the Islamic Isawa of Morocco (98). West Africans and "Gypsies," however, spat as a "rite of separation" (98). In Melanesia, Mundugumor spat on captives as an insult (McDowell 1991, 71), while Gnau (Lewis 1980, 76, 83–84, 182–83), Yafar (Juillerat 1996), and Sambia (Herdt 1981, 240–41) spit during male initiation.

12. Spittle is *tsiipmia;* chewed nut is *kisalagwi,* or "chewed floating island." (For the feminine suffix *-agwi,* see chap. 4.) Linguistically, the expectorant is feminine.

13. Men in Kararau believe that women use menstrual blood in sorcery (not witchcraft); women deny it (Hauser-Schäublin 1977, 116).

14. Conversely, Yafar symbolically coat young men with maternal blood in order to develop their manhood (Juillerat 1996, 398–404).

15. All contact between the iai woman and their alters during naven is mediated by fronds, spittle, and mud. This ritual requirement, which until now has remained unnoticed, evidences the problematic status of self-assertions in the culture, which I discussed in chapter 8.

16. The pidgin word *bagarap* derives from the British-Australian phrase "to bugger up," which in this context, for reasons that will become clear later in the chapter, might best be rendered as "all fucked up."

17. One man, though, reported that the first wife can hear her husband's flatulence since she is a wainjiimot wife. He linked this attribution to the husband's premier sexual experience within marriage. Other men refuted this statement—a few even admitted to refraining from taking meals with all categories of women lest they inadvertently expel gas. They did not, however, inform their female kin of this routine (relatedly, see Herdt 1981, 224; McDowell 1991, 129–30).

18. In this regard, the comments of a woman in Palimbei are suggestive (Weiss 1987b, 183). She stated that the mother gives food to her children; if they have problems, they turn to her. "A child never forgets all that his mother did to insure his well-being." After a pause, she then said, "I know that men are jealous of women," which she fol-

lowed shortly thereafter with the statement, "women have *naven* and the men have initiation."

19. I do not wish to unduly simplify Houseman and Severi's complex logic. They are not claiming that naven merely juxtaposes these different relationships. Rather, they see the ritual as differentiating between the two relational modes *and* establishing a sequential linkage between them. This process, moreover, condenses into a single drama Bateson's two forms of schismogenesis, symmetrical and complementary.

20. On Tubetube island in the Massim, mothers "give birth, nourish and sustain their children. Witches make women barren, steal the lives of children and destroy crops" (Macintyre 1987, 215). For the "destructive mother image" in Melanesian witchcraft, see Stephen (1987); Willis (1995) offers a related, Kleinian inquiry into witchcraft in early modern England, while Roper (1994) focuses on issues relating to preoedipal motherhood and uterine fertility.

21. On Malekula, an island in Vanuatu, men attempt to annihilate their fears of devouring motherhood through boar-sacrifice (Layard 1955).

22. Dundes (1979, 419) concludes that potlatch "is an anal equivalent of female parturition."

23. Gregor (1985, 129) describes similar images among the Mehinaku of the Amazon.

24. The face of the awan (discussed in chap. 4) also appears on an ancestral island whose ability to bring forth eggs of land is the prize sought by crocodilian ancestors. The presence of the humorous awan during naven appears to mock this masculine goal.

25. Handelman (1981, 367; see also 1991) echoes Bakhtin by writing "the ritual-clown type is continuously completing itself, but it remains permanently unfinished." Ironically, Handelman's (1979) earlier work on naven failed to discuss the awan figure since she is largely absent from Bateson's publications. Yet Handelman (1979, 179–80) did claim correctly that the -*awan* suffix for male matrinames reflects "the immanent transmutability" of the avunculate relationship.

26. For other Sepik clowns, see Mitchell (1992) and especially Hogbin (1970, 58–71) who interpreted a female "spirit monster" on Wogeo Island as pantomiming the gait of a pregnant women; its name, *lewa,* means "mask." Outside the region, on Tubetube, female clowns are "an essential inverse of the antisocial witch" (Macintyre 1992, 143)—yet the witch is herself an inversion of motherhood (see n. 20 this chapter).

27. My use of Lévi-Strauss here is not an endorsement of his universal thesis that women are exchanged as "signs" of masculine privilege during exogamous marriage (see Rubin 1975; Collier and Rosaldo 1981, 315).

28. The concept of "opportunism" (Houseman and Severi 1998, 82), however, is slightly amiss in this context. From Bateson's (1936, 218) perspective, the expansiveness of naven mirrors the "hypertrophic" pattern of Iatmul thought or eidos.

29. Abelam men cultivate long yams as a form of androgenesis (Hauser-Schäublin 1995, 43). They would no more eat their own tubers than commit incest (see also Mead 1940a, 352–53). Instead, men exchange yams with partners in a feast that resembles marriage—but also incest since the meal forges a consubstantial bond between male partners.

30. During major totemic and cosmological rituals, too, women may topple before the costumed impersonations of clan spirits. The sister's son during naven may also step over his mothers' brothers (which I never witnessed), and, in Kararau, brides during wedding processions walk atop other women (Hauser-Schäublin 1977, 96).

Hauser-Schäublin interprets the latter as celebrating not the bride's own birth but her promise to bear children.

31. European folklore also assigns notions of sexuality and incest to images of "stepping over" (Róheim 1922) and, relatedly, lifting the bride over a threshold (Crooke 1902).

32. Chambri also possess a ritual repertoire of birthing inversions. Elder women crawl through the legs of their juniors to communicate "unity through a collapse of generational difference" (Errington and Gewertz 1987c, 158 n. 6; 1987b). Likewise, Mead (1935b, 241) observed "masked figures . . . clowning and pantomiming their way among the groups of dancing women, who periodically dive between their legs, or break their beautifully etched lime-gourds in a shower of white powder."

33. Bateson (1936, 214–15) interpreted public disrobing among Iatmul as variously indicating joy, sorrow, self-abnegation, and exuberance.

Chapter 10

1. Houseman and Severi (1998, 207) analyze nggariik in terms of a wider ritual symmetry between the avunculate and amitate. This perspective is invalid on two accounts for Tambunum. First, as I noted in chapter 9, the father's sister is an entirely peripheral figure during the Eastern Iatmul rite. Second, it dilutes the emotional and semiotic distinctiveness of nggariik by viewing the gesture as merely one of many equal elements in the wider class of ritual actions.

2. Further upriver, uncles do slide their buttocks down the legs of nieces (e.g., Houseman and Severi 1998, 50; relatedly, see Bateson 1936, 17–18).

3. A mother's brother's wife (mbora), for example, can shoulder and then nggariik the avunculate's niece. Yet women in Tambunum do not dance and sing their own private naven as reported by Bateson (1936, 16) for other Iatmul villages.

4. The word nggariik, unless otherwise specified, will refer solely to the uncle's pantomime.

5. Women give birth inside domestic houses while squatting and grasping a horizontal bamboo pole. During delivery, they often scream insults at their husbands who, of course, are nowhere to be seen.

6. Men on Manam Island, attired as women, "pantomimed the 'birth' of a canoe—metaphorically represented by the halyard (moaboa), phallus-shaped piece of wood attached to the mast . . . which they called their 'child'" (Lutkehaus 1995b, 199).

7. Sambia men worry that women's vaginas may overheat and cook their penises, boiling out all of their semen during intercourse (Herdt 1981, 250).

8. While Kristeva is not normally linked to Bateson, she did pay brief tribute to his ideas on logic, paradox, and metalanguage in relation to psychoanalysis (Kristeva 1984).

9. Houseman and Severi (1998, 70–72) argue that the uncle's role in naven is a direct counterpart of the nephew's duty in other ritual settings to identify with matri-spirits by wearing the uncle's totemic masks, blowing his flutes, and so forth. Both dramas, they contend, express different linkages of descent and kinship. Yet this suggestion is valid only if we narrow the meanings of nggariik to a straightforward assertion of moral parturition. As a gesture of defilement and shame, as well as homoerotic taboo and unparalleled emotional intensity, nggariik must instead be situated in a broader cultural symbolism of masculinity rather than a matrix of social organization.

10. D'Amato (1979), despite his undue reliance on Bateson's 1958 Epilogue, is on the right track when he argues that naven sacrifices the identity of the sister's son.

11. Ilahita Arapesh men, swept away by Christian millenarianism, divulged their cult secrets to women. Women's response? That "men's ritual understandings were variously irrelevant, hostile, and fraudulent; mostly, though, they were unimpressed" (Tuzin 1997, 161).

12. The myths and obscenities of Ilahita Arapesh men reveal a related image: an *anus dentatus* (Tuzin 1997, 81). Eastern Iatmul have no such notion. Nonetheless, it is suggestive that the rear entrance of a house mother in Tambunum, which can be envisioned as her anus, may be surrounded by ornamental crocodile teeth (chap. 5).

13. Here, the logic behind the maternal role of the uncle during nggariik includes the brother-sister identification. At the same time, the nephew identifies with his father and portrays the uncle's "husband" (Bateson 1936, chap. 14).

14. Paul's (1991) "anti-oedipal" theory of social integration cites Dundes (1976b) and builds on Freud (1921).

15. Newton (1987) sees a parallel between naven and a Manambu rite that protects brothers from supernatural danger if they commit incest with their sisters. One Manambu man, echoing the anxieties of his Iatmul peers, reported that a women's vagina "permanently gapes open" after incest, "like a devouring mouth" (1987, 255).

16. As Houseman and Severi (1998) detail, both naven and Bateson's analysis bear relation to Lévi-Strauss's (1963b, 40–49) famous "atom of kinship." Yet this atom, I maintain, offers limited insight into nggariik since it presupposes a static configuration of dichotomous gender and allows for little psychodynamic desire (see also Gillison 1987).

Epilogue

1. Tuzin (1992b, 258), drawing on Devereux's (1953) "Laius complex," argues that the arrows shot toward the solar breast are "an act of masculine power and assertion against a feminine threat that is, by psychodynamic reckoning, castrative." For "protection and guidance," the Yafar youth has but one choice: "commit himself to membership in the solidary male society."

2. The scholarly literature on masculinity, which is also discussed by Tuzin (1997) with regard to another Sepik society, is vast and growing, e.g., Brandes (1980), Fogel, Lane, and Liebert (1986), Herzfeld (1985), Gilmore (1987a), Hudson and Jacot (1991), Breen (1993), Schofield (1993), Brod and Kaufman (1994), Cornwall and Lindisfarne (1994), Eilberg-Schwartz (1994), Frosh (1994), Badinter (1995), Almeida (1996), Kimmel (1996), Mosse (1996), Smith (1996), and Boyarin (1997).

References

Ackerman, Charles. 1976. Omaha and "Omaha." *American Ethnologist* 3:555–72.

Aitken, Thomas C. 1983. Marriage and Bride Price. *Bikmaus* 44:17–23.

Allen, Benedict. 1987. *Into the Crocodile Nest: A Journey inside New Guinea.* London: Paladin.

Allen, Michael. 1988. The 'Hidden Power' of Male Ritual: The North Vanuatu Evidence. In *Myths of Matriarchy Reconsidered,* ed. D. Gewertz, 74–96. Sydney: University of Sydney Press.

———. 1998. Male Cults Revisited: The Politics of Blood versus Semen. *Oceania* 68:189–99.

Almeida, Miguel Vale de. 1996. *The Hegemonic Male: Masculinity in a Portuguese Town.* Providence: Berghahn Books.

Andresen, Jeffry J. 1980. Rapunzel: The Symbolism of the Cutting of Hair. *Journal of the American Psychoanalytic Association* 28:69–88.

Anthony, E. James. 1981. Shame, Guilt, and the Feminine Self in Psychoanalysis. In *Object and Self: A Developmental Approach,* ed. S. Tuttman, C. Kaye, and M. Zimmerman, 191–234. New York: International Universities Press.

Apte, Mahadev L. 1985. *Humor and Laughter: An Anthropological Approach.* Ithaca: Cornell University Press.

Bachelard, Gaston. 1964. *The Psychoanalysis of Fire.* Trans. Alan C. M. Ross. Boston: Beacon. (Orig. French ed. 1938.)

Badinter, Elisabeth. 1997. *XY: On Masculine Identity.* New York: Columbia University Press.

Bakhtin, Mikhail. 1984a. *Rabelais and His World.* Trans. Helene Iswolsky. Bloomington: Indiana University Press.

———. 1984b. *Problems of Dostoevsky's Poetics.* Trans. Caryl Emerson. Minneapolis: University of Minnesota Press.

Bakwin, H. 1940. Review of *Naven. Psychoanalytic Quarterly* 9:555–57.

Barlow, Kathleen. 1985. The Social Context of Infant Feeding in the Murik Lakes of Papua New Guinea. In *Infant Care and Feeding in the South Pacific,* ed. L. B. Marshall, 137–54. New York: Gordon and Breach.

———. 1990. The Dynamics of Siblingship: Nurturance and Authority in Murik Society. In *Sepik Heritage: Tradition and Change in Papua New Guinea,* ed. N. Lutkehaus, C. Kaufmann, W. E. Mitchell, D. Newton, L. Osmundsen, and M. Schuster, 325–36. Durham: Carolina Academic Press.

———. 1992. "Dance When I Die!": Context and Role in the Clowning of Murik Women. In *Clowning as Critical Practice: Performance Humor in the South Pacific,* ed. W. E. Mitchell, 58–87. Pittsburgh: University of Pittsburgh Press.

———. 1995. Achieving Womanhood and the Achievements of Women in Murik Society: Cult Initiation, Gender Complementarity, and the Prestige of Women. In *Gender Rituals: Female Initiation in Melanesia,* ed. N. C. Lutkehaus and P. B. Roscoe, 85–112. New York: Routledge.

Barlow, Kathleen, and David Lipset. 1997. Dialogics of Material Culture: Male and Female in Murik Outrigger Canoes. *American Ethnologist* 24:4–36.

Barth, Frederik. 1975. *Ritual and Knowledge among the Baktaman of New Guinea.* Cambridge: Cambridge University Press.

———. 1990. The Guru and the Conjurer: Transaction in Knowledge and the Shaping of Culture in Southeast Asia and Melanesia. *Man,* n.s., 25:640–53.

Bataille, Georges. 1986. *Erotism: Death and Sensuality.* Trans. Mary Dalwood. San Francisco: City Lights Books. (Orig. French ed. 1962.)

———. 1992. *Theory of Religion.* Trans. Robert Hurley. New York: Zone Books. (Orig. French ed. 1973.)

Bateson, Gregory. 1931. Head Hunting on the Sepik River. *Man* 31:49.

———. 1932. Social Structure of the Iatmul People of the Sepik River. *Oceania* 3:245–90, 401–52.

———. 1935a. Culture Contact and Schismogenesis. *Man* 35:178–83.

———. 1935b. Music in New Guinea. *The Eagle* (St. John's College, Cambridge) 48:158–70.

———. 1936. *Naven: A Survey of the Problems Suggested by a Composite Picture of the Culture of a New Guinea Tribe Drawn from Three Points of View.* Cambridge: Cambridge University Press.

———. 1941. The Frustration-Aggression Hypothesis and Culture. *Psychological Review* 48:350–55.

———. 1946. Exhibition Review: Arts of the South Seas. *Art Bulletin* 28:119–23.

———. 1949. Bali: The Value System of a Steady State. In *Social Structure: Studies Presented to A.R. Radcliffe-Brown,* ed. M. Fortes, 35–53. Oxford: Clarendon Press.

———. 1958. *Naven: A Survey of the Problems Suggested by a Composite Picture of the Culture of a New Guinea Tribe Drawn from Three Points of View.* 2d rev. ed., with a new Epilogue. Stanford: Stanford University Press.

———. Unpublished. Iatmul fieldnotes. Library of Congress, Washington, D.C. Courtesy of the Institute for Intercultural Studies, Inc., New York.

Bateson, Gregory, and Mary Catherine Bateson. 1987. *Angel's Fear: Toward an Epistemology of the Sacred.* New York: Macmillan.

Bateson, Gregory, D. D. Jackson, J. Haley, and J. Weakland. 1956. Toward a Theory of Schizophrenia. *Behavioral Science* 1:251–64.

Bateson, Gregory, and Margaret Mead. 1942. *Balinese Character: A Photographic Analysis.* New York: New York Academy of Science.

Battaglia, Debbora. 1990. *On the Bones of the Serpent: Person, Memory, and Mortality in Sabarl Island Society.* Chicago: University of Chicago Press.

Benedict, Ruth. 1934. *Patterns of Culture.* New York: New American Library.

———. 1946. *The Chrysanthemum and the Sword.* Boston: Houghton Mifflin.

Bennett, Lynn. 1983. *Dangerous Wives and Sacred Sisters: Social and Symbolic Roles of High-Caste Women in Nepal.* New York: Columbia University Press.

Berg, Charles. 1951. *The Unconscious Significance of Hair.* London: Allen and Unwin.

Berman, Morris. 1981. *The Reenchantment of the World.* Ithaca: Cornell University Press.

Bettelheim, Bruno. 1954. *Symbolic Wounds: Puberty Rites and the Envious Male.* New York: Free Press.

Biersack, Aletta. 1983. Bound Blood: Paiela 'Conception' Theory Interpreted. *Mankind* 14:85–100.

———. 1996. Word Made Flesh: Religion, the Economy, and the Body in the Papua New Guinea Highlands. *History of Religions* 36:86–111.

———. 1998. Horticulture and Hierarchy: The Youthful Beautification of the Body in the Paiela and Porgera Valleys. In *Adolescence in Pacific Island Societies,* ed. G. Herdt and S. C. Leavitt, 71–91. Pittsburgh: University of Pittsburgh Press.

Bloch, Maurice, and S. Guggenheim. 1981. Compadrazgo, Baptism, and the Symbolism of Second Birth. *Man* 16:376–86.

Bonnemere, Pascale. 1990. Considérations relatives aux représentations des substances corporelles en Nouvelle-Guinée. *L'Homme* 114:101–20.

Boon, James A. 1984. Folly, Bali, and Anthropology, or Satire across Cultures. In *Text, Play, and Story,* ed. E. Bruner, 156–77. Washington: Proceedings of the American Ethnological Society for 1983.

———. 1985. Mead's Mediations: Some Semiotics from the Sepik, by way of Bateson, on to Bali. In *Semiotic Mediations,* ed. B. Mertz and R. Parmentier, 333–57. New York: Academic Press.

Borneman, Ernest. 1976. *The Psychoanalysis of Money.* New York: Urizen Books.

Bourdieu, Pierre. 1977. *Outline of a Theory of Practice.* trans. Richard Nice. Cambridge: Cambridge University Press. (Orig. French ed. 1972.)

Bowden, Ross. 1982. Lévi-Strauss in the Sepik: A Kwoma Myth of the Origin of Marriage. *Oceania* 52:294–302.

———. 1983a. Kwoma Terminology and Marriage Alliance: The 'Omaha' Problem Revisited. *Man,* n.s., 18:745–65.

———. 1983b. *Yena: Art and Ceremony in a Sepik Society.* Oxford: Pitt Rivers Museum.

———. 1984. Art and Gender Ideology in the Sepik. *Man,* n.s., 19:445–58.

———. 1988. Kwoma Death Payments and Alliance Theory. *Ethnology* 27:271–90.

———. 1991. Historical Ethnography or Conjectural History? *Oceania* 61:218–35.

Bowers, C. A. 1990. Implications of Gregory Bateson's Ideas for a Semiotic of Art Education. *Studies in Art Education* 31:69–77.

Boyarin, Daniel. 1997. *Unheroic Conduct: The Rise of Heterosexuality and the Invention of the Jewish Man.* Berkeley: University of California Press.

Brandes, S. 1980. *Metaphors of Masculinity: Sex and Status in Andalusian Folklore.* Philadelphia: University of Pennsylvania Press.

Breen, Dana. 1993. *The Gender Conundrum: Contemporary Psychoanalytic Perspectives on Femininity and Masculinity.* New York: Routledge.

Briggs, Charles. 1993. Personal Sentiments and Polyphonic Voices in Warau Women's Ritual Wailing: Music and Poetics in a Critical and Collective Discourse. *American Ethnologist* 95:929–57.

Brison, Karen J. 1991. Community and Prosperity: Social Movements among the Kwanga of Papua New Guinea. *Contemporary Pacific* 3:325–55.

————. 1992. *Just Talk: Gossip, Meetings, and Power in a Papua New Guinean Village.* Berkeley: University of California Press.

————. 1995. Changing Constructions of Masculinity in a Sepik Society. *Ethnology* 34:155–75.

Brod, Harry, and Michael Kaufman. 1994. *Theorizing Masculinities.* London: Sage.

Broucek, Francis J. 1982. Shame and Its Relationship to Early Narcissistic Developments. *International Journal of Psycho-Analysis* 63:369–78.

Brown, Paula. 1987. New Men and Big Men: Emerging Social Stratification in the Third World, A Case Study from the New Guinea Highlands. *Ethnology* 26:87–106.

Burton, R. V., and J. W. M. Whiting. 1961. The Absent Father and Cross-Sex Identity. *Merrill-Palmer Quarterly* 73:960–61.

Busby, Cecilia. 1997. Permeable and Partible Persons: A Comparative Analysis of Gender and Body in South India and Melanesia. *Journal of the Royal Anthropological Institute,* n.s., 3:261–78.

Carroll, Michael P. 1986. *The Cult of the Virgin Mary: Psychological Origins.* Princeton: Princeton University Press.

————. 1987. Heaven-Sent Wounds: A Kleinian View of the Stigmata in the Catholic Mystical Tradition. *Journal of Psychoanalytic Anthropology* 10:17–38.

Carson, Janet, and Stephen Hugh-Jones. 1995. *About the House: Lévi-Strauss and Beyond.* Cambridge: Cambridge University Press.

Charles, Lucile Hoerr. 1945. The Clown's Function. *Journal of American Folklore* 58:25–34.

Chasseguet-Smirgel, Janine. 1970. *Female Sexuality: New Psychoanalytic Views.* Ann Arbor: University of Michigan Press. (Orig. French ed. 1964.)

————. 1985. *The Ego Ideal: A Psychoanalytic Essay on the Malady of the Ideal.* New York: W.W. Norton.

Chodorow, Nancy. 1978. *The Reproduction of Mothering: Psychoanalysis and the Sociology of Gender.* Berkeley: University of California Press.

Chowning, Ann. 1987. 'Women Are Our Business': Women, Exchange and Prestige in Kove. In *Dealing with Inequality: Analysing Gender Relations in Melanesia and Beyond,* ed. M. Strathern, 130–49. Cambridge: Cambridge University Press.

Cixous, Hélène. 1981. Castration or Decapitation? Trans. Annette Kuhn. *Signs* 7:41–55. (Orig. French ed. 1976.)

Clark, Jeffrey. 1995. Shit Beautiful: Tambu and Kina Revisited. *Oceania* 65:195–211.

Clay, Brenda Johnson. 1977. *Pinikindu: Maternal Nurture, Paternal Substance.* Chicago: University of Chicago Press.

————. 1986. *Mandak Realities: Person and Power in New Ireland.* New Brunswick, N.J.: Rutgers University Press.

Cohler, Bertram J. 1992. Intent and Meaning in Psychoanalysis and Cultural Study. In *New Directions in Psychological Anthropology,* ed. T. Schwartz, G. M. White, and C. A. Lutz, 269–93. Cambridge: Cambridge University Press.

Coiffier, Christian. 1992a. Rituels et identité culturelle Iatmul (Vallée du Sépik-Papouasie Nouvelle-Guinée). *Bulletin de L'École Française d'Extrême-Orient* 79:131–48.

————. 1992b. Changements des représentations relatives à l'habitat chez les Iatmul de Papouasie Nouvelle-Guinée. *Journal de la Société des Océanistes* 94:45–56.

————. 1995. "Les îles flottantes du fleuve Sépik": Note concernant l'article de Henri

Lavondès: Jules Verne, les Polynésiens et le motif de l'île mouvante. *Journal de la Société des Océanistes* 100–101:238–40.

Coleman, Mary. 1985. Shame: A Powerful Underlying Factor in Violence and War. *Journal of Psychoanalytic Anthropology* 8:67–79.

Collier, Jane, and Michelle Z. Rosaldo. 1981. Politics and Gender in Simple Societies. In *Sexual Meanings: The Cultural Construction of Gender and Sexuality,* ed. S. B. Ortner and H. Whitehead, 275–329. New York: Cambridge University Press.

Collier, Jane, and Sylvia Junko Yanagisako, eds. 1987. *Gender and Kinship: Essays towards a Unified Analysis.* Stanford: Stanford University Press.

Connell, John. 1979. The Emergence of a Peasantry in Papua New Guinea. *Peasant Studies* 8:103–37.

Connell, R. W. 1995. *Masculinities.* Berkeley: University of California Press.

Cornwall, Andrea, and Nancy Lindisfarne, eds. 1994. *Dislocating Masculinity: Comparative Ethnographies (Male Orders).* New York: Routledge.

Counts, David R., and Dorothy A. Counts. 1992. Exaggeration and Reversal: Clowning among the Lusi-Kaliai. In *Clowning as Critical Practice: Performance Humor in the South Pacific,* ed. W. E. Mitchell, 88–103. Pittsburgh: University of Pittsburgh Press.

Crapanzano, Vincent. 1980. *Tuhami: Portrait of a Moroccan.* Chicago: University of Chicago Press.

Creed, Gerald W. 1984. Sexual Subordination: Institutionalized Homosexuality and Social Control in Melanesia. *Ethnology* 23:157–76.

Creighton, Millie R. 1990. Revisiting Shame and Guilt Cultures: A Forty-Year Pilgrimage. *Ethos* 18:279–307.

Crooke, B. A. 1902. The Lifting of the Bride. *Folk-Lore* 13:226–51.

Crumrine, N. Ross. 1969. Capakoba, the Mayo Easter Ceremonial Impersonator: Explanations of Ritual Clowning. *Journal for the Scientific Study of Religion* 8:1–22.

Csordas, Thomas J. 1990. Embodiment as a Paradigm for Anthropology. *Ethos* 18:5–47.

Curtain, Richard L. 1988. The Colonial State, Migrant Labor, and Class Formation in Papua New Guinea. In *New Perspectives on Social Class and Socioeconomic Development in the Periphery,* ed. N. W. Keith and N. Z. Keith. New York: Greenwood Press.

Daelemans, Sven, and Tullio Maranhao. 1990. Psychoanalytic Dialogue and the Dialogical Principle. In *The Interpretation of Dialogue,* ed. T. Maranhao, 219–41. Chicago: University of Chicago Press.

D'Amato, John. 1979. The Wind and the Amber: Notes on Headhunting and the Interpretation of Accounts. *Journal of Anthropological Research* 35:61–84.

Da Matta, Roberto. 1983. An Interpretation of Carnaval. *SubStance* 37/38:162–70.

Davis, Natalie Zemon. 1975. *Society and Culture in Early Modern France.* Stanford: Stanford University Press.

Delaney, Carol. 1998. *Abraham on Trial: The Social Legacy of Biblical Myth.* Princeton: Princeton University Press.

Derrida, Jacques. 1978. Structure, Sign, and Play in the Discourse of the Human Sciences. In *Writing and Difference,* 278–93. Trans. Alan Bass. Chicago: University of Chicago Press. (Orig. French ed. 1966.)

Devereux, George. 1953. Why Oedipus Killed Laius: A Note on the Complementary Oedipus Complex in Greek Drama. *International Journal of Psycho-Analysis* 34:132–41.

———. 1960. Retaliatory Homosexual Triumph over the Father: A Clinical Note on the Counteroedipal Sources of the Oedipus Complex. *International Journal of Psycho-Analysis* 41:157–61.

———. 1966. The Cannibalistic Impulses of Parents. *Psychoanalytic Forum* 1:114–24, 129–30.

———. 1978. Ethnopsychoanalytic Reflections on the Notion of Kinship. In *Ethnopsychoanalysis: Psychoanalysis and Anthropology as Complementary Frames of Reference*, 177–215. Berkeley: University of California Press. (Orig. French ed. 1965.)

De Vos, George A., and Marcelo M. Suarez-Orozco. 1987. Sacrifice and the Experience of Power. *Journal of Psychoanalytic Anthropology* 10:309–40.

Doane, Janice, and Devon Hodges. 1992. *From Klein to Kristeva: Psychoanalytic Feminism and the Search for the "Good Enough" Mother*. Ann Arbor: University of Michigan Press.

Dollard, John. 1937. Review of *Naven* by Gregory Bateson. *American Sociological Review* 2:567.

Doniger, Wendy. 1989. Review Article: Structuralist Universals versus Psychoanalytic Universals. *History of Religions* 28:267–81.

———. 1993. When a Lingam Is Just a Good Cigar: Psychoanalysis and Hindu Sexual Fantasies. *Psychoanalytic Study of Society* 18:81–103.

Douglas, Mary. 1966. *Purity and Danger: An Analysis of the Concepts of Pollution and Taboo*. London: Routledge and Kegan Paul.

———. 1970. *Natural Symbols: Explorations in Cosmology*. London: Barrie and Rockliff.

Dundes, Alan. 1962. Earth-Diver: Creation of the Mythopoeic Male. *American Anthropologist* 64:1032–51. (Reprinted in *Reader in Comparative Religion: An Anthropological Approach*, ed. W. A. Lessa and E. Z. Vogt, 4th ed., 174–85. New York: Harper Collins, 1979.)

———. 1963. Summoning Deity through Ritual Fasting. *American Imago* 20:213–20.

———. 1976a. Projection in Folklore: A Plea for Psychoanalytic Semiotics. *Modern Language Notes* 91:1500–1533. (Reprinted in *Interpreting Folklore*, 33–61. Bloomington: Indiana University Press, 1980.)

———. 1976b. A Psychoanalytic Study of the Bullroarer. *Man*, n.s., 11:220–38. (Reprinted in *Interpreting Folklore*, 176–98. Bloomington: Indiana University Press, 1980.)

———. 1979. Heads or Tails: A Psychoanalytic Study of Potlatch. *Journal of Psychological Anthropology* 2:395–424. (Reprinted in *Parsing through Customs: Essays by a Freudian Folklorist*, 47–81. Madison: University of Wisconsin Press, 1987.)

———. 1983. Couvade in Genesis. In *Studies in Aggadah and Jewish Folklore*, ed. K. Ben-Ami and J. Dan, 35–53. Jerusalem: Magnes Press. (Reprinted in *Parsing through Customs: Essays by a Freudian Folklorist*, 145–66. Madison: University of Wisconsin Press, 1987.)

———. 1984. *Life Is Like a Chicken Coop Ladder: A Study of German National Character through Folklore*. Detroit: Wayne State University Press.

———. 1986. The Flood as Male Creation. *Journal of Psychoanalytic Anthropology* 9:359–72. (Reprinted in *The Flood Myth*, ed. A. Dundes, 167–82. Berkeley: University of California Press, 1988.)

———. 1992. Wet and Dry, the Evil Eye: An Essay in Indo-European and Semitic Worldview. In *The Evil Eye: A Casebook*, ed. A. Dundes, 257–312. Madison: University of Wisconsin Press.

———. 1993. Gallus as Phallus: A Psychoanalytic Cross-Cultural Consideration of the Cockfight as Fowl Play. *Psychoanalytic Study of Society* 18:23–65. (Reprinted in *The Cockfight: A Casebook*, ed. A. Dundes, 241–82. Madison: University of Wisconsin Press, 1994.)

———. 1997a. *Two Tales of Crow and Sparrow: A Freudian Folkloristic Essay on Caste and Untouchability*. Lanham: Rowman and Littlefield.

———. 1997b. Traditional Male Combat: From Game to War. In *From Game to War and Other Psychoanalytic Essays on Folklore*, 25–45. Lexington: University Press of Kentucky.

Durkheim, Émile. 1995. *The Elementary Forms of Religious Life*. Trans. Karen E. Fields. New York: Free Press. (Orig. French ed. 1912.)

Edmunds, Lowell. 1985. *Oedipus: The Ancient Legend and Its Later Analogues*. Baltimore: Johns Hopkins University Press.

Edmunds, Lowell, and Alan Dundes, eds. 1983. *Oedipus: A Folklore Casebook*. New York: Garland.

Ehrenreich, Barbara. 1987. Foreword. In *Male Fantasies. Volume 1: Women, Floods, Bodies, History*. Klaus Theweleit, ix–xvii. Minneapolis: University of Minnesota Press.

Eilberg-Schwartz, Howard. 1994. *God's Phallus: And Other Problems for Men and Monotheism*. Boston: Beacon.

Eilberg-Schwartz, Howard, and Wendy Doniger, eds. 1995. *Off with Her Head! The Denial of Women's Identity in Myth, Religion, and Culture*. Berkeley: University of California Press.

Eliade, Mircea. 1958. *Patterns in Comparative Religion*. New York: Meridian.

Elkin, A. P. 1938. Review of *Naven*. *Oceania* 8:373–75.

Elliston, Deborah A. 1995. Erotic Anthropology: "Ritualized Homosexuality" in Melanesia and Beyond. *American Ethnologist* 22:848–67.

Epstein, A. L. 1979. Tambu: The Shell-Money of the Tolai. In *Fantasy and Symbol: Studies in Anthropological Interpretation*, ed. R. H. Hook, 149–205. London: Academic Press.

———. 1984. *The Experience of Shame in Melanesia: An Essay in the Anthropology of Affect*. Royal Anthropological Institute of Great Britain and Ireland, Occasional Paper No. 40.

———. 1992. *In the Midst of Life: Affect and Ideation in the World of the Tolai*. Berkeley: University of California Press.

Errington, Frederick, and Deborah Gewertz. 1987a. The Confluence of Powers: Entropy and Importation among the Chambri. *Oceania* 58:99–113.

———. 1987b. The Remarriage of Yebiwali: A Study of Dominance and False Consciousness in a Non-Western Society. In *Dealing with Inequality: Analysing Gender Relations in Melanesia and Beyond*, ed. M. Strathern, 63–88. Cambridge: Cambridge University Press.

———. 1987c. *Cultural Alternatives and a Feminist Anthropology: An Analysis of Culturally Constructed Gender Interests in Papua New Guinea*. Cambridge: Cambridge University Press.

———. 1989. Tourism and Anthropology in a Post-Modern World. *Oceania* 60:37–54.

———. 1995. *Articulating Change in the "Last Unknown."* Boulder: Westview.

———. 1996a. The Individuation of Tradition in a Papua New Guinean Modernity. *American Anthropologist* 98:114–26.

——. 1996b. On PepsiCo and Piety in a Papua New Guinea "Modernity." *American Ethnologist* 23:476–93.

Etchegoyen, R. Horacio, and Jorge L. Ahumada. 1990. Bateson and Matte-Blanco: Biologic and Bi-logic. *International Review of Psycho-Analysis* 17:493–502.

Eyre, Stephen L. 1992. Alliance through the Circulation of Men: A System of Name-Assigned Residence. *Ethnology* 31:277–90.

Fajans, Jane. 1983. Shame, Social Action, and the Person among the Baining. *Ethos* 11:166–80.

——. 1985. The Person in Social Context: The Social Character of Baining "Psychology." In *Person, Self, and Experience: Exploring Pacific Ethnopsychologies,* ed. G. M. White and J. Kirkpatrick, 367–97. Berkeley: University of California Press.

——. 1997. They Make Themselves: Work and Play among the Baining of Papua New Guinea. Chicago: University of Chicago Press.

Feldman, Harold. 1959. The Problem of Personal Names as Universal Elements in Culture. *American Imago* 16:237–50.

Firth, Stewart. 1983. *New Guinea under the Germans.* Port Moresby: Web Books.

Flax, Jane. 1990. *Thinking Fragments: Psychoanalysis, Feminism, and Postmodernism in the Contemporary West.* Berkeley: University of California Press.

Flugel, J. C. 1924. Polyphallic Symbolism and the Castration Complex. *International Journal of Psycho-Analysis* 5:155–96.

Fogel, Gerald I., Frederick M. Lane, and Robert S. Liebert. 1986. *The Psychologies of Men: New Psychoanalytic Perspectives.* New York: Basic Books.

Foley, William. 1986. *The Papuan Languages of New Guinea.* Cambridge: Cambridge University Press.

Forge, Anthony. 1966. Art and Environment in the Sepik. *Proceedings of the Royal Anthropological Institute for Great Britain and Ireland for 1965,* 23–31.

——. 1969. Moon Magic. *New Society* 355 (July): 87–88.

——. 1971. Marriage and Exchange in the Sepik: Comments on Francis Korn's Analysis of Iatmul Society. In *Rethinking Kinship and Marriage,* ed. R. Needham, 133–44. London: Tavistock.

——. 1972. The Golden Fleece. *Man,* n.s., 7:527–40.

——. 1973. Style and Meaning in Sepik Art. In *Primitive Art and Society,* ed. A. Forge, 170–92. London: Oxford University Press.

Fortes, Meyer. 1969. *Kinship and the Social Order: The Legacy of Lewis Henry Morgan.* Chicago: Aldine.

——. 1974. The First Born. *Journal of Child Psychology and Psychiatry* 15:81–104.

Fortune, Reo F. 1939. Arapesh Warfare. *American Anthropologist* 41:22–41.

Foucault, Michel. 1978. *History of Sexuality,* vol. 1. New York: Vintage.

——. 1979. *Discipline and Punish: The Birth of the Prison.* New York: Vintage.

Fox, James J. 1971. Sister's Child as Plant: Metaphors in an Idiom of Consanguinity. In *Rethinking Kinship and Marriage,* ed. R. Needham, 219–52. London: Tavistock.

Fox, James, ed. 1993. *Inside Austronesian Houses: Perspectives on Designs for Living.* Canberra: Australian National University.

Freud, Sigmund. 1900. *The Interpretation of Dreams.* In *The Standard Edition of the Complete Psychological Works of Sigmund Freud,* vols. IV and V, trans. and ed. James Strachey, 1958. London: Hogarth. (Hereafter referred to as *SE.*)

——. 1908. Character and Anal Eroticism. In *SE,* vol. 9, 167–75.

——. 1910. A Special Type of Choice of Object Made by Men. In *SE,* vol. 11, 163–75.

―――. 1912. On the Universal Tendency to Debasement in the Sphere of Love. In *SE*, vol. 11, 177–90.

―――. 1913. *Totem and Taboo.* In *SE*, vol. 13, 1–160.

―――. 1917. Mourning and Melancholia. In *SE*, vol. 14, 237–58.

―――. 1918. From the History of an Infantile Neurosis. In *SE*, vol. 17, 1–123.

―――. 1921. Group Psychology and the Analysis of the Ego. In *SE*, vol. 18, 67–143.

―――. 1922. Medusa's Head. In *SE*, vol. 18, 273–74.

―――. 1930. *Civilisation and Its Discontents.* In *SE*, vol. 21, 57–145.

―――. 1932. The Acquisition and Control over Fire. In *SE*, vol. 22, 183–93.

―――. 1938. Splitting of the Ego in the Defensive Process. In *SE*, vol. 23, 271–78.

Frosh, Stephen. 1994. *Sexual Difference: Masculinity and Psychoanalysis.* New York: Routledge.

Frye, Northrop. 1957. *Anatomy of Criticism.* Princeton: Princeton University Press.

Gallop, Jane. 1982. *The Daughter's Seduction: Feminism and Psychoanalysis.* Ithaca: Cornell University Press.

Geertz, Clifford. 1966a. Person, Time, and Conduct in Bali. Yale Southeast Asia Program, Cultural Report Series, #14. (Reprinted in *The Interpretation of Cultures*, 360–411. New York: Basic Books, 1973.)

―――. 1966b. Religion as a Cultural System. In *Anthropological Approaches to the Study of Religion*, ed. M. Banton, 1–46. London: Tavistock. (Reprinted in *The Interpretation of Cultures*, 87–125. New York: Basic Books, 1973.)

―――. 1972. Deep Play: Notes on the Balinese Cockfight. In *Daedalus* 101:1–37. (Reprinted in *The Interpretation of Cultures*, 412–53. New York: Basic Books, 1973.)

―――. 1988. *Works and Lives: The Anthropologist as Author.* Stanford: Stanford University Press.

Gell, Alfred F. 1975. *Metamorphosis of the Cassowaries: Umeda Society, Language and Ritual.* London: Athlone Press.

―――. 1992a. *The Anthropology of Time: Cultural Constructions of Temporal Maps and Images.* Oxford: Berg.

―――. 1992b. Inter-Tribal Commodity Barter and Reproductive Gift-Exchange in Old Melanesia. In *Barter, Exchange and Value: An Anthropological Approach,* ed. C. Humphrey and S. Hugh-Jones, 142–68. Cambridge: Cambridge University Press.

Gewertz, Deborah B. 1977a. "On Whom Depends the Action of the Elements": Debating among the Chambri People of Papua New Guinea. *Journal of the Polynesian Society* 86:339–53.

―――. 1977b. The Politics of Affinal Exchange: Chambri as a Client Market. *Ethnology* 16:285–98.

―――. 1978. The Myth of the Blood-Men: An Explanation of Chambri Warfare. *Journal of Anthropological Research* 34:577–88.

―――. 1982. The Father Who Bore Me. In *Rituals of Manhood: Male Initiation in Papua New Guinea,* ed. G. H. Herdt, 286–320. Berkeley: University of California Press.

―――. 1983. *Sepik River Societies: A Historical Ethnography of the Chambri and Their Neighbors.* New Haven: Yale University Press.

―――. 1984. The Tchambuli View of Persons: A Critique of Individualism in the Works of Mead and Chodorow. *American Anthropologist* 86:615–29.

―――. 1991. Symmetrical Schismogenesis Revisited? *Oceania* 61:236–39.

Gewertz, Deborah B., and Frederick K. Errington. 1991. *Twisted Histories, Altered Con-*

texts: Representing the Chambri in a World System. Cambridge: Cambridge University Press.

Gillison, Gillian. 1980. Images of Nature in Gimi Thought. In *Nature, Culture and Gender,* ed. C. MacCormack and M. Strathern, 143–73. Cambridge: Cambridge University Press.

———. 1987. Incest and the Atom of Kinship: The Role of the Mother's Brother in a New Guinea Highlands Society. *Ethos* 15:166–202.

———. 1994. Symbolic Homosexuality and Cultural Theory: The Unconscious Meaning of Sister Exchange among the Gimi of Highland New Guinea. In *Anthropology and Psychoanalysis: An Encounter through Culture,* ed. S. Heald and A. Deluz, 210–24. London: Routledge.

Gilmore, David D. 1987a. *Aggression and Community: Paradoxes of Andalusian Culture.* New Haven: Yale University Press.

———. 1987b. Introduction: The Shame of Dishonor. In *Honor and Shame and the Unity of the Mediterranean,* ed. D. D. Gilmore, 2–21. Washington, D.C.: American Anthropological Association.

———. 1987c. Honor, Honesty, Shame: Male Status in Contemporary Andalusia. In *Honor and Shame and the Unity of the Mediterranean,* ed. D. D. Gilmore, 90–103. Washington, D.C.: American Anthropological Association.

———. 1990. *Manhood in the Making: Cultural Concepts of Masculinity.* New Haven: Yale University Press.

———. 1996. Sexual Imagery in Spanish Carnival. In *Denying Biology: Essays on Gender and Pseudo-Procreation,* ed. W. Shapiro and U. Linke, 27–50. Lanham: University Press of America.

Girard, René. 1977. *Violence and the Sacred.* Trans. Patrick Gregory. Baltimore: Johns Hopkins University Press. (Orig. French ed. 1972.)

———. 1987. Discussion. In *Violent Origins: Walter Burkert, René Girard, and Jonathan Z. Smith on Ritual Killing and Cultural Formation,* ed. R. G. Hamerton-Kelly, 106–45. Stanford: Stanford University Press.

Gluckman, Max. 1945. *Rituals of Rebellion in South-East Africa.* Manchester: Manchester University Press.

———. 1956. *Custom and Conflict in Africa.* Oxford: Basil Blackwell.

Godelier, Maurice. 1986. *The Making of Great Men: Male Domination and Power among the New Guinea Baruya.* Trans. Rupert Swyer. Cambridge: Cambridge University Press. (Orig. French ed. 1982.)

Godelier, Maurice, and Marilyn Strathern, eds. 1991. *Big Men and Great Men: Personifications of Power.* Cambridge: Cambridge University Press.

Goodale, Jane C. 1995. *To Sing with Pigs Is Human: The Concept of the Person in Papua New Guinea.* Seattle: University of Washington Press.

Gorer, Geoffrey. 1936. Aspects of Primitive Culture. Review of *Naven* by Gregory Bateson. *Listener,* December 30.

Gottlieb, Alma. 1989. Hyenas and Heteroglossia: Myth and Ritual among the Beng of Côte d'Ivoire. *American Ethnologist* 16:487–501.

Green, André. 1992. The Oedipus Complex as Mutterkomplex. Trans. Alan Sheridan and Kenneth Hoyle. In *Shooting the Sun: Ritual and Meaning in West Sepik,* ed. B. Juillerat, 144–72. Washington, D.C.: Smithsonian Institution Press.

Greenson, Ralph R. 1968. Dis-Identifying from Mother: Its Special Importance for the Boy. *International Journal of Psycho-Analysis* 49:370–74.

Gregor, Thomas. 1985. *Anxious Pleasures: The Sexual Lives of an Amazonian People.* Chicago: University of Chicago Press.

————. 1988. "She Who Is Covered with Feces": The Dialectics of Gender among the Mehinaku of Brazil. In *Dialectics and Gender: Anthropological Approaches,* ed. R. R. Randolph, D. M. Schneider, and M. N. Diaz, 80–90. Boulder: Westview.

Gutmann, Matthew C. 1997. Trafficking in Men: The Anthropology of Masculinity. *Annual Review of Anthropology* 26:385–409.

Haddon, A. C. 1937. An Ethno-Psychological Study: Review of *Naven* by Gregory Bateson. *Cambridge Review* (January 29): 217.

Hallpike, Christopher R. 1969. Social Hair. *Man*, n.s., 4:256–64.

Handelman, Don. 1979. Is Naven Ludic? Paradox and the Communication of Identity. *Social Analysis* 1:177–91.

————. 1981. The Ritual-Clown: Attributes and Affinities. *Anthropos* 76:321–70.

————. 1991. Symbolic Types, the Body, and Circus. *Semiotics* 85:205–25.

Harries-Jones, Peter. 1995. *A Recursive Vision: Ecological Understanding and Gregory Bateson.* Toronto: University of Toronto Press.

Harrison, Simon. 1982. Yams and the Symbolic Representation of Time in a Sepik River Village. *Oceania* 53:141–62.

————. 1983. *Laments for Foiled Marriages: Love Songs from a Sepik River Village.* Port Moresby: Institute of Papua New Guinea Studies.

————. 1984. New Guinea Highland Social Structure in a Lowland Totemic Mythology. *Man*, n.s., 19:389–403.

————. 1985a. Concepts of the Person in Avatip Religious Thought. *Man*, n.s., 20:115–30.

————. 1985b. Names, Ghosts and Alliance in Two Sepik River Societies. *Oceania* 56:138–46.

————. 1985c. Ritual Hierarchy and Secular Equality in a Sepik River Village. *American Ethnologist* 12:413–26.

————. 1987. Cultural Efflorescence and Political Evolution on the Sepik River. *American Ethnologist* 14:491–507.

————. 1989a. The Symbolic Construction of Aggression and War in a Sepik River Society. *Man*, n.s., 24:583–99.

————. 1989b. Magical and Material Polities in Melanesia. *Man*, n.s., 24:1–20.

————. 1990. *Stealing People's Names: History and Politics in a Sepik River Cosmology.* Cambridge: Cambridge University Press.

————. 1993a. *Mask of War: Violence, Ritual and the Self in Melanesia.* Manchester: Manchester University Press.

————. 1993b. Commerce of Cultures in Melanesia. *Man*, n.s., 28:139–58.

————. 1995a. Four Types of Symbolic Conflict. *Journal of the Royal Anthropological Institute*, n.s., 1:255–72.

————. 1995b. Transformations of Identity in Sepik Warfare. In *Shifting Contexts: Transformations in Anthropological Knowledge,* ed. M. Strathern, 81–97. London: Routledge.

Hauser-Schäublin, Brigitta. 1977. *Frauen in Kararau: Zur Rolle der Frau bei den Iatmul am Mittelsepik, Papua New Guinea.* Basel: Basler Beiträge zur Ethnologie 18.

————. 1983. The Mai-Masks of the Iatmul, Papua New Guinea: Style, Carving, Process, Performance and Function. *Oral History* 11:1–53 (Port Moresby, Papua New Guinea).

————. 1989. The Fallacy of "Real" and "Pseudo" Procreation. *Zeitschrift für Ethnologie* 114:179–94.

————. 1990. In the Swamps and on the Hills: Traditional Settlement Patterns and House Structures in the Middle Sepik. In *Sepik Heritage: Tradition and Change in Papua New Guinea,* ed. N. Lutkehaus, C. Kaufman, W. E. Mitchell, D. Newton, L. Osmundsen, and M. Schuster, 470–79. Durham: Carolina Academic Press.

————. 1995. Puberty Rites, Women's Naven, and Initiation: Women's Rituals of Transition in Abelam and Iatmul Culture. In *Gender Rituals: Female Initiation in Melanesia,* ed. N. C. Lutkehaus and P. B. Roscoe, 33–53. New York: Routledge.

Hays, Terrence. 1988. 'Myths of Matriarchy' and the Sacred Flute Complex of the Papua New Guinea Highlands. In *Myths of Matriarchy Reconsidered,* ed. D. Gewertz, 98–120. Sydney: University of Sydney Press.

Herdt, Gilbert. 1981. *Guardians of the Flutes: Idioms of Masculinity.* New York: Columbia University Press.

————. 1982a. Fetish and Fantasy in Sambia Initiation. In *Rituals of Manhood: Male Initiation in Papua New Guinea,* ed. G. H. Herdt, 4–98. Berkeley: University of California Press.

————. 1984a. Ritualized Homosexual Behavior in the Male Cults of Melanesia, 1862–1983: An Introduction. In *Ritualized Homosexuality in Melanesia,* ed. G. Herdt, 1–81. Berkeley: University of California Press.

————. 1987. Transitional Objects in Sambia Initiation Rites. *Ethos* 15:40–57.

————. 1989. Self and Culture: Contexts of Religious Experience in Melanesia. In *The Religious Imagination in New Guinea,* ed. G. Herdt and M. Stephen, 15–40. New Brunswick, N.J.: Rutgers University Press.

————. 1997a. Male Birth-Giving in the Cultural Imagination of the Sambia. *Psychoanalytic Review* 84:217–26.

————. 1997b. *Same Sex, Different Cultures: Gays and Lesbians across Cultures.* Boulder: Westview.

Herdt, Gilbert, ed. 1982b. *Rituals of Manhood: Male Initiation in Papua New Guinea.* Berkeley: University of California Press.

————. 1984b. *Ritualized Homosexuality in Melanesia.* Berkeley: University of California Press.

Hereniko, Vilsoni. 1994. Clowning as Political Commentary: Polynesia, Then and Now. *Contemporary Pacific* 6:1–28.

————. 1995. *Woven Gods: Female Clowns and Power in Rotuma.* Honolulu: University of Hawaii Press.

Héritier, Françoise. 1982. The Symbolics of Incest and Its Prohibition. In *Between Belief and Transgression: Structuralist Essays in Religion, History, and Myth,* ed. M. Izard and P. Smith, 152–79. Trans. John Leavitt. Chicago: University of Chicago Press. (Orig. French ed. 1979.)

Hershman, P. 1974. Hair, Sex and Dirt. *Man,* n.s., 9:274–98.

Herskovits, Melville, and Frances Herskovits. 1958. Sibling Rivalry, the Oedipus Complex, and Myth. *Journal of American Folklore* 71:1–15.

Hertz, Robert. 1960. A Contribution to the Study of the Collective Representation of Death. In *Death and the Right Hand,* ed. R. Needham, 27–86. Trans. Rodney and Claudia Needham. Glencoe: Free Press. (Orig. French ed. 1909.)

————. 1973. The Pre-eminence of the Right Hand: A Study in Religious Polarity. In

Right and Left: Essays on Dual Symbolic Classification, ed. R. Needham, 3–31. Trans. Rodney Needham. Chicago: University of Chicago Press. (Orig. French ed. 1909.)

Herzfeld, M. 1985. *The Poetics of Manhood: Contest and Identity in a Cretan Mountain Village*. Princeton: Princeton University Press.

Hiatt, L. R. 1971. Secret Pseudo-Procreation Rites among the Australian Aboriginals. In *Anthropology in Oceania*, ed. L. Hiatt and C. Jayawardena, 143–62. Canberra: Australian Institute of Aboriginal Studies.

Hieb, Louis A. 1972. Meaning and Mismeaning: Toward an Understanding of the Ritual Clown. In *New Perspectives on the Pueblos,* ed. A. Ortiz, 163–95. Albuquerque: University of New Mexico Press.

Hiltebeitel, Alf, and Barbara D. Miller. 1998. *Hair: Its Power and Meaning in Asian Cultures*. Albany: State University of New York Press.

Hobbes, Thomas. 1958. *Leviathan*. H. W. Schneider, ed. Indianapolis: Bobbs-Merrill. (Orig. 1651.)

Hodge, Bob. 1989. National Character and the Discursive Process: A Study of Transformations in Popular Metatexts. *Journal of Pragmatics* 13:427–44.

Hogbin, Ian. 1970. *The Island of Menstruating Men: Religion in Wogeo, New Guinea*. Scranton: Chandler.

Hollan, Douglas. 1992. Cross-Cultural Differences in the Self. *Journal of Anthropological Research* 48:283–300.

Honigman, John J. 1942. An Interpretation of the Social-Psychological Functions of the Ritual Clown. *Journal of Personality* 10:220–26.

Hoskins, Janet. 1996. Introduction: Headhunting as Practice and Trope. In *Headhunting and the Social Imagination in Southeast Asia*, ed. J. Hoskins, 1–49. Stanford: Stanford University Press.

Houseman, Michael, and Carlo Severi. 1994. *Naven ou le Donner à Voir: Essai d'Interprétation de l'Action Rituelle*. Paris: CNRS-Éditions, Éditions de la Maison des Sciences de l'Homme.

———. 1998. *Naven or the Other Self: A Relational Approach to Ritual Action*. Leiden: Brill.

Hudson, Liam, and Bernadine Jacot. 1991. *The Way Men Think: Intellect, Intimacy and the Erotic Imagination*. New Haven: Yale University Press.

Inger, Ivan B. 1983. A Dialogic Perspective for Family Therapy: The Contributions of Martin Buber and Gregory Bateson. *Journal of Family Therapy* 15:293–314.

Ingham, John M. 1996a. *Psychological Anthropology Reconsidered*. Cambridge: Cambridge University Press.

———. 1996b. Oedipality in Pragmatic Discourse: The Trobriands and Hindu India. *Ethos* 24:559–87.

Irigaray, Luce. 1985. *This Sex Which Is Not One*. Trans. Catherine Porter with Carolyn Burke. Ithaca: Cornell University Press. (Orig. French ed. 1977.)

Irwin, Alexander C. 1993. Ecstasy, Sacrifice, Communication: Bataille on Religion and Inner Experience. *Soundings* 76:105–28.

Jackson, Jean E. 1996. Coping with the Dilemmas of Affinity and Female Sexuality: Male Rebirth in the Central Northwest Amazon. In *Denying Biology: Essays on Gender and Pseudo-Procreation*, ed. W. Shapiro and U. Kinke, 89–127. Lanham: University Press of America.

Jaffe, Daniel S. 1968. The Masculine Envy of Woman's Procreative Function. *Journal of the American Psychoanalytic Association* 16:521–48.

Jay, Nancy. 1992. *Throughout Your Generations Forever: Sacrifice, Religion, and Patriarchy.* Chicago: University of Chicago Press.

Jensen, Gordon D., and Luh Ketut Suryani. 1992. *The Balinese People: A Reinvestigation of Character.* Kuala Lumpur: Oxford University Press.

Johnson, Allen, and Douglass Price-Williams. 1996. *Oedipus Ubiquitous: The Family Complex in World Folk Literature.* Stanford: Stanford University Press.

Johnson, Mark. 1992. *The Body in the Mind: The Bodily Basis of Meaning, Imagination, and Reason.* Chicago: University of Chicago Press.

Jorgensen, Dan. 1980. What's in a Name? The Meaning of Meaninglessness in Telefolmin. *Ethos* 8:349–66.

———. 1983a. The Facts of Life, Papua New Guinea Style. *Mankind* 14:1–12.

———. 1983b. Mirroring Nature? Men's and Women's Models of Conception in Telefolmin. *Mankind* 14:57–65.

———. 1990. Secrecy's Turn. *Canberra Anthropology* 13:40–47.

Juillerat, Bernard. 1988. "An Odor of Man": Melanesian Evolutionism, Anthropological Mythology and Matriarchy. *Diogenes* 144:65–91.

———. 1991. Complementarity and Rivalry: Two Contradictory Principles in Yafar Society. Trans. Nora Scott. In *Big Men and Great Men: Personifications of Power,* ed. M. Godelier and M. Strathern, 130–41. Cambridge: Cambridge University Press.

———. 1992. "The Mother's Brother Is the Breast": Incest and Its Prohibition in the Yafar Yangis. In *Shooting the Sun: Ritual and Meaning in West Sepik,* ed. B. Juillerat, 20–124. Washington, D.C.: Smithsonian Institution Press.

———. 1996. *Children of the Blood: Society, Reproduction and Cosmology in New Guinea.* Trans. Nora Scott. Oxford: Berg. (Orig. French ed. 1986.)

———. 1999. Séparation, retour, permanence: Le lien maternel dans le rite *naven* des Iatmul. *L'Homme* 151:151–79.

Jung, C. G. 1956. *Symbols of Transformation: An Analysis of the Prelude to a Case of Schizophrenia.* Trans. R. F. C. Hull. Princeton: Princeton University Press. (Orig. German ed. 1952.)

Kaberry, Phyllis M. 1940–41. The Abelam Tribe, Sepik District, New Guinea: A Preliminary Report. *Oceania* 11:345–67.

Kahn, Miriam. 1986. *Always Hungry, Never Greedy: Food and the Expression of Gender in a Melanesian Society.* Cambridge: Cambridge University Press.

Kakar, Sudhir. 1978. *The Inner World: A Psychoanalytic Study of Childhood and Society in India.* Delhi: Oxford University Press.

Kan, Sergei. 1989. *Symbolic Immortality: The Tlingit Potlatch of the Nineteenth Century.* Washington, D.C.: Smithsonian Institution Press.

Karp, Ivan. 1987. Laughter at Marriage: Subversion in Performance. In *Transactions of African Marriage,* ed. D. Parkin and D. Nyamwaya, 137–54. Manchester: Manchester University Press.

Kaufmann, Christian. 1985. Postscript: The Relationship between Sepik Art and Ethnology. In *Authority and Ornament: Art of the Sepik River, Papua New Guinea,* ed. S. Greub, 33–47. Basel: Tribal Art Centre.

Keesing, Roger M. 1982. Introduction. In *Rituals of Manhood: Male Initiation in Papua New Guinea,* ed. G. H. Herdt, 1–43. Berkeley: University of California Press.

———. 1991. Experiments in Thinking about Ritual. *Canberra Anthropology* 14:60–74.

Kessel, Ralph. 1971. *Logic and Social Structure: A Critical Revaluation of Bateson's Naven:*

The Iatmul Tribe of New Guinea. Miscellaneous Series, no. 25, Museum of Anthropology, University of Northern Colorado–Greeley.

Kimmel, Michael. 1996. *Manhood in America: A Cultural History.* New York: Free Press.

Kinston, Warren. 1987. The Shame of Narcissism. In *The Many Faces of Shame,* ed. D. L. Nathanson, 214–45. New York: Guilford Press.

Kitahara, M. 1974. Living Quarter Arrangements in Polygyny and Circumcision and Segregation of Males at Puberty. *Ethnology* 13:401–13.

Kittay, Eva Feder. 1995. Mastering Envy: From Freud's Narcissistic Wounds to Bettelheim's Symbolic Wounds to a Vision of Healing. *Psychoanalytic Review* 82:125–58.

Klein, Melanie. 1975. The Psycho-Analysis of Children, trans. Alix Strachey. In *The Writings of Melanie Klein,* Vol. II. New York: Free Press. (Orig. 1932.)

Knauft, Bruce M. 1985. *Good Company and Violence: Sorcery and Social Action in a Lowland New Guinea Society.* Berkeley: University of California Press.

———. 1987. Homosexuality in Melanesia. *Journal for Psychoanalytic Anthropology* 10:155–91.

———. 1989a. Bodily Images in Melanesia: Cultural Substances and Natural Metaphors. In *Fragments for a History of the Human Body,* ed. M. Feher et al., 199–270. New York: Urzone.

———. 1989b. Imagery, Pronouncement, and the Aesthetics of Reception in Gebusi Spirit Mediumship. In *The Religious Imagination in New Guinea,* ed. G. Herdt and M. Stephen, 67–98. New Brunswick, N.J.: Rutgers University Press.

———. 1990. Melanesian Warfare: A Theoretical History. *Oceania* 60:250–311.

———. 1993. *South Coast New Guinea Cultures: History, Comparison, Dialectic.* Cambridge: Cambridge University Press.

———. 1997. Gender Identity, Political Economy and Modernity in Melanesia and Amazonia. *Journal of the Royal Anthropological Institute,* n.s., 3:233–59.

Korn, Francis. 1971. A Question of Preferences: The Iatmul Case. In *Rethinking Kinship and Marriage,* ed. R. Needham, 99–132. London: Tavistock.

Kracke, Waud H. 1978. *Force and Persuasion: Leadership in an Amazonian Society.* Chicago: University of Chicago Press.

Krause, Inga-Britt. 1993. Family Therapy and Anthropology: A Case for Emotions. *Journal of Family Therapy* 15:35–56.

Kristeva, Julia. 1982. *Powers of Horror: An Essay on Abjection.* Trans. Leon S. Roudiez. New York: Columbia University Press. (Orig. French ed. 1980.)

———. 1984. Un docteur subtil. *La Quinzaine Littéraire* 419 (June 16–30, 1984): 14–15.

Kuklick, Henrika. 1991. *The Savage Within: The Social History of British Anthropology, 1885–1945.* Cambridge: Cambridge University Press.

Kuper, Adam. 1983. *Anthropology and Anthropologists: The Modern British School.* London: Routledge and Kegan Paul.

———. 1988. *The Invention of Primitive Society: Transformations of an Illusion.* London: Tavistock.

Kurtz, Stanley M. 1991. Polysexualization: A New Approach to Oedipus in the Trobriands. *Ethos* 19:68–101.

———. 1992. *All the Mothers Are One: Hindu India and the Cultural Reshaping of Psychoanalysis.* New York: Columbia University Press.

———. 1993. A Trobriand Complex. *Ethos* 21:79–103.

Lacan, Jacques. 1968. *Speech and Language in Psychoanalysis.* Trans. Anthony Wilden. Baltimore: Johns Hopkins Press. (Orig. French ed. 1956.)

Lachmann, Renate. 1988. Bakhtin and Carnival: Culture as Counter-Culture. *Cultural Critique* 11:115–52.

Lattas, Andrew. 1989. Trickery and Sacrifice: Tambarans and the Appropriation of Female Reproductive Powers in Male Initiation Ceremonies in West New Britain. *Man,* n.s., 24:451–69.

Layard, John. 1955. Boar-Sacrifice. *Journal of Analytical Psychology* 1:7–31.

———. 1959. Homo-Eroticism in Primitive Society as a Function of the Self. *Journal of Analytical Psychology* 4:101–15.

Laycock, D. C. 1965. *The Ndu Language Family (Sepik District, New Guinea).* Linguistic Circle of Canberra Publications C 1.

Leach, Edmund. 1958. Magical Hair. *Journal of the Royal Anthropological Institute* 88:147–64.

Leavitt, Stephen C. 1991. Sexual Ideology and Experience in a Papua New Guinea Society. *Social Science and Medicine* 33:897–907.

———. 1998. The Bikhet Mystique: Masculine Identity and Patterns of Rebellion among Bumbita Adolescent Males. In *Adolescence in Pacific Island Societies,* ed. G. Herdt and S. C. Leavitt, 173–94. Pittsburgh: University of Pittsburgh Press.

Leenhardt, Maurice. 1979. *Do Kamo: Person and Myth in the Melanesia World.* Trans. Masia Miller Gulati. Chicago: University of Chicago Press. (Orig. French ed. 1947.)

Levine, Jacob. 1961. Regression in Primitive Clowning. *Psychoanalytic Quarterly* 30:72–83.

Lévi-Strauss, Claude. 1963a. Split Representation in the Art of Asia and America. In *Structural Anthropology,* 245–73. Trans. Claire Jacobson and Brooke Grundfest Schoepf. New York: Basic Books. (Orig. French ed. 1944–45.)

———. 1963b. Structural Analysis in Linguistics and Anthropology. In *Structural Anthropology,* 31–66. Trans. Claire Jacobson and Brooke Grundfest Schoepf. New York: Basic Books. (Orig. French ed. 1945.)

———. 1969. *The Elementary Structures of Kinship.* Trans. James Harle Bell, John Richard von Sturmer, and Rodney Needham. Boston: Beacon. (Orig. French ed. 1949.)

———. 1988. *The Jealous Potter.* Trans. Bénédicte Chorier. Chicago: University of Chicago Press. (Orig. French ed. 1985.)

Lewis, Gilbert. 1980. *A Day of Shining Red: An Essay on Understanding Ritual.* Cambridge: Cambridge University Press.

Lewis, Helen Block. 1987. Shame and the Narcissistic Personality. In *The Many Faces of Shame,* ed. D. L. Nathanson, 93–132. New York: Guilford Press.

Lewis, Nolan D. C. 1928. The Psychology of the Castration Reaction. *Psychoanalytic Review* 15:174–77.

Lidz, Theodore, and Ruth Wilmanns Lidz. 1977. Male Menstruation: A Ritual Alternative to the Oedipal Transition. *International Journal of Psycho-Analysis* 58:17–31.

———. 1989. *Oedipus in the Stone Age: A Psychoanalytic Study of Masculinization in Papua New Guinea.* Madison, Conn.: International Universities Press.

Limón, José. 1989. Carne, Carnales and the Carnivalesque: Bakhtinian Bathos, Disorder and Narrative Discourse. *American Ethnologist* 16:471–86.

Lindenbaum, Shirley. 1987. The Mystification of Female Labors. In *Gender and Kinship:*

Essays toward a Unified Analysis, ed. J. F. Collier and S. J. Yanagisako, 221–43. Stanford: Stanford University Press.

Lindstrom, Lamont. 1984. Doctor, Lawyer, Wise Man, Priest: Big-Men and Knowledge in Melanesia. *Man,* n.s., 19:291–301.

———. 1990. *Knowledge and Power in a South Pacific Society.* Washington, D.C.: Smithsonian Institution Press.

Lipset, David M. 1982. *Gregory Bateson: The Legacy of a Scientist.* Boston: Beacon.

———. 1990. Boars' Tusks and Flying Foxes: Symbolism and Ritual of Office in the Murik Lakes. In *Sepik Heritage: Tradition and Change in Papua New Guinea,* ed. N. Lutkehaus, C. Kaufmann, W. E. Mitchell, D. Newton, L. Osmundsen, and M. Schuster, 286–97. Durham: Carolina Academic Press.

———. 1997. *Mangrove Man: Dialogics of Culture in the Sepik Estuary.* Cambridge: Cambridge University Press.

Loewald, H. W. 1951. Ego and Reality. *International Journal of Psycho-Analysis* 32:10–18.

———. 1979. The Waning of the Oedipus Complex. In *Papers on Psychoanalysis,* 384–404. New Haven: Yale University Press.

Losche, Diane. 1995. The Sepik Gaze: Iconographic Interpretation of Abelam Form. *Social Analysis* 38:47–60.

———. 1997. What Do Abelam Images Want from Us? Plato's Cave and Kwatbil's Belly. *Australian Journal of Anthropology* 8:35–49.

Lutkehaus, Nancy Christine. 1990. Hierarchy and 'Heroic Society': Manam Variations in Sepik Social Structure. *Oceania* 60:179–95.

———. 1995a. *Zaria's Fire: Engendered Moments in Manam Ethnography.* Durham: Carolina Academic Press.

———. 1995b. Gendered Metaphors: Female Rituals as Cultural Models in Manam. In *Gender Rituals: Female Initiation in Melanesia,* ed. N. C. Lutkehaus and P. B. Roscoe, 183–204. New York: Routledge.

Lutkehaus, Nancy Christine, and Paul B. Roscoe, eds. 1995. *Gender Rituals: Female Initiation in Melanesia.* New York: Routledge.

MacCormack, Carol, and Marilyn Strathern, eds. 1980. *Nature, Culture and Gender.* Cambridge: Cambridge University Press.

Macintyre, Martha. 1987. Flying Witches and Leaping Warriors: Supernatural Origins of Power and Matrilineal Authority in Tubetube Society. In *Dealing with Inequality: Analysing Gender Relations in Melanesia and Beyond,* ed. M. Strathern, 206–28. Cambridge: Cambridge University Press.

———. 1992. Reflections of an Anthropologist Who Mistook Her Husband for a Yam: Female Comedy on Tubetube. In *Clowning as Critical Practice: Performance Humor in the South Pacific,* ed. W. E. Mitchell, 130–44. Pittsburgh: University of Pittsburgh Press.

MacKenzie, Maureen A. 1991. *Androgynous Objects: String Bags and Gender in Central New Guinea.* Chur, Switzerland: Harwood.

MacRae, Donald G. 1975. The Body and Social Metaphor. In *The Body as a Medium of Expression,* ed. J. Benthall and T. Polhemus, 59–73. New York: E. P. Dutton.

Mahler, Margaret. 1963. Thoughts about Development and Individuation. *Psychoanalytic Study of the Child* 18:307–24.

———. 1971. A Study of the Separation-Individuation Process and Its Possible Applications to Borderline Phenomena in the Psychoanalytic Situation. *Psychoanalytic Study of the Child* 26:403–24.

Malinowski, Bronislaw. 1916. Baloma: The Spirits of the Dead in the Trobriand Islands. *Journal of the Royal Anthropological Institute* 45. (Reprinted in *Magic, Science and Religion, and Other Essays*, 149–254. Prospect Heights, Ill.: Waveland, 1992.)

———. 1927. *Sex and Repression in Savage Society.* Chicago: University of Chicago Press.

———. 1929. *The Sexual Life of Savages in North-Western Melanesia.* New York: Harvest.

———. 1936. Preface. *We, the Tikopia*, R. Firth, xxi–xxv. London: George Allen and Unwin.

Manenti, François. 1992. Yangis: Enacting the Unconscious. Trans. Alan Sheridan and Kenneth Hoyle. In *Shooting the Sun: Ritual and Meaning in West Sepik*, ed. B. Juillerat, 173–90. Washington, D.C.: Smithsonian Institution Press.

Marcus, George E. 1985. A Timely Rereading of Naven: Gregory Bateson as Oracular Essayist. *Representations* 12:66–82.

Markarius, L. 1970. Ritual Clowns and Symbolic Behaviour. *Diogenes* 69:44–73.

Marksbury, Richard A. 1993. *The Business of Marriage: Transformations in Oceanic Matrimony.* Pittsburgh: University of Pittsburgh Press.

Marriott, McKim. 1976. Hindu Transactions: Diversity without Dualism. In *Transaction and Meaning*, ed. B. Kapferer, 109–42. Philadelphia: Institute for the Study of Human Issues.

Marshall, Mac, ed. 1982. *Through a Glass Darkly: Beer and Modernization in Papua New Guinea.* Boroko, Papua New Guinea: Institute for Applied Social and Economic Research.

Mauss, Marcel. 1979. The Notion of Body Techniques. In *Sociology and Psychology*, 97–123. Trans. Ben Brewster. London: Routledge and Kegan Paul. (Orig. French ed. 1935.)

———. 1990. *The Gift: The Form and Reason for Exchange in Archaic Societies.* Trans. W. D. Halls. New York: Routledge. (Orig. French ed. 1925.)

McCall, Dwight L., and Robert G. Green. 1991. Symmetricality and Complementarity and Their Relationship to Marital Stability. *Journal of Divorce and Remarriage* 15:23–32.

McDowell, Nancy. 1976. Kinship and Exchange: The Kamain Relationship in a Yuat River Village. *Oceania* 57:36–48.

———. 1977. The Meaning of Rope in a Yuat River Village. *Ethnology* 16:175–83.

———. 1978. The Flexibility of Sister Exchange: Case Studies. *Oceania* 48:207–31.

———. 1980. It's Not Who You Are But How You Give That Counts: The Role of Exchange in a Melanesian Society. *American Ethnologist* 7:58–69.

———. 1984. Complementarity: The Relationship between Male and Female in the East Sepik Village of Bun, Papua New Guinea. In *Rethinking Women's Roles*, ed. D. O'Brien and S. Tiffany, 32–52. Berkeley: University of California Press.

———. 1990. Intergenerational Exchange in Diachronic Context: A Melanesian Example. *Anthropos* 85:393–401.

———. 1991. *The Mundugumor: From the Field Notes of Margaret Mead and Reo Fortune.* Washington, D.C.: Smithsonian Institution Press.

Mead, Margaret. 1935a. Book Review of Róheim, *The Riddle of the Sphinx. Character and Personality* 4:85–90.

———. 1935b. *Sex and Temperament in Three Primitive Societies.* New York: William Morrow.

———. 1937. Public Opinion Mechanisms among Primitive Peoples. *Public Opinion Quarterly* 1:5–16.

———. 1938. The Mountain Arapesh, Part I. An Importing Culture. *Anthropological Papers of the American Museum of Natural History* 36:139–349. (Reprinted in *The Mountain Arapesh II: Arts and Supernaturalism,* 1–206. Garden City, N.Y.: Natural History Press, 1970.)

———. 1940a. The Mountain Arapesh, Part II. Supernaturalism. *Anthropological Papers of the American Museum of Natural History* 37:317–451. (Reprinted in *The Mountain Arapesh II: Arts and Supernaturalism,* 207–480. Garden City, N.Y.: Natural History Press, 1970.)

———. 1940b. Character Formation in Two South Seas Societies. *Transactions of the American Neurological Association for 1940,* 99–103.

———. 1940c. Conflict of Cultures in America. *Proceedings of the Annual Conference of the Middle States Association of Colleges and Secondary Schools,* 30–44.

———. 1941. Administrative Contributions to Democratic Character Formation at the Adolescent Level. *Journal of the National Association of Deans of Women* 4:51–57.

———. 1943. The Family in the Future. In *Beyond Victory,* ed. R. N. Anshen, 66–87. New York: Harcourt, Brace.

———. 1947. Age Patterning in Personality Development. *American Journal of Orthopsychiatry* 17:231–40.

———. 1949. *Male and Female: A Study of the Sexes in a Changing World.* New York: Dell.

———. 1950. Some Anthropological Considerations Concerning Guilt. In *Feelings and Emotions: The Mooseheart Symposium in Cooperation with The University of Chicago,* ed. M. L. Reymert, 362–73. New York: McGraw-Hill.

———. 1952. Some Relationships between Social Anthropology and Psychiatry. In *Dynamic Psychiatry,* ed. F. Alexander and H. Ross, 401–48. Chicago: University of Chicago Press.

———. 1954. Research on Primitive Children. In *Manual of Child Psychology,* 2d ed., ed. L. Carmichael, 735–80. New York: John Wiley and Sons.

———. 1964. *Continuities in Cultural Evolution.* New Haven: Yale University Press.

———. 1972. *Blackberry Winter: My Earlier Years.* New York: William Morrow.

———. 1977. *Letters from the Field, 1925–1975.* New York: Harper and Row.

———. 1978. The Sepik as a Culture Area: Comment. *Anthropological Quarterly* 51:69–75.

Mead, Margaret, and Gregory Bateson. 1991. "Bathing Babies in Three Cultures." Film. (Orig. ca. 1954.)

Meeker, Michael E., Kathleen Barlow, and David M. Lipset. 1986. Culture, Exchange, and Gender: Lessons from the Murik. *Cultural Anthropology* 1:6–73.

Meigs, Anna S. 1976. Male Pregnancy and the Reduction of Sexual Opposition in the New Guinea Highlands. *Ethnology* 15:393–407.

———. 1984. *Food, Sex, and Pollution: A New Guinea Religion.* New Brunswick, N.J.: Rutgers University Press.

———. 1987. Semen, Spittle, Blood and Sweat: A New Guinea Theory of Nutrition. In *Anthropology in the High Valleys: Essays on the New Guinea Highlands in Honor of Kenneth E. Read,* ed. L. L. Langness and T. E. Hays, 27–44. Novato, Calif.: Chandler and Sharp.

Meiser, Leo. 1955. The "Platform" Phenomenon along the Northern Coast of New Guinea. *Anthropos* 50:265–72.

Metraux, Rhoda. 1976. Eidos and Change: Continuity in Process, Discontinuity in Product. In *Socialization in Cultural Communication,* ed. T. Schwartz, 201–16. Berkeley: University of California Press.

———. 1978. Aristocracy and Meritocracy: Leadership among the Eastern Iatmul. *Anthropological Quarterly* 51:47–58.

———. 1990. Music in Tambunum. In *Sepik Heritage: Tradition and Change in Papua New Guinea,* ed. N. Lutkehaus, C. Kaufmann, W. E. Mitchell, D. Newton, L. Osmundsen, and M. Schuster, 523–34. Durham: Carolina Academic Press.

Mimica, Jadran. 1993. Review Article: The Foi and Heidegger: Western Philosophical Poetics and a New Guinea Life-World. *Australian Journal of Anthropology* 4:79–95.

Mitchell, William E. 1992. Horrific Humor and Festal Farce: Carnival Clowning in Wape Society. In *Clowning as Critical Practice: Performance Humor in the South Pacific,* W. E. Mitchell, 145–66. Pittsburgh: University of Pittsburgh Press.

Moore, Sally Falk. 1964. Descent and Symbolic Filiation. *American Anthropologist* 66:1308–20.

Morgenthaler, Fritz. 1987. Kwandemi. In *Conversations au bord du fleuve mourant: Ethnopsychanalyse chez les Iatmouls de Papouasie/Nouvelle-Guinée,* ed. F. Morgenthaler, F. Weiss, and M. Morgenthaler, 56–143. Carouge-Genève: Éditions Zoé.

Morgenthaler, Marco. 1987a. Wamoun et le groupe des jeunes hommes. In *Conversations au bord du fleuve mourant: Ethnopsychanalyse chez les Iatmouls de Papouasie/Nouvelle-Guinée,* ed. F. Morgenthaler, F. Weiss, and M. Morgenthaler, 194–202. Carouge-Genève: Éditions Zoé.

———. 1987b. Ngaoui. In *Conversations au bord du fleuve mourant: Ethnopsychanalyse chez les Iatmouls de Papouasie/Nouvelle-Guinée,* ed. F. Morgenthaler, F. Weiss, and M. Morgenthaler, 204–39. Carouge-Genève: Éditions Zoé.

Mosse, George L. 1996. *The Image of Man: The Creation of Modern Masculinity.* Oxford: Oxford University Press.

Muensterberger, Warner. 1962. The Creative Process: Its Relation to Object Loss and Fetishism. *Psychoanalytic Study of Society* 2:161–85.

Nachman, Steven R. 1982. Anti-Humor: Why the Grand Sorcerer Wags His Penis. *Ethos* 10:117–35.

———. 1986. Discomfiting Laughter: Schadenfreude among Melanesians. *Journal of Anthropological Research* 42:53–67.

Nadar, Laura. 1988. Post-Interpretive Anthropology. *Anthropological Quarterly* 61: 149–59.

Nadel, S. F. 1937. The Typological Approach to Culture. *Character and Personality* 5:267–84.

———. 1938. Review of *Naven. Man* 38:44–46.

Nash, Jill. 1978. Women and Power in Nagovisi Society. *Journal de la Société des Océanistes* 34:119–26.

Newton, Douglas. 1973. Why Is the Cassowary a Canoe Prow? *Art Journal* 3:41–45.

———. 1987. Shields of the Manambu (East Sepik Province, Papua New Guinea). *Baessler-Archiv,* Neue Folge 35:249–59.

———. 1997. Materials for a Iatmul Chronicle, Middle Sepik River (East Sepik Province, Papua New Guinea). *Baessler-Archiv,* Neue Folge 45:367–85.

Nuckolls, Charles W. 1995. The Misplaced Legacy of Gregory Bateson: Toward a Cultural Dialectic of Knowledge and Desire. *Cultural Anthropology* 10:367–94.

———. 1996. *The Cultural Dialectics of Knowledge and Desire.* Madison: University of Wisconsin Press.

Obeyesekere, Gananath. 1981. *Medusa's Hair: An Essay on Personal Symbols and Religious Experience.* Chicago: University of Chicago Press.

———. 1984. *The Cult of the Goddess Pattini.* Chicago: University of Chicago Press.

———. 1990. *The Work of Culture: Symbolic Transformation in Psychoanalysis and Anthropology.* Chicago: University of Chicago Press.

O'Flaherty, Wendy Doniger. 1980. *Women, Androgynes, and Other Mythical Beasts.* Chicago: University of Chicago Press.

Ogan, Eugene. 1966. Drinking Behavior and Race Relations. *American Anthropologist* 68:181–88.

———. 1986. "Taim Bilong Sipak": Nasioi Alcohol Use, 1962–1978. *Ethnology* 25:21–33.

O'Hanlon, Michael. 1989. *Reading the Skin: Adornment, Display and Society among the Wahgi.* London: British Museum.

Onians, Richard Broxton. 1951. *The Origins of European Thought about the Body, the Mind, the Soul, the World, Time, and Fate: New Interpretations of Greek, Roman and Kindred Evidence also of Some Basic Jewish and Christian Beliefs.* Oxford: Oxford University Press.

Ortner, Sherry. 1974. Is Female to Male as Nature Is to Culture? In *Woman, Culture and Society,* ed. M. Z. Rosaldo and L. Lamphere, 67–88. Stanford: Stanford University Press.

———. 1997. *Making Gender: The Politics and Erotics of Culture.* Boston: Beacon.

Panoff, F. 1970. Food and Faeces: A Melanesian Rite. *Man* 5:237–52.

Parin, Paul, Fritz Morgenthaler, and Goldy Parin-Matthey. 1980. *Fear Thy Neighbor as Thyself: Psychoanalysis and Society among the Anyi of West Africa.* Trans. Patricia Klamerth. Chicago: University of Chicago Press. (Orig. German ed. 1971.)

Parker, Richard G. 1981. *Bodies, Pleasures and Passions: Sexual Culture in Contemporary Brazil.* Boston: Beacon.

Paul, Robert A. 1982. *The Tibetan Symbolic World: Psychoanalytic Explorations.* Chicago: University of Chicago Press.

———. 1987. The Question of Applied Psychoanalysis and the Interpretation of Cultural Symbolism. *Ethos* 15:82–103.

———. 1989. Psychoanalytic Anthropology. *Annual Review of Anthropology* 18:177–202.

———. 1990. Bettelheim's Contribution to Anthropology. *Psychoanalytic Study of Society* 15:311–34.

———. 1991. Freud's Anthropology: A Reading of the "Cultural Books." In *The Cambridge Companion to Freud,* ed. J. Neu, 267–86. Cambridge: Cambridge University Press.

———. 1996a. *Moses and Civilization: The Meaning behind Freud's Myth.* New Haven: Yale University Press.

———. 1996b. Symbolic Reproduction and Sherpa Monasticism. In *Denying Biology: Essays on Gender and Pseudo-Procreation,* ed. W. Shapiro and U. Linke, 51–73. Lanham: University Press of America.

Piers, Gerhart, and Milton B. Singer. 1953. *Shame and Guilt: A Psychoanalytic and a Cultural Study.* Springfield, Ill.: Charles C. Thomas.

Pollmann, Tessel. 1990. Margaret Mead's Balinese: The Fitting Symbols of the American Dream. *Indonesia* 49:1–35.

Poole, Fitz John Porter. 1982. The Ritual Forging of Identity: Aspects of Person and Self in Bimin-Kuskusmin Male Initiation. In *Rituals of Manhood: Male Initiation in Papua New Guinea*, ed. G. H. Herdt, 99–154. Berkeley: University of California Press.

———. 1984. Symbols of Substance: Bimin-Kuskusmin Models of Procreation, Death, and Personhood. *Mankind* 14:191–216.

———. 1985. Coming into Social Being: Cultural Images of Infants in Bimin-Kuskusmin Folk Psychology. In *Person, Self, and Experience: Exploring Pacific Ethnopsychologies*, ed. G. M. White and J. Kirkpatrick, 183–242. Berkeley: University of California Press.

———. 1987. Morality, Personhood, Tricksters, and Youths: Some Narrative Images of Ethics among Bimin-Kuskusmin. In *Anthropology in the High Valleys: Essays on the New Guinea Highlands in Honor of Kenneth E. Read*, ed. L. L. Langness and T. E. Hays, 283–366. Novato, Calif.: Chandler and Sharp.

Powdermaker, Hortense. 1940. Review of *Naven*. *American Anthropologist* 42:162–64.

Radcliffe-Brown, A. R. 1937. Review of *Naven*. *American Journal of Sociology* 43:172–74.

———. 1940. On Joking Relationships. *Africa* 13:195–210.

Rapport, Nigel. 1997. Steps to a Recursive Vision of Living Systems. *Social Anthropology* 5:313–21.

Read, Kenneth E. 1955. Morality and the Concept of the Person among the Gahuku-Gama. *Oceania* 25:233–82.

Reik, Theodor. 1946. The Puberty Rites of Savages. In *Ritual: Psycho-Analytic Studies*. New York: Farrar, Straus.

Rieber, Robert W., ed. 1989. *The Individual, Communication, and Society: Essays in Memory of Gregory Bateson*. Cambridge: Cambridge University Press.

Rieber, Robert W., and Harold J. Vetter. 1995. The Double-Bind Concept and Gregory Bateson. In *The Psychopathology of Language and Cognition*, 135–49. New York: Plenum.

Róheim, Geza. 1922. The Significance of Stepping Over. *International Journal of Pycho-Analysis* 3:302–26.

———. 1932. Psycho-Analysis of Primitive Cultural Types. *International Journal of Psycho-Analysis* 13:1–224.

———. 1934. *The Riddle of the Sphinx*. London: Hogarth Press.

———. 1943. *The Origin and Function of Culture*. New York: Nervous and Mental Disease Monographs.

Roper, Lyndal. 1994. *Oedipus and the Devil: Witchcraft, Sexuality, and Religion in Early Modern Europe*. New York: Routledge.

Roscoe, Paul. 1995a. In the Shadow of the Tambaran: Female Initiation among the Ndu of the Sepik Basin. In *Gender Rituals: Female Initiation in Melanesia*, ed. N. C. Lutkehaus and P. B. Roscoe, 55–82. New York: Routledge.

———. 1995b. Familiar Partners? The Mountain Arapesh and the Westermarck Effect. *Journal of Anthropological Research* 51:347–62.

———. 1995c. Of Power and Menace: Sepik Art as an Affecting Presence. *Journal of the Royal Anthropological Institute* 1:1–22.

Roscoe, Paul, and Richard Scaglion. 1990. Male Initiation and European Intrusion in the Sepik: A Preliminary Analysis. In *Sepik Heritage: Tradition and Change in Papua New Guinea,* ed. N. Lutkehaus, C. Kaufmann, W. E. Mitchell, D. Newton, L. Osmundsen, and M. Schuster, 14–23. Durham: Carolina Academic Press.

Ross, Mary E. 1982. The Concept of Liminality in Two Tribal Rituals. *American Imago* 39:133–48.

Rubel, Paula G., and Abraham Rosman. 1978. *Your Own Pigs You May Not Eat: A Comparative Study of New Guinea Societies.* Chicago: University of Chicago Press.

Rubin, Gayle. 1975. The Traffic in Women: Notes on the "Political Economy" of Sex. In *Toward an Anthropology of Women,* ed. Rayna R. Reiter, 157–210. New York: Monthly Review Press.

Ruddle, K., D. Johnson, P. K. Townsend, and J. D. Rees. 1978. *Palm Sago: A Tropical Starch from Marginal Lands.* Honolulu: East-West Center.

Scaglion, Richard. 1986. Sexual Segregation and Ritual Pollution in Abelam Society. In *Self, Sex, and Gender in Cross-Cultural Fieldwork,* ed. T. L. Whitehead and M. E. Conaway, 151–63. Urbana: University of Illinois Press.

———. 1990. Spare the Rod and Spoil the Woman? Family Violence in Abelam Society. *Pacific Studies* 13:189–204.

Schieffelin, Edward L. 1983. Anger and Shame in the Tropical Forest: On Affect as a Cultural System in Papua New Guinea. *Ethos* 11:181–91.

———. 1985. Anger, Grief, and Shame: Towards a Kaluli Ethnopsychology. In *Person, Self, and Experience: Exploring Pacific Ethnopsychologies,* ed. G. M. White and J. Kirkpatrick, 168–82. Berkeley: University of California Press.

Schindlbeck, Markus. 1980. *Sago bei den Sawos (Mittelsepik, Papua New Guinea): Untersuchungen über die Bedeutung von Sago in Wirtschaft, Sozialordnung und Religion.* Basel: Basler Beiträge zur Ethnologie 19.

Schmidt, Jürg. 1990. The Response to Tourism in Yensan. In *Sepik Heritage: Tradition and Change in Papua New Guinea,* ed. N. Lutkehaus, C. Kaufmann, W. E. Mitchell, D. Newton, L. Osmundsen, and M. Schuster, 241–44. Durham: Carolina Academic Press.

Schmidt, Jürg, and Christin Kocher-Schmidt. 1992. *Söhne des Krokodils: Männer-hausrituale und Initiation in Yensan, Zentral-Iatmul, East Sepik Province, Papua New Guinea.* Basel: Basler Beiträge zur Ethnologie 36.

Schneider, David M. 1984. *A Critique of the Study of Kinship.* Ann Arbor: University of Michigan Press.

Schofield, Richard. 1993. Ritualistic Initiation and the Development of Male Identity. *Progress: Family Systems Research and Therapy* 2:61–74.

Schuster, Meinhard. 1985. The Men's House, Centre and Nodal Point of Art on the Middle Sepik. In *Authority and Ornament: Art of the Sepik River, Papua New Guinea,* ed. S. Greub, 19–26. Basel: Tribal Art Centre.

Schwartz, Theodore. 1973. Cult and Context: The Paranoid Ethos in Melanesia. *Ethos* 2:153–74.

Schwimmer, Eric. 1984. Male Couples in New Guinea. In *Ritualized Homosexuality in Melanesia,* ed. G. H. Herdt, 248–91. Berkeley: University of California Press.

Serpenti, Laurent. 1984. The Ritual Meaning of Homosexuality and Pedophilia among the Kimam-Papuans of South Irian Jaya. In *Ritualized Homosexuality in Melanesia,* ed. G. Herdt, 292–317. Berkeley: University of California Press.

Shapiro, Warren. 1989. The Theoretical Importance of Pseudo-Procreative Symbolism. *Psychoanalytic Study of Society* 14:71–88.

Sheets-Johnson, Maxine. 1990. *The Roots of Thinking*. Philadelphia: Temple University Press.

Shils, Edward. 1972. *The Constitution of Society*. Chicago: University of Chicago Press.

Shurcliff, Sidney Nichols. 1930. *Jungle Islands: The "Illyria" in the South Seas: The Record of the Crane Pacific Expedition, Field Museum of Natural History, Chicago, Illinois*. New York: G. P. Putnam's Sons.

Shweder, Richard A., and Edmund J. Bourne. 1984. Does the Concept of the Person Vary Cross-Culturally? In *Culture Theory: Essays on Mind, Self, and Emotion*, ed. R. A. Shweder and R. A. LeVine, 158–99. Cambridge: Cambridge University Press.

Silverman, Eric Kline. 1993. *Tambunum: New Perspectives on Eastern Iatmul (Sepik River, Papua New Guinea) Kinship, Marriage, and Society*. Ph.D. thesis, University of Minnesota. Ann Arbor, Mich.: University Microfilms International.

———. 1996. The Gender of the Cosmos: Totemism, Society and Embodiment in the Sepik River. *Oceania* 67:30–49.

———. 1997. Politics, Gender, and Time in Melanesia and Aboriginal Australia. *Ethnology* 36:101–21.

———. 1998. Indigenous Mapping in Papua New Guinea. In *The History of Cartography, Vol. 2, Book 3: Cartography in the Traditional African, American, Arctic, Australian, and Pacific Societies*, ed. D. Woodward and G. Malcolm Lewis, 423–42. Chicago: University of Chicago Press.

———. 1999. Art, Tourism, and the Crafting of Identity in the Sepik River (Papua New Guinea). In *Unpacking Culture: Art and Commodity in Colonial and Postcolonial Worlds*, ed. R. Phillips and C. Steiner, 51–66. Berkeley: University of California Press.

———. 2001a. From Totemic Space to Cyberspace: Transformations in Sepik River and Aboriginal Australian Myth, Knowledge and Art. In *Emplaced Myth: Space, Narrative, and Knowledge in Aboriginal Australia and Papua New Guinea*, ed. A. Rumsey and J. Weiner, 189–214. Honolulu: University of Hawaii Press.

———. 2001b. Tourism in the Sepik River of Papua New Guinea: Favoring the Local over the Global. *Pacific Tourism Review* 4. Special Issue, "Local Perspectives on Global Tourism in South East Asia and the Pacific Region," ed. H. Dahles, 105–19.

———. n.d. Sepik River Selves in a Changing Modernity: Sahlins, Schismogenesis, and Psychodynamic Desire. (Revised version of a paper presented at the 1998 Annual Meeting of the American Anthropological Association, Philadelphia.)

Simmel, Georg. 1950. *The Sociology of Georg Simmel*. Trans. and ed. Kurt H. Wolff. New York: Free Press.

Smith, Michael French. 1982. Bloody Time and Bloody Scarcity: Capitalism, Authority, and the Transformation of Temporal Experience in a Papua New Guinea Village. *American Ethnologist* 9:503–18.

———. 1994. *Hard Times on Kairiru Island: Poverty, Development, and Morality in a Papua New Guinea Village*. Honolulu: University of Hawaii Press.

Smith, Paul, ed. 1996. *Boys: Masculinities in Contemporary Culture*. New York: Harper-Collins.

Spain, David H. 1992. Oedipus Rex or Edifice Wrecked? Some Comments on the Universality of Oedipality and on the Cultural Limitations of Freud's Thought. In *Psychoanalytic Anthropology after Freud: Essays Marking the Fiftieth Anniversary of Freud's Death*, ed. D. H. Spain, 198–224. New York: Psyche Press.

Spearritt, Gordon D. 1982. The Pairing of Musicians and Instruments in Iatmul Society. *Yearbook for Traditional Music* 14:106–25.

Spiro, Melford E. 1951. Culture and Personality: The Natural History of a False Dichotomy. *Psychiatry* 14:19–46.

———. 1965. Religious Systems as Culturally Constituted Defense Mechanisms. In *Context and Meaning in Cultural Anthropology,* ed. M. E. Spiro, 100–113. New York: Free Press.

———. 1973. The Oedipus Complex in Burma. *Journal of Nervous and Mental Disease* 157:389–95.

———. 1982a. *Oedipus in the Trobriands.* Chicago: University of Chicago Press.

———. 1982b. Collective Representations and Mental Representations in Religious Symbol Systems. In *On Symbols in Anthropology: Essays in Honor of Harry Hoijer,* ed. J. Maquet, 45–72. Malibu: Udena Publications.

———. 1992. Oedipus Redux. *Ethos* 20:358–76.

———. 1993. Is the Western Conception of the Self "Peculiar" within the Context of the World Cultures? *Ethos* 21:107–53.

Staalsen, Philip. 1966. The Phonemes of Iatmul. *Pacific Linguistics A* 7:69–76.

———. 1969. The Dialects of Iatmul. *Pacific Linguistics A* 22:69–84.

———. 1972. Clause Relationships in Iatmul. *Pacific Linguistics A* 31:45–69.

Stallybrass, Peter, and Allen White. 1986. *The Politics and Poetics of Transgression.* Ithaca: Cornell University Press.

Stanek, Milan. 1983a. *Sozialordnung und Mythik in Palimbei: Bausteine zur ganzheitlichen Beschreibung einer Dorfgemeinschaft der Iatmul East Sepik Province, Papua New Guinea.* Basel: Basler Beiträge zur Ethnologie 23.

———. 1983b. Les travestis rituels des Iatmul. In *Océanie: Le masque au long cours,* ed. F. Lupu, 163–93. Paris: Ouest-France.

———. 1983c. Les Iatmul. In *Océanie: Le masque au long cours,* ed. F. Lupu, 157–62. Paris: Ouest-France.

———. 1990. Social Structure of the Iatmul. In *Sepik Heritage: Tradition and Change in Papua New Guinea,* ed. N. Lutkehaus, C. Kaufmann, W. E. Mitchell, D. Newton, L. Osmundsen, and M. Schuster, 266–73. Durham: Carolina Academic Press.

Starcke, August. 1921. The Castration Complex. *International Journal of Psycho-Analysis* 2:179–201.

Stephen, Michele. 1987. Contrasting Images of Power. In *Sorcerer and Witch in Melanesia,* ed. M. Stephen, 249–304. Victoria: Melbourne University Press.

———. 1995. *A'aisa's Gifts: A Study of Magic and the Self.* Berkeley: University of California Press.

Stoller, Robert H., and Gilbert H. Herdt. 1982. The Development of Masculinity: A Cross-Cultural Contribution. *Journal of the American Psychoanalytic Association* 30:29–53.

Strathern, Andrew. 1977a. Melpa Food-Names as an Expression of Ideas on Identity and Substance. *Journal of the Polynesian Society* 86:503–11.

———. 1977b. Flutes, Birds, and Hair in Hagen (PNG). *Anthropos* 84:81–87.

———. 1977c. Why Is Shame on the Skin? In *The Anthropology of the Body,* ed. J. Blacking, 99–110. London: Academic Press.

———. 1982. Hidden Names. *Bikmaus* 3:72–79.

———. 1996. *Body Thoughts.* Ann Arbor: University of Michigan Press.

Strathern, Marilyn. 1979. The Self in Self-Decoration. *Oceania* 44:241–57.

————. 1984. Marriage Exchanges: A Melanesian Comment. *Annual Review of Anthropology* 13:41–73.

————. 1988. *The Gender of the Gift: Problems with Women and Problems with Society in Melanesia*. Berkeley: University of California Press.

————. 1991. *Partial Connections*. Savage, Md.: Rowman and Littlefield.

Strathern, Andrew, and Marilyn Strathern. 1971. *Self-Decoration in Mount Hagen*. London: Duckworth.

Swadling, Pamela. 1990. Sepik Prehistory. In *Sepik Heritage: Tradition and Change in Papua New Guinea*, ed. N. Lutkehaus, C. Kaufmann, W. E. Mitchell, D. Newton, L. Osmundsen, and M. Schuster, 71–86. Durham: Carolina Academic Press.

Synnott, Anthony. 1993. *The Body Social: Symbolism, Self and Society*. London: Routledge.

Synnott, Anthony, and David Howes. 1992. From Measurement to Meaning: Anthropologies of the Body. *Anthropos* 87:147–66.

Tarachow, Sidney. 1951. Circuses and Clowns. *Psychoanalysis and the Social Sciences* 3:171–85.

Telban, Borut. 1993. Having Heart: Caring and Resentment in Ambonwari, Papua New Guinea. *Ethnology* 3:158–77.

————. 1996a. *Hierarchy of Social Institutions in a Sepik Society*. Manchester Papers in Social Anthropology 4.

————. 1996b. Shit and Greed: Or Why Ambonwari Men Deny Defecating. Paper presented at the Third Conference of the European Society for Oceanists. Copenhagen.

————. 1997a. Being and 'Non-Being' in Ambonwari (Papua New Guinea) Ritual. *Oceania* 67:308–25.

————. 1997b. Body, Being and Identity in Ambonwari, Papua New Guinea. In *Common Worlds and Simple Lives: Constituting Knowledge in Pacific Societies*, ed. V. Keck, 55–70. Oxford: Berg.

Theweleit, Klaus. 1987. *Male Fantasies*. Vol. 1, *Women, Floods, Bodies, History*, trans. Stephen Conway. Minneapolis: University of Minnesota Press. (Orig. German ed. 1977.)

Thurnwald, Richard. 1916. *Banaro Society: Social Organization and Kinship System of a Tribe in the Interior of New Guinea*. Memoirs of the American Anthropological Association, vol. 3, 253–391.

————. 1934. Adventures of a Tribe in New Guinea (The Tjimundo). In *Essays Presented to C.G. Seligman*, ed. E. E. Evans-Pritchard et al., 345–60. London: Kegan Paul, Trench, Trubner and Co.

Townsend, G. W. L. 1968. *District Officer: From Untamed New Guinea to Lake Success, 1921–46*. Sydney: Pacific Publications.

Townsend, Patricia K. 1984. Reproduction, Pregnancy and Birth in Kararau. (An abbreviated English translation of Hauser-Schäublin 1977, chap. 6, pt. 2). Unpublished. Boroko, Papua New Guinea: Institute for Applied Social and Economic Research.

Trawick, Margaret. 1988. Spirits and Voices in Tamil Song. *American Ethnologist* 15:193–215.

————. 1990. *Notes on Love in a Tamil Family*. Berkeley: University of California Press.

————. 1992. Desire in Kinship: A Lacanian View of the South Indian Familial Self. In *Psychoanalytic Anthropology after Freud: Essays Marking the Fiftieth Anniversary of Freud's Death*, ed. D. H. Spain, 49–62. New York: Psyche Press.

Trompf, G. W. 1994. *Payback: The Logic of Retribution in Melanesian Religions.* Cambridge: Cambridge University Press.

Turner, James West. 1991. Sorcery, Sin, and Power in Melanesia. *Anthropos* 86:427–41.

Turner, Victor. 1967a. Color Classification in Ndembu Ritual: A Problem in Primitive Classification. In *The Forest of Symbols,* 59–92. Ithaca: Cornell University Press.

———. 1967b. Betwixt and Between: The Liminal Period in *Rites de Passage.* In *The Forest of Symbols,* 93–111. Ithaca: Cornell University Press.

———. 1969. Liminality and Communitas. In *The Ritual Process,* 94–130. Ithaca: Cornell University Press.

Tuzin, Donald F. 1972. Yam Symbolism in the Sepik: An Interpretive Account. *Southwestern Journal of Anthropology* 28:230–53.

———. 1974. Social Control and the Tambaran in the Sepik. In *Contention and Dispute,* ed. A. L. Epstein, 317–51. Canberra: Australian National University.

———. 1975. The Breath of a Ghost: Dreams and the Fear of the Dead. *Ethos* 3:555–78.

———. 1976. *The Ilahita Arapesh: Dimensions of Unity.* Berkeley: University of California Press.

———. 1977. Reflections of Being in Arapesh Water Symbolism. *Ethos* 5:195–223.

———. 1978. Sex and Meat-Eating in Ilahita. *Canberra Anthropology* 1:82–93.

———. 1980. *The Voice of the Tambaran: Illusion and Truth in Ilahita Religion.* Berkeley: University of California Press.

———. 1982. Ritual Violence among the Ilahita Arapesh: The Dynamics of Moral and Religious Uncertainty. In *Rituals of Manhood: Male Initiation in Papua New Guinea,* ed. G. Herdt, 321–55. Berkeley: University of California Press.

———. 1989. The Organization of Action, Identity, and Experience in Arapesh Dualism. In *The Attraction of Opposites: Thought and Society in the Dualistic Mode,* ed. D. Maybery-Lewis and U. Almagor, 277–96. Ann Arbor: University of Michigan Press.

———. 1992a. Sago Subsistence and Symbolism among the Ilahita Arapesh. *Ethnology* 31:103–14.

———. 1992b. Revelation and Concealment in the Cultural Organization of Meaning: A Methodological Note. In *Shooting the Sun: Ritual and Meaning in West Sepik,* ed. B. Juillerat, 251–59. Washington, D.C.: Smithsonian Institution Press.

———. 1995. Art and Procreative Illusion in the Sepik: Comparing the Abelam and the Arapesh. *Oceania* 65:289–303.

———. 1997. *The Cassowary's Revenge: The Life and Death of Masculinity in a New Guinea Society.* Chicago: University of Chicago Press.

Valentine, C. A. 1963. Men of Anger and Men of Shame: Lakalai Ethnopsychology and Its Implications for Sociopsychological Theory. *Ethnology* 2:441–77.

Van Baal, J. 1966. *Dema: Description and Analysis of the Marind-anim Culture (South New Guinea).* The Hague: Martinus Nijhoff.

———. 1984. The Dialectics of Sex in Marind-anim Culture. In *Ritualized Homosexuality in Melanesia,* ed. G. Herdt, 128–66. Berkeley: University of California Press.

Van Gennep, Arnold. 1960. *Rites of Passage.* Trans. Monika B. Vizedom and Gabrielle L. Caffe. Chicago: University of Chicago Press. (Orig. French ed. 1909.)

Wagner, Roy. 1972. *Habu: The Innovation of Meaning in Daribi Religion.* Chicago: University of Chicago Press.

———. 1977. Analogic Kinship: A Daribi Example. *American Ethnologist* 4:623–42.

————. 1986. *Asiwinarong: Ethos, Image, and Social Power among the Usen Barok of New Ireland*. Princeton: Princeton University Press.

————. 1987. Daribi and Barok Images of Public Man: A Comparison. In *Anthropology in the High Valleys: Essays on the New Guinea Highlands in Honor of Kenneth E. Read*, ed. L. L. Langness and T. E. Hays, 163–83. Novato, Calif.: Chandler and Sharp.

————. 1991. The Fractal Person. In *Big Men and Great Men: Personifications of Power in Melanesia*, ed. M. Godelier and M. Strathern, 159–73. Cambridge: Cambridge University Press.

Walens, Stanley. 1981. *Feasting with Cannibals: An Essay on Kwakiutl Cosmology*. Princeton: Princeton University Press.

Wassmann, Jurg. 1990. The Nyaura Concepts of Space and Time. In *Sepik Heritage: Tradition and Change in Papua New Guinea*, ed. N. Lutkehaus, C. Kaufmann, W. E. Mitchell, D. Newton, L. Osmundsen, and M. Schuster, 23–35. Durham: Carolina Academic Press.

————. 1991. *Song to the Flying Fox: The Public and Esoteric Knowledge of the Important Men of Kandingei about Totemic Songs, Names, and Knotted Chords (Middle Sepik, Papua New Guinea)*. Boroko, Papua New Guinea: National Research Institute.

Weakland, John H. 1994. Metalogue: What Is Mental Illness? With Apologies and Homage to Gregory Bateson. *Journal of Systemic Therapies* 13:70–73.

Weiner, Annette. 1976. *Women of Value, Men of Renown: New Perspectives on Trobriand Exchange*. Austin: University of Texas Press.

Weiner, James F. 1984. Sunset and Flowers: The Sexual Dimension of Foi Spatial Orientation. *Journal of Anthropological Research* 40:577–88.

————. 1986. Blood and Skin: The Structural Implications of Sorcery and Procreation Beliefs among the Foi. *Ethnos* 51:71–87.

————. 1988a. *The Heart of the Pearl Shell. The Mythological Dimensions of Foi Sociality*. Berkeley: University of California Press.

————. 1988b. Durkheim and the Papuan Male Cult: Whitehead's Views on Social Structure and Ritual in New Guinea. *American Ethnologist* 15:567–73.

————. 1991. *The Empty Place: Poetry, Space, and Being among the Foi of Papua New Guinea*. Bloomington: Indiana University Press.

————. 1993. To Be at Home with Others in an Empty Place: A Reply to Mimica. *Australian Journal of Anthropology* 4:233–44.

————. 1995a. *The Lost Drum: The Myth of Sexuality in Papua New Guinea and Beyond*. Madison: University of Wisconsin Press.

————. 1995b. Anthropologists, Historians and the Secret of Social Knowledge. *Anthropology Today* 11:3–7.

Weiss, Florence. 1981. *Kinder schildern ihren Alltag: Die Stellung des Kindes im ökonomischen System einer Dorfgemeinschaft in Papua New Guinea (Palimbei, Iatmul, Mittelsepik)*. Basel: Basler Beiträge zur Ethnologie 21.

————. 1987a. Kinembe. In *Conversations au bord du fleuve mourant: Ethnopsychanalyse chez les Iatmouls de Papouasie/Nouvelle-Guinée*, ed. F. Morgenthaler, F. Weiss, and M. Morgenthaler, 21–55. Carouge-Genève: Éditions Zoé.

————. 1987b. Magendaua. In *Conversations au bord du fleuve mourant: Ethnopsychanalyse chez les Iatmouls de Papouasie/Nouvelle-Guinée*, ed. F. Morgenthaler, F. Weiss, and M. Morgenthaler, 144–93. Carouge-Genève: Éditions Zoé.

————. 1987c. Kwaigambou. In *Conversations au bord du fleuve mourant: Ethnopsych-*

analyse chez les Iatmouls de Papouasie/Nouvelle-Guinée, ed. F. Morgenthaler, F. Weiss, and M. Morgenthaler, 240–92. Carouge-Genève: Éditions Zoé.

———. 1990. The Child's Role in the Economy of Palimbei. In *Sepik Heritage: Tradition and Change in Papua New Guinea*, ed. N. Lutkehaus, C. Kaufmann, W. E. Mitchell, D. Newton, L. Osmundsen, and M. Schuster, 337–42. Durham: Carolina Academic Press.

———. 1994a. Rapports sociaux de sexe et structures socio-économiques dans la société Iatmul. In *Rapports sociaux de sexe et cérémonie du naven chez les Iatmul de Nouvelle Guinée*. Lausanne: Institut d'anthropologie et de sociologie.

———. 1994b. Die Unterdrückung der Fraueninitiation: Zum Wandel des Ritualsystems bei den Iatmul. In *Geschichte und Mündliche Überlieferung in Ozeanien*, ed. B. Hauser-Schäublin, 237–59. Basler: Beiträge zur Ethnologie 37.

Weiss, Wendy A. 1990. Challenge to Authority: Bakhtin and Ethnographic Description. *Cultural Anthropology* 5:414–30.

Wesley-Smith, Terence, and Eugene Ogan. 1992. Copper, Class, and Crisis: Changing Relations of Production in Bougainville. *Contemporary Pacific* 4:245–67.

Whitehead, Harriet. 1987. Fertility and Exchange in New Guinea. In *Gender and Kinship: Essays toward a Unified Analysis*, ed. J. F. Collier and S. J. Yanagisako, 244–67. Stanford: Stanford University Press.

Whiting, John W. M. 1941. *Becoming a Kwoma: Teaching and Learning in a New Guinea Tribe*. New Haven: Yale University Press.

Whiting, J. W. M., R. Kluckhohn, and A. Anthony. 1958. The Function of Male Initiation Ceremonies at Puberty. In *Readings in Social Psychology*, ed. E. E. Maccoby, T. Newcomb, and E. Hartley, 359–70. 3d ed. New York: Holt.

Wikan, Unni. 1990. *Managing Turbulent Hearts: A Balinese Formula for Living*. Chicago: University of Chicago Press.

Wilden, Anthony. 1972. *System and Structure: Essays in Communication and Exchange*. London: Tavistock.

Williams, Jeffery P. 1995. Tracing Iatmul Foreigner Talk. *Journal of Linguistic Anthropology* 5:90–92.

Williamson, Margaret Holmes. 1980. Omaha Terminology and Unilateral Marriage on the Sepik. *American Ethnologist* 7:530–48.

———. 1983. Sex Relations and Gender Relations: Understanding Kwoma Conception. *Mankind* 14:13–23.

———. 1985. Incest, Exchange, and the Definition of Women among the Kwoma. *Anthropology* 8:1–14.

Williamson, Margaret Holmes, and Roy Wagner. 1990. Desperately Seeking Structures: Or, the Futility of Form without Context. *Anthropologica* 32:205–19.

Willis, Deborah. 1995. *Malevolent Nurture: Witch-Hunting and Maternal Power in Early Modern Europe*. Ithaca: Cornell University Press.

Winnicott, D. W. 1953. Transitional Objects and Transitional Phenomena. *International Journal of Psycho-Analysis* 34:89–97.

———. 1967. The Location of Cultural Experience. *International Journal of Psycho-Analysis* 48:368–72.

Wolff, Kurt H. 1944. A Critique of Bateson's *Naven*. *Journal of the Royal Anthropological Institute* 74:59–74.

Wormsley, W. E. 1981. Tradition and Change in Imbonggu Names and Naming Practices. *Names* 28:183–94.

Wurmser, Leon. 1981. *The Mask of Shame*. Baltimore: Johns Hopkins University Press.

Young, Michael W. 1971. *Fighting with Food: Leadership, Values and Social Control in a Massim Society*. Cambridge: Cambridge University Press.

———. 1983. *Magicians of Manumanua: Living Myth in Kalauna*. Berkeley: University of California Press.

———. 1987. The Tusk, the Flute and the Serpent: Disguise and Revelation in Goodenough Mythology. In *Dealing with Inequality: Analysing Gender Relations in Melanesia and Beyond*, ed. M. Strathern, 229–54. Cambridge: Cambridge University Press.

Index

Abelam (people), 75–76

Accountability, 119. *See also* Responsibility

Adoption, 192n. 22

Affinal relations, 100–102. *See also* Brother-in-law relationship; Daughter-in-law; Kinship; Marriage; Son-in-law

Aggression, male, 25, 48, 51, 141, 164; labor as, 77–78; and sexuality, 60, 63, 70. *See also* Naven rite; Violence; Warfare

Agwi. See Floating islands

Alcohol, 183n. 17, 196n. 10

Ambonwari (people), 148

Anal birth/parturition. *See* Birth/Parturition, anal "birth"

Anal clitoris, 127, 169

Ancestor heroes myth, 22, 27, 30. *See also* Myths

Androgyny, 11, 31–33, 88–89, 163–64. *See also* Gender

Apingari, Linus, 56, 67, 72, 95, 110

Arapesh (people), 32, 74, 148, 195n. 29

Architectural mothers, 7, 12, 64–80; and canoes, 76–78; and female body, 66, 70–71; and labor costs, 73–74; and male cult house, 75, 78–80; and marriage, 101; and myths of masculinity, 67–70, 75, 117; and oedipality, 71–74; orificial imagery of, 70–71 (*see also* Vagina dentata); and patrilineage, 64–66, 74–76; and reproduction, 66–71; and sociocosmic body, 67

Art/aesthetics, 75–76; body adornment, 53, 73; cult house adornment, 78–79; headhunting, 117; house adornment, 66–67; Mai spirits, 58; tsamboe, 68; warfare adornment, 119–21; wood carvings, 55, 69. *See also* Awan figure/spirit; Colors; Flutes *(wainjiimot)*

Avatip (village), 22, 45, 46, 77, 92, 121, 188, 201n. 15

Avoidance relationships, 101

Avunculate *(wau). See* Mother's brother *(wau)*

Awan figure/spirit, 57, 67, 156, 185n. 23, 199nn. 24–25; during naven, 152–54; and motherhood, 55–58, 152–54

Bakhtin, Mikhail, 2–3, 7, 10, 38, 99, 153, 165, 180n. 9; on lower bodily stratum, 6, 145, 152, 155. *See also* Dialogism; Grotesque versus moral body

Bamboo flutes. *See* Flutes *(wainjiimot)*

Banaro nuptial rite, 124–25

Barlow, Kathleen, 9, 103, 114, 154, 192nn. 21, 30

Bateson, Gregory, 17, 75, 77, 104, 137, 182n. 11; and anal clitoris concept, 127, 169; on botanical metaphor, 83–84; on bridewealth, 100, 101; on homoeroticism, 39, 170; on incest, 171, 172; on kinship, 87; on male initiation, 38, 185n. 23, 189n. 25; on male interaction, 62–63; on marriage, 122, 190n. 29, 194n. 16; on motherhood, 96, 99; on

Bateson, Gregory (*continued*)
naven rite, 2–3, 4, 62–63, 135, 137, 139, 146, 156, 157–58, 165, 180n. 5, 199n. 28; on parenting, 99; on procreative wind, 51; on ritual transvestism, 133, 135, 139, 163; on riverine culture, 17; on schismogenesis, 3, 4, 93–94, 182n. 8; on sexual shame, 47; on toilet training, 196n. 14; on tshambela, 123, 128

Bathing, 70, 87, 95, 97, 125–27, 143

Betel nut spittle, 147–49, 152, 166; magic of, 120, 142, 145

Bettelheim, Bruno, 181n. 15

Birds, women as, 35, 56, 67, 83

Birth/Parturition, 10, 20, 41, 157, 188n. 5; anal "birth," 37, 52, 127, 162–65, 167; in ritual, 38–39, 200n. 32; and taboo, 99, 104. *See also* Male initiation; Nggariik gesture

Blood, menstrual. *See* Maternal blood; Menstrual blood

Boas, Franz, 7

Body, 1–2, 47–63; architecture as female, 66, 70–71; bones, 48–49; as canoe, 77; and cultural dialogism, 5–7; eyes, 56; grotesque versus moral body, 2, 6, 10; hair, 48, 58; imagery of, 5–7; lower bodily stratum, 6, 145, 152, 155; materiality of, 47–49; and mystery of motherhood, 56–57; and names, 52–56; nose, 58; and sago palm, 18–19, 48, 49, 51; and sexuality, 58–63; teeth, 48, 186n. 3; tongue, 60, 113; and white foods, 49–51; womb/belly *(iai)*, 66, 73. *See also* Anal clitoris; Bathing; Grotesque versus moral body; Male initiation; Menstrual blood; Naven rite; Sexuality; Vagina *(wangu)*; Vagina dentata

Bones, 48–49

Botanical metaphors: and kinship, 83–85, 190n. 3; men as trees, 20, 54, 55, 83, 84–85

Breadfruit, myth of, 50–51

Breast milk, 49, 53, 145, 186n. 8

Breasts, eroticism of, 61

Brideservice, 101, 109

Bridewealth *(waingga)*, 100, 107, 108, 193n.

6, 194n. 22; and father-son tension, 101, 102, 172. *See also* Marriage

Brother-in-law relationship, 88–90

Brother-sister bond, 88, 171, 191n. 14. *See also* Father's sister; Mother's brother *(wau)*

Buffoonery in ritual, 135. *See also* Clowning/Comedy; Humor; Mockery

Bullroarers *(yartwai)*, 34, 37, 42, 52, 184n. 16

Cannibalism, 120, 121

Canoes and masculinity, 64, 76–78, 117; and firstborn, 72; in naven rite, 143, 155

Capitalism and identity, 26

Castration fear, 39, 49–51, 58, 71, 163, 201n. 1

Chambri (people), 45, 51, 79, 135, 191n. 17, 200n. 32

Childbirth. *See* Birth/Parturition

Children, 192nn. 26–28; discipline of, 96–97; in naven rite, 152, 153–54, 155; and patrinames, 53, 54; weaning of, 97, 138, 192n. 28. *See also* Father-son relationship; Mother-child bond

Christianity, 25–26

Cicatrization, 38. *See also* Male initiation

Clans, 20–21. *See also* Kinship; Patriclans

Cleanliness. *See* Bathing

Clowning/Comedy, 40, 152–54, 199n. 26. *See also* Awan figure/spirit; Humor; Mockery; Sexual joking

Clumsiness, physical, 125–27

Coconuts: myth of, 49–51; as villages, 84

Coital/Procreative fluids, 18–19, 47, 48. *See also* Semen

Colors: black, 158; red, 142, 145; white, 142; yellow, 55–56, 66. *See also* Betel nut spittle; Menstrual blood; White foods paradox

Concealment, psychology of, 118–21. *See also* Secrecy in male ritual

Conception, 47, 53. *See also* Reproduction

Connell, R. W., 177

Cosmic creation, 41, 67

Cosmic spaces, 21–23

Cosmology, 27. *See also* Myths

Cowives, 91, 121

Creation myth, 21, 27, 29–30

Crocodile spirits *(wai wainjiimot)*, 34, 78, 126, 148; and male initiation, 37, 38, 71, 197n. 21; Mendangumeli, 86, 87, 191n. 6; and reproduction, 30, 31, 51, 52, 60, 66, 68

Cross-cousins *(kaishe)*, 62, 107, 188nn. 32–33

Culpability, 120, 124. *See also* Responsibility

Cult house. *See* Male cult house

Cultural symbolism, 136; and bodily imagery, 5–7; gendered perspective, 10–11; psychoanalytic perspective, 7–10

Culture and modernity, 24, 174

D'Amato, John, 135

Daughter-in-law, 94, 102–3, 108–9

Death, 53, 85, 95, 110, 175–76. *See also* Head-hunting; Homicide; Killing

Defecation. *See* Excrement; Feces; Mud and anal birth

Defloration rite of Banaro, 124–25

Dependency, shame of, 34, 123, 128

Derrida, Jacques, 124

Devereux, George, 171, 201n. 1

Dialogism, 2, 5–7, 177; between motherhood and masculinity, 19, 51, 55, 57, 70, 83, 115; maternal 31, 198; versus misogyny, 98; in naven rite, 136, 139, 140; in nggariik gesture, 167, 173. *See also* Bakhtin, Mikhail; Grotesque versus moral body

Dmoiawan, 72, 97, 142

Dogs, symbolism of, 67–68, 102

Domestic violence, 25, 91

Douglas, Mary, 85

Dream-work, Freudian, 8–9. *See also* Freud, Sigmund

Dundes, Alan, 37, 38, 52, 86, 151

Durkheim, Émile, 5, 6, 116, 129

Eagle brothers myth, 137–39, 158

Ehrenreich, Barbara, 176

Elder men, 53, 90, 91. *See also* Leadership, male; Patriclans

Elder women. *See* Awan figure/spirit; Iai (elder) women

Elective marriage, 105

Eliade, Mircea, 85

Embarrassment, 97, 156. *See also* Humiliation; Shame *(wup)*

Epstein, A. L., 151

Eroticism: of female breast, 61; passive, 47; same-sex, 39–40, 170; taboos, 47. *See also* Sexuality

Errington, Frederick, and Deborah B. Gewertz, 26

Europeans, contact with, 23

Excrement, 37, 70, 149, 152, 165, 167; in myth, 146. *See also* Feces; Mud and anal birth; Nggariik gesture; Toilet training; Wind, procreative

Expectoration. *See* Spitting/expectorating

Fantasy, mythopoetic, 8, 9. *See also* Myths

Fatherhood, 9, 53–54, 95, 99; in naven rite, 147; in nggariik, 172, 173. *See also* Patrilineage

Father's mother's brother's son's daughter (FMBSD), 73, 105–6, 194n. 17. *See also* Iai (elder) women

Father-son relationship, 72–74, 90–92, 99, 110; and bridewealth, 101, 102, 172. *See also* Oedipality

Father's sister, 88, 91, 164

Feces, 52, 126, 146–48, 172; as food, 127–29, 149, 151, 165–66. *See also* Cannibalism; Excrement; Mud and anal birth

Feeding/Food, 72; breastmilk, 49, 145, 186n. 8; competitive, 128–29; and father-child relationship, 72–73; gifts of, 40, 151; and masculinity, 38, 49–51, 118, 126; maternal, 50–51, 57, 95, 192n. 12; by maternal uncle, 57, 165; sago (palm), 17–20, 48, 53; spouses, 65. *See also* Feces; Greed/Selfishness; Sago palm; White foods paradox

Femininity, 17, 67, 89, 101, 190n. 1; and canoes, 77. *See also* Architectural mothers; Sexuality; Women

Fertility, 118; female, 18–19, 35, 41, 85, 163; male envy of, 10, 37, 52, 105. *See also* Motherhood

Fire, hearths, 52, 72, 75, 76

Fish traps and nets, 54, 158, 190n. 31

Flatulence, male, 12, 126, 148, 198n. 17; and procreation, 37, 51–52

Floating islands *(agwi)*, 56, 60, 66, 67, 79, 86

Flooding, 17, 85–87. *See also* Sepik River

Flutes *(wainjiimot)*, 33–37, 51–52, 62, 104

FMBSD. *See* Father's mother's brother's son's daughter

Food. *See* Feeding/Food

Forge, Anthony, 75

Fortes, Meyer, 74

Fortune, Reo, 3

Foucault, Michel, 5

Freud, Sigmund, 6, 113, 151, 156, 158; on culture, 174; dream-work of, 8–9

Frye, Northrop, 112, 161

Funerary rites, 77, 85, 128

Gamboromiawan, 32, 33, 66, 107

Gebusi (people), 110

Gender, 10–11; and cosmic space, 22; and identity, 10–11, 88–90; and primal theft, 33–37; and totemism, 31–33. *See also* Androgyny

Gendered substance, 47–49. *See also* Menstrual blood; Semen

Gender roles, mockery of, 162

Gender transformation/Transvestism, 3, 133, 135, 139–40, 163. *See also* Male mother

Gewertz, Deborah B., 26, 135

Gift-giving, 36, 92, 124, 128, 172; food as, 40, 151. *See also* Bridewealth *(waingga)*

Gilmore, David D., 71, 177

Girard, René, 155, 196n. 12

Grandparent relationship, 53, 90, 91

Greed/Selfishness, 102–3

Greenson, Ralph R., 9

Groomwealth *(numbun)*, 108. *See also* Bridewealth

Grotesque motherhood, 133, 143, 156, 166. *See also* Moral motherhood; Motherhood

Grotesque versus moral body, 2, 5–7, 10, 159, 175; in architecture, 70, 74, 79; in feeding, 128–29; in homicides, 118; joking, 113; in male initiation, 38; in men's nostalgia, 99; in myth of sago, 18, 20; in naven, 133, 151, 154, 155, 156, 158; in nggariik, 165, 166, 167

Hair. *See* Body

Handelman, Don, 135, 160, 199n. 25

Harrison, Simon, 65, 77, 118–19, 120–21, 195n. 4. *See also* Avatip

Hauser-Schäublin, Brigitta, 43, 101–2, 104, 110, 121; on female sexuality, 59–60, 139; on gender and violence, 187nn. 21–22; on male initiation, 38, 39; on sacred flutes, 35, 36; on witches, 126; on women's labor, 192n. 23

Head-hunting, 58, 104, 116–18. *See also* Homicide; Warfare

Herdt, Gilbert, 41, 63, 171, 187n. 28

Hereditary partnerships. *See* Tshambela partners

Héritier, François, 155

Heroism in naven rite, 157, 158

Hertz, Robert, 65, 180n. 7

Hobbes, Thomas, 5, 6

Homicide, 101, 104, 110, 116–18, 137; responsibility for, 119–21. *See also* Head-hunting; Warfare

Homicide tassels *(tambointsha)*, 58, 117, 121, 125, 141

Homoeroticism. *See* Sexuality

Hornbill myth, 32–33

Houseman, Michael, 136, 137, 139, 161, 200nn. 1, 9; on kinship, 143, 149

Houses. *See* Architectural mothers

House spirits, 67

Humiliation, 97, 122–23, 128; in naven rite, 12, 88–89, 127, 133, 141–43, 148; in nggariik gesture, 161, 163, 167–69. *See also* Shame *(wup)*

Humor, 40, 114, 125, 141, 160. *See also* Mockery; Sexual joking

Iai marriage, 105–15, 122, 143, 144, 194nn. 17–20; and oedipality, 109–13, 172; sexual joking in, 113–15; and violence, 107–8. *See also* Marriage

Iai women, 5, 20, 99, 154; in naven rite, 140, 141–46, 150–51, 154, 156–57, 168, 197n. 5, 198n. 15. *See also* Awan figure/spirit; Father's mother's brother's son's daughter (FMBSD)

Identity: and body, 47, 48; and concealment, 118–21; and culpability, 124; egocentric and sociocentric, 121–22; female, 17, 67, 89, 101, 190n. 31; and gender, 10–11, 88–90; male (*see* Masculinity); modern, 26; in naven rite, 136; personhood, 26, 69, 87–88, 106, 144; self-, 10, 112–13; totemic, 28–29, 54, 67, 73. *See also* Kinship; Personhood; Shame *(wup)*

Ilahita Arapesh (people), 70, 98, 119, 122, 190n. 3, 201n. 12; and Christianity, 25, 201n. 11; oedipal issues of, 73, 90. *See also* Arapesh (people)

Incest, 74, 92, 137, 155, 158, 201n. 15; and oedipality, 110, 114, 144, 171–72, 173, 175

Income, 26

Inheritance, 73–74. *See also* Names

Initiation rites. *See* Male initiation

Jay, Nancy, 167

Joking. *See* Humor; Mockery; Sexual joking

Juillerat, Bernard, 9, 39, 150, 161, 175; on naven rite, 136–37, 138–40, 144, 158

Kaishe (cross cousins), 62, 107, 188nn. 32–33

Kandingei (village), 31, 38

Kararau (village), 36, 39, 50, 102, 104

Kau. See Ritual heat

Killing, 104, 117, 118, 187n. 21. *See also* Death; Head-hunting; Homicide

Kinship, 12, 83–90; ambiguity in, 87–90; botanical metaphors for, 83–85; brother-sister bond, 88, 171, 191n. 4; cross cousins, 62, 107, 188nn. 32–33; dualism in, 149–50; grandparents, 53,

90, 91; identifications, 87–88; and marriage, 136–37; matrifiliation/motherhood, 21, 87, 91–92, 94–99; patrilineage, 20–21, 27, 28, 90–94, 172–73. *See also* Marriage; Tshambela partners

Knauft, Bruce M., 110

Knowledge, mythic, 42–43; inside/outside, 41, 54; layered, 22–23

Koski, 31

Kristeva, Julia, 166

Kwianalagwi (ancestress) myth, 11, 18–20, 31, 143, 163

Kwoiyen (nameless persons), 53

Kwoma (people), 62, 186n. 8, 192n. 28

Labor: men's, 23–24, 77–78; women's, 95–96, 192n. 23

Lacan, Jacques, 112

Land versus water, 54–55

Layard, John, 171

Leadership, male, 75–76, 183n. 6. *See also* Patrilineage

Leenhardt, Maurice, 11, 32, 54

Levine, Jacob, 153

Lévi-Strauss, Claude, 69–70, 100, 155, 171, 180n. 12, 201n. 16

Lime gourds and masculinity, 125

Lindenbaum, Shirley, 170–71

Lipset, David M., 7, 9, 103, 113, 128, 179n. 2, 181n. 4. *See also* Murik

Losche, Diane, 184n. 12

Lutkehaus, Nancy, 179n. 2, 196n. 5, 200n. 6

Magendaua, 146

Magic, 41, 60, 76, 119–21; of betel nut spittle, 120, 142, 145; pregnancy, 50, 68; as ritual heat *(kau)*, 57, 58, 78–79, 119, 120; sorcery, 24–25, 66–67. *See also* Power, mystical; Witchcraft

Maibut, Dominick, 59

Mai spirits, 58

Male cult, 9, 68, 74, 104, 113; and awan figure, 55; and reproduction, 29–31, 51–52

Male cult house, 24, 46, 119, 189n. 22; as architectural mother, 78–80; as canoe, 77; code of conduct for, 78, 129;

Male cult house (*continued*)
  furnishings of, 74–76; and naven,
  148–49; and nggariik, 168–69; and sexuality, 170; sitting platforms, 54–55
Male initiation, 24, 184nn. 19–21, 185n. 23,
  197n. 21; as anal birth, 38; and awan
  mask, 57, 185n. 23; brutality of, 39; and
  cannibalism, 121; and castration, 39;
  and cicatrization, 38, 148; and crocodile
  spirits, 37, 38, 71, 197n. 21; and fathers,
  99; and feeding, 38; and homoeroticism, 39–40, 170; as mocked by women
  during naven rites, 148–49; and
  nggariik, 170; origin myth of, 37–38; as
  replicating childbirth, 38–39, 71, 163;
  role of mother's brother, 77
Male mother, 18, 55, 88–89, 91, 114, 162. *See
  also* Mother's brother *(wau)*
Male personhood, 121, 122. *See also* Masculinity
Malinowski, Bronislaw, 88
Manambu (people). *See* Avatip (village)
Manam Island, 22, 52. *See also* Lutkehaus,
  Nancy
Marriage, 3–4, 12, 100–115, 195n. 29; and
  affinal relations, 100–102; Banaro
  defloration rite, 124–25; and
  bridewealth, 100, 101, 193n. 6, 194n. 22;
  daughters-in-law, 94, 102–3, 108–9; and
  homoeroticism, 170–71; and kinship,
  136–37; and masculinity, 101–2, 144; and
  motherhood, 7, 106–9; and oedipality,
  106, 109–13; polygyny, 103, 121–22; regulation of, 192n. 1, 194n. 16; selfhood in,
  112–13; sexuality in, 70, 103, 104–5; sexual joking in, 113–15; sister-exchange,
  105, 110; wife's role in, 103–5. *See also* Iai
  marriage; Polygyny
Martial ethos, 15. *See also* Violence; Warfare
Masculinity, 25, 69, 75, 88–90, 156, 157,
  176–77; and canoe-building, 76–78; and
  castration fears, 49–51; and clumsi-
  ness/cleanliness, 125–27; and excrement, 126; and feminine husbands,
  88–90; and food, 49–51, 126, 127–29;
  and homoeroticism, 62; and marriage,
  101–2, 105, 107, 144; and martial
  ethos/warfare, 15, 78, 116–18; and motherhood, 1–2, 9, 11, 71, 159; and naming,
  28; and polygyny, 121–22; and psychology of concealment, 118–21; rituals of,
  46 (*see also* Male initiation; Naven rite;
  Nggariik gesture). *See also* Flatulence,
  male; Sexuality; Shame *(wup)*
Masturbation, 61
Maternal blood, 47, 48, 52, 60, 117, 164. *See
  also* Menstrual blood
Matrifiliation, 21, 87, 91–92
Matrinames, 52–54, 55. *See also* Names
Mauss, Marcel, 5, 69, 129
Mboey Nagusamay (patriclan), 21
Mead, Margaret, 15, 36, 127, 145, 179n. 3;
  on bloodletting, 32; on Iatmul success,
  23, 24; on identity, 10, 29, 89; on male
  womb envy, 2; on marriage, 195n. 29;
  on motherhood, 9, 87, 91–92, 96, 97–98;
  on parenting, 192n. 26; on schismogenesis, 3; on sexuality, 61, 79, 187n. 22,
  188nn. 8, 35; on women and masculinity, 49; on women's work, 95–96
Melanesia: bodily imagery in, 6–7; gender
  in, 32; selfhood in, 112–13
Men: ambivalence toward women, 102–3,
  109–10; bravado/swagger of, 196nn.
  10–11; castration fears of, 39, 49–50, 58,
  163, 201n. 1; and cosmic space, 22–23;
  elder, 53, 90, 91; female pollution of, 19,
  20, 56, 99, 151; flatulence of, 12, 37,
  51–52, 126, 147–48, 198n. 17; labor of,
  23–24, 77–78; and marital sexuality, 103,
  104–5; and marriage, 101–5, 114–15; as
  metaphorical trees, 20, 55, 83, 84–85,
  190n. 3; and modernity, 24–28; motherhood ideal of, 1–2, 11, 87, 94, 97, 107, 115;
  naven rite behavior of, 3, 156; responsibility of, 119–21, 123–25; ritual humiliation of, 141–43, 148; secrecy of, 148–49,
  167–68; and totemic debates, 43–45. *See
  also* Male cult; Masculinity; Naven rite;
  Nggariik gesture
Mendangumeli (crocodile spirit), 86, 87,
  191n. 6
Menstrual blood, 19, 47, 48, 56, 126, 142,

145–46, 149, 152, 156, 165; and witch-craft, 126–27. *See also* Maternal blood

Menstruation, 99, 104, 145, 150

Metraux, Rhoda, 97

Mockery: in naven rite, 3, 133, 162; self-, 124; women's, 1, 5, 156, 167–68. *See also* Bakhtin, Mikhail; Clowning/Comedy; Gender transformation/Transvestism; Humor; Sexual joking

Modernity, 23–28; and culture, 24, 174; and men, 24–28; and tourism, 25, 26

Mogua (patriclan), 21

Moieties, 182n. 7, 184n. 19

Moral body. *See* Grotesque versus moral body

Morality: avuncular, 92; and individual desire, 6

Moral motherhood, 57, 69, 74, 76, 79, 95–99

Mother-child bond, 9, 35, 94–99, 198n. 18; in eagle brothers myth, 137–39

Motherhood: and awan figure, 55–56, 152–54; breast milk, 49, 145, 186n. 8; as canoe, 77; and father-son bond, 91–92, 110; grotesque, 133, 143, 156, 166; and iai women, 142; insults in, 96; male ideal of, 1–2, 11, 87, 94, 97, 107, 115; and marriage, 7, 106–9; and masculinity, 138–39, 159; moral, 57, 69, 74, 76, 79, 95–99; mysteries of, 56–57; mythic, 11, 18–20, 31, 35, 143, 163; Nazi fantasy of, 176; and nurturing foods, 49, 50–51, 57, 95, 128, 165, 192n. 22; and oedipality, 86–87, 109–13; phallic, 36–37; pregnancy magic, 50, 68; and ritual mud smear-ing, 146–49; and ritual spitting, 141–42, 145–46; ritual "stepping over" of, 155–57; riverine image of, 17; and sexuality, 61, 142; ubiquitous, 177. *See also* Architectural mothers; Birth/Parturition; Male mother; Naven rite; Nggariik gesture; Phallic motherhood

Mother's brother *(wau)*, 21, 57, 88, 91–94, 106–7, 114, 135, 166; as canoe, 77; compared to iai, 114; as male mother, 18, 55, 114; and naming, 53; in naven rite, 142,
155; and nggariik gesture, 3, 4, 62, 161, 162–65, 165–67, 172, 201n. 13; ritual role of, 77, 133, 135, 136, 142, 159; and shame, 127, 128. *See also* Male mother

Mouth. *See* Orality

Mud and anal birth, 37. *See also* Feces

Mud smearing, 5, 146–49, 152, 166

Muensterberger, Warner, 163

Mundjiindua, 42–43

Mundugumor (people), 96

Murik (people), 30, 35, 41, 47, 71, 79, 154, 190n. 27, 192n. 22, 197n. 17, 198n.6; and maternal nurture, 98, 192n. 22. *See also* Barlow, Kathleen; Lipset, David M.

Mystical power and totemism, 42–45

Myths, 8, 9; ancestral heroes, 22, 27, 30; aquatic, 15, 21; cassowary, 111; clitoris, 127; creation, 21, 27, 29–30; eagle broth-ers, 137–39, 158; feces, 146; flood, 86–87; hornbill, 32–33; motherhood, 11, 18–20, 31, 35, 143, 163; of naven, 172; oedipality, 73–74; pigs, 111; of primal theft, 104; sago palm, 11, 17–20, 31, 49; snake-child, 68–69, 165. *See also* Creation myth; Hornbill myth

Names: gender symbolism of, 54–55; of houses, 67; in iai marriage, 106; and male cult, 30; matrinames, 52–54, 55; and patrilineage, 27, 28, 52–55, 88; totemic, 27–29, 40–41, 43–44, 183nn. 3, 8

Naven (Bateson), 2, 135

Naven rite, 77, 129, 133–58, 197nn. 4–5, 199n. 19; and affinal relations, 144; avuncular role in, 53, 92, 94, 140; Bateson on, 2–3, 4, 135, 137, 139, 156, 157–58, 165, 180n. 5; canoes in, 143, 155; dancing, 142; and eagle brothers myth, 137–39; as "going on view," 157–58; iai women's role in, 140, 141–46, 150–51, 154, 156–57, 197n. 5, 198n. 15; incest theme in, 137, 155, 156, 158, 201n. 15; and kinship ties, 136, 137; male humiliation in, 12, 88–89, 127, 133, 141–43, 145, 146–47, 148, 149, 150–51; male and female roles com-pared, 161–62; as men's response to motherhood, 156–57; motherhood

Naven rite (*continued*)
debased in, 155–57; mud smearing in, 146–49, 151, 152, 166; myth of, 172; obscuring self, 146, 154; Oedipus complex, 144, 145; sexual aggression, 141; sexual joking, 141; spitting, 141–42, 145–46 (*see also* Betel nut spittle); thrashings, 141, 144; transvestism in, 133, 135, 139–40; witch, 149–50; women mocking male initiation, 148–49, 151–52; Yafar and Yangis compared, 175–76. *See also* Awan figure/spirit; Nggariik gesture
Nazism and motherhood, 176
Nephew (*laua*): in naven rite, 77, 91, 114, 127, 140, 154, 159; and exchanges with uncle, 106–7; and masculinity, 135; and nggariik gesture, 159, 160–61, 165, 171–73. *See also* Mother's brother (*wau*)
Newton, Douglas, 201n. 15
Ngawi, Henry, 86
Nggariik gesture, 133, 140, 155, 156, 159–73, 200n. 1; as anal birth, 162–63, 164; and excrement, 165–66; and father, 172, 173; and homoerotic taboo, 62, 155, 168–70, 171, 201n. 9; and iai, 168; and masculinity, 163–64, 166–67; and mother's brother, 3, 4, 62, 161, 162–65, 172, 201n. 13; and patrilineage, 172–73; as sacrifice, 167; tragic emotions in, 159–61, 163, 164–65, 166, 167, 168; women's mockery of, 156, 167–68
Nuptial rite, 124–25. *See also* Marriage
Nurturance, 20, 57. *See also* Feeding/Food

Obeyesekere, Gananath, 8, 173, 174, 176
Oedipality, 9–10, 53, 69, 86–87, 171–73, 181n. 14; and architectural mothers, 71–74; and father-son relationship, 72–74, 90–92, 198n. 10; and incest, 110, 114, 144, 171–72, 173; and marriage, 106, 109–13; and mother in myth, 139; and nggariik gesture, 171–73; and patrilineage, 90–92, 172–73; and primal theft myth, 36. *See also* Incest

Orality, 70–71, 98, 103, 145
Ornamentation, warfare, 120

Palimbei (village), 57, 146, 149, 164–65
Parenting, 96, 99. *See* Fatherhood; Motherhood
Parturition. *See* Birth/Parturition
Paternal aunt as "father," 91, 164
Paths, gendered, 22
Patriclans, 20–21, 75, 182nn. 6–7. *See also* Kinship
Patrilineage, 20–21, 27, 28, 90–94, 172–73; and architecture, 64–66, 74–75
Patrinames, 27, 28, 52–55, 88. *See also* Names
Paul, Robert A., 8, 9, 52, 170, 180n. 12
Personhood, 10–11, 26, 69, 106, 144. *See also* Gender; Identity; Masculinity; Shame (*wup*)
Personified scepters (*tshumbuk*), 120
Phallic motherhood, 36, 79, 86, 114, 119, 144, 163. *See also* Grotesque motherhood
Pity (*miwi*), 160; in naven, 155. *See also* Tragic emotions in nggariik gesture
Pollution, female, 56, 72; in warfare, 117–18
Polygyny, 103, 121–22
Postpartum taboo, 99, 103, 104. *See also* Birth/Parturition
Potlatch, 151
Power, mystical, 42–45, 46, 119. *See also* Magic; Witchcraft
Pregnancy: magic, 50, 68; power of, 118
Preoedipality, 9, 71, 92. *See also* Oedipality
Primogeniture, 64, 72–73, 75
Procreation, 29, 51–52, 117, 167. *See also* Reproduction; Sexual intercourse
Procreative fluids. *See* Coital/Procreative fluids; Semen
Prohibitions, 78–79, 105. *See also* Taboos
Psychoanalysis, 7–10; and concealment, 118–21; and naven rite, 137; projection, 70; splitting concept, 70–71; symbolic interpretation, 68–69, 71, 73–74, 129,

137, 139, 140, 144–45, 150, 158, 174, 175–76. *See also* Freud, Sigmund

Radcliffe-Brown, A. R., 87, 114
Rape: female, 78, 79, 187n. 22; male, 63
Raw and cooked food, 72
Reik, Theodor, 74
Reproduction: and architectural mothers, 66–71; and female identity, 37; male, 117, 118; and male cult, 29–31, 51–52. *See also* Procreation; Birth/Parturition
Reproductive substances, 47. *See also* Semen
Residences. *See* Architectural mothers
Responsibility, 117, 118–21, 123–25
Retribution *(vai)*, 40, 106, 185n. 25
Ritual: rites of reversal, 5. *See also* Male initiation; Naven rite; Totemism
Ritual condensation, 136
Ritual heat *(kau)*, 57, 58, 78–79, 119, 120, 145. *See also* Magic
Ritual partnerships, 62. *See also* Male cult; Tshambela partners
Ritual power, 119
Ritual sacra. *See* Bullroarers *(yartwai)*; Flutes *(wainjiimot)*
River and water motif, 15–17, 66. *See also* Sepik River

Sacred knowledge, 42
Sago palm, 48, 51, 53, 68, 84; myth of, 11, 17–20, 31, 49
Sambia (people), 49, 171
Sawos, 100, 182n. 12
Scarification, 37–38. *See also* Male initiation
Schismogenesis, 3, 4, 116, 135, 144, 179n. 4, 182n. 8; complementary, 191n.18; symmetrical, 93–94, 129, 199n.19
Secrecy in male ritual, 167–68
Secret names, 41. *See also* Names
Selfhood, 10, 112–13. *See also* Identity; Personhood
Semen, 47, 48, 49, 52, 53–54, 56, 60, 117, 142, 171, 186n. 8
Separation-individuation, 69, 139. *See also* Identity; Personhood

Sepik River, 15, 21, 22, 23, 85, 181n. 1
Severi, Carlo, 136, 137, 161, 200nn. 1, 9; on kinship, 143, 149
Sexual intercourse, 18–19, 20, 79, 145; anal, 169–70; and reproductive fluids, 48, 49
Sexuality, 58–63, 67, 102, 187n. 22; female, 58–60, 61, 63, 71; flutes as male, 35; homoerotic, 39–40, 61–63, 127, 169–70, 171, 196n. 16, 200n. 9; and male aggression, 60, 63, 70, 127; marital, 70, 103, 104–5, 118; masturbation, 61; orgasm, 60; in sago myth, 18–20; violence/rape, 78–79, 187n. 22. *See also* Anal clitoris
Sexual joking, 60, 113–15, 141, 195n. 31
Sexual salute, 169, 172. *See also* Nggariik gesture
Sexual taboos. *See* Orality; Sexuality
Shame *(wup)*, 47, 122–25, 127–28, 196n. 9, 200n. 9; and homoeroticism, 61, 169, 170, 196n. 16; in naven rite, 4, 157, 160–61, 163, 173. *See also* Humiliation
Shapiro, Warren, 151
Shui Aimasa (patriclan), 21, 50
Siblings: brother-brother, 64–65, 71–72, 90, 105, 184n. 19, 191n. 12; brother-sister, 87, 88–89, 171, 191n. 14; in myth of naven, 137–39
Sister-exchange marriage, 105, 110, 170
Sister's husband *(iando)*, 89
Sister's son. *See* Nephew
Smith, Michael French, 26
Snake and eel (totemic ancestors), 22
Snake-child myth, 68–69, 165
Social body, 5
Social bond, 136
Socialization and motherhood, 98
Social life and totemism, 45
Social order: and architectural motherhood, 64–66, 74–76; bond, 136; and oedipality, 73; patriclan, 75; and ritual, 5–6; spaces, 20–21; and totemism, 45. *See also* Clans; Kinship
Social spaces, 20–21
Social structure, 74–76
Society of the Divine Word, 25
Son-in-law, 101. *See also* Daughter-in-law

Sons and fathers. *See* Father-son relationship
Sorcery, 24–25, 66–67. *See also* Magic; Witchcraft
Spanish men and masculinity, 71
Spear as phallic symbol, 44, 172
Spirits: household, 67; and identity, 28; impersonation of, 34; *kaiek*, 28; male cult house, 75, 119; *nggwalndu*, 75; *sabi*, 68, 199. *See also* Awan figure/spirit; Crocodile spirits *(wai wainjiimot)*
Spirit world, 22. *See also* Myths; Totemism
Spitting/expectorating, 120, 141–42, 145–46
Splitting (psychoanalytic defense), 70–71, 150
Spousal abuse, 25, 91
Stanek, Milan, 137, 157, 164
Stools in cult house, 74–76, 155
Strathern, Marilyn, 10, 11, 32, 139
Symmetrical schismogenesis. *See* Schismogenesis, symmetrical

Taboos: affinal relations, 101, 171; body, 49; erotic, 47, 71; of male identity, 4, 37; menstruating/postpartum women, 99, 104; pregnancy, 49, 54; prohibitions, 78–79, 105. *See also* Incest; Sexuality
Tambointsha. See Homicide tassels
Tarachow, Sydney, 153
Tchambuli (people), 79. *See also* Chambri
Teeth, 48, 186n. 3. *See also* Body; Vagina dentata
Telban, Borut, 148
Testicles and virility, 49–51. *See also* Castration fear
Theweleit, Klaus, 176
Thurnwald, Richard Christian, 124–25
Toilet training, 95, 126, 196n. 14. *See also* Excrement; Feces
Tokpisin (pidgin), 23
Toponomy. *See* Names
Totemism, 22, 27–46, 84; aquatic, 21; and debating, 43–45, 119; and gender, 31–33; and identity, 28–29, 54, 67, 73; in male initiation, 37–40; and mystical power,

42–45, 46; and mythic floating islands, 56, 60, 66, 67, 86; and name recitations, 27–29, 40–41, 43–44, 183nn. 3, 8; and reproduction, 29–31; sacred flute theft, 33–37; and social life, 45–46. *See also* Magic; Ritual heat
Tourism, 25, 26
Trade networks, 15, 26
Tragic emotions in nggariik gesture, 159–61, 163, 164–65, 167, 168, 175. *See also* Humiliation; Weeping/Tears in ritual
Transactional gender, 11
Transvestism. *See* Gender transformation/Transvestism
Trawick, Margaret, 112, 113, 179n. 4
Trees as male metaphor, 20, 54–55, 75, 83, 84–85. *See also* Botanical metaphors
Trobriand Islands, 47, 88
Trompf, G. W., 124
Tsagi. *See* Totemism
Tshambela partners, 146, 151, 156, 195nn. 1–2, 196n. 7; and food exchange, 126, 128, 129; and masculinity, 116–17, 118; and shame, 122–24
Tuatmeli (mythic hero), 21, 44, 93, 119
Tuzin, Donald F., 119, 122, 159, 168, 169, 201n. 1; on masculinity and motherhood, 70, 98

Vabindu, 45–46
Vagina dentata: cult house, 79, 151; house, 70
Vagina *(wangu)*, 31–33, 145
Vai (retribution), 40, 78, 101, 106, 120, 185n. 25
Vendigarlagwa (ancestress), 79
Violence, 59, 68, 118, 120; domestic, 25, 91; and iai marriage, 107–8, 111. *See also* Rape; Warfare

Wagner, Roy, 67
Wai wainjiimot. See Crocodile spirits *(wai wainjiimot)*
Wangu (totemic pit/vagina), 31–33
Warfare, 44, 68, 76, 104–5, 120, 129; and masculinity, 15, 78, 116–18. *See also* Con-

cealment, psychology of; Head-hunting; Homicide
Wassmann, Jurg, 41, 51
Water: as female metaphor, 75, 84–86; motif, 15–17, 21. *See also* Flooding; River and water motif; Sepik River
Wealth, 26, 103, 151, 196n. 14. *See also* Bridewealth; Gift-giving
Weaning of children, 97, 138, 148, 192n. 28
Weeping/Tears in ritual, 161, 164–65
Weiner, James F., 10, 32, 42, 77, 112–13, 139
Weiss, Florence, 94, 95, 125, 137, 146, 157, 192n. 27
White foods paradox, 49–51. *See also* Colors
Whiting, John W. M., 90
Wife's brother *(tawontu),* 89
Wife's role in marriage, 103–5
Wind, procreative, 51–52. *See also* Flatulence, male
Winnicott, D. W., 137, 177
Witchcraft, 126, 150, 196n. 15, 199n. 20. *See also* Magic; Power, mystical; Sorcery
Wolibunaut (food exchanges), 128–29
Women: as bird people, 35, 56, 67, 83; botanical metaphors for, 83–84, 190n. 3; and canoe ownership, 77; and cosmic space, 22–23; identity of, 17, 67, 89, 101, 190n. 31; and initiation, 184n. 18; labor of, 95–96, 192n. 23; male ambivalence toward, 103, 109–10; and male cult, 39, 46, 76; in marriage, 103–5; mockery of manhood by, 167–68; mythic knowledge of, 42–43; naven rite behavior of, 3, 4, 162, 200n. 13; Nazi fantasy of, 176; pollution of men by, 99; and primal theft myth, 33–37; rape of, 78–79, 187n. 22; and reproductive totems, 30–31; and sexuality, 19, 58–60, 61, 63; water metaphor for, 17, 84–86. *See also* Architectural mothers; Femininity; Fertility, female; Motherhood; Naven rite; Nggariik gesture; Wife's role in marriage
Work. *See* Labor
World War II, 24
Wyngwenjap (patriclan), 21, 22

Yafar (people), 61, 73–74, 175–76, 192n. 28; and Yangis rite, 175–76
Yambukenandi (village father), 78
Yellow (color) and women, 56, 66
Young, Michael W., 149